THE EDUCATION OF BLACKS

IN THE SOUTH, 1860–1935

JAMES D. ANDERSON

THE EDUCATION OF

BLACKS IN THE SOUTH,

1860–1935

THE UNIVERSITY OF NORTH CAROLINA PRESS

CHAPEL HILL AND LONDON

The paper in this book meets the guidelines
for permanence and durability of the
Committee on Production Guidelines for Book Longevity
of the Council on Library Resources.

92 91 90 89 88   5 4 3 2 1

Library of Congress Cataloging-in-Publication Data

Anderson, James D., 1944–
The education of Blacks in the South, 1860–1935 / by James D.
Anderson.
p. cm.
Bibliography: p.
Includes index.
ISBN 0-8078-1793-7 (alk. paper). ISBN 0-8078-4221-4 (pbk.: alk. paper)
1. Afro-Americans—Education—Southern States—History—19th
century. 2. Afro-Americans—Education—Southern States—
History—20th century. I. Title.
LC2802.S9A53   1988   87-35196
370'.0889073075—dc19   CIP

To my mother, Annie Byrd Anderson;

and in memory of my grandmother, Mary Eliza Matthews;

my brother, Leon Anderson;

and my father, Fred Anderson

CONTENTS

TABLES AND FIGURES

TABLES

FIGURE

ILLUSTRATIONS

ACKNOWLEDGMENTS

I wish to express my gratitude to the many persons who assisted and encouraged me in the preparation of this book. I gratefully acknowledge the advice and suggestions of those who read all or portions of the manuscript. Darlene Clark Hine, V. P. Franklin, Robert L. Harris, David B. Tyack, O. Vernon Burton, Hoda Zaki, and Frederic C. Jaher gave generously of their time and knowledge to my work and suggested new directions for research. My colleagues and friends at the University of Illinois have put in so much time, effort, and hard criticism that I could not begin to thank them. Anyway, to Clarence J. Karier, Paul C. Violas, William Trent, Steven Tozer, Ralph Page, Joe R. Burnett, and Terry Denny, your advice and encouragement were extremely helpful. I also wish to thank my good friend and former colleague at Indiana University, B. Edward McClellan, for his advice and support.

A number of graduate students read portions of this study as mimeographed classroom reading assignments. I owe them a debt for their honest feedback. Their questions gave me a great deal to think about. Particularly, I wish to thank my doctoral students, Brenda Jackson, Linda Perkins, Dale Tatalovich, Larry Parker, Warren Chapman, Stafford Hood, Guy Senese, Alexis Freeman, Carolyne White, Casey Machula, and Bernard Ray. They offered good suggestions and continued encouragement over the years. That helps as much as anything. I would like to acknowledge also the long-standing support of my friends Hakim Muhummad and Mikal Kariem.

An important debt to my early teachers is the most difficult to acknowledge in written words. They were my exemplars, and without them my academic development would not have been possible. Honor and respect to my teachers Herman Hughes, Eunice O. Outland, J. C. McCampbel, E.W. Underwood, and J. T. Parker who kept the faith and brought me through the dark path. I am also grateful to Haywood L. Strickland and Joffre T. Whisenton for picking up where they left off. They contributed much to this final product.

I would like to offer special thanks to Marsha May, who typed all drafts of the manuscript. She put in much hard work on this book, and her dedication and professionalism will always be cherished. Jean Bettridge, my research assistant, gave significant aid in the development of the bibliography, and I gratefully acknowledge her assistance. She did excellent work.

A special thanks and debt of gratitude are due my research assistant, Carrie Geyer Franke, who read and critiqued the entire manuscript. Her suggestions, corrections, and additions contributed significantly to the quality of this book. She worked hard under very difficult conditions and demonstrated an impressive quality of scholarship and professional character. I am also grateful to Mary Prignano for helping to correct the galleys.

I particularly want to thank several librarians for their very able assistance. Vera Mitchell and Rosemary Stevenson of the University of Illinois and Beth Howse, Ann Shockley, and Jessie Carney Smith of Fisk University helped to make this work possible. And I wish to thank William Hess of the Rockefeller Archive Center.

For Teresa Fisher, words cannot convey the depths of appreciation for your support, understanding, and encouragement.

THE EDUCATION OF BLACKS

IN THE SOUTH, 1860–1935

INTRODUCTION

THE HISTORY of American education abounds with themes that represent the inextricable ties between citizenship in a democratic society and popular education. It is crucial for an understanding of American educational history, however, to recognize that within American democracy there have been classes of oppressed people and that there have been essential relationships between popular education and the politics of oppression. Both schooling for democratic citizenship and schooling for second-class citizenship have been basic traditions in American education. These opposing traditions were not, as some would explain, the difference between the mainstream of American education and some aberrations or isolated alternatives. Rather, both were fundamental American conceptions of society and progress, occupied the same time and space, were fostered by the same governments, and usually were embraced by the same leaders.

Appropriately, it was Thomas Jefferson who first articulated the inseparable relationships between popular education and a free society. If a nation expected to be ignorant and free, he argued, it expected the impossible. To the legislature of Virginia in 1787 Jefferson proposed a popular educational system that would offer three years of public schooling to every white child of the commonwealth and then send the brightest male youngsters on to grammar school and college at public expense. But what of the enslaved children who constituted about 40 percent of the total number of Virginia's children and who along with enslaved adults formed the basis of wealth for Jefferson, as well as for the state of Virginia? It was believed that Virginia's peace, prosperity, and "civilization" depended as much, if not more, on the containment and repression of literate culture among its enslaved population as it did on the diffusion of literate culture among its free population.

These two contradictory traditions of American education emerged during the first half of the nineteenth century and clashed with each other until well into the twentieth century. Both legacies flow into our own present. They reflect fundamentally, though not exclusively, the long struggle between two social systems—slavery and peasantry on one hand, and capitalism and free labor on the other. The successful campaign to contain and repress literacy among enslaved Americans triumphed just as the crusade for popular education for free people began to flourish. Between 1800 and 1835, most of the southern states enacted legislation making it a crime to teach enslaved children to read or write. In contrast, a massive campaign to achieve popular schooling for free Americans developed between 1830 and 1860, and out of this campaign emanated designs for state systems of public education. By the end of the antebellum period a majority of the states had established public school systems, and nearly half of the nation's free children were already getting some formal education. Still, it was not until the latter part of the nineteenth century that the organization, scope, and role of schooling were transformed into a carefully articulated structure of free tax-supported public institutions.

In 1863, the enslaved Americans were emancipated whereby they temporarily joined the ranks of the nation's free citizens at the very moment that public educational systems were being developed into their modern form. For a brief period during the late 1860s and 1870s, as free laborers, citizens, and voters, the ex-slaves entered into a new social system of capitalism, Republican government, and wage labor. Their campaign for first-class citizenship, however, was successfully undermined by federal and state governments and by extralegal organizations and tactics. Soon after the late 1870s, blacks were ruthlessly disfranchised; their civil and political subordination was fixed in southern law, and they were trapped by statutes and social customs in an agricultural economy that rested heavily on coercive control and allocation of labor. From the end of Reconstruction until the late 1960s, black southerners existed in a social system that virtually denied them citizenship, the right to vote, and the voluntary control of their labor power. They remained an oppressed people. Black education developed within this context of political and economic oppression. Hence, although black southerners were formally free during the time when American popular education was transformed into a highly formal and critical social institution, their schooling took a different path.

This book tells the story of the unique system of public and private education that was developed by and for black southerners between 1860 and 1935. It examines the structure, ideology, and content of black education as part and parcel of the larger political subordination of blacks, for it was the social system in which blacks lived that made their educational institutions so fundamentally different from those of other Americans. Education within this social context was not necessarily deleterious, nor was all of black education repressive in reality. Indeed, a central theme in the history of the education of black Americans is the persistent struggle to fashion a system of formal education that prefigured their liberation from peasantry.) The book begins with the movement by ex-slaves to develop an educational system singularly appropriate to defend and extend their emancipation. Within this movement the basic form, philosophy, and subject matter of black education reflected the ex-slaves' intent to restructure and control their lives. Yet their struggle to defend and advance themselves was undertaken as oppressed people. Apart from this conception we cannot appreciate fully the choices they made, the greatness of their triumphs, and their ultimate failure to dominate the course of their educational development. As black southerners lost political and economic power, they lost substantial control of their educational institutions, especially in the public sector, and the shape and character of their education took a different turn. As detailed in Chapter 2, this system of second-class education for blacks did not just happen. It was the logical outgrowth of a social ideology designed to adjust black southerners to racially qualified forms of political and economic subordination. The ex-slaves, however, persisted in their crusade to develop systems of education compatible with their resistance to racial and class subordination. This effort set the stage for the bitter national debate about the social purposes of black education that unfolded at the turn of the century; it is detailed in Chapter 3. A description of how these educational movements and ideologies were translated into institutional behavior is presented in Chapters 4 through 7. This section of the book begins with a study of black teacher training institutions, followed by a detailed examination of the structure and content of black common schools and high schools, ending with a study of black higher education.

This approach reflects two primary goals. First, this volume seeks to give meaning to educational movements and ideologies as they influenced the basic organization and substance of educational institutions. Second, it seeks to provide a detailed documentation of the actual structure and content of each level of black education. So often the histories of black education attend excessively to the growth of intellectual currents and ideological debate, leaving the readers without a clear, concise, and comprehensive understanding of what actually existed in the way of elementary schools, normal schools, secondary schools, and colleges. This approach makes it difficult, if not impossible, for readers to understand how politics, power, and ideology shaped the framework and opportunity structure of black educational institutions and how these institutions differed from the educational institutions of other Americans. This volume examines both the ideological and institutional nature of schooling in the black South and the interplay of both in the education of an oppressed class of American citizens.

I

EX-SLAVES AND THE RISE

OF UNIVERSAL EDUCATION

IN THE SOUTH,

1860–1880

FORMER SLAVES were the first among native southerners to depart from the planters' ideology of education and society and to campaign for universal, state-supported public education. In their movement for universal schooling the ex-slaves welcomed and actively pursued the aid of Republican politicians, the Freedmen's Bureau, northern missionary societies, and the Union army. This uprising among former slaves was the central threat to planter rule and planters' conceptions of the proper roles of state, church, and family in matters of education. The South's landed upper class tolerated the idea of pauper education as a charity to some poor white children, but state-enforced public education was another matter. The planters believed that state government had no right to intervene in the education of children and, by extension, the larger social arrangement. Active intervention in the social hierarchy through public education violated the natural evolution of society, threatened familial authority over children, upset the reciprocal relations and duties of owners to laborers, and usurped the functions of the church. During the period 1860 to 1880, other classes of native white southerners, including small farmers, industrialists, and laborers, showed little inclination to challenge the planters on these questions. Indeed, specific economic, political, social, and psychological relationships bound southern whites in general to the ideological position of the planter regime. The result was a postwar South that was extremely hostile to the idea of universal public education. The ex-slaves broke sharply with this position. With the aid of Republican politicians, they seized significant influence in state governments and laid the first foundation for universal public education in the South. This chapter tells the story of the ex-slaves' struggle for universal schooling, why they pursued it, how they organized to defend their common interests, how they coped with the resistance of opposing social

classes, and finally, how they gained the cooperation of sympathetic social groups.

Blacks emerged from slavery with a strong belief in the desirability of
learning to read and write. This belief was expressed in the pride with
which they talked of other ex-slaves who learned to read or write in
slavery and in the esteem in which they held literate blacks. It was expressed in the intensity and the frequency of their anger at slavery for
keeping them illiterate. "There is one sin that slavery committed against
me," professed one ex-slave, "which I will never forgive. It robbed me of
my education." The former slaves' fundamental belief in the value of
literate culture was expressed most clearly in their efforts to secure
schooling for themselves and their children. Virtually every account by
historians or contemporary observers stresses the ex-slaves' demand for
universal schooling. In 1879 Harriet Beecher Stowe said of the freedmen's campaign for education: "They rushed not to the grog-shop but to
the schoolroom—they cried for the spelling-book as bread, and pleaded
for teachers as a necessity of life." Journalist Charles Nordhoff reported
that New Orleans's ex-slaves were "almost universally . . . anxious to
send their children to school." Booker T. Washington, a part of this
movement himself, described most vividly his people's struggle for education: "Few people who were not right in the midst of the scenes can
form any exact idea of the intense desire which the people of my race
showed for education. It was a whole race trying to go to school. Few
were too young, and none too old, to make the attempt to learn." When
supervising the first contrabands at Fortress Monroe in 1861, Edward L.
Pierce "observed among them a widespread desire to learn to read."[1]

The foundation of the freedmen's educational movement was their
self-reliance and deep-seated desire to control and sustain schools for
themselves and their children. William Channing Gannett, a white American Missionary Association teacher from New England, reported that
"they have a natural praiseworthy pride in keeping their educational
institutions in their own hands. There is jealousy of the superintendence
of the white man in this matter. What they desire is assistance without
control." The values of self-help and self-determination underlay the ex-
slaves' educational movement. To be sure, they accepted support from
northern missionary societies, the Freedmen's Bureau, and some southern whites, but their own action—class self-activity informed by an ethic
of mutuality—was the primary force that brought schools to the children of freed men and women. This underlying force represented the culmination of a process of social class formation and development that
started decades before the Civil War. "Emancipation," as Herbert Gutman showed, "transformed an established and developed subordinate
class, allowing ex-slave men and women to act on a variety of class

beliefs that had developed but been constrained during several generations of enslavement." Hence the South's postbellum movement for universal education is best understood as an expression of the ex-slaves'
beliefs and behavior. External assistance notwithstanding, the postwar
campaign for free schooling was rooted firmly in the beliefs and behavior
of former slaves. W. E. B. DuBois was on the mark when he said: "Public
education for all at public expense was, in the South, a Negro idea."
Such a view of postbellum southern education acknowledges the important contributions of northerners but recognizes the ex-slaves as the principal challenge to the region's long-standing resistance to free schooling.[2]

Most northern missionaries went south with the preconceived idea
that the slave regime was so brutal and dehumanizing that blacks were
little more than uncivilized victims who needed to be taught the values
and rules of civil society. They were bent on treating the freedmen almost
wholly as objects. Many missionaries were astonished, and later cha-
grined, however, to discover that many ex-slaves had established their
own educational collectives and associations, staffed schools entirely
with black teachers, and were unwilling to allow their educational movement to be controlled by the "civilized" Yankees. In vital respects, missionary propaganda continued in spite of the social reality that contradicted it, but some of the more insightful Yankees began to appreciate
ex-slaves as creative participants in the postbellum social process. John
W. Alvord, the national superintendent of schools for the Freedmen's
Bureau, was one of those perceptive Yankees. His growing awareness of
a distinctly black perspective on educational and social matters was
probably a result of his work, which compelled him to travel across the
South and thereby afforded him a view of the depth and breadth of ex-
slaves' values and behavior.

In September 1865, Alvord was appointed inspector of schools for the
bureau. The title was later changed to general superintendent of schools.
In July 1865 Alvord appointed a superintendent of schools for each
southern state to help compile records on the bureau's educational activities. Alvord had traveled through nearly all the Confederate states by
December 1865 and filed his first general report on the Freedmen's Bureau schools in January 1866. In this document he gave special attention
to the practice of "self-teaching" and "native schools" among the freed
men and women. "Throughout the entire South," Alvord reported, "an
effort is being made by the colored people to educate themselves." "In
the absence of other teaching they are determined to be self-taught; and
everywhere some elementary text-book, or the fragment of one, may be
seen in the hands of negroes." Not only were individuals found teaching
themselves to read and write, but Alvord also discovered a system of
what he chose to call "native schools," one of which he found at Golds-

boro, North Carolina: "Two colored young men, who but a little time before commenced to learn themselves, had gathered 150 pupils, all quite orderly and hard at study." Further, Alvord discovered that "no white man, before me, had ever come near them." Hence native schools were common schools founded and maintained exclusively by ex-slaves. Two of Alvord's findings must be heavily emphasized. First, he found "native schools," in his own words, "throughout the entire South." Second, he discovered many of them in places that had not been visited by the Freedmen's Bureau or northern benevolent societies. Alvord, realizing that his findings did not square with existing perceptions of "the character of the Negro," took "special pains" to ascertain the facts on native schools. Such schools were found in "all the large places I visited," and they were "making their appearance through the *interior* of the entire South." After receiving much testimony from his field agents, "both oral and written," Alvord estimated in 1866 that there were "at least 500 schools of this description . . . already in operation throughout the South." This estimate, he warned his readers, was not an "overstatement." Alvord had little doubt about the significance of his findings: "This educational movement among the freedmen has in it a self-sustaining element." This "self-sustaining" activity was rooted firmly in the slave experience and began to surface before the war's end.[3]

Before northern benevolent societies entered the South in 1862, before President Abraham Lincoln issued the Emancipation Proclamation in 1863, and before Congress created the Bureau of Refugees, Freedmen and Abandoned Lands (Freedmen's Bureau) in 1865, slaves and free persons of color had already begun to make plans for the systematic instruction of their illiterates. Early black schools were established and supported largely through the Afro-Americans' own efforts. The first of these schools, according to current historiography, opened at Fortress Monroe, Virginia, in September 1861, under the leadership of Mary Peake, a black teacher. Primary historical sources, however, demonstrate that slaves and free persons of color started schools even before the Fortress Monroe venture. In July 1864, for instance, the black *New Orleans Union* commemorated the founding of the Pioneer School of Freedom, established in New Orleans in 1860, "in the midst of danger and darkness." Some schools predated the Civil War period and simply increased their activities after the war started. A black school in Savannah, Georgia, had existed unknown to the slave regime from 1833 to 1865. Its teacher, a black woman by the name of Deveaux, quickly expanded her literacy campaign during and following the war. It was this type of "self-sustaining" behavior that produced the native schools Alvord observed throughout the South in 1866.[4]

Herbert Gutman's pioneering work on this subject demonstrates fur-

*Zion School in Charleston, South Carolina, established in December
1865, had an entirely black administration and teaching staff. By
December 1866 it had 13 teachers, an enrollment of 850 students, and
an average daily attendance of 720 pupils. Wood engraving in* Harper's
Weekly, *15 December 1866.*

ther that the native schools of Fortress Monroe, Savannah, and New
Orleans were not isolated occurrences. Such schools were also begun
among refugees in Alexandria, Virginia. A white teacher did not work
with Afro-Americans in Alexandria until October 1862, by which time
they had already established several schools. "In April 1863," wrote
Gutman, "about four hundred children attended such schools." Likewise, he documented schools for rural ex-slaves in northeastern South
Carolina. In 1867 Camden blacks, largely through their own individual
and collective efforts, established twenty-two schools in which more
than four thousand children were instructed. Schooling also made significant progress among blacks in Sumter, Marion, Darlington, Sim-
monsville, Florence, Kingstree, Chetau, Bennettsville, and Timonville,
South Carolina. Ex-slaves contributed their money and labor to help
make these schools possible, and they organized responsible committees
to supervise the schools.[5]

What happened in Alexandria, Virginia, before 1865 and in northeastern South Carolina in 1866 and 1867 occurred elsewhere in the
South. Afro-Americans over the entire region contributed significantly to
the origin and development of universal schooling. Even where the Union

army and Freedmen's Bureau were heavily involved in the education of refugees and ex-slaves, the long-term success of schooling depended mainly on Afro-Americans. The activities of Louisiana refugees and ex-slaves illustrate the importance of such involvement. Blacks began establishing small private schools between 1860 and 1862. Though these first schools were inadequately financed and haphazardly run, attempts were made to organize them on a systematic basis. After Union forces occupied New Orleans in 1863, however, the federal Commission of Enrollment presided over blacks' educational activities. According to historian John W. Blassingame, Major General Nathaniel P. Banks "instituted the most thorough of all systems for educating the freedmen in his Department of Gulf (Louisiana, Mississippi, Alabama, and Texas)." In October 1863, Banks authorized the Commission of Enrollment to take a census of Afro-Americans in the Gulf states and to establish schools for blacks in New Orleans. On 22 March 1864, he established a Board of Education to organize and govern the spread of black schools. In September 1864, the black *New Orleans Tribune* reported that Banks's effort had already resulted in 60 schools with "eight thousand scholars and more than one hundred teachers." By December 1864, the Board of Education was operating 95 schools with 9,571 children and 2,000 adults, instructed by 162 teachers. This system of schooling extended beyond the New Orleans area. The *Tribune* reported, in July 1864, that teachers were "sent to instruct black pupils in rural areas." In 1865 the Freedmen's Bureau took control of this school system, which then included 126 schools, 19,000 pupils, and 100 teachers.[6]

Such historical evidence has been wrongly used to attribute the freedmen's school movement to Yankee benevolence or federal largesse. The events that followed the Freedmen's Bureau takeover, however, underscore Gutman's observation that the ex-slaves' educational movement was rooted deeply within their own communal values. The Board of Education and later the Freedmen's Bureau maintained these schools through federal contributions and by levying a property tax. In 1866, allegedly to reduce the financial costs to the bureau, its officials temporarily closed all black schools under their authorization, and the general tax for freedmen's education was suspended by military order. The effect of this change was catastrophic. Alvord recorded the actions of Louisiana's ex-slaves: "The consternation of the colored population was intense. . . . They could not consent to have their children sent away from study, and at once expressed willingness to be assessed for the whole expense." Black leaders petitioned Yankee military officers to levy an added tax upon their community to replenish the bureau's school fund. Petitions demanding the continuation of universal schooling poured in from all over Louisiana. As Alvord recounted: "I saw one [petition], from plantations across the river, at least 30 feet in length, representing 10,000 negroes. It was affecting to examine it and note the names and marks (x) of such a long list of parents, ignorant themselves, but begging that their children might be educated, promising that from beneath their present burdens, and out of their extreme poverty, they would pay for it." Such actions reveal the collective effort and shared values of the ex-slaves who built and sustained schools across the postwar South.[7]

Much more than federal largesse made free schooling a reality among Louisiana's ex-slaves. After the bureau withdrew its support, the freedmen took control of the educational system and transformed federal schools into local free schools. The *New Orleans Tribune* reported that as soon as the bureau's failures were recognized, educational associations "were organized in various parts of the state, at least in its principal cities, to promote the cause of education, and with the particular view of helping the children of parents in reduced circumstances to attend schools." One such association, the Louisiana Educational Relief Association, was organized in June 1866. Its primary aim was to "disseminate the principle of education, by assisting poor children whose friends are unable to do so." The board of trustees could "lease or buy such school property as may be deemed judicious, and examine and employ teachers." Louisiana's freedmen believed themselves primarily responsible for providing education for their children. "Each race of men, each class in society, have [sic] to shape their own destinies themselves," wrote J. Willis Menard, secretary of the Louisiana Educational Relief Association. Although acknowledging the support of the Freedmen's Bureau and northern benevolent societies, Menard maintained that the ex-slaves' survival and development rested largely on their own shoulders: "The colored people are called today to mark out on the map of life with their *own hands* their future course or locality in the great national body politic. Other hands cannot mark for them; other tongues cannot speak for them; other eyes cannot see for them; they must see and speak for themselves, and make their own characters on the map, however crooked or illegible." That Menard's feelings were not unusual is revealed through the behavior of Louisiana's freedmen from 1866 to 1868. During this period they developed a parallel system of free schools. Even when the bureau reopened its schools, private schools for black pupils continued to spring up outside its control. Enrollment in such schools grew rapidly and actually exceeded the number registered in the bureau's system. In January 1867 there were sixty-five private schools in New Orleans enrolling 2,967 pupils; the bureau maintained fifty-six schools with 2,527 pupils enrolled. Free schooling was sustained in Louisiana largely as a result of the ex-slaves' collective efforts.[8]

The relationship between black self-activity and educational changes in the postwar South is further illustrated by the behavior of Georgia's ex-slaves. In December 1864 a committee of Afro-American leaders in Savannah met with Secretary of War Edwin M. Stanton and General William T. Sherman to request support for the education of Georgia's liberated blacks. Out of this conference evolved a plan for establishing an organized system of free schools. In 1865 Afro-American leaders formed the Georgia Educational Association to supervise schools in districts throughout the state, to establish school policies, and to raise funds to help finance the cost of education. Freedmen's Bureau officials described the aims and structure of this association:

> To associate the efforts of the people, the prominent educators in the State, the agents of northern societies, and such officers of the government as are authorized to aid the work, and to unite in such a manner as shall exclude any subject at all likely to divide their efforts or direct them from their one great and desirable object. To secure this end, subordinate associations are established as far as practicable. By this means a thorough union is formed and a prompt and constant communication with the parent society is had. Connected with the State association is a State board of education, which . . . is a general executive committee.

Through this association Georgia's Afro-Americans sustained in full or part the operation of more than two-thirds of their schools. In the fall of 1866, they financed entirely or in part 96 of the 123 day and evening schools. They also owned 57 of the school buildings. Such accomplishments fulfilled the primary purpose of the Georgia Educational Association, "that the freedmen shall establish schools in their own counties and neighborhoods, to be supported entirely by the colored people." In Savannah, for instance, there were 28 schools in 1866, and 16 of them, reported the black *Loyal Georgian*, were "under the control of an Educational Board of Colored Men, taught by colored teachers, and sustained by the freed people." These beliefs and behavior were consistent with the activities of ex-slaves in Virginia, South Carolina, and Louisiana.[9]

Significantly, Georgia's black educational leaders were critical of popular misconceptions, which attributed the schooling of ex-slaves to Yankee benevolence. The *Loyal Georgian*, official newspaper of the Georgia Educational Association, rejected explicitly the argument that Yankee teachers brought schooling to the freedmen. In February 1866, though defending Yankee teachers against southern white criticism, the *Loyal Georgian* also expressed its hope that missionary teachers were not in the South "in any vain reliance on their superior gifts, either of intelligence or benevolence; or in any foolish self-confidence that they have a special call to this office, or special endowments to meet its demands." Historian Jacqueline Jones has demonstrated that northern teachers in Georgia were "taken aback to discover that some blacks preferred to teach in and operate their own schools without the benefit of northern largesse." Similarly, Ronald E. Butchart has shown that ex-slaves, in general, initiated and supported education for themselves and their children and also resisted external control of their educational institutions. In 1867, for instance, the *Freedmen's Record* complained about the tendency of ex-slaves to prefer sending their children to black-controlled private schools rather than supporting the less expensive northern white-dominated "free" schools. A white observer noted that "in all respects apart from his or her competency to teach—they will keep their children out of school, and go to work, organize and [*sic*] independent school and send their children to it." It is no wonder, then, that some missionaries complained of the ex-slaves' lack of gratitude "for the charity which northern friends are so graciously bestowing." The ex-slaves' educational movement became a test of their capacity to restructure their lives, to establish their freedom. Although they appreciated northern support, they resisted infringements that threatened to undermine their own initiative and self-reliance.[10]

In other important ways ex-slaves initiated and sustained schools whether or not northern aid was available. The "Sabbath" school system, about which little is known, provides a particularly clear study of educational activities operated largely on the strength of the ex-slave community. Frequently, Sabbath schools were established before "free" or "public" schools. These church-sponsored schools, operated mainly in evenings and on weekends, provided basic literacy instruction. "They reached thousands not able to attend weekday schools," writes historian Samuel L. Horst. In January 1866, in his first report to the Freedmen's Bureau, Alvord commented:

Sabbath schools among freedmen have opened throughout the entire South; all of them giving elementary instruction, and reaching thousands who cannot attend the week-day teaching. These are not usually included in the regular returns, but are often spoken of with special interest by the superintendents. Indeed, one of the most thrilling spectacles which he who visits the southern country now witnesses in cities, and often upon the plantations, is the large schools gathered upon the Sabbath day, sometimes of many hundreds, dressed in clean Sunday garments, with eyes sparkling, intent upon elementary and Christian instruction. The management of some of these is admirable, after the fashion of the best Sunday schools of white children, with faithful teachers, the majority of whom it will be noticed are colored.

Some of Alvord's findings are especially worthy of emphasis. Sabbath schools were common in ex-slave communities across the South immediately following the war's end. In 1868 Alvord described the scope of Sabbath schools in North Carolina: "In all the cities of the State, in most of the smaller towns, and in many of the rural districts, Sabbath schools are established and well conducted." Although white religious societies sponsored some Sabbath schools for ex-slaves, the system was largely black-dominated, relied on local black communities for support, and generally had all-black teaching staffs. The importance of the Sabbath schools varied across states and localities. In some areas they constituted the only viable system of free instruction. T. K. Noble, Freedmen's Bureau superintendent of education in Kentucky, said in 1867: "The places of worship owned by the colored people are almost the only available school houses in the State."[11]

It is important, therefore, to emphasize another of Alvord's observations, that the Sabbath schools, often spoken of with special interest by the state superintendents, were not usually included in the regular bureau reports. C. E. Compton, the bureau's superintendent of education in Tennessee, reported in 1870 that "many children attend Sabbath schools at colored churches of which no report is received." The Freedmen's Bureau kept statistics from 1866 to 1870. These records include almost exclusively schools under the auspices of northern societies. Hence, ex-slaves laid a significantly larger foundation for universal education than is accounted for in official reports and in the histories of southern education. James M. McPherson writes, "At no time were more than 10 percent of the freedmen of school age attending the [missionary] societies' schools." Meyer Weinberg concludes that, in 1870, "nine out of ten black children still remained outside any school." These estimates, however accurate for schools reporting to the bureau, do not include data on the black church-operated schools. In 1869 Alvord asked his field agents to estimate numbers of teachers and enrollments in Sabbath schools. These reports, admittedly conservative in their estimates, enumerated 1,512 Sabbath schools with 6,146 teachers and 107,109 pupils. Sabbath schools continued to grow in the black community long after Reconstruction. In 1868 the African Methodist Episcopal church (AME), for example, enrolled 40,000 pupils in its Sabbath schools. By 1885, the AME church reported having "200,000 children in Sunday schools" for "intellectual and moral" instruction. These Sunday schools were not devoted entirely to Bible study. As Booker T. Washington recalled from

This school on St. Helena Island in South Carolina was typical of the Sabbath and free schools attended by ex-slaves in the period immediately following the Civil War. Courtesy of the National Archives.

his own experience, "the principal book studied in the Sunday school
was the spelling book." The Sabbath schools represent yet another remarkable example of ex-slaves seeking, establishing, and supporting
their own schools.[12]

It was such local activities by ex-slaves that spurred the establishment
of widespread elementary and literacy education and provided the grass-
roots foundation for the educational activities of northern missionary
societies and the Freedmen's Bureau. To be sure, ex-slaves benefited
greatly from the support of northern whites; but they were determined to
achieve educational self-sufficiency in the long run with or without the
aid of northerners. Their self-determination has escaped the attention of
all but a few historians. The larger significance of their behavior, however, did not go unnoticed by Freedmen's Bureau superintendent John
Alvord, one of the most perceptive Yankee observers of postwar southern educational changes. As early as January 1866, Alvord noted the
"self-sustaining element" in the ex-slaves' educational movement. He
quickly recognized the organization and discipline that underlay the
school campaign. In July 1866 he reported "that the surprising efforts of
our colored population to obtain and [*sic*] education are not spasmodic."
"They are growing to a habit," he continued, "crystalizing into a system,
and each succeeding school-term shows their organization more and
more complete and permanent." Initially, Alvord did not know what to
make of these "surprising efforts." Foreshadowing the interpretations of
some later historians, in January 1866 he attributed the ex-slaves' campaign for schooling to "the natural thirst for knowledge common to all
men," a desire to imitate educated whites, an attraction to the mystery of
literate culture, the practical needs of business life, and the stimulating
effects of freedom. By July, however, Alvord pointed to a more fundamental motive for the freedmen's behavior: "They have within themselves . . . a vitality and hope, coupled with patience and willingness to
struggle, which foreshadows with certainty their higher education as a
people in the coming time." Universal education was certain to become a
reality in black society, not because ex-slaves were motivated by childlike, irrational, and primitive drives, but because they were a responsible
and politically self-conscious social class. Alvord, therefore, was confident that the ex-slaves' educational movement would not soon fall into
decline: "Obstacles are yet to be encountered. Perhaps the most trying
period in the freedmen's full emancipation has not yet come. But we can
distinctly see that the incipient education universally diffused as it is, has
given these whole four millions an impulse onward never to be lost. They
are becoming conscious of what they can do, of what they ultimately *can*
be. . . . Self-reliance is becoming their pride as it is their responsibility."
The great efforts blacks made to establish schools for their own children

soon after the war and to establish state-supported systems of public education for all children reflected both their self-reliance and distinct educational and social philosophy. These ideals had been cultivated in large part during their long ordeal of slavery.[13]

Ultimately, the formation and development of the ex-slaves' beliefs and behavior regarding universal education in the postwar South will have to be understood as part of a process that started decades before the Civil War. For, as Herbert Gutman has demonstrated, the choices so many freed men and women made immediately upon their emancipation, before they had substantial rights by law, had their origins in the ways their ancestors had adapted to enslavement. Hence, before the reason why Afro-Americans emerged from slavery with a particular desire for literacy can be understood, slavery and especially slave literacy await refined and detailed study. That is beyond the primary scope of this chapter, but a few examples might illuminate the social context of slave literacy and, therefore, black consciousness of literate culture. The way slaves and other southern social classes thought about literacy and education developed along with the modes in which they actually learned or experienced it. That experience for slaves was vastly different in most important respects from the experiences of planters, white small farmers, industrialists, and poor whites. During the three decades before the Civil War slaves lived in a society in which for them literacy was forbidden by law and symbolized as a skill that contradicted the status of slaves. As former slave William Henry Heard recalled: "We did not learn to read nor write, as it was against the law for any person to teach any slave to read; and any slave caught writing suffered the penalty of having his forefinger cut from his right hand; yet there were some who could read and write." Despite the dangers and difficulties, thousands of slaves learned to read and write. By 1860 about 5 percent of the slaves had learned to read. Many paid a high price for their literacy. Thomas H. Jones, a slave in mid-nineteenth-century North Carolina, learned how to read while hiding in the back of his master's store. "It seemed to me that if I could learn to read and write," said Jones, "this learning might, nay, I really thought it would point out to me the way to freedom, influence and real secure happiness." As he became more engrossed in his pursuit of literate culture and careless about concealing it, Jones was surprised one morning by the sudden appearance of his master. Having only a second to react, Jones threw his book behind some barrels in the store, but not before his master had seen him throw something away. The slaveowner assumed that Jones had been stealing items from the stockroom and ordered him to retrieve whatever he had thrown away. "I knew if my book was discovered that all was lost, and I felt prepared for any hazard or suffering rather than give up my book and my hopes of improvement," recalled Jones. He endured three brutal whippings to conceal his pursuit of literacy. In another instance a slave by the name of Scipio was put to death for teaching a slave child how to read and spell, and the child was severely beaten to make him "forget what he had learned." The former slave Ferebe Rogers was married by a slave, Enoch Golden, who persisted throughout his life in spreading literacy among his fellow slaves. "On his dyin' bed he said he been de death o' many a nigger 'cause he taught so many to read and write," said Rogers. Elizabeth Sparks was part of a group of rebel slaves who held secret literacy sessions in the slave quarters. The gatherings, known among slaves as "stealin' the meetin'," were attended by free blacks who attempted to teach slaves to read and write. Although slaves became literate in a variety of ways, including at the hands of slaveowners, probably the typical experience was characterized by former slave Louisa Gause: "No child, white people never teach colored people nothin, but to be good to dey massa en mittie, what learnin dey would get in dem days dey been get it at night; taught demselves." No other class of native southerners had experienced literacy in this context. Hence emancipation extruded an ex-slave class with a fundamentally different consciousness of literacy, a class that viewed reading and writing as a contradiction of oppression.[14]

In the history of black education the political significance of slave literacy reaches beyond the antebellum period. Many of the educators and leaders of the postbellum years were men and women who first became literate under slavery. Moreover, many prominent post–Civil War black educators who were not literate as slaves received their initial understanding of the meaning of literacy under slavery. Such black leaders as Frederick Douglass, Bishop Henry M. Turner, Bishop Isaac Lane, Bishop Lucius H. Holsey, and P. B. S. Pinchback and educators Isaac M. Bergman, Bishop John Wesley Gaines, W. S. Scarborough, and Lucy C. Lancy are some of the prominent nineteenth-century figures who became literate in the antebellum South. Their ideas about the meaning and purpose of education were shaped partly by the social system of slavery under which they first encountered literacy. After slavery many of the leading black educators emerged from among the rebel literates, those slaves who had sustained their own learning process in defiance of the slaveowners' authority. They viewed literacy and formal education as means to liberation and freedom.

Postslavery experiences continued to reinforce and shape a distinctive Afro-American consciousness of literate culture. "Every little negro in the county is now going to school and the public pays for it," wrote one disgruntled planter. "This is a hell of [a] fix but we can't help it, and the best policy is to conform as far as possible to circumstances." Such responses emphasized the planters' persistent beliefs that literate culture contradicted the status of black southerners. Many postslavery developments provided ex-slaves with compelling reasons to become literate. The uses and abuses of written labor contracts made it worthwhile to be able to read, write, and cipher. Frequently, planters designed labor contracts in ways that would confuse and entrap the ex-slaves. As the Freedmen's Bureau superintendent observed, "I saw one [labor contract] in which it was stipulated that one-third of seven-twelfths of all corn, potatoes, fodder, etc., shall go to the laborers." Hence when a middle-aged black woman was asked why she was so determined to learn to read and write, she replied, "so that the Rebs can't cheat me." The enfranchisement of black males also gave ex-slaves an impulse to become literate. "At the place of voting they look at the ballot-box and then at the printed ticket in their hands, wishing they could read it," reported Alvord in 1867. Education for the freedmen could serve as a safeguard against fraud and manipulation.[15]

More fundamentally, the ex-slaves' struggle for education was an expression of freedom. It was, as Ronald Butchart maintains, an effort of an oppressed people "to put as great a distance between themselves and bondage as possible." The *New Orleans Black Republican* proclaimed in April 1865: "Freedom and school books and newspapers, go hand in hand. Let us secure the freedom we have received by the intelligence that can maintain it." This proclamation was signed by prominent black leaders of New Orleans, including Thomas S. Isabelle, C. C. Antoine, S. W. Rogers, Professor P. M. Williams, and A. E. Barber. Similarly, in 1867, the black Equal Rights Association of Macon, Georgia, resolved: "That a Free school system is a great need of our state, and that we will do all in our power by voice and by vote to secure adoption of a system." That same year black leaders Henry M. Turner, T. G. Campbell, John T. Costin, and Thomas P. Beard formed the Black Republican party of Georgia. The organization declared that "Free Schools and churches are the guardians of civil and religious liberty." Northern observers quickly noted that education stood as "the token and pledge" of blacks' emancipation. Even adult ex-slaves were, as the Freedmen's Bureau superintendent recorded, "earnestly seeking that instruction which will fit them for their new responsibilities." For the freedmen, universal schooling was a matter of personal liberation and a necessary function of a free society.[16]

Thus ex-slaves did much more than establish a tradition of educational self-help that supported most of their schools. They also were the first among native southerners to wage a campaign for universal public education. From its small beginnings in 1860 and with the help of the Freedmen's Bureau and northern benevolent societies, the school system was virtually complete in its institutional form by 1870. According to historian Henry Allen Bullock, fourteen southern states had established 575 schools by 1865, and these schools were employing 1,171 teachers for the 71,779 Negro and white children in regular attendance. School attendance was not uniform across cities and towns, but it was visible in enough places to signal a fundamental shift in southern tradition. In 1866 Alvord reported his findings on the level of ex-slaves' school attendance: "The average attendance is nearly equal to that usually found at the North. For instance, in the District of Columbia, the daily attendance at the public school is but forty-one (41) percent; while at the colored schools of the District it is seventy-five (75) percent. In the State of New York, the daily attendance at the public school averages forty-three (43) percent. At the colored schools in the city of Memphis it is seventy-two (72) percent; and in Virginia eighty-two (82) percent." In Louisiana over 60 percent of all black children from five to twelve years of age were enrolled in school by 1865. The ex-slaves' school enrollment suffered a setback in 1868, rose again in 1869, and leveled off in 1870. In the entire South in 1870, about one-fourth of the school-age ex-slaves attended "public" schools. Reliable data are not available to determine Sabbath school attendance rates, but it seems probable from scattered evidence that Sabbath schools increased their enrollment throughout the 1870s and 1880s. The freedmen's initiative in starting schools and their remarkable attendance rates made it evident that "free" schooling was fast becoming a customary right in the postwar South.[17]

The ex-slaves' most fundamental challenge to the planters' ideology and structure of schooling, however, went beyond the practice of universal schooling as a customary right. They played a central role in etching the idea of universal public education into southern state constitutional law. As DuBois demonstrated, "The first great mass movement for public education at the expense of the state, in the South, came from Negroes." Black politicians played a critical role in establishing universal education as a basic right in southern constitutional conventions during congressional Reconstruction. Under the Military Reconstruction Acts passed in 1867, Congress empowered the generals of the armies of occupation to call for new constitutional conventions in which blacks were to participate along with whites. Black politicians and leaders joined with Republicans in southern constitutional conventions to legalize public education in the constitutions of the former Confederate states. By 1870, every southern state had specific provisions in its constitution to assure a public school system financed by a state fund. And even when white southerners regained control of state governments, they kept the central features of educational governance and finance created by the ex-slave–Republican coalition. Ex-slaves used their resources first in a grass-roots movement to build, fund, and staff schools as a practical right; then they joined with Republicans to incorporate the idea into southern state constitutional law. With these actions they revolutionized the South's position regarding the role of universal public education in society.[18]

The freedmen's educational revolution bred a counterrevolution. Postwar southern economic and social development, including educational reform, was heavily influenced by the persistent domination of the planter class. Traditional historiography has contended that the Civil War and emancipation brought about the downfall of the prewar planter class. The most recent historical scholarship, however, demonstrates convincingly the extent to which wealth and power in the postwar South continued to rest in the planters' hands. What actually occurred was not the downfall or destruction of the old planter class but rather its persistence and metamorphosis. Plantation land tended to remain in the hands of its prewar owners.[19]

The persistence and tenacity of the planter class throughout the war and Reconstruction, contends Jonathan Wiener, laid the basis for its continued domination of the southern political economy in the 1870s and 1880s. As a consequence, the South took the "Prussian road to industrial capitalism—a delayed industrialization under the auspices of a backward agrarian elite, the power of which was based on a repressive system of agricultural labor." In 1880, 75.4 percent of the South's labor force was in agriculture. Black agricultural laborers constituted more than 40 percent of the South's total agricultural labor force and formed a clear majority in several southern states. Agriculture accounted for only 23.3 percent of the work force in the Northeast and 54.5 percent in the North Central region. The planters' approach to labor control posed a formidable threat to the ex-slaves' educational movement. Elsewhere in the nation, particularly the industrial Northeast, dominant classes had already committed themselves to tax-supported public education, partly as a means to train and discipline an industrial work force. Freedmen's Bureau Superintendent Alvord, echoing the northern idea of universal schooling for the laboring classes, proclaimed to the South in 1866: "Popular education cannot well be opposed; free labor is found to be more contented with its privileges." But southern planters did not share northern ideas on free labor or popular education. Postwar planters complained that their "free" laborers were unreliable, failed to comply with the terms of their labor contracts, and would not obey orders. Most important, schooling most emphatically was not the answer to southern labor problems. "The South could not supply by schools," said one southern writer in 1868, "the restraining, correcting, elevating influences" cultivated and maintained by slavery. When Carl Schurz toured the South in late 1865, he found the planters believing that "learning will spoil the nigger for work." Faced with the possibilities of moving toward a northern-style system of free labor and mass literacy or remaining with their coercive mode of labor allocation and control, the planters chose the labor-repressive system, which rested at least partially on the absence of formal schooling among agricultural and domestic laborers.[20]

Hence at war's end the planters attempted to reestablish the plantation system with only minor modifications. With the overseer renamed "manager" or "agent," the planters tried to force ex-slaves to work the postwar plantation in antebellumlike work gangs. The planters needed above all a resumption of work on the part of black laborers in numbers and involving costs similar to those prevailing in the pre-war era. This desire was thwarted when ex-slaves withdrew a substantial portion of their labor power. By greatly reducing the number of days worked and the number of hours worked each day, they created a serious labor shortage. According to economic historians Roger L. Ransom and Richard Sutch, upon emancipation the supply of black labor fell to two-thirds its prewar level. This reduced labor supply had a profound impact on the ability of the South to produce cotton. It represented a severe financial blow to the planter class. Therefore, ex-slaves gained some power in the labor market to insist upon educational and economic changes in the South's social hierarchy. Planters, however, generally favored a policy of strict labor control and discouraged the education of freedmen.[21]

In the immediate postwar years, ex-slaves, sometimes assisted by northern troops, were able to use their labor power to give weight to their educational demands. In January 1866 Alvord noted:

> If they are to be retained as laborers in the rural districts, [educational] opportunities must be furnished on the plantations. More than one instance could be already given where a school in the interior has been started from this motive. . . . The head of one of the largest of the timber and turpentine enterprises in South Carolina told me that he formerly had hired only men, but he had now learned that he must have their families too, and that this could only be done by allowing them patches of land, treating them properly, paying them well, and *giving them schools.*

In 1866 and 1867, Freedmen's Bureau officials observed the widespread emergence of the "educational clause" in labor contracts between planters and ex-slaves. In July 1867 Frank R. Chase, the bureau's superintendent of education for Louisiana, reported: "Many of the freedmen made it a special clause of their contract this year, that they should have the benefit of schools. But the planter was only willing to have colored teachers employed, thinking that such schools would amount to little or nothing. In this they are mistaken, as many of the most prosperous

schools in the State are taught by competent colored teachers." Such
reports from bureau officials throughout the South convinced Alvord
that "the educational clause in the contracts . . . is rapidly becoming
universal." Hence, he continued, "Schools are everywhere springing up
from the soil itself at the demand of those who till it—a state of things
which localizes the benefits of education in a fixed, permanent society."
Because ex-slaves understood that their labor power was essential for the
restoration of southern agriculture to its prewar level of prosperity, they
demanded not only fair wages for their work but educational opportunities as well. This practice, at least for a brief period in the postwar years,
enabled some plantation ex-slaves to experience the benefits of schooling. Some planters, desiring to secure and stabilize a needed supply of
laborers, even shielded freedmen's schools from harassment by white
terrorists. Schools on the plantations were usually financed by the ex-
slaves, but a few were paid for by planters.[22]

In general, the ex-slaves were unable to reconcile the planters to the
idea of black education. It has been argued that the most intelligent and
successful planters usually supported Negro education and that the most
bitter opposition came from the white lower classes. To be sure, militant
opposition did come from lower-class whites, but it came also from
planters. A few planters did accept or tolerate the idea of universal education among the ex-slaves, and so did a few poor whites. As a class,
however, the planters reacted decisively to the freedmen's educational
movement; they were opposed to black education in particular and
showed substantial resistance to the very idea of public schooling for the
laboring classes. The planters' opposition to black education surfaced
early. In 1864 the *New Orleans Tribune* reported that Louisiana planters
were strongly opposed to the ex-slaves' educational movement. In the
country parishes, white teachers were "condemned and scorned" and
landlords "refused to rent buildings for school purposes, and to board
the teachers." In 1867 Louisiana's superintendent of education complained that "a large majority of the planters are opposed to the education of the freedmen." An example from 1871 illustrates the point with
much greater force. General John Eaton, commissioner of the new Federal Bureau of Education, sent out three thousand questionnaires to laborers and employers regarding the benefits of universal education in the
South. Concerning the replies, he wrote: "A large number have been
received, and the writers were unanimous in their testimony as to the
value of education to every class of laborers, with one striking exception,
namely, the southern planters; the majority of whom did not believe in
giving the Negro any education." Planters resisted in various ways the
ex-slaves' pursuit of universal schooling. Henry Allen Bullock found that
Virginia planters in 1865 "were seeking to prevent Negro parents from

sending their children to school by threatening to put them out of their houses." Alabama whites who employed ex-slaves as domestics would terminate the employment of servants whose children attended school. Similarly, in 1869 the Freedmen's Bureau school superintendent for northwestern Louisiana and northern Texas discovered that "many of the planters will not allow colored children on their places to go to school at all, even when we have started those which are convenient." The planters, with few exceptions, viewed black education as a distinct threat to the racially qualified form of labor exploitation upon which their agrarian order depended.[23]

The planters' heavy use of child labor contributed significantly to their opposition to black education. During good crop years black school terms were so short and irregular that children hardly had time to learn to read and write. "Owing to unusual employment of children this season in gathering crops, especially cotton, which was very abundant, many schools did not open until December," reported John Alvord in 1870. Many parents fought this infringement upon their children's educational opportunities, but others conceded to the planters' interests.[24]

Despite the ex-slaves' early success in laying the foundation for universal education in the South, planters presented severe obstacles to those who endeavored to establish an elaborate bureaucratic system of free public schooling. Between 1869 and 1877, the planter-dominated white South regained control of the state governments. The moment of broad retrenchment came with the disputed presidential election of 1876 and the settlement that resulted in the Compromise of 1877. Southerners agreed to the election of Rutherford B. Hayes, and Republicans agreed to remove federal troops from the South. With both state authority and extralegal means of control firmly in their hands, the planters, though unable to eradicate earlier gains, kept universal schooling underdeveloped. They stressed low taxation, opposed compulsory school attendance laws, blocked the passage of new laws that would strengthen the constitutional basis of public education, and generally discouraged the expansion of public school opportunities. The planters' resistance virtually froze the ex-slaves' educational campaign in its mid-1870s position. "At the beginning of the twentieth century," wrote Horace Mann Bond, "the condition of the schools for Negro children in the South was but slightly improved over their condition in 1875." Indeed, between 1880 and 1900, the number of black children of school age increased 25 percent, but the proportion attending public school fell.[25]

The planters gained further control over black education as they increased their supervision and control over the ex-slave laboring class. The semiautonomous position and newly acquired economic power of freedmen in the labor market had buttressed their educational move-

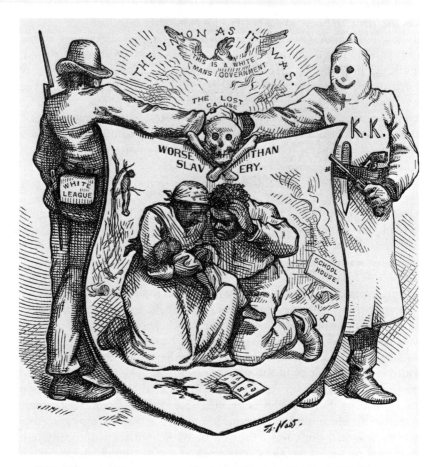

This Thomas Nast cartoon that appeared in Harper's Weekly, 24 *October 1874, depicts the southern white reaction to the ex-slave crusade for universal schooling. Note the fallen school book and the schoolhouse burning in the background while an ex-slave is being lynched. Courtesy of the Library of Congress.*

ment, but as landlords regained control over black labor, the force and autonomy of the campaign for universal schooling were severely weakened. The planters established a system of coercive labor designed to reduce wages, to restrict labor mobility, to protect individual planters from competition with other employers, and to force blacks to sign repressive labor contracts. Historians William Cohen, Pete Daniel, and Jonathan Wiener discovered a variety of state laws and local customs aimed at helping planters acquire, hold, and exploit black labor virtually at will. Enticement laws passed by ten southern states from 1865 to 1867 were the most common measures aimed at controlling the black labor force. "Enticement statutes," writes Cohen, "established the proprietary claims of employers to 'their' Negroes by making it a crime to hire away a laborer under contract to another man." Many other laws facilitated the recruitment and retention of black labor. Vagrancy laws, passed by all the former Confederate states except Tennessee and Arkansas in 1865 and 1866, gave local authorities a "virtual mandate to arrest any poor man who did not have a labor contract." Such statutes enabled police to round up "idle" blacks in times of labor scarcity, and, except in North Carolina, they provided for the hiring out of convicted offenders. Those jailed on charges of vagrancy could sign a "voluntary" labor contract with their former employer or some other white man who agreed to post bond. Workers who had no surety often wound up on chain gangs and were forced to labor through the convict-lease system.[26]

The planters favored a labor-repressive system of agricultural production. They had little incentive to use education and technology to increase efficiency and productivity or to use schooling as a means to train and discipline a more efficient work force. The postwar planters held to the beliefs and behavior of over two centuries of slavery; they did not trust the system of "free labor." Force, rather than rational free choice, was the basis of the South's political economy. Hence the region's slow development in education was in substantial part the result of the planters' stubborn adherence to a set of values inconsistent with democracy, modernization, rapid industrialization, and free schooling. To be sure, other factors militated against rapid educational change. Fundamentally, however, the South's slow rate of educational development and the planters' particular opposition to black education sprang from their clear economic and ideological interests in preserving the racially qualified system of coercive agricultural labor. Both race and class conflict existed between white planters and their black agricultural laborers.

Even though the long-term gains in public education for ex-slaves proved to be small and slow, their organized efforts and ideological imperatives laid the foundation for universal education in the South. Between 1860 and 1880 no organized challenge to the planters' interests came from the region's white middle or lower classes. Both groups were not only economically dependent on the planters, as were the ex-slaves, but also subservient to the planters' interests. Freedmen's Bureau officials were particularly alarmed by lower-class whites' general apathy toward public education. Bureau officials recognized that some planters were hostile to the idea of public education for poor whites. Louisiana's superintendent in 1869 observed planters' opposition to "the education of freedmen and poor whites." "In the parish of Franklin," he reported, "public sentiment, as to the education of freedmen and poor whites, is very decidedly against it." Unlike the ex-slaves, however, "the whites take little or no interest in educational matters, even for their own race." Throughout the bureau's history, its officials contrasted ex-slave and lower-class white attitudes toward public education. In 1866 Alvord noted: "We make no invidious comparisons of the ignorant freedman, and the ignorant Anglo-Saxon of the South. We only say the former has most creditably won his present position; and he has done it by good conduct, and rapid improvement under that instruction we are now reporting." In 1869 a bureau state school superintendent observed: "As a class they [ex-slaves] are eager to learn, while the poor whites are indifferent." Poor whites were not so much indifferent as they were bound to the planters' regime. Before the war poor children were unable to afford private schooling and only rarely had the opportunity to attend charity institutions. In the immediate postwar years the region's poor whites, in general, were still too closely tied to the planters' interests and ideology to pursue a different conception of education and society. White laborers and small farmers when organized in the Farmers' Alliance and Populist party challenged the planters' opposition to universal schooling only in the late 1880s. Ex-slaves, or black native southerners, had struggled for universal schooling over two decades before the Populist campaigns of the late 1880s and 1890s. The ex-slaves' campaign also predated the organized movement for free schooling by southern middle-class progressives. The South's white middle classes, unorganized and subservient to planter interests throughout the nineteenth century, did not begin their campaign for universal education until the dawn of the twentieth century. Hence, surrounded by planters who were hostile to public education, middle-class professionals who allied themselves with planter interests, and lower-class whites who were largely alienated from mass education, ex-slaves were the only native group to forge ahead to commit the South to a system of universal schooling in the immediate postwar years.[27]

Clearly, the freedmen's educational movement had an impact that reached far beyond their own communities. Their initiative forced whites of all classes to confront the question of universal schooling. From the Freedmen's Bureau superintendent came testimony that "the white population of the South feels the power of the [freedmen's] schools." "The poor whites are provoked by hearing Negroes read, while they are ignorant; and it is my belief that they will now receive schools, if furnished them, as never before," wrote Alvord in 1866. Further, "The educated class are not slow to perceive that their schools must be reopened, or fall behind humiliated, and that new schools must now be organized on a more popular plan than heretofore." Mass education was necessary for

white children, insisted Robert Mills Lusher, white school superintendent of Louisiana, so that they would be "properly prepared to maintain
the supremacy of the white race." The ex-slaves' initiative in establishing
and supporting a system of secular and Sabbath schools and in demanding universal public education for all children presented a new challenge
to the dominant-class whites—the possibility of an emerging literate
black working class in the midst of a largely illiterate poor white class.
This constituted a frontal assault on the racist myth of black inferiority,
which was critical to the maintenance of the South's racial caste system.
The planters, unable to wipe out the educational gains made by ex-slaves
between 1860 and 1870, had to take a more liberal posture regarding
universal education among whites of all classes. Moreover, poor whites
became less indifferent toward the idea of public education. Thus the
Populist demands for free schooling in the late 1880s and 1890s, as well
as the middle-class educational reforms of the early twentieth century,
were indebted to the ex-slaves' educational movement of the 1860s and
1870s.[28]

In the late 1870s and early 1880s, one could already detect a slight
shift in southern white attitudes regarding universal schooling in general
and particularly for black children. Southern whites began realizing the
improbability of reversing the gains made by freedmen during the Civil
War and Reconstruction years. Hence a growing, although small, minority of prominent southern whites began speaking in favor of universal
schooling for the region's laboring classes, including Afro-Americans.
Foremost among these whites were those promoting limited or rapid
southern industrialization. Although traditional planters continued to
favor a repressive system of agricultural labor and to discourage working-class literacy, proponents of southern industrialization increasingly
viewed mass schooling as a means to produce efficient and contented
labor and as a socialization process to instill in black and white children
an acceptance of the southern racial hierarchy. In 1877 Thomas Muldrop Logan, former Confederate general and industrialist in Richmond,
Virginia, spoke before the American Social Science Association on the
question of education in the southern states. Logan, who became one of
the South's most prominent railroad magnates, articulated a rationale
for supporting working-class and Afro-American schooling that came to
characterize the thinking of many dominant-class whites in the late nineteenth and early twentieth centuries. "Wherever public schools have
been established," argued Logan, "the industrial classes, becoming more
intelligent, have proved more skillful and efficient; and all competing
countries must likewise establish public schools, or be supplanted in the
markets of the world." Logan was well aware of the planters' argument
against black schooling, "that when the freedman regards himself quali-

fied to earn a support by mental work, he is unwilling to accept manual labor." Logan believed, however, that maintenance of caste distinctions and division of labor were possible if blacks were offered industrial education such as was practiced at the Hampton Normal and Agricultural Institute of Virginia. By training blacks "to perform, efficiently, their part in the social economy, this caste allotment of social duties might prove advantageous to southern society, as a whole, on the principle of a division of labor applied to races." These views were echoed by famous and little-known southern industrialists as they testified before a subcommittee of the United States Senate Committee on Education and Labor in 1883.[29]

But the prevailing philosophies of black education and the subjects taught in black schools were not geared to reproduce the caste distinctions or the racially segmented labor force desired by Logan and many other postbellum white industrialists. The black teachers, school officials, and secular and religious leaders who formed the vanguard of the postwar common school movement insisted that the ex-slaves must educate themselves, gather experience, and acquire a responsible awareness of the duties incumbent upon them as citizens and as male voters in the new social order. Their thinking on these questions indicated virtually no illusions about the power of schooling to ameliorate fundamental economic inequalities. Rather, it reflected their belief that education could help raise the freed people to an appreciation of their historic responsibility to develop a better society and that any significant reorganization of the southern political economy was indissolubly linked to their education in the principles, duties, and obligations appropriate to a democratic social order. Ex-slave communities pursued their educational objectives by developing various strata, but the one they stressed the most was leadership training. They believed that the masses could not achieve political and economic independence or self-determination without first becoming organized, and organization was impossible without well-trained intellectuals—teachers, ministers, politicians, managers, administrators, and businessmen.

Toward this end the black leaders and educators adopted the New England classical liberal curriculum, so the subjects taught in post–Civil War black elementary, normal, and collegiate schools did not differ appreciably from those taught in northern white schools. Students in elementary schools received instruction in reading, spelling, writing, grammar, diction, history, geography, arithmetic, and music. Normal school students took this standard English curriculum with additional courses in orthography, map drawing, physiology, algebra, and geometry, as well as the theory and practice of teaching. The college curriculum varied slightly among institutions, but the classical course leading to the B.A. usually required Latin, Greek, mathematics, science, philosophy, and, in a few cases, one modern language. Black leaders did not view their adoption of the classical liberal curriculum or its philosophical foundations as mere imitation of white schooling. Indeed, they knew many whites who had no education at all. Rather, they saw this curriculum as providing access to the best intellectual traditions of their era and the best means to understanding their own historical development and sociological uniqueness. To be sure, a study of the classical liberal curriculum was not a study of the historical and cultural forces that enabled Afro-Americans to survive the most dehumanized aspects of enslavement. Yet that curriculum did not necessarily convince black students that they were inferior to white people.³⁰

For example, Richard Wright, one of the brightest and most influential educators of the post-Reconstruction era, found in his study of the classics solid evidence to counter claims of black inferiority. Wright was a student in an American Missionary Association school in Atlanta in 1868 when a group of visitors from the North, including General Oliver O. Howard, asked the black pupils what they should tell their friends in New England about the Georgia freedmen. Replied the young Wright, "Tell them we are rising." Wright graduated from Atlanta University in 1876 and in 1880, at age twenty-seven, he was principal of the Augusta, Georgia, "Colored High School" (later named E. A. Ware High School), the only public high school for blacks in the state. In 1883 principal Wright was sworn and examined by the U.S. Senate Committee on Education and Labor regarding conditions for education and work among blacks in Georgia. Senator Henry W. Blair of New Hampshire, the committee's chairman, queried Wright about the comparative inferiority and superiority of races. Drawing upon his understanding of the classics, Wright replied:

It is generally admitted that religion has been a great means of human development and progress, and I think that about all the great religions which have blest this world have come from the colored races—all. . . . I believe too, that our methods of alphabetic writing all came from the colored race, and I think the majority of the sciences in their origin have come from the colored races. . . . Now I take the testimony of those people who know, and who, I feel are capable of instructing me on this point, and I find them saying that the Egyptians were actually woolly-haired negroes. In Humboldt's Cosmos (Vol. 2, p. 531) you will find that testimony, and Humboldt, I presume, is pretty good authority. The same thing is

stated in Herodotus, and in a number of other authors with whom
you gentlemen are doubtless familiar. Now, if that is true, the idea
that this negro race is inherently inferior, seems to me to be at least a
little limping.

Wright's study of the classical liberal tradition led him to conclude that
"these differences of race, so called, are a mere matter of color and not
of brain." For such educators as Wright, the classical course was not so
much the imposition of an alien white culture that would make blacks
feel inferior as it was a means to understanding the development of the
Western world and blacks' inherent rights to equality within that world.
Thus, with few exceptions, both the schools founded and sustained by
black churches and secular organizations as well as those founded by
northern missionary societies taught a basic English education supplemented with the classical courses at the normal school and collegiate
levels.[31]

During the immediate postwar years the more conservative missionary
societies made some attempts to superimpose upon the common school
curriculum a set of readers designed specifically and exclusively for ex-
slave children. The American Tract Society of the American Missionary
Association published the largest collection of these materials. Such
readers as *The Freedmen's Primer*, *The Freedmen's Spelling Book*, *The
Lincoln Primer*, and the *First*, *Second* and *Third Freedmen's Readers*
contained social values designed to inculcate in the ex-slaves an acceptance of economic and racial subordination. These books portrayed
blacks in subservient roles and frequently assumed that blacks were morally and mentally inferior. Their use of such books to propagate ideas
of racial subordination betray the conservative missionaries' perception
that the appropriate regressive social values were not already contained
in the New England common school course. Whether these special books
had any widespread and long-range impact is extremely doubtful. First,
even in the most conservative missionary schools the basic pattern of
freedmen's education followed that of northern public schools. Second,
the missionary-sponsored common school structure was much too weak
and fragmented to affect the instruction of large numbers of ex-slaves. In
1870 the American Missionary Association, for instance, sustained 157
common schools. That number had declined to 70 in 1871 and to 13 in
1874. By the mid-1870s, the northern societies had already reduced their
involvement in black southern education, particularly in the area of common schools. After this period, they concentrated their efforts and financial aid primarily on normal and higher education. Their normal schools
and colleges offered the traditional classical liberal curriculum. This em-

phasis was important in determining curricular trends in black common
schools because missionary colleges trained the bulk of black teachers
until well into the twentieth century.[32]

The short-range purpose of black schooling was to provide the masses
of ex-slaves with basic literacy skills plus the rudiments of citizenship
training for participation in a democratic society. The long-range purpose was the intellectual and moral development of a responsible leadership class that would organize the masses and lead them to freedom and
equality. Being educated and literate had an important cultural significance to Afro-Americans, and they pursued these goals in opposition to
the economic and ideological interest of the planter-dominated South.
Despite what seemed like overwhelming opposition to their educational
campaigns, the masses of Afro-Americans persisted in becoming literate.
Their 95 percent illiteracy rate in 1860 had dropped to 70 percent in
1880 and would drop to 30 percent by 1910. The former slaves were
becoming literate; the process could be slowed but it could not be
stopped or reversed.[33]

By 1880, many white southerners saw that any attempt to reverse the
thrust of the ex-slaves' school campaigns would invite greater black resistance and possibly northern intervention. They began to make an uneasy
peace with the Reconstruction-era educational reforms. Most did not
agree with the idea of universal education for both races any more than
they agreed with the Fifteenth Amendment and universal franchise for all
men. They could agree, however, that it was politically unwise to attempt
to repeal the legal basis of either. A particular class of southern whites
began thinking more about controlling and restricting the expansion of
public schooling in the black South and the possibility of adapting it to
the region's traditional social structure and racial mores. Their interest in
the schooling of Afro-American children differed in social origin and
purpose from the ex-slaves' educational movement and even from the
interests of the most conservative missionary societies. They called for
the special instruction of the former slaves in a manner that could not be
adapted from the curriculum and teaching materials of the classical liberal tradition. A full curriculum of special instruction for black students
was being developed at that time by Samuel Armstrong at the Hampton
Normal and Agricultural Institute in Hampton, Virginia. This new curriculum offered the possibility of adapting black education to the particular needs and interests of the South's dominant-class whites. Hence
those southern and northern whites who thought it wiser to redirect the
social purpose of freedmen's education rather than attempt to destroy it
rallied to this new model of special instruction. This aspect of the ex-
slaves' struggle for universal education—the development of a special

form of industrial education for Afro-Americans—provoked more controversy than any other issue in black education during the late nineteenth and early twentieth centuries. As the period 1860 to 1880 was characterized by efforts to establish the legal, institutional, and moral foundation of universal schooling for ex-slaves, the quarter century following was characterized by movements to transform the content and purpose of instruction in black education.[34]

2

THE HAMPTON MODEL

OF NORMAL SCHOOL INDUSTRIAL

EDUCATION, 1868–1915

IT IS ONE of the great ironies of Afro-American history that the ideological and programmatic challenge to the ex-slaves' conception of universal schooling and social progress was conceived and nurtured by a Yankee, Samuel Chapman Armstrong, and a former slave, Booker T. Washington. But even as the leaders of the ex-slave class struggled to build an educational system to help reinforce their conceptions of freedom and social order, there was born in Hampton, Virginia, in 1868, a conjuncture of educational pedagogy and social ideology of different origins and character. Armstrong represented a social class, ideology, and world outlook that was fundamentally different from and opposed to the interests of the freedmen. Thus in his establishment of the Hampton Normal and Agricultural Institute, he was neither unconscious nor contrarious, but honest. The institute's curriculum, values, and ethos represented his social class and ideology as properly as the moral foundation of the Sabbath schools, free schools, public schools, and colleges represented the social and cultural values of the ex-slaves. The ex-slaves struggled to develop a social and educational ideology singularly appropriate to their defense of emancipation and one that challenged the social power of the planter regime. Armstrong developed a pedagogy and ideology designed to avoid such confrontations and to maintain within the South a social consensus that did not challenge traditional inequalities of wealth and power. In time these two ideologies and programs of black education collided, and Armstrong's prized pupil, Booker T. Washington, was at the center of the confrontation. Washington founded Tuskegee Normal and Industrial Institute in 1881, and by the turn of the century, the "Hampton-Tuskegee Idea" represented the ideological antithesis of the educational and social movement begun by ex-slaves. The strife between these two ideologies and systems of education did not subside until the late 1920s, when Hampton and Tuskegee radically reformed their curricula and moved closer to the ideological mainstream of black education.[1]

The traditional emphasis on Hampton as a trade or technical school has obscured the fact that it was founded and maintained as a normal school and that its mission was the training of common school teachers for the South's black educational system. The Hampton-Tuskegee curriculum was not centered on trade or agricultural training; it was centered on the training of teachers. A condition for admission to Hampton was the "intention to remain through the whole course and become a teacher." This goal was achieved because approximately 84 percent of the 723 graduates from Hampton's first twenty classes became teachers. Moreover, Hampton did not offer any trade certificates until 1895, twenty-seven years after the school's founding. This was long after it had been embraced by northern and southern white educational reformers as the most appropriate form of education to assist in bringing racial peace, political stability, and material prosperity to the American South. Still, in 1900, only 45 of Hampton's 656 students were enrolled in its trade school division, and only 4 students were listed as majoring in agriculture. These programs were secondary and relatively insignificant. From its inception until well into the twentieth century, Hampton was almost wholly devoted to teacher training. A normal school became confused with trade training and economic development because Armstrong, and later Washington, employed a unique manual labor routine and an ideology of "self-help" as the practical and moral foundation of their teacher training process. Both established farms and small shops to give their prospective teachers the required manual labor experience. In these routinized work situations, however, the development of persons skilled in trades or farming was a secondary aim, seldom acquired by the students. The primary aim was to work the prospective teachers long and hard so that they would embody, accept, and preach an ethic of hard toil or the "dignity of labor." Then, and only then, believed Armstrong, could his normal school graduates develop the appropriate values and character to teach the children of the South's distinctive black laboring class.[2]

As a normal school Hampton was markedly different in structure and content from black teachers' colleges and liberal arts colleges. Like other normal schools of the nineteenth century, Hampton offered a curriculum of two or three years in length and did not grant a bachelor's degree. Moreover, the completion of a four-year secondary school curriculum was not required for admission to Hampton and other normal schools. Most of Hampton's beginning students arrived with a less than adequate elementary school education and successfully completed the normal school program with an education equivalent in quality to that of a fair tenth grade program. A good high school offered a superior academic program. In contrast to the normal school's precollegiate academic program, a teachers' college or department was a state, municipal, or incorporated private institution or an independent unit of a recognized college or university having at least one four-year unified curriculum. It was devoted also to the preparation of teachers but required for admission to its curriculum a standard four-year secondary program and granted a standard bachelor's degree. Hampton was neither a college nor a trade school but a normal school composed of elementary school graduates who were seeking two additional years of schooling and teacher preparation courses so that they might qualify for a common school teaching certificate. Normal school students tended to be much less educated, older, and more economically disadvantaged than college students. Further, unlike students pursuing trade and technical training, normal school students sought professional education courses to achieve their major goal of becoming elementary school teachers.

Thus Hampton should be analyzed more in the context of post–Civil War black normal school training than as part of the era's general trend toward technical, trade, and manual education. Unlike Hampton's concern with teacher training, the late nineteenth-century industrial education movement did not include the training of teachers but instead stressed three basic types of vocational training. First, and of the highest status, were the schools of applied science and technology, whose purpose was to train engineers, architects, chemists, and the like for professional work in the emerging technology-based economy. A second and widely different class of industrial schools encompassed the trade schools, organized to train workers in industry and to educate them for their prospective individual occupations in life. In contrast to technical schools, which trained the overseers and superintendents of labor, the trade schools sought to educate individual operatives. The third class of schools consisted of those in which manual instruction was introduced, mainly as a supplement to the traditional academic curriculum, to promote habits of industry, thrift, and morality. Several years before Hampton was established, institutions such as Mt. Holyoke Seminary for Women, Wellesley College, and Oberlin College had required students to do some manual labor to acquire fixed habits of industry and to provide financial support for the colleges. At such schools simple manual training was not a basic part of the instructional program; at Hampton, manual labor formed the core of the teacher training program and intruded into every aspect of both curricular and extracurricular activities.[3]

Hampton's manual labor routine was designed partly to teach students steady work habits, practical knowledge, and Christian morals. Most important, however, Armstrong viewed industrial education primarily as an ideological force that would provide instruction suitable for adjusting blacks to a subordinate social role in the emergent New South. Significantly, he identified Hampton with the conservative wing of southern reconstructionists who supported new forms of external control over blacks, including disfranchisement, segregation, and civil inequality. Armstrong's philosophy of "Black Reconstruction," widely publicized as the "Hampton Idea," essentially called for the effective removal of black voters and politicians from southern political life, the relegation of black workers to the lowest forms of labor in the southern economy, and the establishment of a general southern racial hierarchy. He expected that the work of adjusting blacks to this social arrangement would be carried out by indigenous black educators, particularly teachers and principals, aided by Hampton-styled industrial normal schools, state departments of education, local school boards, and northern white philanthropists. Hence Hampton developed an extensive manual labor routine because the school's faculty believed that a particular combination of hard work, political socialization, and social discipline would mold appropriately conservative black teachers. In 1888 Atticus G. Haygood, the general agent of the John F. Slater Fund, touched upon Hampton's central mission when he stated that the school's faculty viewed industrial training as the best intellectual and moral discipline for "those who are to be teachers and guides of their people." Haygood went to the heart of the matter. Hampton's teacher training program and its attendant political values focused mainly on the relationship of black "teachers and guides" to the larger issues of southern political and economic reconstruction.[4]

Hampton's ideological and pedagogical framework was derived mainly from the racial, political, and economic views of Armstrong, the principal from 1868 until his death in 1893, and from Hollis Burke Frissell, the vice-principal and chaplain from 1880 to 1893, who succeeded Armstrong and served as principal until 1917. Armstrong, with the help of the American Missionary Association, founded Hampton Institute in April 1868. Four years after the institute was established he initiated and edited the *Southern Workman*, an illustrated monthly, to present his views on the freedmen's place in the developing New South. The paper was created ostensibly as Hampton's official news organ; but from the outset, Armstrong aimed to create a forum much more far-reaching than a typical school newspaper. As he wrote to his friend and Hampton trustee Robert C. Ogden, "We mean to push it by mail, up and forwards—think of this—the paper may become, and I mean it will be a power." The *Southern Workman* became a "power," especially among northern philanthropists and southern white moderates, who favored elementary school and normal school education for blacks and who were basically opposed to black higher education, equal job opportunities, civil equality, and equal political rights. Although Armstrong attempted to promote the *Southern Workman* as a nonpolitical "instructive month-ly," the paper, which expressed vividly his ideas of black reconstruction, sided with conservative political groups who wanted to disfranchise the freedmen and create a legal and customary racial hierarchy. Two years after the founding of the *Southern Workman*, a black newspaper con-cluded that Armstrong's monthly had "become so conservative that it leans the other way," meaning that it had become reactionary.[5]

To Armstrong, the removal of black people from any effective role in southern politics was the first step toward "proper" reconstruction. He wrote almost exclusively of the immorality and irresponsibility of black voters; he excoriated black politicians and labeled the freedmen's enfran-chisement as dangerous to the South and the nation. In his view, the "Colored people" could "afford to let politics severely alone." He main-tained, for instance, that black participation in politics in South Carolina resulted in a "shameless legislature" that had "ruined the credit of a great state." Armstrong instructed black leaders to stay out of politics because they were "not capable of self-government," and he blamed the black voters for creating situations which "no white race on this earth ought to endure or will endure." "The votes of Negroes have enabled some of the worst men who ever figured in American politics to hold high places of honor and trust," argued Armstrong. "Such votes mar-shalled by cunning knavery are dangerous to the country in proportion to their numbers." Thus he advised black men to refrain from voting and urged "every colored leader" to refuse public office for generations to come.[6]

Armstrong waged a campaign against black political rights that should have embarrassed a self-proclaimed "friend of the Negro race," and oc-casionally it apparently did. He stated in 1876 that he did not intend to "denounce as such every colored man who takes part in politics." In 1882 he even admitted that a few "colored politicians" could be "trusted." But these isolated statements tended to appear when Arm-strong perceived that black political power was disintegrating. He was convinced that the withdrawal of Union soldiers from the South in 1877 meant the end of black influence in southern politics. In 1879, however, William Mahone, with the aid of black voters, led Virginia's Readjusters to victory in the state legislative elections. After assuming full control of Virginia's government in 1881, the Readjusters pumped money into pub-lic education and enacted several measures to please their black support-ers, including abolishing the whipping post and the poll tax and creating Virginia Normal and Collegiate Institute in Petersburg. Armstrong was greatly disturbed by the continuing black participation in Virginia politics. In 1879 he stated angrily that "the colored vote was reappearing as a political force." When this vote influenced the 1879 elections in Virginia, few "rebels" were more reactionary than Samuel Armstrong: "The Colored vote has suddenly the balance of power and gives victory to the readjusters. There is a split in Conservative ranks. Ex-Confederate leaders are arrayed against each other. The heroes of the war are replacing one-legged soldiers who fought under them with colored men who might have fought against them." In Armstrong's view, this "calamity" threatened "Virginia's honor or standing in the markets of the world." The black race, he warned, "will act up to its light, but its best light is dim and therefore unsafe." The masses were "weak and blind," and "their so-called leaders" were, according to Armstrong, "ignorant, immoral preachers or selfish politicians."[7]

Armstrong insisted that the freedmen should refrain from participating in southern political life because they were culturally and morally deficient and therefore unfit to vote and hold office in "civilized" society. He fell heir to a particular theory of racial subordination while growing up as the son of a missionary in the Hawaiian Islands. His father, Richard Armstrong, entered Hawaii as a missionary in 1831 and by 1840 was minister of public instruction; he eventually became president of the Board of Education. Samuel Armstrong was told that his father's missionary career was "noble work for the savage race." This missionary inheritance was reinforced and consolidated in the milieu of the postwar South. The southern "darkies," like the Polynesian "savages," were "so possessed with strange notions" that they had to be "most carefully watched over." The "darkies" were "emotional in their nature," improvident by habit, and "not capable of self-government." The Hampton principal easily shifted his missionary views from the Polynesians to the black southerners. Indeed, he observed that "there was worked out in the Hawaiian Islands the problem of emancipation, and civilization of the dark-skinned Polynesian people in many respects like the Negro race." In both instances, Armstrong maintained that it was the duty of the superior white race to rule over the weaker dark-skinned races until they were appropriately civilized. This civilization process, in Armstrong's estimate, would require several generations of moral and religious development.[8]

In his political and educational thought, Armstrong attributed the "barbarism" of dark-skinned people largely to historical and environmental conditions. He occasionally invoked genetic arguments in his attempt to rationalize the dominance of whites over blacks. But the heredity concept set unchangeable patterns that did not readily support the moral and social goals of educational reform movements. Mental or academic achievement was more measurable and came much sooner than moral development, thus supporting more rapid social change than Armstrong was willing to concede. To justify his position that all blacks, educated and noneducated, be excluded indefinitely from active participation in southern politics, Armstrong proclaimed moral development instead of mental development as the chief criterion for political enfranchisement. He believed exclusive white rule was justified because whites had developed exceptionally "in moral strength, in guiding instincts, in power to 'sense things' in the genius for this or that." The Negro, on the other hand, could not "see the point of life clearly, he lacks foresight, judgment and hard sense." The critical problem with the black race, according to Armstrong, was "not one of brains, but of right instincts, of morals and hard work." The freedmen's chief misfortunes were "low ideas of honor, and morality, want of foresight and energy, and vanity." In short, Armstrong contended that the white race was mentally and morally strong, and the black race was mentally capable but morally feeble. He attributed the moral capacity of the different races to historically determined conditions: "The [American] white race has had three centuries of experience in organizing the forces about him, political, social and physical. The Negro has had three centuries of experience in general demoralization and behind that, paganism." This historical legacy, Armstrong argued, robbed the black race of the moral wisdom and foresight necessary for responsible political activity.[9]

Armstrong used concepts such as "guiding instincts" and "moral strength" with slight regard for definition or accurate meaning. But despite the theoretical poverty of his social philosophy, it was a convenient doctrine to support his Reconstruction policy of white rule and black disfranchisement. In 1877, when three black men were elected from the Hampton district to serve in the Virginia state legislature, Armstrong commented: "This district will be represented in both houses by men of intelligence, but of no moral standing." In his view, "political ambition had proved unhealthy for the brightest minds of the [black] race." Until a moral foundation was broadly laid, he counseled, "no sensible colored man could wish to see his race take a leading part in government." In the long run, however, the black race could "develop those guiding instincts and institutions that the Anglo-Saxon has reached through ages of hard experience." Moral intuition was largely automatic, instinctive, and culturally determined. Groups lacking it could acquire it over time but "only by a series of experimental tests, which must of necessity include successive generations." Because the Anglo-Saxon race was morally strong, precisely because of its unique historical experiences, it seemed logical to Armstrong that whites would preside over the ex-slaves' gradual evolution into "civilized" life.[10]

In posing morality, rather than intelligence, as the criterion for admis-

sion to the body politic, Armstrong rejected the idea of literate culture as
either a civilizing force or appropriate preparation for morally responsible citizenship. In his cultural theory of racial subordination, mental
aptness was not an important measure of moral development; on the
contrary, it was a characteristic of primitive existence. As Armstrong put
it, "Most savage races are not mentally sluggish. The African Zulu tests
the wit and resources of an educated missionary. The Polynesian canni-
bal is a natural orator and takes to law and theology with readiness. The
Aborigines of Australia are quickwitted." Similarly, Armstrong observed
that black children were mentally "capable of acquiring knowledge to
any degree, and to a certain age, at least, with about the same facility as
white children." "Most savage people," Armstrong explained, "are not
like 'dumb driven cattle;' yet their life is little better than that of brutes
because the moral nature is dormant." Thus, as long as the Negro's
moral nature remained underdeveloped, Armstrong believed that it was
the whites' duty to prevent blacks from voting and running for political
office. In establishing moral development as the decisive cultural basis of
political and civil equality, Armstrong, wittingly or unwittingly, ideologi-
cally precluded even property-owning and educated blacks from participation in the body politic. Property and education, he argued, could be
acquired in a generation, but moral development, and by extension
readiness for parliamentary government, took centuries.[11]

To apprehend fully Armstrong's preoccupation with black political
development it is imperative to recall that those southerners defined in
law and custom as "Negroes" constituted over one-third of the region's
population. In 1870, as illustrated in Table 2.1, black persons formed a
majority of the total population in Louisiana, Mississippi, and South
Carolina. In Alabama, Florida, Georgia, and Virginia the black populations ranged from 42 to 49 percent of the totals. North Carolina and
Tennessee reported 37 and 26 percent of their populations as black persons, and Texas reported 31 percent. These citizens and voters deserved a
considerable share of the region's political power and the lion's share in
some states and districts. That blacks might achieve their fair share of
political power was Armstrong's nightmare and a problem he wished to
solve in the realm of education and culture, rather than through political
struggle.

Armstrong had much in common with the white planters of the South,
who, in general, believed that blacks should be politically disfranchised
and fitted for the physical drudgery of unskilled farm and domestic labor. But he differed from them on the question of universal schooling.
The planters believed that schooling would raise blacks' political and
economic aspirations and ruin them as agricultural and domestic laborers. Armstrong held a deep faith in the powerful capacity of moral and

TABLE 2.1

Number and Percent of Blacks in Total Population of Southern States, 1870–1930

State	1870 Number	1870 Per-cent	1880 Number	1880 Per-cent	1890 Number	1890 Per-cent	1900 Number	1900 Per-cent	1910 Number	1910 Per-cent	1920 Number	1920 Per-cent	1930 Number	1930 Per-cent
Alabama	475,510	47.7	600,103	47.5	678,489	44.8	827,307	45.2	908,282	42.5	900,652	38.4	944,834	35.7
Arkansas	122,169	25.2	210,666	26.3	309,117	27.4	366,856	28.0	442,891	28.1	472,220	27.0	478,463	25.8
Delaware	22,794	18.2	26,442	18.0	28,386	16.8	30,697	16.6	31,181	15.4	30,335	13.6	32,602	13.7
Florida	91,689	48.8	126,690	47.0	166,180	42.5	230,730	43.7	308,669	41.0	329,487	34.0	431,828	29.4
Georgia	545,142	46.0	725,133	47.0	858,815	46.7	1,034,813	46.7	1,176,987	45.1	1,206,365	41.7	1,071,125	36.8
Kentucky	222,210	16.8	271,451	16.5	268,071	14.4	284,706	13.3	261,656	11.4	225,938	9.8	226,040	8.6
Louisiana	364,210	50.1	483,655	51.5	559,193	50.0	650,804	47.1	713,784	43.1	700,257	38.9	776,326	36.9
Maryland	175,391	22.5	210,230	22.5	215,657	20.7	235,064	19.8	232,250	17.9	244,479	16.9	276,379	16.9
Mississippi	444,201	53.7	650,291	57.5	742,559	57.6	907,630	58.5	1,009,487	56.2	935,184	52.2	1,009,718	50.2
Missouri	118,071	6.9	145,350	6.7	150,184	5.6	161,234	5.2	157,452	4.8	178,241	5.2	223,840	6.2
North Carolina	391,650	36.6	531,277	38.0	561,018	34.7	624,469	33.0	697,843	31.6	763,407	29.8	918,647	29.0
South Carolina	415,814	58.9	604,332	60.7	688,934	59.8	782,321	58.4	835,843	55.2	864,719	51.4	793,681	45.6
Tennessee	322,331	25.6	403,151	26.1	430,678	24.4	480,243	23.8	473,088	21.7	451,758	19.3	477,646	18.3
Texas	253,475	31.0	393,384	24.7	488,171	21.8	620,722	20.4	690,049	17.7	741,694	15.9	854,964	14.7
Virginia	512,841	41.9	631,616	41.8	635,438	38.4	660,722	35.6	671,096	32.6	690,017	29.9	650,165	26.8
West Virginia	17,980	4.1	25,886	4.2	32,690	4.3	43,499	4.5	64,173	5.3	86,345	5.9	114,893	6.6

Source: U.S. Bureau of the Census, Negroes in the United States, 1920–32 (Washington, D.C.: U.S. Government Printing Office, 1935), pp. 9–10, 15.

industrial education to socialize blacks to understand and accept their disfranchisement and to make them more productive laborers. As the right moral education would ultimately prepare blacks for self-government, he believed, the right industrial training would make them an economic asset instead of a burden to the South. Hence the other fundamental dimension of Armstrong's educational and social philosophy focused on the methods and content to develop black teachers and leaders who would prepare the black masses for efficient service in racially prescribed occupational niches.

When Armstrong maintained, as he frequently did, that the black race was "low but not degraded," he usually meant that it was the habit of labor, acquired under slavery, that saved the race from complete "moral ruin." "The Negro has one source of strength," he argued, "the habit of industry acquired in the time of slavery." This source of strength was important to Armstrong's platform of southern economic reconstruction. "Southerners must make the best of Negro labor," he said, "they cannot afford to do otherwise, with them it is that or none." In Armstrong's view, northern capital and cheap black labor were critical to southern economic reconstruction and reunion with the Northeast. "The Eastern states have the capital and experience," he announced in 1875, "while the South has the cheap labor; to bring the two together is to cement a real peace between the sections." This union, he believed, was hindered mainly by the political and racial turmoil in the South, which discouraged capital investments from the Northeast. To Armstrong, the debate over black political participation "kindled the passions of war" and blocked the "swift return of southern prosperity through immigration and capital from the North." The return of order and prosperity in the South was largely dependent upon "the rapidity with which the power of the politician is undermined by the gradual growth of the moneyed classes, whose pecuniary interests depend upon peace, and upon the respect and goodwill of the rest of the world, outside the South." Realizing that the racial upheaval in the postwar South resulted in "scarcity of capital" and "demoralized labor," Armstrong consistently called for racial peace and political stability, but nearly always at the expense of southern blacks. Because northern capitalists would not eagerly invest in a region characterized by labor disorders and race riots, "liberalism must be organized into outward forms to induce northern men and capital to cross the border lines of the southern states." He urgently demanded a quick resolution of political and racial conflict so that economic leaders could set in motion the wheel of material prosperity.[12]

Armstrong attempted to organize Hampton Institute as a model for the emerging southern economy. Early on, he appealed for small businessmen to experiment with student and community labor. In December 1877 he explored the idea of engaging the Hampton students in the manufacturing of cotton clothing for northern markets. Armstrong instructed Charles Whiting, a white member of the Hampton staff, "to work up Negro labor, compete with New York labor in manufacturing for northern markets." The students regularly performed hard labor for cheap rates in the school's workshops. According to the 1880 annual report, the school's Knitting Department produced "fifteen thousand dozen pairs of mittens for S. B. Pratt and Company of Boston, who sell them chiefly in the Northwest." The young men in the trade school department were also required to make products for the market economy. Advertising the manufacture of doors, sashes, and blinds for the general market, Armstrong reported that the workshop did a prosperous business of "six thousand dollars a month, cutting over two million feet of lumber every year." On several occasions he invited entrepreneurs to take advantage of the "cheap labor in and out of the institution; students are paid from six to ten cents per hour."[13]

These work experiments extended beyond the typical industrial educational activities of the era. The Hampton model resembled the industrial training that first appeared during the 1820s in the reform schools established in New York City, Boston, and Philadelphia. Like the reformatories, Hampton sometimes contracted student labor to outside entrepreneurs who assigned the students routine and repetitive tasks similar to those done by unskilled factory or agricultural laborers. Tileston T. Bryce, Hampton's financial agent, opened a meat-packing and canning factory on the institute's grounds in 1879. After two years he reported employing "hundreds of poor people" in "the large canning business," both student and community laborers. In a similar experiment, C. D. Cake, a white Virginia businessman, employed "ten colored and five Indian students," who "cut daily from six to eight thousand feet of yellow pine lumber." The Hampton staff observed the adaptation of black workers in these industries and developed theories that supported the extension of white dominance over black labor. After observing black workers in his canning factory, Bryce reported: "I have found that the colored people, if the same chance be given them, work as diligently as the whites but not so intelligently. With intelligent direction they are admirable laborers, obeying orders and willingly; but when they attempt the direction of their own labor, it is apt to amount to but little."[14]

In an attempt to convince black leaders and workers to remain in the South as cheap and contented laborers, Armstrong and his associates spread propaganda that white opposition to black participation in southern politics was not a barrier to black opportunity in the educational and economic arenas. He insisted that "there was no power and little disposition on the part of leading white conservatives to prevent the colored people from acquiring wealth and education." Indeed, he argued that "competition in the North" held back skilled Afro-American workers "more than prejudice at the South." Southern black mechanics, according to Armstrong, had "a fair field." Armstrong's propaganda well illustrates the economic consciousness that he expected Hampton-trained teachers and leaders to model for the black community. Booker T. Washington, his devoted student, often told black southerners that "when one comes to business pure and simple, stripped of all ideas of sentiment, the Negro is given almost as good an opportunity to rise as is given to the white man." Like Armstrong, the Tuskegee principal forthrightly claimed that "the black man has a better chance in the South than in the North" for economic progress. Thus, "In spite of all talk of exodus," said Washington in 1885, "the Negro's home is permanently in the South." Washington epitomized the type of black educator Armstrong desired to train and in whom Armstrong wanted the black working class to place its trust. It is safe to say that the educational theory and method at Hampton were formulated to train an army of Booker T. Washingtons.[15]

The Hampton-Tuskegee philosophy, which requested black southerners to eschew politics and concentrate on economic development, was not, as it has been hailed, a great compromise. It was the logical extension of an ideology that rejected black political power while recognizing that the South's agricultural economy rested on the backs of black agricultural workers. The United States Bureau of the Census did not classify agricultural laborers by race in the 1870 and 1880 censuses. But the data from the 1890 census, as shown in Table 2.2, documented the substantial presence of black workers in southern agriculture. In the Deep South (Alabama, Florida, Georgia, Louisiana, Mississippi, and South Carolina) black agricultural workers ranged from 48 to 68 percent of the totals, and they were from 23 to 40 percent of the totals in Delaware, Arkansas, Maryland, North Carolina, Tennessee, Texas, and Virginia. Because the South's economy was essentially agricultural, its prosperity depended heavily on black workers. The philosophy that embraced blacks as agricultural laborers and rejected them as voters and politicians was a one-way street, not a compromise. From Armstrong's standpoint, it addressed the region's most fundamental social realities—political power and economic development. In both instances he sought to preserve the region's traditional inequalities of wealth and power. His major task was to carry this message to black southerners and seek to obtain their conscious or half-conscious complicity in their own victimization.

The great educational question absorbing Armstrong's attention and intruding itself into every aspect of Hampton Institute was the nature and role of teachers in shaping the social, economic, and political con-

TABLE 2.2

Black Workers as a Percentage of All Workers in Agricultural
Occupations by Southern States, 1890–1930

State	1890	1900	1910	1920	1930
Alabama	57	54	53	47	45
Arkansas	34	34	38	36	34
Delaware	23	21	23	21	21
Florida	48	49	51	43	42
Georgia	54	53	56	53	46
Kentucky	12	9	8	8	1
Louisiana	67	64	61	56	54
Maryland	33	28	29	27	26
Mississippi	68	69	70	65	65
Missouri	4	3	2	3	4
North Carolina	39	35	37	36	36
South Carolina	68	68	69	66	62
Tennessee	26	22	23	20	19
Texas	25	23	23	22	20
Virginia	40	34	34	32	30
West Virginia	4	1	2	1	1

Source: U.S. Bureau of the Census, *Twelfth Census of the United States, 1900*, cxxxv–
cxxxvi; Henry Gannett, *Occupations of the Negroes* (Baltimore, 1895); U.S. Bureau of
Education, *Negro Education: A Study of the Private and Higher Schools for Colored
People in the United States* (Washington, D.C.: U.S. Government Printing Office, 1917),
1:98; U.S. Bureau of the Census, *Fifteenth Census of the United States* (Washington, D.C.:
U.S. Government Printing Office, 1933), vol. 4, Table 11, p. 874.

sciousness of the black masses. Armstrong expected the sociopolitical
views embodied in the Hampton Idea to be propagated among the black
masses primarily by black teachers. He conjectured that schools and
churches were the best institutions to socialize or "civilize" the black
population. They were viewed as agencies of amelioration and control,
and they were the agencies under which most of the freedmen were
organized. Therefore, said Armstrong, "Let us make the teachers and we
will make the people." Surely the teachers and the people could be easily
molded because they were "in the early stages of civilization." "Our
students," stated Armstrong, "are docile, impressible, imitative and earnest, and come to us as a *tabula rasa* so far as real culture is concerned." Hampton was designed to form an ideological foundation in
these "blank minds" and return them to the outside world not as "pol-
ished scholars" but as "guides and civilizers, whose power shall be that

of character and example, not of sounding words." Armstrong believed that Hampton Institute had taken "a new departure" in the education of freedmen; it was a "civilizing power" that would encourage through its exemplars the "right ideas of life and duty."[16]

Armstrong's 1880 call, "Politicians to the background and school-masters to the front," echoed at once his disdain for black politicians and his vision of black teachers propagating the Hampton Idea of economic efficiency throughout the Afro-American South. His was not merely another naive view of the ameliorative and modifying powers of common schooling. Armstrong's emphasis on the training of teachers or "guides" had even deeper roots in his awareness that black teachers could mold the ideologies of the black masses. As he reasoned, black teachers were "usually the best educated of their society, are leaders of its thought, and give it tone by their superior wisdom and culture." Moreover, "The colored teacher is looked up to for his wisdom, is often chosen magistrate or other local dignitary, and is sometimes the only source of information from the outside world." Armstrong's concern with the potential role of black teachers in the black community led him to consider the forces that enhanced and threatened his aims. He feared the influence of black teachers and ministers who rejected the ideological discipline he propagandized. "The real trouble of the colored teachers," he complained, "is with a class of preachers, politicians, and editors of their own race who resent the introduction of intelligent ideas into religion and into the relations of life. They could easily be conciliated by substituting Latin for labor." Armstrong opposed the existing system of college and normal school training for blacks and campaigned relentlessly for the Hampton model.[17]

Armstrong sought to regulate the flow and quality of black teachers through careful admissions processes and independent boarding schools. In 1881 he asked Virginia and other southern public school officials to notify Hampton Institute of "worthy colored youth" who would make the best teachers. Through this process conservative whites could "do much to select wise leaders for the colored race." The teachers would be bound to the white establishment, and "any conflict of the races will be impossible." These recruits would be properly trained in independent boarding schools like Hampton. The "average Negro student," according to Armstrong, needed a boarding school so that his teachers could "control the entire twenty-four hours of each day—only thus can old ideas and ways be pushed out and new ones take their place." "When his whole routine of life is controlled," Armstrong believed, "the Negro pupil is like clay in the potter's hands." From this "clay" he intended to "create a class or guild who will be a nucleus of civilization" and would transmit the Hampton doctrines of politics and economics to the black race.[18]

Armstrong viewed his own brand of industrial education as the appropriate pedagogy to mold the economic and political consciousness of prospective black leaders and educators. Hampton's curriculum, therefore, was not intended primarily to create "small individualistic entrepreneurs" or to offer "Negroes the technical training necessary for effective competition in an industrial age." It was designed mainly to train black ideologues, who were expected to exemplify and propagate Armstrong's philosophy of southern Reconstruction to the Afro-American working class. "The Negroes, who are to form the working classes of the South," he maintained, "must be taught not only to do their work well, but to know what their work means." But first it was necessary to condition the personalities and attitudes of the teachers. Armstrong believed that "a teacher does more by virtue of what he is than of what he says; the most powerful constructive influence is indirect." He envisioned Hampton students as the embodiment of "habits of living and labor . . . in order that graduates may be qualified to teach others these important lessons of life." To him, hard labor was the first principle of civilized life, and he drilled his students in manual labor routines so that they could effectively teach the value of routinized labor to the black masses. "If you are the right sort of man you will engage in any sort of labor, and dignify it," declared Armstrong. Indeed, "A man had better work for nothing and find himself than to spend his time in idling and loafing." Therefore, he instructed blacks to "plow, hoe, ditch, grub; do anything rather than nothing." To be sure, Armstrong was not opposed to teaching trades to a few individuals, but he primarily sought to cultivate through his graduates a nonskilled or semiskilled black work force that would support the southern economy. If the South were to achieve industrial and agricultural greatness, black workers needed to be taught to "love" labor and to understand the meaning of work more than they needed trade or technical skills. Consequently, Armstrong was almost exclusively concerned with the ideological and psychological value of industrial teacher training.[19]

Routine and repetitive manual labor activities were developed to screen and condition students to serve as missionaries of the Hampton Idea. Armstrong held a lifelong suspicion of highly educated blacks, believing that their aspirations were vain and dysfunctional to his views of southern Reconstruction. His idealized student was a hard worker with elementary education and industrial training. He did not believe that highly educated blacks would remain as "civilizers" among the rural masses. "There is such a thing as over-education," he warned. "A highly

The prospective female teachers of Hampton Institute (top) were compelled to do field work in order to internalize the value of hard work that they were expected to transmit to their students. The normal school students (bottom) found that plowing was an important part of Hampton's teacher preparation program. Courtesy F. B. Johnston Collection, Library of Congress.

educated Negro is as little likely as a highly educated white man to do a work against which his tastes and sensibilities would every day rebel." The highly educated could not serve as models for the masses, who, according to Armstrong, were destined to plow, hoe, ditch, and grub. Therefore, manual labor rather than scholarship became Hampton's chief criterion for educational excellence. "One who shirks labor may be a fine mathematician," noted Armstrong, but "the blockhead at the black board may be a shining example in the cornfield." The idealized "blockhead" or "plodders," as they were called, became the standard by which all students were evaluated. In 1882 Armstrong reported: "A good labor record has often saved one from being dropped as incompetent while one brilliant in studies is sometimes sent away for inefficiency in the shop or farm." The students with good labor records were thought the best potential exponents of the Hampton Idea. Vice-Principal H. B. Frissell, after visiting Hampton graduates in the field, reported in 1885 "that very frequently the dull plodder at Hampton is the real leader of his people toward better things, while the bright scholar who was our pride and delight at school, because of his mental acuteness, either yields to temptation or leaves school work for the more tempting offers of clerkships or political appointments." Similarly, Armstrong argued that "the plodding ones make good teachers."[20]

Hampton's industrial teacher training system consisted of three main areas: the elementary academic program, the manual labor system, and a strict social discipline routine. The entire operation was systematically ordered to provide moral and intellectual discipline to a conservative black teachers corps; however, each division emphasized certain specifics. The academic program, aside from preparing students to teach grade school and to pass varied state teachers' certification examinations, was planned mainly for the ideological training of potential Hampton missionaries. The manual labor system, organized to shape attitudes and build character through steady, hard labor, was designed to connect the theoretical and practical lessons. The daily discipline routine served to rid the school of students at variance with the Hampton Idea.

The Hampton academic program consisted of an English course of study embracing reading and elocution, elementary mathematics, history, literature, moral science, and political economy. Armstrong excluded classical studies because he believed that such training stimulated "vanity" in black students, which propelled them toward high-flown notions of politics and professional life. Hampton sought to impress upon its students their "true" place in the southern social order largely through courses in political economy, civil government, and practical morality. Whereas the other academic courses were taught by white women teachers, these courses were taught by Armstrong and Hollis

Frissell with assistance from Tileston T. Bryce. Armstrong began the courses in the 1870s with triweekly talks on the important economic and political questions of the era. In 1882 he reported that the political economy course included the "discussion of labor, wages, money value, and the tariff." The course was developed to promote proper relations between capitalists and laborers, and the courses in practical morals and civil government were aimed at correcting the students' "wrong notions" regarding the "rights of persons and property, the origins of these rights, and how they may be violated."[21]

The *Southern Workman*, the main text in the political economy course, was used in all reading classes. Armstrong recommended the paper to other "colored normal schools and colleges." He was particularly satisfied with Tileston T. Bryce's series of articles on political economy that were eventually gathered into the Hampton textbook *Economic Crumbs, or Plain Talks for the People about Labor, Capital, Money, Tariff, etc.* In 1878 Bryce initiated a series of essays that were structured around questions which appeared repeatedly on the students' senior examination in political economy. The Hampton students, examined annually by a committee appointed by the Board of Trustees, were required to answer the following questions: "What is labor? Who are the laboring classes? Show how all men are mutually dependent. What are wages? Who determines the price of wages? What is capital? Show the relationship of capital to labor. How are all men capitalists?" Bryce's essays on these questions were consistent with the basic premises of the Hampton Idea.[22]

Bryce saw no inherent or legitimate conflict between capital and labor. It was erroneous "to speak of the 'laboring classes' as distinct divisions of society" because "every man who puts forth any exertion, in order to obtain something in return, is a laborer." If the expression "laboring classes" had any distinctive meaning, it signified "free men as opposed to slaves." Bryce concluded that there were "no class feelings to irritate, no color line to fight over":

> The most pernicious quack, who peddles political nostrums, is he who attempts to excite the multitude by declaring that "all the ills that flesh is to heir" come from the employers of labor. People of this sort hold it as an axiom that there is an unending feud between capital and labor; and that the former ever seeks to extinguish the latter. Some of these mischief-makers, assuming this statement to be true, are logical enough to declare that labor should try to extinguish capital. This is the doctrine of communism. Now if there be two things in this world between which the utmost amity should exist, and between which the most intimate reciprocal relations do exist, they are Capital and Labor.

Thus, contended Bryce, labor unions were conspiracies to defy the laws of economics and to get something for nothing. Those who interfered with the workplace by violence or threats were labeled "either slave-catchers or thieves."[23]

"The bottom idea of capital," Bryce argued, "is that somebody has saved something." A man with only an "extra shirt" was "to that extent a capitalist." It was natural, however, for some men to have more capital than others, and it was "no more unjust, than that one man should be stronger, taller, or more healthy than another." "The majority of people accept such as the natural state of things," he continued, "and the minority, who decline to accept it, are found among the vicious, who have squandered all they had, the improvident, who never labor for more than mere existence." These views were supported by other Hampton textbooks.[24]

Thomas Jesse Jones, an instructor of social studies at Hampton Institute and later director of the Phelps-Stokes Fund, described the purpose and function of social studies in the Hampton curriculum. Jones explained that Armstrong and his co-workers gave "a very important place" to such subjects as "political economy, civil government, moral science and general history." These subjects were aimed primarily at teaching Hampton's students the "right" ideas of citizenship, the duties of laborers, and the history of race development. History, for instance, was designed as a study of the "evolution of races" and was aimed at giving the pupils "a new notion of race development." Jones contended that black students arrived at Hampton with common-sense notions of the problems of racial subordination. "Their acquaintance with the race problem has made them precocious in their knowledge of social forces controlling and limiting the development of races. The white youth grows to manhood without feeling any of the limitations which the colored youth feels all his life." But, Jones continued, "while the colored youth is more conscious of social forces than the white, his views are not natural." From Jones's vantage point, black students' views of "race development" were unnatural because blacks tended to interpret the social limitations imposed on them as arbitrary and unjust. The Hampton faculty taught black students that the position of their race in the South was not the result of oppression but of the natural process of cultural evolution. In other words, blacks had evolved to a cultural stage that was two thousand years behind that of whites and, therefore, they were naturally the subordinate race. In this respect, Washington learned his lessons well while attending Hampton. As he said in 1900 before the General Conference of the African Methodist Episcopal church, "My friends, the white man is three thousand years ahead of us, and this fact we might as well face now as well as later, and that at one stage of his development, either in Europe or America, he has gone through every stage of development that I now advocate for our race." Thus although Washington was opposed to depriving blacks of the legal right of franchise, he advised, like Armstrong, "that in their present condition it is a mistake for them to enter actively into general political agitation and activity." This conception of "race development" was a key component of the Hampton-Tuskegee retrogressive social philosophy.[25]

According to Jones, each social study at Hampton contributed "to this picture of the evolution of races." When the Hampton program of social studies worked successfully, a black student, "instead of regarding the difficulties of his race as the oppression of a weaker by the stronger, he interprets them as the natural difficulties which almost every race has been compelled to overcome in its upward movement." Booker T. Washington could not have said it any better. The ideology of both the Hampton and Tuskegee programs of social studies served to conceal the arbitrary, unjust, and oppressive nature of black subordination in the South. What worried Armstrong and his co-workers, as Jones implied, was the probability that prospective black teachers and leaders might translate the social outlook implicit in their traditions and day-to-day experiences into a conception of politics that defined the South's racially qualified form of working-class subordination as arbitrary, unnatural, and unjust.[26]

Armstrong was always pleased with the results of the senior class examination because "the students got a higher percentage of correct answers in Political Economy than in any other of the several branches." Black students came to Hampton, according to Armstrong, thinking "much of the rights of the laborers and little of those of the capitalist"; they viewed the two classes "as being opposed to one another." Clearly, such thinking diverged from the Hampton Idea, and the school's staff labored to "correct" it. There is no way of determining how many students were converted to Armstrong's doctrines of political economy. But the educational thought of the two most well-known Hampton graduates, Booker T. Washington and Robert R. Moton, parroted the Hampton doctrines. Doubtless other educators at the time, black and white, propagandized similar views. The point, however, is that Hampton was deliberately teaching prospective black leaders and educators economic values that were detrimental to the objective economic interests of black workers. Black domestics, sharecroppers, and factory laborers were not capitalists, and their objective economic interests, as many of them realized, were fundamentally different from and opposed to those of the southern bosses and landlords who ruled over them. Thus, when Hampton trained leaders such as Booker T. Washington to counsel blacks to remain in the South as cheap and contented agricultural laborers and to refrain from political activity, it contributed to the development of a conservative Afro-American leadership, which did not foster the political and economic improvement of black workers and voters. The Hampton social and educational ideology was inherently opposed to the political and economic advancement of black southerners and therefore oppressive, in the objective sense that it was ranged against the development of social ideas that might have encouraged blacks to pursue basic political and social justice.[27]

The relationship of black religious and moral development to the southern social order was another major concern of the Hampton faculty. To Frissell and Armstrong, the "old-time" Negro religion hindered the development of a "new" political economy. It was too removed from questions of practical social responsibility. Armstrong commented: "There is plenty of religion, such as it is, among both parents and scholars, but it is too often a religion that regards more the emotional part of the nature than the moral, and so aids little in the work of checking the evil tendencies of these growing lives." In Armstrong's view, the separation of black religion from moral responsibility was nicely illustrated in the tale of the devout old "Auntie" who attended church regularly without allowing one poor old goose (that she had stolen) to "come between her and her blessed Lord." In discussing black religion and moral strength in 1877, Armstrong told the American Missionary Association that "pastors and deacons all sell whiskey and lead loose lives without scandal; an ex-jail bird returns to his former social position; in politics and in society, character goes for little or nothing."[28]

Behind Armstrong's moral rationale lay more mundane considerations for political and economic reconstruction. He viewed black ministers as eschewing hard labor in favor of political and professional life. He believed that "at least two-thirds" of the ministers were represented by one who explained in a cotton field on a warm day, "O Lord, de work is so bad, de cotton is so grassy, and de sun am so hot, I b'leave dis darkey am called to preach." Such "exemplars" could not be expected to convey the Hampton doctrines of industry and hard labor to the black community. The Hampton staff, therefore, sought to train a corps of teachers who would counteract "the bad leadership of demagogues, whose chief temptation is to get a living by something else than hard work." Frissell attributed black conceptions of social responsibility to the slave experience: "Having been so grossly wronged, their thoughts have been fixed upon their dues from others more than on what is due others from themselves." To "correct their wrong notions," Frissell gave regular instruction on the importance of holding to a contract, on the origin and rights of property and person, and on the duties of citizenship. The Hampton staff labeled this course Practical Morals.[29]

As the academic courses were arranged to influence the students' political and economic ideology, the manual labor system was developed to reinforce consciousness through the formation of habits and character. The manual labor system was a central factor in admission and retention policy and in the students' day-to-day existence. Hampton advertised for "country youth who don't mind hard work." To acquire more "strong, able bodied young men" for the heavier farm and mill work, in 1888 Armstrong created a "special class" who "could not pass the entrance examination, but who were desirable from the work standpoint." Because the entrance examination was mainly a literacy test, it is reasonable to assume that many of these students were semiliterate. They were admitted mainly to work, and after two years in the "Preparatory class" they entered the regular normal school curriculum. Meanwhile, brilliant students considered "indifferent and careless workmen" were "discharged from the farm and usually from the school in consequence." In the nineteenth century, Hampton graduated only one-fifth of its students, and many of those expelled were disqualified because of bad work habits and "weakness of character." The first three months of the school term were considered the "weeding out" session when approximately 20 percent of the new students were dismissed. During the entire three-year course, according to Armstrong, there was "frequent leaving of students for disciplinary, pecuniary, domestic, and other reasons."[30]

All Hampton students were required to work because nonworkers were viewed as "an aristocracy ruinous to manual-labor schools." The amount of work, however, varied according to the student's curriculum. Those who were admitted directly into the normal school to qualify as teachers for graded schools were required to work two ten-hour days per week during their three years of study. They were paid from seven to ten cents per hour or one dollar to one dollar and fifty cents per week. These earnings were credited to the students' accounts for the cost of board, washing, room rent, and tuition, which amounted to approximately ten dollars per month. Thus the students were invariably deficient, and to earn additional credit they agreed to work any time "for any number of days not exceeding twelve [consecutive]." The trade students, generally about sixty males in simple mechanical training, worked six ten-hour days every week for three years and then entered the normal school for two additional years. Such students were also given a normal school certificate until 1895, when Hampton began awarding trade certificates.[31]

The heart of Hampton's manual labor program was established in 1879, when Armstrong created the night school with Booker T. Washington as principal. It opened with 36 students who were required to labor ten hours per day, six days per week, eleven months per year for

two years. Two years of night school work were equivalent to one year of
the normal school course. In their last two years of normal school the
students had to study four days and work two days during each week.
More than any other division, the night school implemented Armstrong's
social philosophy. By 1893, it enrolled 305 of Hampton's 541 black
students. The admissions to the regular or day school declined significantly during the 1880s, and consequently, "the Night School became
the main-feeder of the Day School." It functioned as a sifter for the
normal school by giving the Hampton staff ample opportunity to assess the students' character, industrial habits, and political attitudes before admitting them to the regular normal school. To work from seven
o'clock in the morning until six o'clock at night, and then study from
seven o'clock until nine, was, as Booker T. Washington said, "an under-
taking that few young men would be willing to stick to, through all the
seasons of the year."[32]

Night school students were chiefly farm laborers, domestic servants,
and mill hands. "Much of the labor that goes into our industries," reported Armstrong, "is neither skilled labor nor apprentice labor, but is
made up of the great body of unskilled laborers who come here to work
a year or two at whatever work the school may be able to give them."
Male students worked in the sawmill, on the farm, in the kitchens as
dishwashers and pantry boys, in the dining rooms as waiters, and in the
cottages and smaller buildings as house boys. Female students received
less regular training and were encouraged to do little except "plain sewing, plain washing and ironing, scrubbing, mending, etc." In the words of
the Hampton faculty, the students learned "how to work steadily and
regularly, to attend promptly at certain hours to certain duties," and they
"gained new ideas of the value of manual labor." As Armstrong put it in
his last report, "We do not mean to say that much is not learned by every
faithful student in these departments; he or she will be a better cook,
laundress, or farmer, and surely much needed lessons in promptness, and
thoroughness are inculcated, but still the object in view is not to teach a
trade but to get the work done." Such jobs were no more instructive in
ideas and skills of "self-help" and "self-sufficiency" than the hoeing,
picking, mining, washing, and ironing that black southerners had done
as slaves for centuries. Armstrong required his prospective teachers to
perform the same routinized drudgery as the working class that they
were destined to instruct so that the teachers would stand as exemplars
of the "dignity of labor." His great fear was that black pupils, under
teachers trained in the literary or academic tradition, might come to view
formal schooling as an avenue to escape hard toil. Hampton's emphasis
on the moral value of hard labor in contrast to technical and skill training evidenced Armstrong's concern with the economic adjustment rather

*Female students in Hampton Institute's teacher preparation program
(top) learned to sew as part of their training in the ethic of routinized
hard labor and in occupations prescribed for black women in the South.
The cooking class (bottom) was designed to teach similar lessons.
Courtesy of the Library of Congress.*

than advancement of black southerners. Hampton's theme, "Education for Life," meant the training of blacks to adjust to the life that had been carved out for them within an oppressive social order.[33]

Armstrong had a lifelong distrust of highly educated black persons, and at Hampton he used his power to deemphasize the "black scholar" and to place on a pedestal the "dull plodders." The night school was developed particularly to reproduce "dull plodders." The Hampton faculty described the students as "mostly grown men and women . . . willing to spend their days in hard work on the farm or at the mill," for a chance to enter the normal school curriculum. One night school director, Anna G. Baldwin, reported that the students, most in their early twenties, were "often the best workers" but "the dullest scholars." The demanding work day undoubtedly retarded the students' academic progress. Armstrong, however, maintained that "nothing essential in study is lost, and much that is essential to success in life is gained." Yet the teachers in the academic department constantly complained about low academic achievement, some regarding it a "puzzling mathematical problem" how the night school students could learn anything significant. Baldwin recalled that an ambitious boy could "be overheard conjugating a verb while hoeing in the garden, or perched on a fence watching the cows, [and] meanwhile furtively study his reader." Similarly, night school principal Booker T. Washington reported that "one was noticed to carry a broken piece of slate about with him on which he could work examples while the wheelbarrow of dirt he had loaded, was being emptied." Washington, to illustrate the effectiveness of the night school work routine, quite innocent of satire, stated "their books were in their hands at every spare moment." Indeed, Armstrong had stood the educational process on its head; spare time was used for study and regular time devoted to hard labor.[34]

The "dull plodders" received praise and special treatment from the Hampton faculty. In the summer of 1885, approximately two hundred applicants were refused by Hampton's admission office. Many initial rejects were reconsidered, but only those physically able to take vacant positions in the sawmill and to do the heavier farm work were taken. The Hampton staff certainly had good reason to announce, "There is a certain amount of grit and pluck needed for doing successful work in the night classes." The survivors were held up as model students. As H. B. Frissell explained in 1885, Hampton gave special recognition to successful night school students:

There must always be here the double standard of judging students, by which their moral worth is taken into account even more than their intellectual advancement. What will this student do for the

upbuilding of his race? is the question we are obliged to ask everyone placed under our care. During the past year, students have been
asked to leave the school, whose scholarship was of the best, because it was felt that they lacked in moral earnestness. . . . At the
last anniversary exercises, a young man spoke as the valedictorian of
his class who by no means led his fellows in scholarship, but had
notably taken the lead in Christian Manhood.

Character or "moral earnestness," however, was judged by the students'
willingness to perform "ten hours' drudgery" in unskilled or semiskilled
occupations. The study of mathematics or classical lore for hours on end
was not considered an index of hard labor or moral strength.[35]
Finally, for those students lacking in "moral earnestness," a rigid system of social discipline was instituted to remove the unfit. Armstrong
established a "Daily Order of Exercises," which occupied nearly every
minute of the students' time. They reported for morning inspection at
5:45, had breakfast and prayer from 6:00 to 6:30, worked or studied
during the day with scarcely a half hour to themselves, went to supper
and evening prayers from 6:00 to 6:45 P.M., and, if in night school,
retired to their dormitories thoroughly fatigued after evening study from
7:00 to 9:00. Male students were required to participate in military drill
and to march to and from classes. Beret-Captain Henry Romeyn, who
commanded the Hampton Cadets in 1878, stated that the military drill
was "not intended to make soldiers out of our students, nor to create a
warlike spirit," but to "create ideas of neatness, order, system, obedi-
ence, and produce a better manhood." In Romeyn's view, the drill cultivated a "respect for order and properly constituted authority, that, in
general, would do much to keep down the dangerously increasing com-
munistic elements in the midst of the population of our country." All
students submitted to a system of demerits for infractions of the social
code. This routine enabled the teachers to observe the students' adaptation to the Hampton program. Many pupils were expelled for small
infractions of the social code. One student was dismissed permanently
after receiving reprimands for "using profane language," "not having
room in order," "absence from church without permission," and "having
light on after hours without authority." Another student, accused of "not
rising during singing at morning prayers and causing disturbance by
laughing," was suspended for the year 1879. Many other students met a
similar fate as Hampton sought to instill a respect for order and "properly" constituted authority.[36]
The Hampton model of industrial education was viewed with suspicion and resentment by significant segments of the black community.
The black students who experienced the Hampton routine delivered an

important critique. Historians have failed to analyze the industrial education programs from this perspective. Yet for Hampton, and probably for many other institutions, the most intimate assessment of industrial education, in practice, came from this group. Moreover, when it is considered that nearly all of Hampton's "rebel" students were probably dismissed during the "weeding-out" season, the protest of those who remained is particularly insightful and illuminating.

A significant number of the Hampton students attacked the school's industrial program at its most vulnerable points. Many came to Hampton with the understanding that they would learn skilled trades for future livelihood. But because Hampton was designed primarily to train conservative teachers and leaders, some students were disappointed with the absence of technical training and the low level of trade training. William W. Adams, having heard that "scholars could learn trades" at Hampton, entered the school in 1878 to learn the printing trade. Adams was appalled at the elementary character of the academic program and commented bitterly that he was "not learning anything," merely "going over what I had learned in a primary school." He was more disheartened, however, in discovering that no one would teach him the printing trade. He left in dismay and charged that the school was "greatly overrated." Ten years later, another student complained about the inadequate training in the printing division. As Thomas Mann wrote to Armstrong, "Bookbinding is a part of the printer's trade of which we get none. . . . As I wish to become a successful printer, I would like to learn all about the trade." Hampton was capable of offering better training in the printing trade because the school printed the *Southern Workman* and the *African Repository* and operated the Normal School Press. But in 1878 there were no students in the printing trade, and by 1890 there were only eight black students working in the printing office. But the Hampton mission was to train teachers, not printers or shoemakers.[37]

From the vantage point of the student, the trade instruction at Hampton was elementary and limited. A student in the blacksmith department complained in 1888 that there were "six blacksmiths and only two forges," which greatly restricted their practice in heating and hammering metals. John H. Boothe, in his last year of training to become a shoemaker, wrote that he had not received "any instructions on cutting out and fitting shoes." J. F. Satterwhite stated that the students were not trained to make boots, a product that brought significant profits to shoemakers. C. L. Marshall further criticized the shoemaking program for not teaching "sewed work" in the shop. Marshall, like Satterwhite, was displeased with his training in shoemaking. As he informed Armstrong, "The people do not want peg or nail work, but they want sewed work. Should I go home and attempt to set up a shoe shop without any knowledge of sewed work, I don't think I could earn my daily bread." Indeed, a shoemaker who could not make boots or cut, fit, or sew shoes was hardly worthy of the name.[38]

The "carpenters," like the shoemakers, were trained to be handymen rather than craftsmen or artisans. William M. Keffie was annoyed because he and fellow apprentices did not receive "enough practice in the way of building and framing houses." J. A. Colbert, another aspiring carpenter, worked "all day for six days each week" and was dissatisfied with the lack of training in "the use of timber." Apparently, Hampton's program in carpentry involved little more than instruction in making window sashes and frames. The students urged Armstrong to upgrade the work from essentially manual labor to skilled trade training. Perry Shields, writing to Armstrong in 1888, revealed much about the quality of the carpentry course.

> We the boys in the HIW [Huntington Industrial Workshop] need to learn how to build houses, the practice for which, we do not get in the mill. We work in the mill three years, after which we leave, giving others to think that we are carpenters. All of us can't find mills to get employment, hence we will soon find out that building is the chief and only work of our branch by which we can earn a living. So you see that the only thing we learn in that direction is the use of tools and three years are too much time to spend learning merely to use tools. We draw buildings every week and if we had some of the work to do after drawing it we would become self-supporting mechanics. As it is, we begin with making window and door frames and have but few other jobs, but making frames.

Hampton's trade students were acutely aware of the institute's shortcomings. O. H. Hawkins requested "more practical training or instruction pertaining to framing houses and how to get the different levels, angles, etc." Whether it was Jackson M. Mundy requesting mechanical drawing or George Johnson asking for improvements in the sawmill, trade students at Hampton were largely disappointed with their training.[39]

The students' resentment was eventually expressed in a petition of protest issued to the Hampton faculty in the summer of 1887. According to two students, Perry Shields and W. H. Scott, "every apprentice of the school signed his name" to the protest document. The faculty, however, ignored the petition, and Shields informed Armstrong: "We feel that we form a very insignificant part of the working class, from the fact that last summer a letter was written the faculty to which every apprentice of the school signed his name, and from that letter we have heard nothing, for nor against; from such points we lose interest." Likewise, Scott complained to Armstrong: "The petition put through by the trade-boys during the fall was seemingly ignored much to our disappointment." In the letters that followed the petition, the students protested against the menial level of training, hard labor, low wages, and poor working conditions. Realizing that very little educational benefit accrued from the industrial program, the students responded as a discontented working class. Dissatisfaction with overwork was a consistent and pervasive theme in their letters. John H. Boothe, who described the working conditions in terms suitable to characterizing convict labor, said that the students were "confined" in the shops "for a term of three years to work every day except legal holidays and Sundays." Hawkins viewed the students' training not as an educational program but as a process of "toiling at their trade through three years." Scott spoke for many of his fellow students in candid remarks about the work schedule: "It is to be remembered that four years at a trade like ours, working from 7 A.M. to 5:50 P.M., is enough to break down the constitution of a man, much less boys in the bloom of youth."[40]

Hampton's students understood that they were performing hard labor and some, like J. F. Satterwhite, stated simply, "I think we ought to get paid more." Similarly, Roberta Whiting, the mother of a Hampton student, questioned the school's manual labor program, which operated at the expense of both trade and academic training: "I received a letter from my son and he tells me that he has not attended day school since entering your institution. He also mentioned that his work was hard having to milk, and attend to a number of cows every day and that he has to get up at four A.M. to do this and the only time spent in school was at night. I have spoken to my physician and he thinks that amount of work detrimental to the health of a boy his age." James C. Rollins also consulted his physician about the Hampton labor routine. Arriving at the school in "tolerably good health," he informed Armstrong that "my doctor has seriously cautioned me about overworking myself." George Johnson resented the harshness of his boss; Clayton Elks demanded better food; G. G. Spraggins complained of the rain leaking into his shop; and W. Z. Ruth pleaded for improved working conditions.[41]

Publicly, Armstrong propagandized that at Hampton "there was no begging except for more work." The students, however, actually asked for reduced work loads. J. H. Tucker, who may have understood Armstrong's passion for hard labor, could not comprehend why he had to continue painting in the dark merely to complete a ten-hour work routine. Male students particularly requested Armstrong to suspend work hours on Saturdays at four o'clock. According to Hawkins, they wanted the time "to engage themselves in such games, or local pleasures as they think best." Armstrong, however, believing that blacks had no "respect" for labor, insisted upon "the ten hours' drudgery" to put the students "in shape for the struggle of life." But, in the words of Perry Shields, "after working for a long time upon the same old thing in which there is no future," many students lost interest in their training. In sharp protest against the constrictions on the students' intellect and creativity, Shields asserted, "The shop is cold and our minds are straying and our hands freezing—and we cannot retain any interests."[42]

Hampton's students also resented the school's active support of Jim Crow racial practices. In 1878, Hampton's newly formed Alumni Association petitioned the school's faculty regarding its policies and practices of racial subordination. The Alumni Association, which met at Hampton during the May commencement exercises, urged the faculty to "examine carefully" whether black visitors were accorded proper respect. More specifically, the petition charged: "That the graduates of this Institution have been insulted and have had our feelings mortified by public rumors and newspaper articles to the effect that the officers and teachers of this Institution have not, and do not accord to colored visitors the courtesies and hospitalities due them as a race." The Hampton alumni used their own experiences to charge the faculty with racial proscription. As the petition stated, "We the graduates of this Institution, after returning in compliance with the call of our Alma Mater, have had our feelings wounded most grievously by being barred from some of the privileges that ordinary white visitors enjoyed." Much of this protest remained within the confines of the institute; nevertheless, it reveals important student perceptions of the Hampton program. Clearly, many of them realized that Armstrong and his colleagues were trying to convince black people to accept a subordinate social position in the institution and in the society at large.[43]

Hampton's students and alumni were not alone in questioning the relevance of Armstrong's social philosophy to the interests and aspirations of the Afro-American South. Both Frissell and Armstrong acknowledged persistent black opposition to the Hampton Idea. In 1878 Armstrong declared that black criticism of the institute was "no novelty," and in 1879 he admitted that objections to the Hampton program were "common in the colored papers." In 1888 Armstrong further stated: "During the first ten years of our school life our work was looked upon with disfavor by the Negro leaders as providing only a low grade of instruction." H. B. Frissell recalled that "Negro conventions referred to Hampton as a 'slave pen and literary penitentiary.'" The black *Virginia Star* recommended that the government make Hampton "a National Reform School" for its wards. "It is admirably adapted for such, and it would prevent many unwary parents from sending their children there to equip them with a classical education." The *Christian Recorder* of the African Methodist Episcopal church, after criticizing the conservative view of a Hampton student in 1875, asked, "Have Virginia conservatives captured Hampton?"[44]

Black criticisms of Hampton Institute received national attention in the Afro-American press during the late 1870s. In 1876 two black writers for the *People's Advocate*, which was edited in Alexandria, Virginia, by the prominent black journalist John Wesley Cromwell, characterized the Hampton program as an educational experience that sought to affirm the legitimacy of black subordination. After attending the 1876 commencement, one writer, struck by Hampton's pattern of race relations, reported:

> On Commencement Day May 18th visitors were present, white and colored, but not one of the latter was to be seen on the splendid platform of Virginia Hall. The rudest and most ignorant white men and women were politely conducted to the platform; respectable and intelligent colored ladies and gentlemen were shown lower seats where they could neither see nor hear the exercises of the day with any pleasure. To speak in general the colored people and students are made to feel that they must forever remain inferior to their white brethren no matter what their attainments may be.

The reporter concluded that it was "better, far better, yes infinitely better that we have no high schools and colleges, if our youth are to be brought up under such baneful influences." Several days later another reporter for the *People's Advocate*, who had also visited Hampton Institute, commented boldly: "I had rather my boy, should grow up ignorant of letters, than attend an Institution to be taught that Negroes, notwithstanding their acquirements, are and must forever remain inferior to the whites."[45]

This line of criticism continued in 1878, when the prominent black leader Henry M. Turner visited Hampton and reported his impressions of the school in the *Christian Recorder*. In his weekly column "Wayside Dots and Jots," Turner chastised Hampton for its Confederate orientation. He was struck immediately by the pictures of Andrew Johnson and General Robert E. Lee hanging on the walls of the school's chapel and commented acidly: "What [they] had ever done for the colored people I could not tell." Turner attended an advanced class for seniors purportedly in astronomy, and he concluded that "the teacher knew comparatively nothing about it, and the class knew, if possible, less than nothing." He was convinced that Hampton deprived black students of intellectual development, particularly in "algebra, geometry, higher mathematics, Greek, Latin, and Science." He was most upset, however, with Hampton's policy of racial subordination. During his stay, "not a teacher asked me to sit down, made a solitary explanation, gave me a welcome look, nor showed me the civility of a visitor, while I was in the building." In contrast to the treatment he received, Turner observed that "when white visitors come in, chairs were offered them, etc." Turner's treatment at Hampton differed sharply from the cordial receptions he had received at other black schools. Thus he assessed the Hampton teachers and students as follows: "They are either in the whole ex-slave-holders themselves, or are pandering to the spirit of slavery. The graduates they send out cannot be called educated by any means, for they have not near the learning given by a respectable grammar school. . . . Besides, I think colored children are taught to remember, 'You are Negroes,' and as such, 'your place is behind.' "⁴⁶

R. A. Green, editor of the *Virginia Star*, reprinted Turner's editorial and informed his readers that he had received similar treatment while visiting Hampton Institute. A year later the *Louisianian* reported that "General Armstrong, the principal of Hampton Institute, does not seem to stand in high favor with the colored people of the east." The *Louisianian* declared that Armstrong was charged with "curbing the aspirations of his students" and with crushing the manhood of the male students by refusing to hire black professors. "To know and *feel* that he is indeed a man," argued the *Louisianian*, "the Negro should have the black professor side by side with his white brother. This manhood education can never come from white teachers alone, however competent." The *Louisianian* charged that Armstrong "by his educational policy, seems to think that we should only know enough to make good servants."⁴⁷

Even the more moderate wing of black educators and writers criticized industrial education during the 1880s and 1890s. Such black spokesmen as Harry Smith, Alexander Crummell, and Calvin Chase questioned the motives of those who promoted industrial training as the educational model most suitable for Afro-Americans. Initially, it appeared that Crummell, the venerable and learned rector of Washington, D.C.'s St. Luke's Methodist Church, would support the Hampton-styled industrial education movement. In 1887 he published *Common Sense in Common Schooling*, which praised vocational education and stated that higher education was "ruinous [to] well-nigh half of the colored youth who graduate from high schools and colleges." The African Methodist Episcopal church's *Church Review* criticized Crummell's position on the grounds that many whites would "refer to him as endorsing the position they hold, to wit, that the Negro only needs and should therefore only receive an industrial education." The editor of the *Church Review*, however, understood that Crummell meant only to emphasize the value of skilled trades and technical training and did not intend to encourage the Hampton program of Negro industrial education. Crummell confirmed this view when he later wrote, "All the talk about 'industrialism' is with regard to the Negro and Negro education, and there is a lot of white men in the land who pity the Negro but who have never learned to love him, who take up this miserable 'fad,' and are striving by one pretext or another to put this limitation upon our brains and culture."[48]

In the 1890s Harry Smith, editor of the *Cleveland Gazette*, and Calvin Chase, editor of the *Washington Bee*, continued to warn the black community about the dangers of the Hampton-Tuskegee style of industrial education. The *Gazette*, arguing that attainments in the industrial arts would not fit young blacks for the "higher duties of life," reported in 1890 that Hampton graduates were being employed as waiters and porters. Although admitting to the necessity of trade training, the *Gazette* advocated higher and professional training for "the fullest development of the [Negro] mind." Likewise, the *Washington Bee* urged blacks to relegate industrial education to a secondary role and to place top priority on the training of lawyers, doctors, scientists, and other professional persons. Much of the *Bee*'s attack on industrial training focused on Booker T. Washington as he became in the 1890s the leading black spokesman for industrial education. In a typical editorial against Washington and the Hampton-Tuskegee Idea, the *Bee* remarked in 1896: "It is a notorious fact, that the utterances of Mr. Washington are nothing more than to make himself rich by assuring the white people of this country that the negroes [*sic*] place is in the machine shop, at the plow, in the washtub and not in the schools of legal and medical professions; that he [the Negro] has no business to aspire to those places as they are reserved for the proud Caucasian." Significantly, such criticisms, which started in the middle 1870s, long predated the Washington-DuBois debates of the early twentieth century and represented a persistent strain of black protest against the Hampton-Tuskegee Idea for the training of black educators and leaders.[49]

Black protest against the Hampton Idea was directed at that particular form of industrial education; it was not a blanket rejection of vocational and technical training. Black leaders in conjunction with white antislavery leaders were interested in establishing black trade and industrial schools as early as the eighteenth century. This interest increased significantly with the emergence of militant abolitionism and the Negro convention movement of the 1830s. In 1831 black male activists from the major northern urban centers assembled in Philadelphia for the First Annual Convention of the Free People of Color at which they proposed the establishment of a black "Manual Labor College" in New Haven, Connecticut, that would embrace all the mechanic arts and provide a thorough classical education. Early on, it seemed that the proposed trade and technical college would receive general support from the New Haven white community and prove itself a success within a short time.

New Haven whites, however, foreshadowing future opposition to serious black trade and technical training, "were as one in their protest" against the plan and forced the initial project to be abandoned. In 1833, still attempting to realize the goal of a black trade and technical school, black leaders and white abolitionists sought to transfer their resources to an academy in Canaan, Connecticut. But the white townspeople demolished the building that was erected to start a black manual labor college; again, the plan was squelched almost before it began. The project was pursued through the 1840s and 1850s, but no black polytechnic institute was established in the antebellum era. Still, the persistent campaign for such a school underscored black interest in education that could combine a classical liberal course with training in technology and trades. This idea differed sharply from the Hampton program that precluded technical education and did very little with respect to trades. Ironically, when "industrial education" programs developed in black schools during the postbellum period, they never met the long-standing aspirations of Afro-Americans.[50]

The most significant expansion of industrial education in black normal schools and colleges occurred during the 1880s. Its sudden rise was the result primarily of the establishment of the John F. Slater Fund in 1881, which offered financial aid exclusively for the development of black industrial education. Perhaps more than any other factor, the Slater Fund caused several black schools to initiate vocational programs during the 1880s. Many of the schools' reports indicate that the industrial work would not have been possible without the Slater Fund. As badly as most black schools needed money just to scrape by, they could hardly afford to ignore the availability of this new philanthropy, even if it was targeted for low-level industrial training. Indeed, the increased interest in industrial education by black schools indicates, above all else, a pragmatic search for funds, not a commitment to the social and educational philosophy embodied in the Hampton program. Thus, although many schools offered or at least advertised new courses in industrial education, they never allowed it to displace classical liberal academic education.[51]

The sudden rise of industrial education in black schools during the 1880s has often led to the erroneous conclusion that it became the ascendant form of education in black normal schools and colleges and temporarily eclipsed liberal and higher education. Yet a careful analysis of the curriculum reveals that most black colleges relegated industrial education to a subordinate role. Among the black colleges under mission societies, the traditional liberal or classical curriculum remained dominant throughout the nineteenth and early twentieth centuries. Most black colleges were under the direction of four major mission societies: the American Missionary Association, the Freedmen's Aid Society of the Methodist Episcopal church, the American Baptist Home Mission Society, and the Board of Missions for the Freedmen of the Presbyterian Church in the U.S.A. A significant number of black secondary schools and colleges, however, were organized and controlled by black religious organizations. The African Methodist Episcopal church, the Colored Methodist Episcopal church, and the African Methodist Episcopal Zion church established nearly all of the major colleges controlled by black organizations, and their combined voice largely articulated the educational policy of the black community. These institutions never adopted the Hampton-Tuskegee pattern of black industrial education, and they gave low priority to all forms of industrial training. Robert G. Sherer, in a useful study of black secondary and normal schools and colleges in nineteenth-century Alabama, demonstrated that Booker T. Washington was virtually alone in urging that prime emphasis be put on industrial rather than classical liberal education. Sherer concludes correctly that Washington and the Hampton-Tuskegee Idea were "outside the mainstream of black educational thought." Consequently, at the close of the nineteenth century, the proponents of the Hampton Idea found little support for their model of industrial training. In fact, they faced powerful resistance, especially from important leaders in the mission societies.[52]

The northern mission societies generally accepted manual training courses such as printing, carpentry, and blacksmithing for student work programs, the teaching of skilled trades, and character development, but they tended to view such courses as relatively insignificant for intellectual and leadership training. The proponents of the Hampton model never accepted the missionary interpretation of industrial training. Samuel Armstrong was one of the first to recognize that the industrial education concept left "a wide opportunity for difference of opinion as to the application of the principle, and these differences go deeper than the surface." There were clear distinctions between the Hampton and the missionary models of industrial education. Whereas Hampton established a system of menial labor to build character and mold the ideology of prospective teachers, missionary schools focused on job training. Teacher training in the missionary schools focused on the classical liberal tradition. At Hampton, industrial training was the core curriculum for all students, whereas the mission societies maintained industrial education as a relatively insignificant adjunct to the classical liberal curriculum. The Hampton model was organized around a conservative sociopolitical ideology that advocated the political disfranchisement and economic subordination of the black race. The mission societies emphasized literary and professional training to develop a black intelligentsia that would fight for political and civil equality. Thus there was far more discord than harmony between the two camps.[53]

The missionary vanguard was headed by Thomas J. Morgan, Henry L. Morehouse, and Malcolm MacVicar of the American Baptist Home Mission Society and Joseph E. Roy and William Hayes Ward of the American Missionary Association. Morgan, a colonel of the Fourteenth United States Colored Infantry during the Civil War and former commissioner of Indian affairs, served as executive secretary of the Baptist Home Mission Society and as editor of the society's influential *Home Mission Monthly* from 1893 to 1902. Morehouse was the executive secretary of the American Baptist Education Society. MacVicar, superintendent of the Home Mission Society's Educational Department from 1890 to 1900, headed the society's Virginia Union University from 1900 to 1904. Ward, one of the most vigorous defenders of black higher education, was for many years chairman of the American Missionary Association's executive committee and was associate editor, 1868–70, superintending editor, 1870–96, and editor, 1896–1913, of the *New York Independent*. His colleague, Roy, was field superintendent of the American Missionary Association. The status of these men in missionary activities and in the larger society enabled them to form a powerful vanguard that stood clearly and unswervingly for black higher education and for the development of advanced technical schools to prepare blacks for executive and administrative posts.[54]

This vocal missionary leadership objected to the Hampton model on the grounds that it undermined the democratic rights of blacks by assuming that black students were destined for a subordinate industrial role in the southern economy. Following a conference on black education in 1895 at the American Social Science Association, Morgan and Ward attacked the "reviving Negrophobia," which opposed the higher education of blacks and laid "special stress upon the necessity of Industrial training." Morgan, through the *Home Mission Monthly*, and Ward, in the *Independent*, "protest[ed] vehemently against any philosophy of education which will restrict the Negro schools to industrial training, or to rudimentary education." Moreover, they suspected "that the prime motive of the white men in the South who urge most strongly the industrial education of the Negroes, is the conviction in their minds that all the Negro needs to know is how to work. This proceeds upon the assumption that the race is doomed to servitude." The Negro industrial education concept, as Morgan and Ward understood it, was "based upon the denial of the humanity of a whole race" and was calculated to make the Negro "absolutely content with his lot as a servant." In contrast to the Hampton model of industrial training, Morgan urged the mission societies to establish for blacks technical departments and schools "to develop among them architects, artists, engineers, master mechanics, superintendents of mines, overseers of mills," and the like. On another occasion, after politely stating his sympathy for Booker T. Washington, Morgan rejected the manual training concept in favor of "the higher grade of industrial training proper, such as is now furnished in Pratt Institute and other similar institutions in the North."[55]

Generally, the missionary leaders were diplomatic in their handling of the industrial education movement, and they attempted to check its growth by vigorously defending the need for black higher education. "Neglect, if you will, the common school education in your missionary labor; neglect, if you must, the industrial education," advised Ward, "but never forget that it is your work to educate leaders." To the mission societies, leadership training meant, above all, higher literary education. According to Morehouse, the Home Mission Society believed in "the thorough humanity of the black man, with divine endowment of all the facilities of the white man; capable of culture, capable of high attainments under proper conditions and with sufficient time; a being not predestined to be simply a hewer of wood and drawer of water for the white race." Morehouse believed that the black race would progress largely through the wise leadership of a gifted intelligentsia, and he therefore placed top priority on the higher education of a black "talented tenth." Morgan also thought that black progress depended on the leadership of "noble and powerful minds raised up from their own ranks." Similarly, MacVicar argued for the highest form of liberal education because the mental development of the black man followed "precisely the same laws as in the case of the white man."[56]

Significantly, the views of the missionary vanguard were shared by white presidents of the mission societies' black colleges and secondary schools. Henry S. DeForest, president of the American Missionary Association's Talladega College, contended "that while all should have the lower education, a great many should receive the higher." As he put it, "Every man may need silver, but the best commerce of the world requires that some should have gold, and a good deal of it." DeForest stated that Talladega had "not forgotten the industrial education"; the college's primary goal, however, was to offer the black students "choice scholarship." George Sale, president of Atlanta Baptist College (Morehouse), informed the white Georgia State Teacher's Association that he objected to "the idea that the education of the Negro should be exclusively or distinctly industrial." If classical studies were valuable for whites, Sale asked, "Why should they not have the same value for Negroes?" E. C. Mitchell, president of Leland University in New Orleans, reasoned that it was purposeless to include industrial training in black colleges because "every village has its Negro mechanics who are patronized both by white and colored employers, and any who wish to learn the trade can do so." He viewed industrial training as a form of "class education" for blacks and argued that it did "not educate, even in trades." Likewise, Presidents Charles F. Meserve of Shaw University, George F. Genung of Richmond Theological Seminary, and MacVicar of Virginia Union University regarded industrial training as relatively insignificant to the higher education of black students.[57]

To be sure, many other college presidents were less adamant in their opposition to industrial training. In fact, most probably considered it a positive adjunct to the black students' general academic program. Even so, they relegated industrial training to a subordinate role in the curriculum. A. C. Osborn, president of Benedict College, saw some usefulness in industrial training, but as he clearly stated, "Benedict is not a trade or industrial school, in that it does not give the industrial work the foremost place." President L. G. Barrett of Jackson College also praised the positive aspects of limited industrial training while emphasizing that his college directed black students "on to higher study." Ward spoke well for the missionary leadership when he said, "Industrial education is good, very valuable, and we give it as an adjunct, but it is not an important thing."[58]

The conflicting ideologies of black education led to some significant confrontations between the missionary and Hampton camps in the late nineteenth century, and the outcome shaped the Hampton's advocates' course of action at the turn of the century. In 1890, following a suggestion of former President Rutherford B. Hayes, Quaker philanthropist Albert K. Smiley organized a conference at his Lake Mohonk resort hotel in the Catskills to discuss the "Negro question." Of this conference Armstrong wrote, "In order to be sure and get the southern white men to come, he [Smiley] decided not to invite any colored people." Modeled on the annual Indian conferences at Mohonk, the conferences of 1890 and 1891 concentrated essentially on Negro education. Samuel C. Armstrong, Hollis B. Frissell, Rutherford B. Hayes, chairman of the Slater Fund, and others argued strongly for the Hampton model as the best form of black education. The words of Armstrong were typical: "The great mass of Negroes must be farmers and they need to be taught to farm intelligently." But regardless of whether blacks were forced to be farmers, the missionary educators objected to imposing second-class industrial training on the black race. Reverend Roy, secretary of the American Missionary Association, after making a brilliant defense of blacks' right to higher education, informed the Hampton supporters that it was "too late in the history of civilization to impose any repression upon any class of people." Similarly, Lyman Abbott, Congregational minister and editor of the *Christian Union* (renamed the *Outlook* in 1893), admonished the conference that it was "not in the province nor in the power of one class to determine the metes and bounds of another class." "I claim, therefore," said Abbott, "the Negroes' right to an education from a, b, up to Syriac, from the multiplication table up to conic sections. Or, if there is anything higher than that, that higher thing, whatever it may be." Ward and MacVicar also supported higher education and equal rights for black people. Even though blacks were barred from the Mohonk conference, the Hampton boosters failed to achieve a consensus in support of industrial normal schools for training black leaders.[59]

Another debate regarding the "instruction of the colored citizens" was held at the 1896 annual conference of the American Social Science Association. The major address was given by Hampton booster H. L. Wayland, editor of the *New York Examiner*, who retired as president of the association in 1894. Wayland took great care to summon distinguished black supporters of the Hampton model, particularly Booker T. Washington and Hugh M. Browne, principal of a black high school in Washington, D.C. He wrote Robert C. Ogden, president of the Hampton Board of Trustees: "On Tuesday evening, September 1, I shall read a paper at the Social Science, at Saratoga, on the higher education of the southern colored, which will be followed by a debate. We hope to have Prof. Washington, who is heartily with us, and I shall ask Mr. Durham and one or two others. . . . Now what I want to say is this, will you not make it a point to be present." Ogden did not attend the conference, but Wayland, Washington, and Browne gave an adequate defense of the Hampton Idea. To these men, as Wayland aptly phrased it, the whole question of black education could be summarized in two words: "These two words are 'Hampton' and 'Tuskegee.'" But Morgan, Atlanta University Professor Silas X. Floyd, and Malcolm MacVicar were not persuaded by the arguments of the Hampton supporters. "I submit," replied Morgan, "that no form of industrial training yet devised can take the place of a college curriculum in giving breadth of knowledge, catholicity of sympathy, power of thought, constructive ability and fitness for leadership." Floyd and MacVicar joined Morgan in rejecting industrial training as an appropriate model of education for the black leadership. Wayland, in describing the results of the debate to Ogden, revealed his frustration over the resistance to the Hampton Idea:

Gen. Morgan and Dr. MacVicar held on to the old theory. I am surprised that they do not take counsel with common sense. Probably they would say, "The Colored people demand Greek and Latin,

and if we do not give it to them, they will go elsewhere." But to that
I would reply, "Both Hampton and Tuskegee have annually more
applications than they can receive." And also it is our duty to give
them what we conscientiously think best, and it is our right to do so
since we pay for it ourselves.

It became increasingly clear to the advocates of the Hampton model that
a powerful cadre of missionary educators and important black leaders
would not accept industrial training as the dominant form of black education. In 1895 and 1896 Wayland was sharply assailed for making
caustic criticisms of black higher education. Even President William
McKinley was chastised by Ward when, in 1898, the president praised
Tuskegee for giving black students instruction in "practical industry"
and for not "attempting the unattainable" by offering higher education.
Ward replied acidly: "What there is 'unattainable' to the Negro, or what
school offers the unattainable, we do not know." The missionary vanguard met well the challenge of the Hampton ideologues and effectively
blocked the spread of the Hampton doctrine in the mission schools; thus
in the late nineteenth century, the Hampton spokesmen found themselves
cut off from the mainstream of black higher education.[60]
     The Hampton Idea was not isolated from the mainstream of American
society, however. In sharp contrast to its rejection by black teachers and
the leaders of black schools and colleges, leading American politicians,
businessmen, and philanthropists came to view Hampton and Tuskegee
as pointing the way toward a national and even worldwide solution of
the "Negro problem." The Hampton Idea was supported actively by
Ulysses S. Grant, Rutherford B. Hayes, James A. Garfield, Theodore
Roosevelt, William Howard Taft, Woodrow Wilson, Andrew Carnegie,
John D. Rockefeller, Jr., Julius Rosenwald, George Eastman, Charles W.
Eliot, Jabez L. M. Curry, and Clark Howell, to name only a few. Through
correspondence and visits to Hampton and Tuskegee, such men had
come to know Hampton's work intimately. They understood correctly
that Armstrong, Frissell, and Washington propounded not merely an
educational theory but a social philosophy. President Garfield said that
Armstrong was working out the race problem "in the only way that will
give us a country without section and a people without a stain." "If there
is any work which every American must believe in," said Theodore Roosevelt, "it is the work you are doing at Hampton and Tuskegee." Harvard
University President Charles W. Eliot said: "Hampton and Tuskegee
have done great good. I know of no educational or philanthropic object which should more commend itself to American patriots." These
two small normal schools, with academic programs comparable to the

quality of instruction in an adequate common school, received national acclaim because of their profoundly conservative approach to the problems of race, labor, and politics in the New South.[61]

Booker T. Washington's rise to national prominence in 1895 breathed new life into the Hampton Idea and accounted in large part for its fame and achievements during the early twentieth century. Indeed, from 1895, when he addressed the opening of the Cotton States and International Exposition at Atlanta, Georgia, to his death in 1915, the Hampton Idea was recognized nationally as the Hampton-Tuskegee Idea. On 18 September 1895, Washington delivered his widely publicized "Atlanta Compromise." He said virtually nothing about education but much about economics, politics, and racial equality. True to the Hampton philosophy, which he learned under Armstrong from 1872 to 1875, Washington stressed the political and economic value of his educational philosophy. Had he lived to hear it, Armstrong would have been proud of the way his favorite student addressed the South's dominant-class whites. He spoke carefully to their greatest fears: that black southerners would persist in their struggle to attain the political power formally granted to them by the Fourteenth and Fifteenth Amendments and that they might choose not to till the region's cotton, tobacco, and sugar fields, or at least withdraw a substantial portion of their labor power. "No race can prosper," said Washington, "till it learns that there is as much dignity in tilling a field as in writing a poem." Washington urged the development of a black laboring class that would "buy your *surplus* land, make blossom the waste places in your fields, and run your factories." These black workers, he promised, would be "the most patient, faithful, law-abiding, and unresentful people that the world has seen." Washington was silent on the questions of black voting and officeholding, and his silence was evidence enough of his willingness to accommodate the practical disfranchisement of black voters. Washington, an ex-slave, embodied the objective conjuncture of race and class that threatened to tear apart the southern social order, and, therefore, his espousal of the Hampton Idea gave it more legitimacy than Armstrong ever did or could have. Somehow, the retrogressive and repressive tenets of the Hampton Idea rang differently when spoken by an ex-slave.[62]

Still, Washington and Tuskegee were Armstrong and Hampton in blackface. "The mission of Tuskegee Institute," said Roscoe Conkling Bruce, the director of the school's Academic Department, "is largely to supply measurably well equipped teachers for the schools." Tuskegee, like Hampton, was primarily a normal school, and Washington, as Armstrong, saw his students as prospective missionaries of the traditional Hampton educational and social philosophy. The student body at both institutes was divided into day students and night students. At Tuskegee, said Bruce, "The night students work in the industries, largely at common labor, all day every day and go to school at night, thus paying their current board bills and accumulating such credits at the Treasurer's office as will later defray their expenses in the day school." The student pay rate remained two and a half cents per hour or one dollar for a forty-hour week, so much hard toil was required of the night students. The day students were divided into two sections that alternated working every other day for three days a week and attending academic classes for three days. Not surprisingly, Louis Harlan discovered that at Hampton and Tuskegee "there was perhaps one graduate for every ten ex-students."[63]

Because the night students worked all day for six days a week and attended school at night, while the day students spent one-half of their time at common labor, Tuskegee's curriculum was also weighted heavily toward the manual labor routine. As at Hampton, academic education was of low quality. Bruce, putting the best possible face on his department, told a Boston audience in 1904 that Tuskegee's lowest day school class was "about the equivalent to a fourth grade in the North" and the senior day school class was comparable to "the first or the second year (barring the foreign languages) in a northern high school." Washington thought that even this standard placed too much emphasis on academic learning, and the following year he and Bruce enforced a directive: "Every academic teacher is appreciably to diminish the amount of time required of his students for the preparation of his subjects." Washington's decision raises a fundamental question. Why did he, as principal of a normal school, whose avowed mission was to train teachers, deliver such a crippling blow to an already weak academic program? Here it is important to recall that Washington was called back to Hampton in 1879 to preside over Armstrong's night school. What he did in 1905 was no different than what Armstrong did in 1879—base the training of teachers primarily on manual labor rather than on academic studies. Washington kept Tuskegee in line with the educational form and content he had received at Hampton.[64]

Both Armstrong and Washington believed strongly in correlating academic and industrial training. In reality this meant academic instruction no higher than the three Rs and what was presupposed by the manual labor routines. As Bruce stated,

> But, the teaching of agriculture, even in its elementary stages, presupposes a considerable amount of academic preparation. To be sure, a flourishing garden may be made and managed by bright-eyed tots just out of the kindergarten, but how can commercial fertilizers

be carefully analyzed by a boy who has made no study of general chemistry?—and how can a balanced ration be adjusted by an illiterate? Similarly, the girl in the laundry does not make soap by rote but by principle; and the girl in the dressmaking shop does not cut out her pattern by luck or guess or instinct or rule of thumb, but by geometry.

Bruce saw in such training the "technical utility of Tuskegee's Academic Department." It is hardly necessary to add again that Tuskegee was not training farmers, laundry women, or dressmakers, but teachers. The teachers were trained in academic skills presupposed by common labor occupations. It is no wonder, then, that Louis Harlan found that "a generation of Tuskegee graduates, not to mention the larger number who left before graduation, murdered the King's English in their letters back to the school." This performance reflected the Hampton glorification of "dull plodders."[65]

When Hampton and Tuskegee are taken on their own terms, as normal schools, there is no logical reason why they should have given priority to technical and trade training. Yet, with all the talk about industrial training, both contemporary observers and later historians mistakenly assumed that trade, technical, and commercial training formed the essence of Washington's educational philosophy. In fact, Tuskegee placed even less emphasis on trade and commercial training than did Hampton. In 1903 Daniel C. Smith, Tuskegee's auditor, made a study of the school's industrial training program. According to Smith, of 1,550 students, "there were only a dozen students in the school capable of doing a fair job as joiners. There were only fifteen boys who could lay brick." "Meanwhile," Smith continued, "the number of students who are doing unskilled drudgery work is increasing, and the number who receive no training through the use of tools is getting to be very large." This finding was not inconsistent with Tuskegee's aims. Nor was Tuskegee's failure to teach commercial or business subjects, despite Washington's preachings about economic development as the only salvation of black Americans. In 1906, in assessing Tuskegee's endeavors in the teaching of business and commercial subjects, Robert E. Park discovered that "there is a large amount of business conducted by the school, but there is no school of business here." There were "a large number of stenographers employed on the ground but stenography and typewriting are not taught here." Three papers and a number of pamphlets were published at Tuskegee, but printing was not taught there. There was not even a formal course in bookkeeping.[66]

From their founding to the late 1920s, Hampton and Tuskegee were

Normal school students at Hampton and Tuskegee were trained in academic skills presupposed by common labor occupations. The captions on a Tuskegee blackboard—Shoemaking, Blacksmithing, Machine, Carpentry—indicate the topics for reading and composition. This practice of correlating the academic and the industrial was known as "dovetailing." Courtesy of the Library of Congress.

Normal school teachers bring the ethics of hard toil and field work directly to the black kindergarten children of Tuskegee's elementary school, the institute's lab school, which was used primarily for practice teaching. Courtesy of the Library of Congress.

not trade schools, nor academic schools worthy of the name, but schools that attempted to train a corps of teachers with a particular social philosophy relevant to the political and economic reconstruction of the South. Their mission and source of strength was to train teachers and leaders who would, as Washington urged, "carry a drop of [Armstrong's] life blood into the darkest corner of the darkest South." Their espousal of this mission gained Hampton and Tuskegee the support of America's leading politicians, businessmen, and philanthropists. But the Hampton-Tuskegee Idea had not won the hearts and minds of the teachers and administrators who controlled black educational institutions.[67]

By the close of the nineteenth century, Hampton supporters recognized that their model of industrial training was relatively insignificant in the overall scheme of black higher education. Yet they were determined to advance the Hampton program as the dominant educational model for the training of black leaders. In 1899 Frissell planned a tour of several southern cities to convert important black leaders to the Hampton Idea. Frissell wrote: "Our trustees have felt strongly that it is important to stir up the colored people to an interest in industrial education." He had no illusions about the black community's view of industrial education. "As you know," he wrote to a friend, "there is a perhaps natural feeling among them against this form of instruction." But to the Hampton ideologues, their form of industrial training represented the best solution to the southern race problem, and they launched a campaign to impose it as a regional system of black education. As Ogden, the president of the Hampton Board of Trustees, declared: "The main hope is in Hampton and Hampton ideas. Our first problem is to support the School; our second to make the School ideas national." Or, as Hampton Trustee Collis Potter Huntington put it, "The only question is, Where shall we get another Booker T. Washington for these other schools?" William H. Baldwin, Jr., the president of Tuskegee Institute Board of Trustees, said to Washington: "I tell you again that your course is the only one, and the work must be organized in other states, and you must do it, and we must get the money."[68]

This dogmatic determination to spread the Hampton model throughout the Afro-American South set the stage for the early twentieth-century struggle over the proper education of black people. Though many historians would come to view this struggle mainly as the Washington-DuBois debate, it is well to remember that the Hampton model was launched in 1868, the year DuBois was born. The Washington-DuBois controversy merely represented one of the last great battles in the long war to determine whether black people would be educated to challenge or accommodate the oppressive southern political economy. DuBois and his colleagues, however, would face a far more powerful and well-organized

Hampton movement than had the missionary and black educators of the late nineteenth century. Beginning in 1898, the Hampton model constantly gained support among northern businessmen-philanthropists and southern whites. The Hampton advocates also picked up additional support in the black community. But the main reason the Hampton movement gained momentum was because its supporters waged a well-organized campaign to spread the Hampton-Tuskegee doctrines.

3

EDUCATION AND THE

RACE PROBLEM IN

THE NEW SOUTH

THE STRUGGLE FOR IDEOLOGICAL HEGEMONY

O F A L L the topics covered in southern black educational history, the reforms and debates that began in the late 1890s and ended around 1915 have been examined most thoroughly. Still, fundamental misunderstandings persist. Indeed, particular distortions and half-truths, which have been developed and repeated in a series of fine monographs, have evolved into the standard interpretation of southern educational reform at the turn of the century. A synopsis of this interpretation would run as follows: philanthropic northerners, perturbed by the social and economic hindrances placed on black southerners by white southerners, sought "to cushion the Negro against the shock of racism and to keep public education open as an avenue of Negro advancement." These philanthropists, less concerned about constitutional rights and social equality than were the radical Republicans of the Reconstruction era, hoped to form an alliance with the South's conservative upper class to protect black southerners from rampant racism. But, according to this school of thought, the northern philanthropists fatally miscalculated the depth and force of the white supremacy movement and soon found themselves overpowered by it. Consequently, they were deflected from their original aim to challenge racism by "good will, tact, and hard work," and they compromised with the region's white supremacists to "save for the former slaves what could be salvaged."[1]

What could be salvaged, the story continues, was a system of universal common schooling for black children which would serve as the last avenue of black advancement in an otherwise oppressive society. This is, of course, a peculiar interpretation because it is difficult to comprehend how a subordinate institution such as state-controlled public education might advance a class of people against the racist oppression of government and other dominant social institutions. Yet the philanthropists' support of universal public education for black children is cited as decisive evidence of their alleged original aim to cushion black southerners against the shock of extreme racism. This brings us to the last phase of the standard interpretation, which sees the emergence of the Hampton-Tuskegee model of black industrial education as the basis of a great compromise. Northern philanthropists, enveloped by the white supremacy movement and largely deflected from their original directions, readjusted their aim and moved to save black public education from total eradication by stressing the value of the Hampton-Tuskegee style of industrial education. In this context the philanthropists' persistently extreme emphasis on the Hampton-Tuskegee philosophy of black education emerges as a politically expedient device to reconcile hostile southern whites to the idea of universal common schooling for black children, and not so much as a unique form of second-class education to reinforce the social oppression of black southerners. The story ends with a partial redemption. Southern white industrialists, middle-class professionals, and school reformers, with little but a nominal connection with the traditional planter regime and poor whites, accepted the idea of minimal schooling for black children so long as the curriculum embodied the basic theory and practices of the Hampton-Tuskegee program.[2]

Historians of the South, on balance, have failed to grasp the fundamental ideological conflicts contained in the late nineteenth- and early twentieth-century southern educational movement. It was not in any significant sense a conflict between extreme racists and moderate racists. There were racists, extreme and moderate, who both supported and opposed the idea of universal public schooling for blacks and whites. There were also extreme and moderate white supremacists who favored a racially restrictive form of universal public education. What separated white southerners from each other, and from the philanthropic northerners as well, were conflicting conceptions of the relationship between political economy and universal education. In other words, they were separated by their particular educational ideologies. A coalition of northern philanthropists and southern whites viewed universal schooling for the laboring classes as complementary to a changing and modern political economy. Believing that the right schooling could train laborers to be better citizens and more efficient workers, they viewed universal education as a sound investment in social stability and economic prosperity. From this standpoint, universal education was not conceived of as transforming the social position of any laboring class, not to mention black southerners, but a means to make society run more efficiently. Consequently, philanthropic and southern white crusaders for universal public education wished to substitute education for older and cruder methods of socialization and control. In pursuit of this goal they collided with the

South's landed upper-class whites and their allies, who depended for their wealth and power on large classes of illiterate, exploited agricultural laborers. The white planters were, at best, ambiguous about the value of universal education as a means to social stability and economic growth. They lived in a society in which agricultural laborers worked for them under direct legal and extralegal compulsion. The planters' views on socializing and controlling labor developed in the context of premodern modes of social control that rested on coercion. They therefore resisted the idea of universal education on the grounds that it would inflate the economic and political aspirations of their workers and thereby spoil good field hands.[3]

Thus because there were white racists of all degrees on all sides of the question, the common denominator of racism is insufficient to place the social and educational ideology of philanthropic northerners and southern white school reformers at one with that of the planter class and its allies. Although white southerners in general shared a belief in white supremacy, they did not share a belief in universal public education for the laboring classes. The philanthropic northerners and southern white school reformers understood this split but did not accept it as fixed and unchangeable. The school reformers sought to convert the South to northeastern standards of social welfare and economic efficiency, including universal education as a better and more subtle means of preparing laborers for work and citizenship. To accomplish this goal they were compelled to challenge the educational and social ideology of the planter regime. Such aims underlay the southern education movement, which proceeded in an organized fashion from 1898 to 1915.

Another basic ideological conflict in the southern education movement was that which separated the northern philanthropists and southern white school reformers from the educational ideas of the region's laboring classes. What historians of the South have termed the southern education movement was in fact the region's third distinctive campaign for universal education. Obviously, the first such campaign began during the Reconstruction era. The ex-slaves were the first native southerners to wrestle with the problem of universal public education. Next came the white small farmers of the late 1880s and 1890s. Rising up during the long depression, members of the Farmers' Alliance and Populist party seized control of state and local governments and made the first substantial gains in public education since the ex-slaves' campaigns during Reconstruction. Both of these educational movements were components of larger social movements that challenged the social power of the South's dominant planter class. In some respects, the turn-of-the-century educational movement also challenged the planters on ideological terrain, but its implications for political and economic changes were far less threatening than those contained in the educational campaigns of the ex-slaves and white small farmers. The new school reformers' central task was to convince the planters that particular forms of education would produce a more productive and contented agricultural work force and to allay suspicion among industrialists that universal schooling would increase competition between whites and blacks for the better urban working-class jobs. The reformers who believed that rudimentary schooling could help upgrade black labor productivity while preparing blacks for racially prescribed social roles threw their influence behind the Hampton-Tuskegee Idea. In particular, they sought to build a universal public education system because they believed that such a system would improve the deportment, the health, the morals, and the efficiency of the region's workers and would socialize the young to the disciplines and values needed to maintain proper race and class relations. In 1899, at the Capon Springs, West Virginia, conference that launched the southern education movement, northern philanthropist William H. Baldwin expressed succinctly this ideology of industrial training for a racially qualified form of class subordination:

> The potential economic value of the Negro population properly educated is infinite and incalculable. In the Negro is the opportunity of the South. Time has proven that he is best fitted to perform the heavy labor in the Southern States. "The Negro and the mule is the only combination, so far, to grow cotton." The South needs him; but the South needs him educated to be a suitable citizen. Properly directed he is the best possible laborer to meet the climatic conditions of the South. He will willingly fill the more menial positions, and do the heavy work, at less wages, than the American white man or any foreign race which has yet come to our shores. This will permit the southern white laborer to perform the more expert labor, and to leave the fields, the mines, and the simpler trades for the Negro.

Baldwin assured his southern audience that the Hampton program would achieve the proper racial hierarchy by teaching black youth to "work with their hands," to have "few wants," and to stay in their "natural environment." The Hampton-Tuskegee curriculum of industrial education was central to the philanthropists' educational ideology, not as a means to reconcile white supremacists to the idea of black public education, but as a program to reinforce the existing structure of the South's political economy and make it run more efficiently.[4]

Therefore, the twin slogans of the southern education movement were universal schooling for all, black and white, and the Hampton-Tuskegee style of industrial education for blacks. Each of these slogans, for different reasons, evoked strong resistance within and without the South. Universal education held one meaning for the northern philanthropists and southern white school reformers and another for the planters. Industrial education held one meaning for the northern philanthropists and their southern white allies and quite another for the black educators and white missionaries who presided over the vast majority of the South's black normal schools, secondary schools, and colleges. These were almost diametrically opposed educational ideologies which arose from different conceptions of political economy and the function of universal schooling in modern society. It was, of course, each group's goal to achieve ideological and political victory over the rest of the field. Any such victory, however, required the development of an educational and social ideology that would appeal to a wide range of social groups within the South and the nation, including the planter class, white small farmers, industrialists, middle-class professionals, black leaders, northern philanthropists, and missionaries. The philanthropists accepted the challenge and officially began their struggle for ideological hegemony in 1898.

The meeting place of northern philanthropists and southern white educational reformers was the Conferences for Education in the South, which convened at Capon Springs, West Virginia, from 1898 to 1900 and met annually at various locations in the South from 1901 to 1914. The first stage of the campaign, 1898 to 1900, focused on fortifying the appropriate educational and social ideology within the coalition of northern philanthropic and southern middle-class school reformers. The second stage, 1901 to 1914, sought to spread the ideology beyond the borders of the coalition to obtain the allegiance of other major social groups. Modeled after the Lake Mohonk conferences on the Negro question, the first three annual meetings were private and informal, and no black persons were invited or permitted to attend. Noticeably absent also were members of northern missionary societies. The Capon Springs coalition, as Louis Harlan has demonstrated, was an intersectional partnership of white northern industrial philanthropists and white southern businessmen and middle-class professional educators. At the center of the philanthropic northerners were Robert C. Ogden, George Foster Peabody, and William H. Baldwin, Jr. Prominent members included Wallace Buttrick and two southerners transplanted to the North, J. L. M. Curry and Walter Hines Page. The southern contingent was headed by a group of North Carolina educational reformers. The key members were Charles Dabney, a University of North Carolina chemistry professor, later president of the University of Cincinnati; Charles D. McIver, president of North Carolina Women's College and president of the Southern Educational Association; and Edwin A. Alderman, president of the University of North Carolina. Other southern members of this coalition were Philander P. Claxton, later federal commissioner of education; Edgar Gardner Murphy, organizer of the Montgomery, Alabama, Conference on the Race Question; and Hollis B. Frissell, principal of Hampton Institute, a northerner transplanted to the South.[5]

The Capon Springs conferences provided an opportunity for philanthropic northerners and southern white educational reformers to rehearse their propaganda in friendly confines. Appropriately, Principal Frissell of Hampton Institute gave the opening address at the First Capon Springs Conference for Southern Education. He maintained that slavery had been a "civilizing" influence on the "barbarous Negroes" and recommended Hampton's model of industrial education as a system that would complete the "education" begun under slavery. J. L. M. Curry, recognized as the Horace Mann of southern educational reform, laid the groundwork for a racially qualified form of dominance and subordination in the South: "The white people are to be the leaders, to take the initiative, to have the directive control in all matters pertaining to civilization, and the highest interests of our beloved land." Still, when Curry spoke of universal education he had in mind common schooling for both blacks and whites, demonstrating that there was no inherent conflict between white supremacy and the advocacy of universal education. At the Second Capon Springs Conference, in 1899, William H. Baldwin, Jr., advised black southerners to accept racial subordination: "Avoid social questions; leave politics alone; continue to be patient; live moral lives; live simply; learn to work . . . know that it is a crime for any teacher, white or black, to educate the negro for positions which are not open to him." Baldwin also saw the Hampton-Tuskegee curriculum of industrial training as the only answer to the race problem. After three annual meetings the northern and southern participants in the Capon Springs conferences recognized that they shared beliefs in universal education, white supremacy, and black industrial training. They also held similar ideas regarding the promotion of public welfare, the training of laboring classes, industrialization, and the efficient organization of society. Having fortified their social and educational ideology from within, they were ready to take on the whole South.[6]

The regionwide southern education movement began in 1901 with a journey by Pullman train of influential and philanthropic northerners to North Carolina. This trip included a public meeting with Governor Charles B. Aycock, a white supremacist who supported the disfranchisement of black voters and universal education for all children. This meeting, the Fourth Conference for Education in the South, was the first of a series of annual organized forums. The enthusiastic group met at Winston-Salem, and the meetings, lasting through three days, were well attended. At this meeting the northern philanthropists gave the floor to white southerners. Charles W. Dabney, then president of the University of Tennessee, declared that "the only solution of the southern problem is free public schools for all the people, blacks and whites alike, and compulsory-attendance laws." He spoke strongly for universal education for black children. "The negro is in the South to stay—he is a necessity for southern industries—and the southern people must educate and so elevate him or he will drag them down." But, cautioned Dabney, "We must use common sense in the education of the negro." Most important, "We must recognize in all its relations that momentous fact that the negro is a child race, at least two thousand years behind the Anglo-Saxon in its development." Blacks, said Dabney, must work out their salvation by practicing the industrial arts. Hence, "Nothing is more ridiculous than the programme of the good religious people from the North who insist upon teaching Latin, Greek, and philosophy to the negro boys who come to their schools." For Dabney, there was only one right way to educate black boys and girls: "General Armstrong, of Hampton, and Principal Washington, of Tuskegee, have worked out a sensible plan for the education of the negro. Our state schools for this race should be modeled after their plan." Similarly, George T. Winston, president of North Carolina's College of Agriculture and Mechanic Arts, advocated universal education and black industrial training. Winston argued that "the Old South was overthrown not by Webster and Greeley and Lincoln, but by the industrial inefficiency of Negro slavery." Therefore, the free black laboring class "must be taught to work, to submit to authority, to respect their superiors . . . the saw and plane and the anvil must take the place of geography." Winston believed that "the entire system of public education for the negro race, from top to bottom, should be industrial." He recommended that the Hampton-Tuskegee program be "duplicated in every southern state—if possible in each Congressional district." Such views were reinforced by Charles D. McIver and G. R. Glenn, Georgia's state superintendent of education.[7]

White delegates from all over the region attended the Fourth Conference for Education in the South. The philanthropic northerners and southern white educators were generally satisfied with the manner in which their social and educational ideology was received by the southern delegates. Thus at the Winston-Salem meeting they decided to subsidize a regionwide public school campaign through the creation of two organizations, the Southern Education Board and the General Education Board. In his 1900–1901 annual report, the U.S. commissioner of education described the Southern Education Board as "an investigating and 'preaching' board for carrying on a propaganda of education" and the General Education Board as a foundation composed of businessmen, "to provide funds and to follow up and give effect to the work of the propagandists." This was an accurate description of the distinct functions of the two boards. Louis Harlan has shown that "the Southern Education Board was a propaganda agency both in the South and the North." It was composed mostly of southern white educators, young men in their thirties and early forties, who "magnified the virtues of the dominant Northeast." This board had among its original members Robert C. Ogden, J. L. M. Curry, Edwin A. Alderman, Charles Dabney, Charles McIver, Hollis B. Frissell, George Foster Peabody, William H. Baldwin, Jr., and Wallace Buttrick. The General Education Board also grew out of the Winston-Salem meeting. Ogden invited John D. Rockefeller, Jr., as a guest on the chartered Pullman train to the Fourth Conference for Education in the South. After visits to Hampton and Tuskegee Institutes and many discussions with educational reformers and philanthropists, the young Rockefeller became sufficiently impressed with the southern education movement to approach his father regarding financial contributions to the school campaigns. The senior Rockefeller responded by creating the General Education Board in 1902. He gave an initial endowment of $1 million, supplemented it by others amounting to $53 million in 1909, and by 1921 had personally donated over $129 million to the General Education Board. Ogden, Peabody, Baldwin, Curry, and Buttrick, all original members of the Southern Education Board, were among the original trustees of the General Education Board. Besides this interlocking directorate, the Peabody Fund and Slater Fund acted largely through the General Education Board. Moreover, agents and supporters of the board directed other foundations established to aid southern educational reform, such as the Anna T. Jeanes Foundation and the Phelps-Stokes Fund, created in 1907 and 1910 respectively. As Louis Harlan aptly stated, the General Education Board acquired "virtual monopolistic control of educational philanthropy for the South and the Negro."[8]

Significantly, the northern reformers who effectively shaped the policy and programs of the Southern Education Board and the General Education Board were originally involved in southern school reform through their nineteenth-century connections with Hampton and Tuskegee Institutes. Robert C. Ogden, the man chiefly responsible for bringing northern philanthropists and southern white educational reformers together, had helped to establish Hampton Institute in 1868. He was Hampton's most active trustee from 1874 to 1894, and from then until his death in 1913, he served as president of the board. Ogden's commitment to the Hampton program reflected his belief that industrial training was the appropriate form of schooling to assist in bringing racial order, political stability, and material prosperity to the American South. He considered Hampton's principal, Samuel C. Armstrong, "the clearest thinker upon Negro education and the race question generally" and viewed Hampton as "one of the greatest successful educational experiments in the country." Hence Ogden labored from the early 1870s to obtain financial support for Hampton's industrial education program and to publicize the school's cause in northern philanthropic circles. His career as a wealthy merchant capitalist in New York City afforded him the opportunity to know important northern philanthropists, and his connections meant the addition of many new donors for Hampton and, later, Tuskegee Institute.[9]

By 1901, when the southern education movement was publicly launched, Ogden was generally recognized by northern philanthropists as the leading reformer interested in the development of southern education, and he soon gained the respect and confidence of southern white educational reformers. From 1901 to 1913 he championed the southern education movement through such powerful positions as president of the Conference for Education in the South, president of both the Southern Education Board and the General Education Board, and president of the Hampton and Tuskegee Institute boards of trustees. In 1906 Ogden was at once president of all five organizations and was ably situated to project the Hampton-Tuskegee program of industrial training into national prominence and favor.[10]

Second only to Ogden in influencing northern philanthropists and southern educational reformers was George Foster Peabody, a wealthy Wall Street banker. He was a full partner in the banking firm of Spencer Trask and Company. As an investment banker with special expertise in railroads and public utilities securities, Peabody worked closely with many of America's wealthy men. He was also very active in politics. In 1904 he was treasurer of the National Democratic Party Committee, and in 1912 he campaigned for Woodrow Wilson's presidential nomination. Wilson offered him the position of secretary of the treasury in 1913, but Peabody declined, maintaining that he could perform greater public service outside of political office. In 1914, however, he accepted appointment as deputy chairman of the New York Federal Reserve Bank.[11]

Peabody, like Ogden, became actively involved in southern education through Hampton Institute. His interest in black industrial education surfaced as early as 1876, when he became impressed with the Hampton program through contact with Samuel Armstrong. Ogden influenced Peabody to join the Hampton Board of Trustees in 1884. Peabody also viewed the Hampton program as the solution to the southern race problem and contributed his investment banking skills toward placing Hampton and Tuskegee on a solid economic foundation. He served briefly as Hampton's treasurer and a longer tenure as financial manager on Hampton's and Tuskegee's investment and endowment committees. Like Ogden, he succeeded in arousing a great deal of enthusiasm among northern millionaires for the Hampton-Tuskegee pattern of industrial education. In the 1920s he helped spearhead a successful campaign to raise $8 million for Hampton and Tuskegee Institutes. The money he secured to expand the Hampton-Tuskegee model of industrial education came largely from northern millionaires such as William E. Dodge, Collis P. Huntington, John D. Rockefeller, and George Eastman, who had come to trust Peabody's judgment on southern educational matters. Peabody, a key founder of the Southern Education Board and the General Education Board, served as treasurer of the former from 1901 to 1914 and of the latter from 1902 to 1909. In vital respects, he was the investment banker of the southern education movement.[12]

William H. Baldwin, Jr., a railroad entrepreneur who employed thousands of black laborers, was the third leading reformer who significantly shaped the direction of the southern education movement. Born in Boston on 5 February 1863, he was educated in the city's public schools and the Roxbury Latin School and graduated from Harvard in 1885. After one year in Harvard's law school Baldwin entered the railroad business under the tutelage of Charles Francis Adams. He rose rapidly in the railroad industry and was appointed vice-president and general manager of J. P. Morgan's Southern Railway Company in 1894. Baldwin became a trustee of Tuskegee Institute the same year and, until his premature death in 1905, worked closely with Booker T. Washington in advancing the growth of that institution. Baldwin went south as an agent of northern capital to take charge of the region's railroads. The centrality of black labor in the railroad industry compelled him to consider the Negro's place in the southern social economy. Like Ogden and Peabody, he became convinced that the Hampton program represented the solution to the "Negro problem," and he used his connections among northern capitalists and southern whites to spread the influence of Hampton and Tuskegee. Baldwin's advocacy of the Hampton Idea meant literally thousands of dollars for black industrial education. As an original trustee of the Southern Education Board and first president of the General Education Board he played a major role in committing northern philanthropy to black industrial education.[13]

The philanthropists were particularly interested in the role of black workers in the southern agricultural economy and the relationship of that economy to the emergent urban-industrial nation. Their interest in black industrial education was not merely or primarily a rationalization for personal economic gains, but the reformers' own investment in Negro cotton tenancy revealed that for them economic and educational concerns fused as part of their broader vision of southern development. The philanthropists were similar to other twentieth-century northern urbanites who "demanded an organized and efficient agricultural sector to supplement the emergent industrial nation." Their concern for southern agricultural prosperity was inextricably bound to a consideration of black farm workers, especially in a period of declining rural population and rapid urban growth. "Our great problem," said Ogden, "is to attach the Negro to the soil and prevent his exodus from the country to the city." In Ogden's view, "The prosperity of the South depend[ed] upon the productive power of the black man." He embraced the Hampton model of black industrial education as a vehicle to hold blacks to southern rural society, stating specifically that Tuskegee's "first and large work" was in the area of "industrial leadership, especially in Agriculture." "The purpose of the Hampton school," said Ogden, "is to furnish district school teachers, well equipped with all the necessary knowledge of domestic science for practical missionary work among the colored people." He believed that the Hampton-Tuskegee program would help fit blacks into the southern agricultural economy as wage laborers, sharecroppers, and domestic workers. Indeed, this was the function of the black school maintained by the Southern Improvement Company, the corporation that owned the philanthropists' cotton plantation of which Ogden was a major stockholder.[14]

Like Ogden, northern philanthropist George Peabody endeavored to convince his southern countrymen that the Hampton-Tuskegee program could help build a strong southern economy on the backs of submissive, nonpolitical, cheap black laborers. Convinced that industrial training would "help the Negro fit his environment," Peabody used his influence to impress upon white southern businessmen the idea of an inseparable relation between black education and the region's material prosperity. "I believe that the South needs their [blacks'] labor and would be practically bankrupt without it," he argued. Thus he informed a prominent Georgia planter and politician that industrially trained black laborers would primarily benefit white investors:

> Have you the least doubt but that if the one million Negroes, constituting nearly one-half of the men, women and children of Georgia were rightly educated to the development of their bodily health and strength and facilities and of the application of the same, which means their minds trained, to have their arms and legs work promptly and accurately in coordination, their moral apprehension rightly trained to know and do the right and avoid the wrong, and their affectional nature encouraged to love and not hate their white neighbors, and to respect and honor their own sexual purity, that they would be worth in dollars and cents to the state of Georgia

more than three times their present value. If this be true, as I am
positively sure that it is, and as the property of the State of Georgia
is so largely owned by the white race, would not the gain to the
white race, under present methods of distribution, be most incalcu-
lable in dollars and cents.[15]

Peabody used his connections to sell the Hampton Idea to the nation's
leaders. In 1918 he wrote to invite his friend President Woodrow Wilson
to make the keynote address at Hampton's fiftieth anniversary celebra-
tion. Based on his "long and wide experience" in southern education,
Peabody explained to Wilson the importance of the Hampton program
to the South's cotton production. "One-ninth of our population is of
Negro blood, and the prosperity of the South and the world's supply of
cotton are intimately bound up with the development of the Hampton
Idea of 'Education for Life,' " he wrote Wilson. Peabody believed that
black people's role in the South was primarily in agricultural labor, and
he advocated the Hampton model of industrial education to train them
for that function.[16]

Baldwin, more than the other reformers, elaborated the philanthropic
vision of black workers' role in regional and national economic development. In 1899, at the Second Conference for Education in the South, he
spoke about the "great black stratum of human beings, with human
intelligence, who can be directed to produce infinite wealth for the
South." Baldwin, who entered the South to organize the Southern Railroad, remained acutely aware of the region's cotton mills and their relationship to increased industrialization. Likewise, he recognized the centrality of black farm workers to the cotton industry, and this concern
also underlaid his interest in the Hampton-Tuskegee program. As he
wrote to southern historian John Spencer Bassett, "I agree with you,
also, that the high price of cotton is going to have a great effect upon the
southern white people. I feel sure with you that the reaction has begun,
and that the economic value of the Negro is going to prove his salvation.
It is for this reason that I have always been so much interested in industrial education." To spread black industrial education, Baldwin urged
northern and southern whites "to build up a secondary school system
under the general control and supervision of Hampton and Tuskegee."[17]

Baldwin also viewed black laborers as a potential force to protect the
South's economy against the onslaught of unionized labor. He believed
that the industrial nations would ultimately engage in economic warfare
and the prospects of an American victory depended significantly on the
nation's ability to assemble quickly a nonunionized, cheap, efficient laboring class. To Baldwin, the South was fortunate because black workers

could be used to break the power of white labor unions. As he wrote to the southern white industrialist N. F. Thompson:

> The union of white labor, well organized, will raise the wages be-yond a reasonable point, and then the battle will be fought, and the Negro will be put in at a less wage, and the labor union will either have to come down in wages, or Negro labor will be employed. The last analysis is the employment of Negro labor in the various arts and trades of the South, but this will not be a clearly defined issue until your competition in the markets of the world will force you to compete with cheap labor in other countries. . . . I believe, as a last analysis, the strength of the South in its competition with other producing nations will lie in the labor of the now despised Negro, and that he is destined to continue to wait for that time.

For this and similar reasons, he struggled to keep black workers in the South by offering them an education that would adapt them to their "natural environment" of unskilled and semiskilled labor and preclude them from pursuing skilled and professional occupations. He praised Tuskegee because there black students were "educated for their environ-ment and not out of it."[18]

Other philanthropists also made it abundantly clear that white indus-trialists and landowners were to be the main beneficiaries of black indus-trial training. In 1904 the Armstrong Association of New York City held a conference to discuss the work of Hampton Institute and "the bearing of industrial education on race problems at the South." Andrew Carne-gie, who had given Tuskegee its first major endowment in 1903, spoke on the economic necessity of training southern black workers:

> We cannot produce cotton enough for the wants of the world. We should be in the position in which South Africa is today but for the faithful, placable, peaceful, industrious, lovable colored man; for industrious and peaceful he is compared with any other body of colored men on the earth—not up to the standard of the colder North in continuous effort, but far in advance of any corresponding class anywhere. South Africa has just had to admit contracted Chi-nese labor, although there are between five and six million of col-ored people there who will not work. We should be in the same condition but for our colored people, who constitute one of the most valuable assets of the Republic, viewed from an economic standpoint. It is certain we must grow more cotton to meet the demands of the world, or endanger our practical monopoly of that indispensable article. Either the efforts of Europe will be successful

to grow in other parts, even at greater cost for a time, or the world will learn to substitute something else for it. We cannot afford to lose the Negro. We have urgent need of all and of more. Let us therefore turn our efforts to making the best of him.

James Hardy Dillard, the Tulane University president who became general agent of the Slater Fund, was similarly impressed with the economic potential of an industrially trained black citizenry. "We of the South," he informed the Southern Educational Association in 1908, "cannot afford to have in our midst any mass of ignorance, and it is to our interest in every way to train the Negroes to thrift and intelligent industry. It will pay us in material advancement." Walter Hines Page, editor of the *Atlantic Monthly* and trustee of the Southern Education Board, said: "I have no sentimental stuff in me about the Negro, but I have a lot of economic stuff in me about the necessity of training him." Similarly, the Tuskegee Institute trustee from New York City declared that black industrial education was not only "good business especially for the South, but good business for the entire country."[19]

Thus historians have revealed only a half-truth in arguing that it was the white South that insisted on a second-class education to prepare blacks for subordinate roles in the southern economy. The northern philanthropists insisted on the same. White supremacists themselves, northern reformers were not perturbed by the southern racism per se. They also viewed black Americans as an inferior and childlike people. Peabody maintained that black people were "children in mental capacity." Likewise, Southern Education Board and General Education Board trustee Wallace Buttrick said: "I recognize the fact that the Negro is an inferior race and that the Anglo-Saxon is the superior race." Ogden also spoke of the black man's "childish characteristics" and argued that blacks were thriftless, careless, shiftless, and idle by disposition. Hence he believed that the Hampton program was good for blacks all over the nation. "I have many times thought that a school of domestic training for colored people in New York City would be of immense advantage, and in certain ways I have had the opportunity to promote the idea in a practical fashion in this city," wrote Ogden in 1903. "The English, Irish, French and Swiss," he continued, "are holding places in domestic service in this city that would naturally belong to the colored people, but the latter are distanced in the competition because of ignorance and easy-going ways." These philanthropists also shared the white southern belief in Negro disfranchisement, even though they opposed movements to repeal the Fifteenth Amendment. As Baldwin, for example, put it, "It seems to me perfectly ridiculous to discuss the question of repealing the XV Amendment. I have always said that it was from many points of view an abso-

Tuskegee's twenty-fifth anniversary was celebrated in part by inscribing the names of key northern industrial philanthropists and political supporters on the institute's lawn. Courtesy of the Library of Congress.

Tuskegee students serve a gathering of the school's white donors and supporters in 1906. This segregated dining on Tuskegee's campus was in keeping with Washington's declaration, "In all things that are purely social we can be as separate as the fingers, yet one as the hand in all things essential to mutual progress." Courtesy of the Library of Congress.

lute mistake in the beginning; but for political and other reasons it is ridiculous to talk about repealing it." Clearly, Baldwin put greater stress on his view that any argument to repeal the amendment was impolitic than he did on its injustice. This was consistent with his advice to blacks to "leave politics alone." Both in their public utterances and private correspondence, the philanthropists consented willingly to southern efforts to disfranchise black voters, as long as such efforts stopped short of attempts to repeal the Fifteenth Amendment. Some white southern leaders, particularly the "progressive" industrialists of the urban South, found virtually no conflict between their own political and economic views and those of the philanthropists. Thus the philanthropists were not a group of antiracist, democratic northerners challenging southern racism by goodwill, tact, and hard work. Rather, white superiority seems to have been one of the few things upon which virtually all of the northern philanthropists and white southerners agreed. The common belief of whites that black human beings were inherently less capable and less worthy, however, did not assure agreement on other important social questions, particularly the role of universal schooling in southern society.[20]

Though the philanthropists obtained support from some of the South's prominent and influential white leaders, the southern white majority and many of its spokesmen were opposed to the southern education movement. Southern opposition to Yankee reform, taxes for education, compulsory school attendance bills, and Negro schooling was voiced by backcountry demagogues, state school superintendents, politicians, industrial capitalists, periodical and newspaper editors, and men in high academic positions. When efforts were made to institute practical educational reforms at the state level, southern resistance was sharp, and what the philanthropists defined as educational and social improvement seldom corresponded to most southerners' definitions of those terms. Among other things, many white southerners resented the northern philanthropic movement as an encroachment upon regional initiative, pride, and independence. Led by the *Charleston News and Courier*, the *Charlotte Observer*, and the powerful *Manufacturer's Record*, the unregenerate southern press excoriated the philanthropic movement as an "insidious attack upon the high spirit of the southern white man." The *Memphis Commercial Appeal* greeted the northern reformers with the comment: "All that the South asks is that the North will mind its own business and keep its missions to itself." Georgia's Governor Allen D. Candler, who attempted in 1898 to cut his state's meager school fund in half, informed the philanthropists in 1901 that "we can attend to the education of the darky in the South without the aid of these yankees." Richard H. Edmonds, a southern businessman of supreme importance and editor of the influential *Manufacturer's Record*, waged the most systematic and sustained attack against philanthropic "meddling" in southern educational affairs. Edmonds and other writers in the *Manufacturer's Record* inveighed against the "southern education scheme" charging that it eroded southern initiative and self-reliance. "The South needs no outside help in the development of its educational system," said the *Manufacturer's Record*, "and the acceptance of such help means the loss of manliness and strength of character." The weekly also argued that state pride would suffer "as no man can feel a pride and claim an interest in educational institutions and schemes fostered and dominated by foreign factors." The *Manufacturer's Record* urged the South to "develop and maintain its schools from funds derived from state taxation and contributions from southern philanthropists." During the early stages of the southern education movement the paper frequently warned the South of the North's "patronizing educational scheme."[21]

Many southern leaders misread the northern-based school reform movement as a subversive scheme to achieve "social equality" for the region's black citizens. Newspaper headlines read: "Millions to Teach Negroes," "Uplifting Dark Races," "Two Races Occupied the Same Gallery," and the like. Philanthropists Robert C. Ogden and Walter H. Page were attacked for promoting social and educational equality. Ogden, receiving the brunt of southern resentment for his close association with Booker T. Washington, was labeled a "Negrophile" for escorting Washington through New York City's Wanamaker clothing store. Thomas Dixon, author of *The Clansman*, a bitter indictment of the black race, was the prime mover behind the stories on Ogden. Dixon wrote that Ogden, a "Negro worshipper, pure and simple . . . conducts the only first-class restaurant in the metropolis where a big, buck Negro is allowed to seat himself with a white man's wife and daughter." The *Manufacturer's Record*, clearly misrepresenting the aims of the southern education movement, contended that the philanthropists ultimately wanted blacks and whites to be "taught in the same schools" and warned that no "tendency to a mingling of the races in the common schools shall be permitted in the South."[22]

The white southern leaders were especially fearful that northern philanthropists would make the blacks discontent with the political and economic roles accorded them in southern society. The *New Orleans Picayune*, with good logic, charged that "just as soon as all the Negroes in the State shall be able to read and write they will become qualified to vote, and it is not to be doubted that they will demand their rights in the primaries with the 14th Amendment to back them up." Similarly, the *Charleston News and Courier* viewed the philanthropic movement as an attempt to educate the Negro "so that in time he shall become a political

factor in the administration of the affairs of the South." From the vantage point of the southern white majority, any system of universal education for blacks, even industrial education, would potentially lead to
universal suffrage. South Carolina's senator Ben Tillman argued that
education would qualify blacks to vote and potential black voters would
"bring strife by trying to regain political power." Many white landowners opposed black schooling on economic grounds because they believed
that reading, writing, and arithmetic would make black workers discontented with unskilled and semiskilled farm labor. In 1905, the North
Carolina state labor commissioner conducted an opinion poll among the
state's white farmers on the question of compulsory school attendance.
The commissioner reported that nine-tenths of the farmers preferred "a
compulsory system if it applied only to the white race, but they do not
desire it to apply to Negroes as they contend that educated Negroes, in
nearly all cases, become valueless as farm laborers." A Virginia landowner put the question frankly: "If we educate the Negro out of being a
laborer, who is going to take his place?" Many southern white employers
clamored for an illiterate, tractable black work force, one with low so-
cioeconomic aspirations, and one that avoided political activity and labor unions. A North Carolina mill owner asserted that it was necessary
to maintain a "large number of illiterate people to perform the labors of
the country." Compulsory education, said A. F. Johnson, chairman of the
Board of Education of Sampson County, North Carolina, "may be fatal
to the cotton crop," which depended "upon the labor of children for
pickers." The millionaire Georgia landowner Colonel James Smith maintained that his own success with illiterate black workers proved that they
needed no education to be satisfactory farm laborers. Governor Robert
Glenn of North Carolina stated in 1905 that the education of black
children had been "a flat failure."[23]

By 1900, in Virginia, belief in the practical destruction of black
schools and the view that black education had caused a serious break-
down in race relations had won the approbation of many leading white
men. Professor Richard H. Dabney of the University of Virginia declared
it foolish for the state to tax itself for the education of the black citizens
it sought to disfranchise. Paul B. Barringer, chairman of the faculty of the
University of Virginia, addressing the tenth annual meeting of the Southern Educational Association in 1900, charged that black southerners had
used their education "as a weapon of political offense" against white
southerners. "Any education will be used by the Negro politically; for
politics, once successful, is now an instinctive form of warfare," he explained. Barringer argued that "whites should cease to support free
schools for the blacks" because "the schools tended to make some negroes idle and vicious" and "others able to compete with the whites."

The *Richmond Dispatch* editorialized that black education had been "a failure and a blunder," a waste of tax dollars, a needless expense that made "hotbeds of arrogance and aggression" out of black schools. Besides, the paper noted bluntly, "Many families distinctly prefer nurses and cooks who cannot read and write." Such themes were repeated endlessly at the turn of the century. "When they learn to spell dog and cat they throw away the hoe," complained Virginia's *Farmville Herald*. Virginia's state superintendent of education, Joseph W. Southall, was reported to have said that "negro education is a failure." All such views were effectively summed up by a white citizen of Richmond, John S. Curtis, who declared that he was in favor of "giving the white child all the education possible, and the black child as little as possible." With opposition to universal education for black children emanating from such prominent white southerners, the philanthropists and school reformers realized that they had encountered a different and contradictory conception of the proper relationship between formal schooling and social development.[24]

The philanthropists were disillusioned by the South's "failure" to comprehend the social and economic "advantages" of industrially trained laboring classes. Concentrating largely on the political and social implications of an educated black laboring class, many white southern politicians and school superintendents often made no significant distinctions between black industrial and academic schooling. In fact, nearly all of the black common schools and the few public high schools supported by public taxation in the South were academic institutions, and none of them were modeled after the Hampton program. The philanthropists recognized and were baffled by the South's lack of enthusiasm for black industrial training. As Peabody complained to a prominent Georgia attorney: "Probably not 5 percent of this southern expenditure for Negro education goes to industrial education to help the Negro fit his environment. The remaining 95 percent is wasted in so-called academic education." The philanthropists were particularly perturbed by the white South's occasional hostility to the Hampton-Tuskegee program. In 1904 Edgar Gardner Murphy, vice-president of the Conference for Education in the South, informed Ogden that "the demagogue is abroad." "I have never seen so much sentiment against the Negro; Tuskegee and Mr. Washington were never so intensely unpopular." The northern reformers could not understand most white southerners' educational ideology. The northerners were convinced that majority opinion in the South was shaped by emotionalism and political demagoguery rather than by enlightened self-interest. Ogden believed that southern whites were "insane upon the Negro question" and that such insanity prevented them from organizing their social and economic institutions to their own benefit.

No southern politician, said Baldwin, would dare have his platform read "Free education for the white man and the Negro," because "the politician, who has always represented the southern leadership, has always played the demagogue and depended almost entirely upon arguments against the Negro in order to gain the popular, good will." Although some southern politicians, such as North Carolina's Governor Charles Aycock, did stand for universal education for both races, the philanthropists could comprehend the deep southern resistance to public schooling for blacks only as a form of political demagoguery.[25]

The southern white opponents of universal schooling were not as emotional or irrational as the philanthropic reformers charged. In fact, they grasped firmly the peculiar nature of their oppressive social order and understood better than the philanthropic northerners what was required to hold it intact. Two characteristics of their opposition evidenced their good insights into the complications of southern society. First, the major concerns reflected constantly in the opposition to universal education were fears of political instability and increased competition between black and white laborers. Second, the opposition to universal education for all children came largely from the states of Virginia, South Carolina, Georgia, Alabama, Florida, Mississippi, and Louisiana. In this context, education was viewed as a two-edged sword. The same instructional process that taught the children of illiterate farm workers to read and write about industrial arts also enabled them to read and sign their names to voting ballots. In these states the majority of the agricultural workers were black, ranging from a low of 40 percent in Virginia to a high of 69 percent in Mississippi. In the same states the black populations ranged from 42 percent of the total in Virginia to 60 percent in South Carolina. Was it possible, in the name of greater industrial efficiency, to make these black populations literate and simultaneously exclude them from voting? And would not their disfranchisement if they were literate require an even greater use of force? White southerners, particularly in these states, feared that increased literacy among black citizens would only add to the latter's demand for equal political rights. In contrast, the educational reformers argued that white dominance could best be maintained by educating blacks to accept or internalize the idea that white southerners had some legitimate right to rule over them. From the reformers' standpoint, the right universal schooling could influence black children to accept the values embodied in the Hampton Idea, so that in time black southerners would acknowledge the legitimacy of the South's racial caste system and submit willingly to its order. White southerners who encountered black southerners daily had good reasons to doubt that blacks were that pliable.

The northern philanthropists failed to grasp the fundamental difference between their society based on class stratification and southern society based on a racially qualified form of the more general subordination of the laboring class. Racism was rampant in both societies, but the organized structures of domination and subordination differed in form and content. The principle of one-man-one-vote held no significant racial implications in New York, where the philanthropists lived, but in South Carolina, where Ben Tillman lived, it meant, theoretically, black control of the state. Hence in South Carolina, as elsewhere in the South, whites stressed coercion as the only safe means of keeping blacks in "their place." They knew that blacks as a class had never submitted willingly to racist oppression or acknowledged the legitimacy of whites to rule over them. Most white southerners, therefore, were naturally suspicious of the philanthropists' claim that blacks could be formally schooled to accept subordinate social and economic roles. Consequently, black education became the ideological medium of conflict between southern whites' wishes for the preservation of traditional, coercive methods of subordination and the educational reformers' demands for modern, subtle forms of social control. The southern white opposition to universal education for both races was tied to entrenched social values, and it especially frustrated the philanthropic northerners.[26]

The northern reformers, however, were inspired by what Baldwin perceived as the "new leaders of southern thought," who were "gradually shaping a new and enlightened public opinion." These new leaders, prominent middle-class professionals who committed themselves to universal education and pledged their support to expanding the Hampton-Tuskegee pattern of black education, included Alderman, Dabney, Aycock, Claxton, McIver, Murphy, and Walter B. Hill. They articulated the interests of many commercial-minded southerners who aligned themselves with the urban-industrial North and who were determined to proselytize their unregenerate countrymen to northern standards of economic efficiency and social organization. These men understood the educational reform movement largely from the vantage point of the philanthropists. Hill made his first visit to Hampton in 1905 with Peabody as his "guide, philosopher and friend." "I was greatly impressed with the excellence of the Hampton work," wrote Hill to Ogden, "certainly I know of no other place where education is so immediately related to life." Convinced of the social and economic necessity of schooling the entire southern population, these men campaigned, as Murphy put it, "to know and to work with one another, in order that the *better* [white] sentiment may gain organization and expression." Through such southern leaders the philanthropists organized state campaigns for compulsory school attendance laws, to legalize taxation for public education, and to arouse public opinion in favor of the Hampton Idea.[27]

Although southern white resistance to philanthropic intervention was powerful, northern reformers found significant white support for their school campaign. Against the early attacks by papers such as the *Charleston News and Courier* and the *Manufacturer's Record*, the philanthropists found powerful advocates in the *Atlanta Constitution, Nashville Banner, Birmingham News, Richmond Times, Raleigh News and Observer*, and the *State* of Columbia, South Carolina. The reformers were also able to establish alliances with some of the region's businessmen and politicians. Upon hearing criticism of the philanthropic movement, Congressman John H. Small of Alabama assured Ogden that "the best sentiment and the best people, those who stand for the best ideals, are with you in this good work." Similarly, T. G. Bush, president of the Mobile and Birmingham Railroad Company, welcomed the philanthropists to Birmingham, Alabama, for their 1904 conference. Another southern white businessman, Belton Gilreath, president of the American Coal Corporation and of the Gilreath Coal and Iron Company, shared the reformers' view of black education. Gilreath, a Tuskegee Institute trustee who employed many black laborers in his coal mines, believed that an industrially trained black working class meant "so much to the future wealth and improved social and industrial conditions of every part of our country where the colored man is to dwell." As he expressed in a letter to Principal Frissell of Hampton Institute, Gilreath worked to obtain southern businessmen's support for the Hampton model of black education:

> I was especially anxious for the businessmen of Birmingham to meet you, and also the large corporate interests, because I feel that the industrial work which you are doing at Hampton, and through the government at Washington, and Tuskegee, which is the outcome of Hampton, is not as fully known at present by the businessmen as it ought to be. Its bearing on our commercial interests and the reflex benefit which we derive in other ways is manifest to my mind, and I think is going to be more fully appreciated in the near future than ever before by our people generally.

Gilreath's belief in universal schooling for blacks was shared by Birmingham's school superintendent, John Herbert Phillips. Reflecting the educational views of the South's growing number of urban white industrialists, Phillips believed that the "enlightened selfishness" of white southerners, as well as their sense of duty, should lead them to provide public schooling for black children. The philanthropists and school reformers found solid support among the region's few progressive urban school administrators. But the South was largely rural, and out in the countryside local governments were dominated by planters who resisted investment in black education.[28]

During the southern education movement, 1901–15, the region resisted educational reforms in the Negro's behalf. Virginia's state political machine, because of its peculiar dependence on railroads and other outside corporations for campaign funds, stressed low taxation and fought against public school appropriations for whites and especially for blacks. The white majority in South Carolina stood solidly against expanding public education for blacks, and the *Charleston News and Courier*, which articulated the interests of the city's capitalists, opposed the compulsory attendance bill of 1900. Even the supporters of compulsory school attendance carefully assured the state that local white officials could exclude blacks from the compulsory school law. North Carolina whites opposed taxation for black schools, and white Georgians generally viewed the "educational awakening" as either Yankee meddling in southern affairs, a cause of high taxation, or a scheme to promote racial equality. Georgia did not pass its compulsory school attendance bill until 1916, and it still allowed local school boards to exempt black children from the law. Southern opposition was further reflected in the meager financial support that the region gave to black education. And it made no difference whether the advocates of black schooling presented themselves as industrial or classical liberal educators. Baldwin, to no avail, informed Edmonds of the *Manufacturer's Record* that northern reformers approached southern education "without sentiment" and were interested in it "only as a great economic sociological question." To the *Raleigh Morning Post*, Baldwin insisted that "the Negro should be taught to work, to work at the trades and in the fields, and a common school education along with their work is not only unharmful but a great benefit to them [and] to their employers." The dominant white South could agree that blacks should be trained to work efficiently in the fields, but it did not see the necessity of sending them to school for that, especially inasmuch as they had performed such tasks for centuries without any schooling. Decades later the South would appreciate more fully the socializing power of public education, but in the early twentieth century the region presented the reformers with a strong rival ideology that virtually assured the retardation of the philanthropists' black industrial education program. Louis Harlan concluded that the Southern Education Board "had almost no effect on the Negro schools."[29]

"With southern prejudice on the one hand and Negro suspicion on the other, we have a delicate course to steer," wrote Ogden to Baldwin in 1903. To expand the Hampton program the industrial philanthropists had to fight on two major fronts. In an effort to obtain more economic and political support for universal schooling in the South, they were compelled to struggle with the region's white leadership. The southern white leadership, on balance, insisted that any large-scale expansion of black education, even industrial education, would set in motion a revolution in race relations that would undermine the South's existing political and economic arrangements. The philanthropists, however, won considerable support among the commercial-minded editors and educators who pushed for a southern alliance with the industrial Northeast. On the other front, the reformers fought to obtain the allegiance of the leading Afro-American intellectuals in an effort to persuade the black community to acknowledge the legitimacy of the Hampton-Tuskegee program. In this endeavor, as with the white South, the philanthropists faced a formidable intelligentsia that, for radically different reasons, opposed the Hampton-Tuskegee philosophy. Many black intellectuals and leaders recognized that the Hampton-Tuskegee program was essentially an educational blueprint for black subordination. In 1904 Ogden correctly noted that "the so-called 'educated' Negroes are more violent than the southern people" in their criticisms of the southern education movement.[30]

To the northern philanthropists, Booker T. Washington loomed as the indispensable agent in their struggle to obtain the support of black intellectuals and leaders. Washington entered Hampton in 1872 aspiring to become a lawyer before Armstrong persuaded him to spend his life spreading the Hampton doctrine. In Armstrong's words, Washington was "the best man we ever had here." Thus in 1881 when Armstrong received a letter from Alabama state commissioners requesting a principal for the newly authorized black normal school at Tuskegee, he enthusiastically recommended Washington. From this post Washington worked closely with northern philanthropists, and following Armstrong's death in 1893, he became the chief spokesman for the Hampton-Tuskegee Idea. Washington fully embraced Armstrong's philosophy of racial progress, which urged Afro-Americans to remain in the South and seek their fortune, primarily in common agricultural and domestic labor. He asserted frequently that blacks had "a better chance in the South than in the North" for economic progress. He also argued that in the southern economy "the Negro is given almost as good an opportunity to rise as is given to the white man." Believing that black workers could control southern agricultural and domestic labor, Washington advocated a paternalistic relationship between them and white employers in which "the material and business interests in the southern communities would become so linked together, so interlaced, that instead of strife there would become peace and union." To prevent racial strife, Washington, like Armstrong, discouraged blacks from voting, running for political office, and pursuing civil equality. In short, Washington's endorsement of the southern racial hierarchy and black industrial training was consistent with the basic premises of the Hampton Idea.[31]

A key factor in Washington's rise to fame was the support of industrial philanthropists, who virtually developed Tuskegee Institute and played the central role in projecting Washington onto the national scene as the new leader of the black race. Through their influence Booker T. Washington and the Hampton-Tuskegee Idea were heavily advertised in national periodicals and magazines during the late nineteenth century. Washington knew full well that Tuskegee would quickly fall were it not for the philanthropists' political and economic support. In 1899 Baldwin was the leading figure in obtaining for Tuskegee twenty-five thousand acres of land through special acts of the United States Congress and the Alabama state legislature. Baldwin then established the Tuskegee Committee on Investment of Endowment Fund with himself as chairman, along with Ogden, Peabody, and J. G. Phelps-Stokes as members. He was also the key person in securing Tuskegee's first significant endowment of $600,000, a gift from Andrew Carnegie in 1903. And when he became chairman of the General Education Board in 1902, Baldwin used his position to provide funds for Tuskegee's annual operating expenses.[32]

Washington's address at the Atlanta Exposition on 18 September 1895 set in motion the ideological struggle between the industrial philanthropists and the black intelligentsia to determine the social purpose of training Afro-American leaders and teachers. As Washington apprehensively faced the southern white audience inside the Exposition Hall, Baldwin paraded nervously around the building anticipating the outcome. In Washington's words: "When I delivered my address at the opening of the Atlanta Exposition in 1895, Mr. Baldwin was in Atlanta, and on the Exposition grounds, but he was not in the building when I spoke. He was so much concerned as to the impression that my address would make upon the audience that, during the entire opening exercises, he walked nervously around the building, waiting impatiently for the close of the exercises, to hear the verdict of those who had listened to my remarks." Washington, Baldwin, and other philanthropists were pleased with the northern and southern white response to the "Atlanta Compromise," but they were not satisfied with the divided black response. In December 1895, the *Christian Recorder* printed an article by C. H. Taylor challenging Washington's philosophy. Taylor, who had recently read the *Philadelphia Standard-Echo*'s editorial, "Is Booker T. Washington Correct?," replied that it was shameful for a Negro to stand up and "make a willing surrender" to southern racism. "What the Negro desires today," said Taylor, "is a Moses who will not lead him to the plow, for he knows the way there, but who will lead him to the point in this country where he can get all his manhood rights under the Constitution." Five months after the young black educator John Hope heard Washington speak at the Atlanta Exposition, he told a Nashville audience that it was "cowardly and dishonest for any of our colored men to tell white people or colored people that we are not struggling for equality." Such black resistance to Washington's program constantly gained support, waxing stronger with each passing year. The *Philadelphia Tribune*, which was sympathetic to Washington, reported in 1899 that some black leaders were denouncing Washington as a "traitor" to his race. According to the *Tribune*, "Booker T. Washington, the famous Negro educator, was roundly criticized at the Afro-American Convention recently assembled at Chicago." By 1899, Washington and the philanthropists realized that they could not easily sell the Hampton Idea to black educators and leaders. Hence they entered the twentieth century prepared to struggle for ideological control of the black intelligentsia.[33]

Washington's training and essential character did not prepare him well for the struggle to gain the allegiance of black intellectuals and leaders. He was not an intellectual and was much more a man of action than an ideologue. Yet his advocacy of a special form of industrial education for Afro-Americans and the political and moral underpinnings of his educational program compelled him to engage forthrightly in a national debate about the appropriate schooling for black children. Washington's educational program, as much as that of his opponents, depended primarily on his ability to persuade the emergent black intellectual or leadership class to propagate and implement a particular social and educational gospel. Hence, despite Washington's concerns about industrial education for the masses, in actuality both he and DuBois were seeking to educate, organize, and direct the same segment of Afro-America, the "talented tenth" or the black intelligentsia. Had DuBois advocated higher education for the few and Washington merely proposed industrial education for the masses, a compromise might have been feasible. Indeed, at the 1904 "Washington-DuBois" conference, DuBois stood on a platform of "higher education of selected youths" and "industrial education for the masses." Both Washington and DuBois, however, looked primarily to the "selected youth" (prospective teachers, editors, ministers, and businessmen) to guide the race's social development. DuBois, of course, stated boldly his interest in the "talented tenth" whereas Washington often kept in the background his central concern with training prospective race leaders. Yet, as Washington explained in 1895, leadership training was the one thing that schools like Tuskegee promised to do well: "It is not a practical thing for the North to educate directly all the Negroes in the South, but it is a perfectly practical and possible thing for the North to help the South to educate the leaders, who in turn will go and reach the masses and show them how to lift themselves up." The philanthropists also viewed Tuskegee as a training center for the black leadership class. As Ogden put it, "The education is too costly to be expended upon the production of domestic servants, and the purpose of the Institution is to supply strong characters well equipped for practical work . . . to go out as leaders among their people." Whatever the secondary concerns of DuBois, the philanthropists, and Washington, they were all concerned primarily with the training of black teachers and leaders and the ideological persuasion of that class. For the exceptional persons to guide the race, DuBois looked to colleges like Atlanta to produce egalitarian social critics and Washington looked to industrial normal schools like Tuskegee to produce leaders who would endorse and advance the Hampton Idea.[34]

The conflict thus became increasingly bitter as the two camps struggled for the allegiance of the very small sphere of black youth who attended normal schools, secondary schools, and colleges. Led by William Monroe Trotter, the fiery editor of the *Boston Guardian*, a significant and influential segment of the black intelligentsia opened the twentieth century with a heated attack on the Hampton-Tuskegee Idea. Trotter bitterly opposed the Hampton-Tuskegee program because "the idea lying back of it is the relegating of a race to serfdom." He insisted that whites generally supported the program because of their belief in the innate mental inferiority of Negroes. Trotter was particularly critical of Washington. "It is bad enough to be enslaved by white men," he said, "without being put under thraldom to a Negro." In 1902, when Washington's daughter Portia had flunked out of Wellesley College, Trotter contended that her misfortune was consistent with her father's "antipathy to anything higher than the three Rs for his 'people.' " Black leaders such as Charles Chesnutt, John S. Durham, John Hope, Bishop Alexander Walters, Bishop Henry M. Turner, Ida Wells-Barnett, Calvin Chase, and W. E. B. DuBois did not agree with Trotter's freewheeling attacks on Washington, but they endorsed Trotter's stand for racial equality, political enfranchisement, equal civil rights, and higher education for black teachers and leaders. They were backed at times by such black periodicals as the *Boston Guardian*, Ida Wells-Barnett's *Conservator*, *Voice of the Negro*, *Washington Bee*, *Chicago Broad Ax*, *West Virginia Pioneer Press*, and *Cleveland Gazette*. In 1905 these black leaders organized themselves into the Niagara Movement, which aggressively and unconditionally demanded for blacks the same civil rights and privileges which other Americans enjoyed.[35]

Similarly, Washington, the philanthropists, and a supporting cadre of black leaders entered the new century determined to discredit their opposition and to unify the race behind the Hampton-Tuskegee program. The

"Tuskegee Machine," as DuBois called the Washington forces, was formidable because it consisted of wealthy white philanthropists, large amounts of capital, large sections of the black press, a cadre of black educators in small industrial schools, and powerful white politicians. The philanthropists, with Washington's assistance, organized an impressive vanguard of black educators to propagate the Hampton-Tuskegee Idea. Included in this leadership were Robert R. Moton and W. T. B. Williams of Hampton Institute; Isaac Fisher, principal of the Colored Branch Normal College in Pine Bluff, Arkansas; W. J. Edwards, principal of Snow Hill Institute in Alabama; Henry A. Hunt, principal of the Fort Valley, Georgia, High and Industrial School; William H. Holtzclaw, principal of the Utica, Mississippi, Industrial and Normal School; and Hugh M. Browne, principal of the Institute for Colored Youth in Cheyney, Pennsylvania. Washington also controlled the black press and used it shrewdly to project a positive image of his campaign to commit blacks to the Hampton-Tuskegee educational and social ideology. Using philanthropic funds, he heavily subsidized the *Boston Colored Citizen* and later *Alexander's Magazine* to counter the influence of Trotter's *Guardian*. In Chicago, where Ida Wells-Barnett's *Conservator* and the *Broad Ax* were attacking him, Washington toyed with the idea of subsidizing a rival newspaper. When such efforts proved unsuccessful, Washington suggested to Baldwin: "One of the most important things to do is first to establish a strong national negro paper which will unify the race and keep it at work along sensible and constructive directions. We could either buy a paper now established and re-organize it, or start a new paper." As Washington admitted to Francis Garrison, he was determined "to keep the race in harmony" with the Hampton-Tuskegee philosophy. Washington and the philanthropists did not establish a new journal, but they secured control over the majority of the *New York Age*'s stock in 1907. To the *Age* and most of the other black journals Washington submitted material for editorials, advised on changes in staff, and persuaded editors to attack or ignore opposing campaigns such as the Niagara Movement and the National Suffrage League. Both were organizations of anti-Washington forces.[36]

The philanthropists and Washington also used a variety of methods to obligate key black intellectuals and leaders to the Hampton-Tuskegee program. The Boston attorney William H. Lewis and the *Age*'s editor T. Thomas Fortune came upon hard times in their personal finances and career goals and came under Washington's influence when he helped them out of difficult situations. In 1902 Baldwin, Ogden, Peabody, and other philanthropists urged DuBois to join Tuskegee's faculty. They were particularly anxious to obtain his considerable talents, for DuBois was the first Afro-American scholar whose work was widely published by influential national periodicals. DuBois, however, became suspicious and refused the offer. Still, Washington proposed early in 1903 that he and DuBois convene a private conference of prominent men for the purpose of uniting black leaders behind certain "fundamental principles" of racial progress. A definite date and place for the meeting—6–8 January 1904, Carnegie Hall in New York City—were set in October 1903. Washington anticipated that the conference was "going to be the most important, serious, and far-reaching in the history of our people." Significantly, DuBois's *The Souls of Black Folk*, with a critical essay on Washington, was published in April 1903. After its publication DuBois was recognized as Washington's chief opponent. In October 1903 Washington wrote to Ogden: "I have evidence which is indisputable that Dr. DuBois is very largely behind the mean and underhanded attacks that have been made upon me during the last six months." DuBois's attacks on the Hampton-Tuskegee Idea, however, were open and above board. As he wrote to Peabody in December 1903, "every energy is being used to put black men back into slavery, and Mr. Washington is leading the way backward." Peabody acknowledged to his fellow philanthropist Ogden that DuBois's letter could not be "called encouraging," but they persisted in organizing the conference to confront Washington's opposition. DuBois instructed his associates that "the main issue of this meeting is Washington; refuse to be side-tracked." The Carnegie Hall meeting became a forum for each side to affirm its ideology. Philanthropists Carnegie, Ogden, Peabody, and others witnessed DuBois and his supporters affirm their unequivocal commitment to black suffrage, equal rights, and higher education. Although Washington and the philanthropists had hoped to achieve a consensus around the Hampton-Tuskegee philosophy, the 1904 conference, financed by Carnegie, failed to harmonize the black intelligentsia. Among his northern supporters Washington characterized the meeting, which appointed the Committee of Twelve to unify the race, as a clear victory for the Tuskegee machine. "I am quite sure," wrote Washington to Baldwin, "that several of the members, perhaps the majority of those who have been in opposition, are either silenced or won over to see the error of their way." DuBois, however, resigned from the Committee of Twelve in protest, refusing to have his demands for black progress "countersigned by Booker Washington or laid out by Robert Ogden." As Trotter aptly put it, "Washington can't settle this controversy behind closed doors, even if [Lyman] Abbott, Carnegie, and Baldwin are there." Indeed, black opposition to Washington and the philanthropists increased sharply after 1904.[37]

Some students of the Washington-DuBois controversy have concluded that the Trotter-DuBois forces were "outgeneraled by that Machiavellian prince of Negroes, Booker T. Washington." Clearly, Washington continued to serve as the Negro power broker for northern philanthropists, but this was mainly because he shared with them the Hampton philosophy of black education. Washington and the philanthropists, however, did not outmaneuver the Trotter-DuBois forces on the ideological front. From 1902 to 1904, the philanthropists attempted to prevent a total break between the Washington and DuBois camps. They failed, and out of their failure grew the radical Niagara Movement in 1905. By forthrightly demanding voting rights, equal educational opportunities, and "the abolition of all caste distinctions," the black Niagarites helped drive a wedge between the philanthropic movement and northern white neoabolitionists. Northern white liberals such as Francis Garrison, William Hayes Ward, Mary White Ovington, and Oswald Garrison Villard became disillusioned with the triumvirate of industrial philanthropists, southern white educational reformers, and Negro accommodationists. They began to attack the conservative coalition and responded affirmatively by establishing the National Association for the Advancement of Colored People (NAACP) in 1910, which, like the Niagara Movement, stood for universal political and civil equality. In 1903, betraying a respect for the important ideological victories won by Washington's opponents, Baldwin informed his fellow philanthropists that "a great deal of harm is being done by Dr. DuBois, and some other people, notably some other Negroes in Boston who have never seen the South." By 1911, Peabody admitted that "the large majority" of blacks followed DuBois. And by 1915, even the pro-Washington *New York Age, Chicago Defender,* and *Indianapolis Freeman* were becoming increasingly critical of the philanthropists' approach to black education. The Trotter-DuBois forces had won the ideological war and prevented the Hampton Idea from becoming the dominant Afro-American educational ideology.[38]

More important than the open opposition to Washington and the Hampton Idea was the undercurrent of sentiment against industrial education emerging throughout the Afro-American South. This opposition never was voiced in newspapers and journals, but it was often reported to Washington and the philanthropists. For example, one of Washington's former students and his trusted associate Isaac Fisher kept him abreast of such developments in Arkansas. Fisher, who had attended Tuskegee from 1893 to 1898, became, in 1902, principal of the Colored Branch Normal College in Pine Bluff, Arkansas, a state-supported normal and land-grant school for black students. In April 1904, Fisher hosted the meeting of the "Presidents of Land Grant Colleges and other Schools." During the conference anti-Washington feeling ran high. As Fisher wrote to Washington:

I believe that I ought to write you of some phases of the meeting: In the first place while I have known of the opposition of many Negroes towards you, I have not appreciated until now how bitter and unfair and widespread is that opposition. I think I do not err at all when I say that every Negro but one attending the meetings is an anti-Washington Negro. In the opening session covert flings at Booker Washington was the order of the day. I remained quiet until I discovered that I was the only Washington man present. This afternoon agricultural education was under discussion. A young woman from Miss Laney's school at Augusta was discussing the need of such training. She made a good impression. When she sat down one of the principals of one of the colored schools here rose and attacked all kinds of industrial education as well as the young woman.

Later that year Fisher informed Washington that Pine Bluff was "bitterly anti-Washington." When Fisher sent three of his female graduates to study industrial training at Tuskegee, "prominent colored citizens" of Pine Bluff "almost begged the parents of these girls not to send them to Tuskegee." Black organizations and communities in general discouraged the development of more Hamptons and Tuskegees. Although black religious and secular organizations created and controlled many private secondary and normal schools and colleges, they were not modeled on the Hampton program, except for a cluster of small industrial normal schools founded by Hampton and Tuskegee graduates. The philanthropic northerners won an important battle in conquering the Tuskegee machine, but they lost the war as black leaders everywhere moved farther away from the Hampton-Tuskegee educational and social ideology.[39]

In the meantime, the industrial philanthropists continued their campaign to expand the Hampton model of black industrial education throughout the Afro-American South. The black opposition was limited primarily to ideological weapons, but the philanthropic movement consisted of wealthy foundations and powerful whites with access to federal and state power. Thus the philanthropists could mount a flexible response to political and ideological setbacks. Step by step, they used their private foundations and government connections to establish educational institutions modeled on the Hampton program. Failing to conquer the existing black secondary and collegiate system, the philanthropists began erecting an alternative industrial normal school and county training school system to train black teachers and leaders for the rural districts. In this movement, the philanthropists drew upon their great wealth and political connections to build the institutions that corresponded to their economic, political, and social interests.

4

NORMAL SCHOOLS AND

COUNTY TRAINING SCHOOLS

EDUCATING THE SOUTH'S BLACK

TEACHING FORCE, 1900−1935

AT THE DAWN of the twentieth century, the various proponents of universal elementary education for black southerners, irrespective of their unique social and educational ideology, recognized a common problem: the infrastructure necessary for a viable black public school system did not exist. Nearly two-thirds of the black children of elementary school age were not enrolled in school, primarily because there were not enough school buildings or seating capacity to accommodate the overwhelming majority of these children. Another serious problem was the great shortage of black teachers. No adequate common schools could be developed until there were black teachers to teach in them because most southern white educators would not teach black children. Northern white missionary teachers, who had contributed significantly to the spread of common schools among ex-slaves during the postwar period, could not be acquired in sufficient numbers, and their presence in the South was statistically insignificant by 1900. If black children were to learn, be it academic or industrial and manual training, they would be taught by black teachers. Hence the proper training of an adequate supply of black teachers was a necessary first step toward the successful expansion of common schooling for black children.

In 1900 the supply of black teachers depended almost entirely upon the private normal schools, secondary schools, and colleges. As illustrated in Table 4.1, over 70 percent of the black normal school students were enrolled in private institutions and 80 percent of those who graduated were from private schools. Seventy-five percent of the black students enrolled in secondary schools, and 55 percent of the high school graduates were in private institutions. Nearly 90 percent of the black college students and 81 percent of the college graduates were in private schools. Altogether the private normal schools, high schools, and colleges claimed 17,541 or 75 percent of the 23,362 black students enrolled in normal, secondary, and collegiate courses, and 1,379 or 66 percent of 2,087 students graduating in 1900 with a normal school certificate, high school diploma, or college degree. These graduates, whether they had received teacher training or not, were filling public school positions. Still there was a great teacher shortage and the annual demand for approximately 7,000 new black teachers was increasing at a much faster rate than the yearly output of about 2,500. In 1900 in the sixteen former slave states there were 26,770 black teachers for the 2,485,737 black children ages five through eighteen, or one black teacher for every 93 black children of school age. The black teaching force in the southern states would have to double if it were to supply one teacher for every 46 black children of school age, a ratio well above the then accepted standard of one teacher for every 30 pupils. The southern black ratio of 93 school-age children per teacher was also well above the southern white ratio of 57 school-age children per teacher. To enroll 75 percent of the black school-age population in 1900, an additional 35,373 teachers were required to provide one teacher for every 30 pupils. Although the magnitude of this teacher shortage declined with each passing year, the basic pattern remained through the first third of the twentieth century.[1]

Significantly, the great shortage of black teachers existed at a moment in history when the philanthropists, white school reformers, and black leaders were locked in a struggle to shape the ideological content of schooling for the black masses. If the system of common schooling for black children had been fairly well developed by 1900, many of the ideological debates among industrial philanthropists, northern missionaries, black leaders, and southern whites might have ended as rhetorical wars. But those interested in shaping the beliefs and behavior of southern black children through formal schooling viewed the great teacher shortage as an opportunity to influence significantly the form and content of black teacher training and thereby contribute directly to the socialization of black children. All groups understood that no system of beliefs could be transmitted to the millions of black schoolchildren except through the ideas and behavior of black teachers. Consequently, during the early twentieth century black teacher training departments became primary battlefields for campaigns to translate particular ideologies of black education into institutional and bureaucratic forces.

The problem of supply and demand of black teachers presented both opportunity and despair. At the beginning of the twentieth century, teachers for the common school system could be produced at little cost. Although southern states, counties, and cities varied in their standards for certifying and hiring teachers, many elementary school teachers had not gone beyond high school. Some normal schools continued the nine-

TABLE 4.1
Black Students and Graduates in Public and Private Normal Schools, High Schools, and Colleges in Southern States, 1900

State	Normal Schools				High Schools				Colleges			
	Students		Graduates		Students		Graduates		Students		Graduates	
	Public	Private	Public	Private	Public	Private	Public	Private	Public	Private	Public	Private
Alabama	659	767	41	26	70	2,007	10	95	0	33	0	4
Arkansas	62	77	0	13	273	308	39	15	0	70	0	4
Delaware	3	0	3	0	0	31	8	0	20	0	1	0
Florida	5	66	5	15	60	306	8	19	0	1	0	0
Georgia	0	384	0	87	79	1,524	13	194	22	290	0	9
Kentucky	73	50	5	18	714	270	93	0	34	36	0	0
Louisiana	25	20	2	15	0	529	0	36	4	35	0	9
Maryland	0	49	0	13	221	199	28	0	0	11	0	0
Mississippi	0	105	0	48	394	1,318	30	36	33	52	8	7
Missouri	0	22	0	22	682	228	72	8	0	13	0	0
North Carolina	253	538	49	123	77	1,544	17	82	39	429	7	36
South Carolina	0	266	0	115	169	1,262	25	62	0	76	0	12
Tennessee	0	660	0	82	425	1,060	67	9	0	297	0	15
Texas	0	97	0	3	553	650	44	17	0	188	0	3
Virginia	154	162	40	41	547	1,201	67	73	27	26	9	7
West Virginia	88	98	11	6	56	186	14	0	0	0	0	0
Totals	1,322	3,361	156	627	4,320	12,623	527	646	179	1,557	25	106

Source: U.S. Commissioner of Education, *Report, 1899–1900*, 2:2504–7, 2514–21.

teenth-century practice of admitting students who had not gone to high school but who passed an examination in common school subjects. States still recognized high schools and junior colleges as adequate teacher preparatory institutions. Consequently, schools that, in many instances, were only slightly above the common school level were graduating students who received jobs as common school teachers. This pattern was especially compatible with the Hampton-Tuskegee industrial normal school model of teacher training, which offered elementary academic education while stressing manual labor practices. Yet many of these traditional low-level teacher certification requirements were being upgraded, and the new trends played into the hands of those who controlled the black four-year colleges. During the early twentieth century states began to require a high school diploma for admission to the normal schools. This step automatically put the normal schools on the college level and led to higher academic and professional standards for training teachers. Meanwhile, nearly all of the colleges and universities developed teacher training programs, and soon larger numbers of their graduates were going into teaching than any other postgraduate occupation. To be sure, the development of teacher training programs for black students in the South evolved at a slower pace, in large part because southern white school authorities were unwilling to enforce equally high standards for black schools. Still, efforts to direct and control the training of black teachers were shaped significantly by the early twentieth-century transformation of teacher preparatory programs.

The existing black educational institutions with possibilities of developing sound departments of teacher education fell into four groups: (1) the sixteen land-grant and seven state normal schools; (2) approximately fifty public high schools and five city normal schools; (3) approximately sixty private colleges; and (4) the more than two hundred private institutions offering secondary and normal courses. The land-grant state agricultural and mechanical schools had unique possibilities for teacher training. Their public ownership and regulation gave them an official status in the school system. But they did not attain adequate provisions for teacher training until after 1920. The state normal schools were scarce and inadequately equipped to train significant numbers of black teachers. Before World War I, only Virginia, Alabama, Maryland, and North Carolina maintained state normal schools, and four of the seven were in the latter state. City normal schools were located in Louisville, Baltimore, Richmond, St. Louis, and Little Rock. The output annually from these schools was insufficient to meet local demands. Practically, then, the supply of black teachers depended almost entirely upon the black private secondary and normal schools and colleges. Having resisted the development of universal common schooling for black children, the South provided very little public support for black teacher training. Moreover, although many of the public facilities for teacher training could be developed, it was obvious that the black private institutions would be needed for some years to come. Because of the strategic place they occupied in the overall structure of black teacher training, these private institutions became prime targets of reform movements to shape and control the form and content of southern black public education during the first third of the twentieth century.

The major struggles for control of black teacher training institutions occurred between the black educators who presided over the private normal and secondary schools and the supporters of the Hampton-Tuskegee model of industrial normal education. The advocates of industrial teacher training were proud of the success of Hampton and Tuskegee, but they were very disappointed with the reality that the Hampton-Tuskegee model of normal school training had not become widely accepted among black private secondary and normal institutions. Because these institutions were training the vast majority of the South's black teaching force, the Hampton-Tuskegee supporters correctly viewed themselves as losing the struggle to implant industrial and manual training as the primary curriculum in black public schools. The black private colleges, whether owned and controlled by black or white organizations, resisted successfully the Hampton-Tuskegee model of teacher training. The black public high schools, which trained many of the teachers for the South's black elementary schools, also resisted by holding to the classical liberal curriculum. The Hampton-Tuskegee advocates considered even the teacher training courses in southern state-supported normal schools too academically oriented. Therefore, in view of the existing structure of black teacher training and the difficulties of redirecting the black colleges in favor of the Hampton-Tuskegee model, northern industrial philanthropists and their allies chose to use their wealth and power to influence small black private secondary and normal schools to eliminate classical liberal curricula and adopt the Hampton-Tuskegee model of industrial normal education.

The philanthropists saw the small private black normal schools and high schools as the most strategic means to supplement the Hampton-Tuskegee supply of industrial teachers. First, they knew that some of the small private schools had been founded by Hampton-Tuskegee graduates and were known as Hampton-Tuskegee offshoots. Second, such institutions depended for their support mainly on voluntary contributions recruited by their financial agents in the North. The federal government offered limited support to industrial education in the poorly equipped black land-grant schools, but neither Tuskegee nor any of the Hampton-Tuskegee offshoots received any federal aid. The white South did little to alleviate the financial burden. In short, the smaller schools faced constant financial crisis year after year. The philanthropic reformers believed that they could exercise much greater control over the structure and content of the small private schools because these schools were not under the control of either missionary societies, black religious organizations, or federal and state authorities.

The efforts made by northern philanthropists to increase the supply of black industrial teachers through the development of small private black normal and high schools has been one of the most neglected aspects of black educational history during the early twentieth century. These efforts provide a concrete picture of the particular translation of their social and educational ideology into institutionalized teacher training programs. Moreover, they help us to see the extent to which the intellectual debates about the purpose of black education reflected a real struggle to control and shape the form and content of black schools. Further, such efforts at the level of particular institutions reveal the individuals and organizations involved, the specific results they sought, the methods and techniques they employed, and the overall impact these developments had on black students, faculty, and administrators. The following case history of the Fort Valley High and Industrial School (the name was changed in 1932 to the Fort Valley Normal and Industrial School and then to Fort Valley State College in 1939) provides a closer view of this aspect of black educational history. The struggle to control and shape black teacher training institutions rested on the assumption that those who shaped the beliefs and behavior of the teachers would also influence heavily the minds and hearts of black schoolchildren.

Located in Fort Valley, Georgia, the center of the state's Black Belt, the Fort Valley High and Industrial School was started in 1890 by Atlanta University graduate John W. Davison. Founded as a private school, the institution was chartered as a public normal and industrial school in 1895. During its first five years, Fort Valley High and Industrial School consisted of one small shanty on four acres of land valued at $800, against which there was a mortgage of $1,000. The school, situated within a one-hundred-mile radius of five hundred thousand black Georgians, had just two teachers and enrolled only one hundred pupils for a mere four-month term. Principal Davison, unable to secure funds from public or private agencies, was forced to invest his own money to maintain the school from year to year. He relied mainly on Fort Valley's black community for additional support. This method of fund-raising, however, proved inadequate, and in 1896 Davison hired James H. Torbert, also a graduate of Atlanta University, as assistant principal and financial agent. Torbert managed to solicit enough funds from local donors to pay off the school's mortgage and to cover his own salary. Still, Davison had to mortgage his home to pay off the school's full indebtedness, and on another occasion he mortgaged his farm to obtain funds for annual expenditures. Fort Valley High and Industrial School entered the twentieth century under severe financial handicaps.[2]

The desperate need for economic assistance pointed the Fort Valley educators north in search of capital from wealthy whites. In this period virtually every black educational institution flooded the North with letter-writing campaigns, school publications, and appeals for financial contributions, and Fort Valley was no exception. Fort Valley, like other small private black schools, relied mainly on its financial agent, who made annual and, in many cases, monthly trips north to solicit donations personally. Torbert, accompanied by a student quartet singing "plantation melodies," conducted door-to-door-appeals, visited fashionable resort hotels and churches, and held fund-raising meetings in northern cities to uncover new sources of financial aid for the struggling Fort Valley school. To Fort Valley's credit, Torbert was one of the most persistent and successful fund-raisers of his day. By 1900, he collected from $3,000 to $5,000 annually. His efforts might well have prevented Fort Valley from closing its doors.[3]

Torbert's fund-raising efforts, though moderately effective in procuring money to cover annual expenditures, did not solve the school's financial woes. The donations were too small substantially to alleviate a desperate fiscal situation. Fort Valley received no aid from Georgia or the federal government, and the local black community could contribute only small gifts. The funds from northern white benefactors, which could be used to cover immediate expenses, were not sufficient to start an endowment or to cover the cost of consistent growth and expansion. There was no money to erect new buildings, to increase salaries, or to hire more staff. In addition, Torbert's fund-raising job was filled with hardships and difficulties that made the process of obtaining northern donations very unstable. As he described it, "Many times I have tramped from door to door, all day with no success and with hardly enough money in my pocket belonging to the school to pay for my night's lodging or get a wholesome meal." Obviously, more reliable and substantial sources of funding were needed to maintain and build a sound educational institution.[4]

With Davison's approval, Torbert sought to solve Fort Valley's financial difficulties by cultivating relationships with whites who could give large, continuous donations to the school. From 1900 to 1904, Torbert campaigned successfully to stack Fort Valley's Board of Trustees with northern industrial philanthropists who were becoming increasingly interested in contributing their capital to southern educational reform. He convinced Philadelphians Theodore J. Lewis and Dr. Joseph H. Schenck to become trustees. Both men were listed in the Philadelphia Blue Book among the city's "prominent" householders. J. H. Hale, a wealthy white from Connecticut with "large orchard interests at Fort Valley, Georgia," also agreed to join the school's Board of Trustees. George Foster Peabody was undoubtedly the most influential philanthropist to join the Fort Valley trustees. Peabody had been interested in the development of southern black education since he was appointed to the Hampton Institute Board of Trustees in 1884. From the outset, Peabody showed strong interest in the development of Fort Valley. He donated $1,000 of the $5,000 needed to erect the main school building and contributed $500 of the $2,500 needed to construct the Children's Training School. Most significantly, however, he brought the school to the attention of the General Education Board, a source that could promise long-term funding.[5]

The shift from small and scattered donations to organized industrial philanthropy eventually had great impact on Fort Valley High and Industrial School. The institution was chartered specifically to promote the "higher and mental and manual training" of black students, but principal Davison was concentrating mainly on the development of a good liberal arts secondary and normal school for the training of black teachers. Both he and Torbert were graduates of Atlanta University, and apparently they intended to model Fort Valley on the Atlanta system. The support received from individuals and northern white churches did not threaten these plans because the money was usually given with no strings attached. But although philanthropic foundations declared it their policy to put no pressure, direct or indirect, upon any institution to conform to a certain course of action, it was well known that northern organizations such as the General Education Board were donating funds almost exclusively to promote the Hampton-Tuskegee model of black industrial education. Hence struggling black private institutions, especially those not committed to the Hampton-Tuskegee model, found it easier to secure funds from northern industrial philanthropists by trumpeting industrial training than by stressing academic education. Such was the case with Fort Valley. The financial appeal made to Peabody and the General Education Board advertised the school as the prospective Tuskegee of Georgia's Black Belt. As the interest of philanthropists increased, Torbert recommended the addition of "a first-class industrial department to the school." "It has been our desire from the beginning," wrote Davison to Peabody in 1902, "to make this an industrial school after the order of Hampton and Tuskegee." Yet, as Torbert wrote to Peabody in 1906, "Davison did not care much for the industrial department." It largely was a department in name only, a means of attracting funds that could be diverted to building Davison's idea of a liberal arts institution.[6]

Organized industrial philanthropists were not easily fooled or misused, however. In 1899 Hollis B. Frissell, Hampton principal who later became a trustee of the General Education Board and the Southern Education Board, warned that too many "sham" schools in the South called themselves "industrial" only because industrial education was popular in the North. The following year Frissell publicly demanded a closer scrutiny of black fund-raisers and warned that philanthropists were disturbed by the prevalence of deception. Similarly, in 1899 railroad industrialist and Tuskegee trustee William H. Baldwin, Jr., called for a reorganization of northern philanthropy to support schools engaged in appropriate industrial training. Baldwin, who became the first president of the General Education Board, urged that such an organization "be recognized by the whole country as a proper channel through which the Negro Industrial Education can be reached successfully." As a consequence of such concerns, northern philanthropic foundations established "school inspectors" and committees to investigate the industrial features of black institutions. Some of these paid inspectors, such as W. T. B. Williams of Hampton Institute, were black. Also, Booker T. Washington and his staff were constantly called upon to evaluate the industrial education curriculum of schools applying for philanthropic aid. This close scrutiny made it particularly difficult for institutions to persuade philanthropists to support fake industrial schools—or even legitimate industrial schools—that gave too much attention to academic training.[7]

From the outset, northern philanthropists had doubts about Fort Valley's commitment to industrial education. Usually when such "unscrupulous imposters" were discovered, philanthropists simply stopped donating funds and severed all ties with the "guilty" institution. But Fort Valley was extremely significant in the philanthropists' campaign to spread industrial education throughout the Afro-American South. They were particularly disturbed that Georgia, with the largest black population in the South, entered the twentieth century with no black teacher training institutions based on the Hampton-Tuskegee model. When the philanthropists discovered Fort Valley, therefore, they set out immediately to make it a model institution for industrial education in Georgia. Peabody visited the school twice "to look it over," and he sent Hollis B. Frissell to assess Fort Valley's potential as an industrial normal school. Peabody thought Fort Valley was in "a good location for a school of central influence in Georgia." He asked Wallace Buttrick, executive officer of the General Education Board, to inspect the school in November 1902. "I am greatly pleased with the institution and am confident that it will improve from year to year," wrote Buttrick. "It is located where there are many Negroes, and this school is a most promising civilizing agency." Because Fort Valley appealed to the philanthropists, they decided not to allow Davison to pursue his own course. As Buttrick wrote to Peabody, "I quite agree with you that we ought to take hold of the Fort Valley work promptly."[8]

The philanthropists moved quickly to direct Fort Valley along the Hampton-Tuskegee model of industrial education. Principal Davison was the first target. They concluded that he needed extensive in-service training in the Hampton program to transform Fort Valley. As a test of his commitment to industrial education, and for him to continue to receive financial support, the philanthropists required Davison to attend Hampton Institute during the summer of 1902 for an orientation to the proper industrial education curriculum. Meanwhile, the philanthropists and other white trustees of Fort Valley were growing increasingly doubtful of Davison's willingness to lead the school in the "right" direction. Fort Valley trustee C. G. Gray, president of the Fort Valley Exchange Bank, informed Peabody that

> Davison, at the suggestion of Professor Cloyd, will leave for Hampton where he will take an industrial course during the summer, and we hope that he will make such progress on these lines as will qualify him for the position he now holds. There is every disposition on the part of the committee to assist Davison rather than to dispose of him, but each of us feel the responsibility of our position and will strive to make this school a success with Davison if possible, but without Davison if absolutely necessary.[9]

By early fall of 1902, the philanthropists were eager to see what lessons Davison had learned from his summer experience at Hampton. Wallace Buttrick informed E. C. Branson, a white trustee who was chairman of Fort Valley's Teachers' Committee, that "Principal Davison is on trial this year." Thus Davison started the year with little support among the philanthropists and white trustees. After a meeting with Davison in September 1902, Buttrick expressed his contempt for the black principal: "I don't like him. He has a furtive glance that is far from assuring." In November 1902, treasurer and trustee C. G. Gray reported that Fort Valley was running smoothly except for "quite a number of foolish suggestions that are frequently made by the Principal." Two months later Gray wrote to Peabody: "I fear that he will never learn that amount of common sense that is so necessary to lead an enterprise like the one we have in mind." Such criticism of Davison's leadership continued during the 1902–3 school term and reached a peak in April 1903. David E. Cloyd, a school inspector for the General Education Board who had investigated Fort Valley, advised the philanthropists to "dismiss Davison instantly."[10]

On 15 May 1903, philanthropist and trustee George Foster Peabody informed Wallace Buttrick that "Mr. Davison is in disfavor and the

Trustees are to have a meeting at Philadelphia." The Philadelphia meet-
ing, attended by Peabody, Buttrick, Schenck, Lewis, Gray, Torbert, and
Davison, was called specifically to decide Davison's future at Fort Valley.
Although there were several black members on the Fort Valley Board of
Trustees, not one of them was invited to the Philadelphia meeting. Dur-
ing the meeting, according to Gray, the white trustees chastised Davison
for poor leadership, whereupon he returned to Fort Valley "very quiet."
The reprimand, however, was merely the tip of the iceberg. While in
Philadelphia, the white trustees had met privately and agreed to seek
Davison's resignation. Buttrick advised Schenck and Lewis to "proceed
cautiously" with plans to remove Davison and revealed that he and
Peabody were already considering a successor for the black principal.
Soon after, Buttrick wrote to Schenck: "When you reach the point where
you think it best to make an attempt to reorganize the school, Mr. Peabody and I have in mind a very competent man and his wife who, it
seems to us, would be eminently qualified to take up that work. We
should want to inquire a little further about him but we have already
made some investigation and all reports are exceedingly favorable."
Schenck replied that he and Lewis would cooperate with Buttrick and
Peabody in efforts to secure Davison's resignation. "As I told you over
the phone when you were last in our city," said Schenck to Buttrick, "it
will be for the interest of the school for Davison to resign." Schenck
further stated, "I cannot see how we are going to make a success of
the school with that man as principal." The philanthropists agreed to
push for Davison's resignation during the summer following the 1902-3
school year. Buttrick quickly made plans to arrive at Fort Valley before
the school's annual trustee meeting in June so that he and the white
trustees could urge Davison to resign the principalship.[11]

   Meanwhile, Davison, having learned of plans to remove him, began to
maneuver for his own survival by vigorously trumpeting the utility and
efficacy of industrial education for the black masses. In a report to the
General Education Board, he proposed to buy four cows so that Fort
Valley boys and girls could learn dairying, "a most useful occupation."
He also recommended the appointment of an "expert laundress" because laundering was a key occupation at which many black females
would work "all their lives." He proclaimed laundering as a "very useful
occupation" that was "much needed in civilized life." Davison promised
to "follow the leading industrial schools: Tuskegee and Hampton," and
invited the General Education Board to help reorganize Fort Valley on
the Hampton-Tuskegee model. The Fort Valley principal even apologized
to Peabody for having the school's motto printed in Latin and explained
that it was only "put in Latin for brevity's sake," not to symbolize a
commitment to classical training. Thus Davison attempted to convince

the philanthropists that he was "no hypocrite" on the question of industrial education.[12]

But praising the virtues of industrial education was one thing; persuading northern philanthropists that he was no hypocrite was quite another. They were not convinced by Davison's instant conversion to the gospel of industrial education and still awaited the opportunity to dismiss him. By 23 June 1903, trustee Gray informed Peabody that he had sufficient support to oust Davison and advised the philanthropists to search for a replacement, "some colored man from the South who has industrial training and is 'chuck full' of common sense." From the philanthropists' standpoint, the June meeting was a success. Two days later, Gray apprised Buttrick of Davison's response: "He came to my office this morning and notified me that he would not be an applicant for the office of principal this year but had made up his mind to leave the place entirely." On the same day, Davison informed Buttrick that he would resign because he understood that the General Education Board and "northern trustees" would withdraw their financial support from the school if he continued as principal. Yet, in a final plea for his job, Davison reminded the philanthropists of his sacrifice and devotion to Fort Valley during its formative stages. They believed, however, that his resignation was a small and necessary price to pay for the development of a solid industrial normal school in Georgia's Black Belt. Buttrick replied to Davison: "I appreciate your earnest labors of many years, and sympathize with you and your disappointment, but I am convinced that your manly offer to resign the principalship will contribute most to the progress of the school."[13]

Thus the philanthropists saw to it that Davison was dismissed because of his failure to model Fort Valley on the Hampton-Tuskegee curriculum, and their actions enable us to assess the depth of their commitment to black industrial education. The philanthropists, according to current historiography, placed heavy emphasis on industrial education so as to reconcile hostile southern whites to tolerate even limited Negro education. Hence it is alleged that grants were made to Hampton-Tuskegee–styled agricultural and domestic training to accommodate southern whites' idea of the Negro's "place" and as a means to save black education from total eradication. Presumably, this policy of respecting the feelings of southern whites, as Merle Curti and Roderick Nash contend, "was not the deliberate aim of the philanthropists and their agents, who instead sought to improve the Negroes' lot." Historians of southern education, on balance, contend that the philanthropists originally went south to support more liberal educational opportunities for Negroes but curbed their aspirations for fear of alienating southern whites, which in turn would thwart the expansion of common schools for black children.

These assumptions, however, are seldom tested against specific relationships among philanthropists, black educational institutions, and southern whites.[14]

Interestingly, Davison, who was unanimously opposed by northern
white philanthropists, received significant support from some important
southern whites. C. M. Carethy, a local white medical doctor and supporter of Fort Valley, insisted that the philanthropists retain Davison
even if the black principal was devoted to classical liberal education.
Carethy argued that academic education was necessary for a good trade
program and he believed that Davison was "as well-fitted as anyone" to
teach academic subjects. Further, Carethy maintained that a reorganization of Fort Valley without Davison was equivalent to "slapping in the
face all the efforts Mr. Davison has put forth for the school." Similarly,
W. J. Scroggs, the white superintendent of the Fort Valley public schools,
wrote in Davison's defense: "He appears to be well-adapted for his work
and as far as I am able to learn he has influence among his people and is
well thought of by the whites." Davison even received support from
George B. Culpepper, a local businessman who worked for the Fidelity
Mutual Life Insurance Company of Philadelphia. Culpepper, "sired by a
secession father, nursed by a rebel mother, and not yet reconstructed," as
he described himself, supported Davison. "I believe in J. W. Davison," he
wrote, "and would like to see him succeed in bringing to his race in this
section whatever of good there is in education." These statements do not
support the argument that philanthropists made grants to Negro industrial education solely to mollify hostile southern whites.[15]

To be sure, many southern whites favored simple agricultural and
manual training as a form of second-class education for blacks. But it
is misleading to assume that northern white philanthropists supported
black industrial training primarily to respect southern white opinion.
Northern philanthropists had their own reasons for supporting the
Hampton-Tuskegee model of industrial education.[16] Thus, even when
southern whites cooperated with black academic institutions, philanthropists withheld their donations because schools failed to conform to
the Hampton-Tuskegee model. The relationship between northern philanthropists and the Georgia State Industrial College (Savannah State)
illustrates this point. Richard R. Wright, Sr., a well-known black educator, was president of Savannah State, a school whose curriculum emphasized academic education and training in selected skilled trades. Wright,
a member of the first graduating class of Atlanta University, was a strong
advocate for the higher literary training of black students and even offered Latin and Greek in the Savannah State curriculum. He managed
to make his brand of academic and industrial education acceptable to
Georgia's all-white Board of Commissioners for Savannah State. North-

ern philanthropists, however, thought the school was much too academic
to merit financial assistance. William H. Baldwin, Jr., visited Savannah in
1900 and concluded that the school's "industrial feature" was not sufficiently emphasized. In 1903 Baldwin's cousin George J. Baldwin (president of the Savannah Electric Company) attempted to get the General
Education Board to support Savannah State, "provided the industrial
feature was made more prominent." William H. Baldwin, then president
of the General Education Board, replied emphatically: "You say we
might be willing to be of assistance to the college, providing the industrial feature was made more prominent. You have hit the nail on the
head. It isn't to make the industrial feature prominent only, however,
that we are interested in doing, but to make it effective. There are lots of
schools in the South that talk a good deal of industrial features, and
really do not mean it, and I am told that is the trouble with the Savannah
institution." For him, Savannah State was too much under the "false
atmosphere" of Atlanta University, which stressed "that a higher education only is of importance to the Negro race." Hence Savannah State was
not among those black institutions favored by northern philanthropy.
Clearly, such policies were not adopted to mollify "hostile" white Georgians who were supporting the institution with state funds. Similarly,
the philanthropists' campaign to transform Fort Valley into a Hampton-Tuskegee–like industrial school was not done to appease southern
whites.[17]

With Davison's resignation in hand, northern philanthropists plunged
vigorously into hiring a new principal for Fort Valley. Although they
stated publicly that institutions would be left to "work out their own
salvation," the strong desire to establish Fort Valley as an industrial
training school for teachers worked against any impulse to respect institutional self-determination. By July 1903, Peabody and Buttrick had
identified two candidates for the Fort Valley vacancy. Peabody recommended Henry Alexander Hunt, who was business manager and director
of trades at Biddle (currently Johnson C. Smith) University, a Presbyterian college for black men in Charlotte, North Carolina. Buttrick, however, was convinced that his nominee, a Mr. Diamond (a Hampton Institute graduate), who was employed at Walden University in Nashville,
Tennessee, was the best man for the job. "He has had the industrial
training which makes him specially capable of directing an Industrial
School, such as Fort Valley aims to be," wrote Buttrick. Diamond was
"a competent man and thoroughly imbued with the Hampton methods
and spirit." The philanthropists submitted their candidates to Booker T.
Washington for his scrutiny. Washington knew very little about Diamond
or Hunt and recommended Tuskegee graduate Isaac Fisher for the Fort
Valley principalship. The philanthropists then considered Fisher and

Diamond their top candidates, and both men were offered the Fort Valley position, but they decided to remain at their respective institutions. Thus the philanthropists were left with their third choice, Henry A. Hunt.[18]

Initially, Peabody and Buttrick were skeptical of Hunt's allegiance to the Hampton-Tuskegee model of industrial education. "I do not know whether Hunt is committed to the idea of Industrial Education," wrote Buttrick, "he may be but, I simply do not know." Like Davison, Torbert, and Wright, Hunt was a graduate of Atlanta University. The philanthropists disliked Wright's brand of industrial education, had coerced Davison to resign because of his halfhearted commitment to industrial training, and, as Buttrick said, did "not expect much from men like Torbert." Moreover, Booker T. Washington had advised them that industrial schools were "not likely to do effective work" unless directed by Hampton or Tuskegee graduates. The philanthropists, made wary by Davison's deception, took a long look at Henry A. Hunt. Fort Valley opened in the fall of 1903 without a principal, and Mr. Miller, head of the school's mechanical shop, served as acting head until February 1904. During this time, however, Hunt convinced Buttrick and Peabody that he was seriously committed to developing an industrial education program at Fort Valley. Hunt emphasized his "mechanical" study at Atlanta University and his experience as head of Biddle University's Industrial and Boarding departments. In addition, wrote Hunt, "I do not know about mechanical work in a theoretical way only, but I'm a practical workman as well, having 'carried the dinner pail' and earned $2.50 per day as a carpenter during vacation seasons while a student." Buttrick was "favorably" impressed. On 5 November 1903, he informed Peabody, "I have a growing conviction that it might be well to secure the services of Mr. Hunt as principal and retain the services of Torbert as vice-principal and soliciting agent." Hunt was hired in November 1903 and began his long career (1904–38) as principal of Fort Valley on 9 February 1904.[19]

From the outset, the philanthropists watched closely Hunt's development of Fort Valley's industrial education program. Peabody directed his friend Walter B. Hill, chancellor of the University of Georgia, to investigate Hunt's educational activities. Hill would arrive at Fort Valley unannounced and question Hunt rigorously about every aspect of the school's industrial program. In his first report, Hill was very critical of Hunt's initial efforts toward the development of industrial training. "I had gone through the buildings and had talked with Mr. Hunt and Mr. McNiel," wrote Hill to Peabody, "and had heard nothing said, and had seen nothing, as to industrial work." Still worse, Hunt had closed down the old industrial shop and made it into a boys' dormitory. Consequently, Hill was "compelled to have some skepticism as to his earnestness in regard to the industrial feature."[20]

Peabody, distressed by Hill's report, requested from Hunt a full explanation of the changes at Fort Valley and warned the principal that philanthropic funding would be forthcoming only if he developed a Hampton-Tuskegee model of industrial education. Peabody stated:

> Write me rather freely respecting your own thought as to the industrial work and your reasons for suspending it in order to make dormitory rooms. I should be glad to take up promptly through Doctor Buttrick as representative of the General Education Board the question of making you a proposition to put the amount necessary for completing the building which is now under way. I think I should be inclined in view of what I now learn to make some condition respecting a proper development of the industrial work which should, I think, grow to be as at Hampton, an essential element in the entire work of the school being correlated to all branches of study.

Obviously, Peabody was using philanthropic capital to pressure Hunt to conform to the Hampton model of industrial education. In this endeavor Peabody sought successfully the cooperation of Buttrick and the General Education Board. "I shall hope that it may seem feasible to you and that you may think it wise," said Peabody to Buttrick, "that definite pressure be brought for the inauguration of immediate industrial work as far as is practicable." Hunt replied that Fort Valley's industrial education system developed slowly because of inadequate resources; he was not opposed to industrial training in principle. "I agree heartily with your idea in the matter of having the industrial feature grow to be an essential element in the work of the school; in fact, I would not have undertaken the work had I not expected this to be the case." As evidence of his commitment to industrial training, Hunt reported his activities in organizing classes in sewing, cooking, carpentry, and gardening. He had also planted two hundred peach trees to provide training in "the care and cultivation of fruit trees." Such activities were especially satisfying to Fort Valley trustee J. H. Hale, the Connecticut owner of Hale's Fruit Company, who possessed large peach orchards in Fort Valley, Georgia.[21]

The philanthropists became pleased with Hunt's attitude toward industrial training. As Buttrick wrote to Hunt in January 1905: "Your letter of January 10 to Mr. Peabody was duly received. I have just had a long conference with him regarding it. The letter is exceedingly satisfactory to us both. You have outlined the situation with great clearness. I am glad to say that I can authorize you to complete and furnish the needed recitation rooms in the new buildings, funds for which will be furnished through the General Education Board." Confident that they had found the right man to implant industrial training in Georgia's Black Belt, the philanthropists cemented a relationship with Hunt in 1905 that lasted into the 1930s. The General Education Board made yearly contributions to help cover Fort Valley's annual expenses and contributed larger sums for buildings, equipment, and other permanent improvements. By 1910, the board was contributing $2,000 annually to cover the school's current expenses; this annual donation increased to $3,500 in 1917, $5,000 in 1920, and peaked at $7,500 in 1924. In addition, the board made substantial contributions to the improvement of Fort Valley's physical plant. In 1928, for example, $100,000 was donated to the school for buildings and equipment. During this entire period Fort Valley was literally starved for financial aid, and the philanthropists, with their immense and desperately needed funds, had within their power the resources to assure Fort Valley's continuation. Hence they held a whip over Fort Valley's administrators and teachers.[22]

Philanthropic domination required and conditioned new types of black trustees, teachers, and students. Because Principal Davison had originally emphasized liberal arts training, the black trustees, teachers, and students attracted to the schools during his era did not fit easily with Hunt's program of simple agricultural and domestic training. Thus when W. T. B. Williams, a black school inspector for the General Education Board, investigated staff relations at Fort Valley in 1906, he discovered some "very positive opposition to Mr. Hunt" among "the colored trustees and a set of the young men teachers of the school." From the philanthropists' standpoint, all such resistance stood in the way of any effective and rapid development of industrial education. Consequently, with Hunt and Torbert's cooperation, the philanthropists mounted a successful campaign to remove from Fort Valley virtually all black trustees and teachers who opposed the new order.[23]

In the spring of 1907, Peabody conveyed to Torbert his growing discontent with Fort Valley's black trustees. Torbert replied: "Mr. Meyers has written me how you feel towards Fort Valley in view of the presence on the Board of Trustees of a number of incompetent members, a matter which you very kindly discussed with me at Lake George last summer. I want to assure you that I see clearly the need of dropping most, if not all of the local colored Trustees, for the reason that they are not the proper kind of material for the school to depend upon and Mr. Hunt thinks likewise." Torbert agreed to use his influence to rearrange Fort Valley's Board of Trustees to "inspire a larger confidence in the school among our northern constituency." Principal Hunt also promised his assistance. The great "purge" of black trustees came in June 1907, when Torbert

and white trustees Matthews and Gray used questionable tactics to remove the black trustees. Torbert described their arbitrary actions to
Peabody:

> The Board was called to meet Friday, but we did not get a quorum.
> By the keenest strategy in parliamentry usages, we took up the mat-
> ter of revising the Board and began the transaction of business with-
> out a quorum. It was embarrassing to take up the matter of revising
> the Board, as those aimed at for elimination were in evidence and
> were contending for what they termed their "rights." But we mas-
> tered the situation by voting that we all tender our resignation and
> appoint a committee of three men to confer and recommend to the
> Board for trustees such men as in their judgment are best suited to
> serve. Col. Matthews, Mr. Hunt and myself compose this commit-
> tee, Col. Matthews naming me chairman of the committee.

The new committee, having secured the resignations of all the trustees
present, refused to recommend the black trustees for appointment.[24]

The search for new trustees reveals that the philanthropists desired
blacks who held to Booker T. Washington's ideology and believed in the
Hampton-Tuskegee model of industrial education. Peabody nominated
W. H. Spencer, a leading black educator in Columbus, Georgia, who was
sympathetic to the industrial education program. Torbert recommended
E. R. Carter, pastor of the Atlanta Friendship Baptist Church and one of
the most influential black clergymen in Georgia. Black educators W. T. B.
Williams and Robert R. Moton of Hampton, and Warren Logan of Tuskegee, Hunt's brother-in-law, were also suggested. The ideological character of these nominations became even clearer when someone, mistakenly perhaps, nominated W. B. Matthews, a black school principal in
Atlanta, Georgia, who was critical of the Washington philosophy. Torbert acted quickly to remove Matthews from the list of nominees and
stated his reasons explicitly: "He has a record of being opposed to
Booker T. Washington and his methods of education. I don't think he is
the man we should desire for a trustee of Fort Valley." The Fort Valley
Board of Trustees was reorganized with Warren Logan, W. H. Spencer,
and E. R. Carter as the new black members. The philanthropists, pleased
with this arrangement, demanded one more major change: they wanted
to remove Lee O'Neal, the black president of the board, and replace him
with a white. Philadelphia trustee James H. Schenck wrote to George
Foster Peabody: "I am convinced that the Fort Valley High and Industrial
School can be made a grand success if we only had a good white man
as President." So Peabody telegrammed Torbert and requested that the
trustees elect Theodore J. Lewis as the new white president. Following
the annual meeting in June 1907, Lee O'Neal wrote to Peabody that

"Mr. Theo. J. Lewis was elected Chairman, according to your directions and also in accord with a telegram received by Mr. Torbert from you." O'Neal was made vice-president.[25]

Parallel to the movement to reorganize Fort Valley's Board of Trustees, Principal Hunt waged his own successful campaign to weed out opposing black teachers. When W. T. B. Williams inspected Fort Valley for the philanthropists in 1906, he recorded that three men teachers stood "aloof" and were not "in sympathy with the working of the school." Williams described these teachers as "young fellows and fully conscious of their own importance" who could not "lose themselves in their work and forget about their rights, restrictions, and the like." Between 1905 and 1908, Hunt dismissed all of these teachers and more. In March 1906, he abruptly terminated the appointment of the music teacher, S. Madora Watts. According to Watts, "Mr. Hunt demanded then and there my resignation, without a moment's notice or alleging any reasons therefor." Later, Hunt replied that she was terminated "for a lack of interest in the conduct and affairs of the school." In February 1907, Levi Nelson, Jr., resigned his teaching position to avoid a violent confrontation with Hunt. "I have tolerated long enough with his thrusts, insinuations, etc., until I can bear no more and feel that for my own sake I had better leave here, for fear if he makes one more funny move, someone will get hurt." Nelson reported that working conditions at the school were very unpleasant because Hunt interfered with the work and rights of several teachers. Similarly, R. T. Bowles complained about Hunt's harassment of the Fort Valley teaching staff. S. A. Grant, a teacher in the academic department, resigned in July 1907. Grant maintained that at least five teachers suffered continuously from Hunt's actions, for no other reason than "an honest difference of opinion as to our social freedom and personal rights." He further charged that "individual action and thought," unless in conformity with Hunt's policies, was exercised at "very great hazard" to one's position in the school. In short, the philanthropists and Hunt dismissed virtually all of the black trustees and teachers who came to Fort Valley under Davison's principalship, especially those not firmly committed to the Hampton-Tuskegee model of industrial education.[26]

As would be expected, educational and leadership changes had a significant impact on Fort Valley students. Since 1890, students from Georgia's Black Belt had enrolled at Fort Valley primarily to obtain a liberal arts education. As Davison told the philanthropists in 1903, black students "came with the notion that school was not the place for anything but the books." Davison reported that only through "persistent effort" could he interest a few students in manual labor, practical farming, and gardening. Hunt soon discovered that Davison was right: "It is a sad thing that so few students choose agriculture." As Fort Valley changed from a liberal arts to an industrial school, however, students were coerced to select industrial programs. Many rebelled against the new emphasis on industrial training. As soon as Davison resigned and Miller, the Fort Valley carpenter, became acting principal, a significant number of students left the school. C. H. Nixon, the black secretary of Fort Valley's Board of Trustees, reported the changes in student enrollment to Peabody:

> The moment he was placed there the people began to complain, notwithstanding the fact that he was placed there until a better man could be secured. The school opened with less than a dozen students while in previous years it has opened with not less than seventy-five or a hundred; up to the present time there are less than forty while every other year at this time the number has reached 200; most of the students of the 9th and 10th grades have entered other schools, feeling that Miller could not instruct them.

Such problems continued over the next three years as Hunt pressured the students to conform to the industrial program. By the spring of 1907, Hunt's campaign threatened to tear the school asunder. Assistant Principal Torbert was especially disturbed by the disappearance of the male students. "Most of the boys," Torbert observed, "had for various reasons left the school and gone either to their homes or to work elsewhere." In the fall of 1907, black teacher Levi Nelson noted that Hunt had "been so rough on the student body as a whole that quite a number have threatened to leave." Undoubtedly, many of the students caught in the transition from liberal arts to industrial training resisted the changes, but in the long run, Hunt admitted students who were more amenable to industrial education.[27]

By 1910, Fort Valley had new black trustees, teachers, and students, and virtually no traces of Davison's regime remained. The school offered industrial training to approximately five hundred black students annually. W. T. B. Williams made a second survey of the school for the General Education Board in 1914 and found Hunt conducting "the most thorough-going industrial school in Georgia." Great pressure was placed on black students to take practical farming and gardening. Hunt contended that it was "absolutely necessary" to give "special inducements" to students interested in industrial training. In 1915 he asked the General Education Board to help Fort Valley purchase fifty-five acres of additional farm land for agricultural training. Particularly, Hunt aimed to convince the local community, "especially the whites," that Fort Valley was "earnest about the matter of teaching students to work." Fort Valley students, like those at Hampton and Tuskegee, were required to spend a considerable amount of their time doing common labor. Every student had to major in some form of menial labor such as laundering, cooking, or the care and cultivation of fruit trees. Special stress was laid on training in agriculture at a time when only 12.8 percent of Georgia's 86,789 black farm operators were owners. Fort Valley's student-teachers were being prepared to socialize their prospective pupils for the role of common laborer for white landowners. This trend pleased northern philanthropists, and Hunt received annual donations from the General Education Board, the Phelps-Stokes Fund, and the John F. Slater Fund. Peabody was convinced that Hunt had implanted industrial education in the "strategic center" of the South. The philanthropists gave Hunt their highest praises for his loyalty to industrial training. "I am proud of the good work you have done and I am bound to say that you have more than fulfilled all the expectations which Mr. Peabody and I had when you were chosen for the position at Fort Valley," wrote Buttrick to Hunt in 1922.[28]

Economic dependency on industrial philanthropy required and conditioned a different kind of black leadership. In choosing Davison's successor, the philanthropists searched for a principal who was willing to accommodate to white authority, agreeable to placing control of Fort Valley in the hands of white authority, and committed to the Hampton-Tuskegee model of industrial normal education. The philanthropists disliked Davison for being "uppity" or too assertive in the presence of whites. Buttrick made private references to the black educator as the "esteemed Davison," and trustee Gray joined with his own sarcastic characterization of the principal as the "illustrious Davison." A school inspector for the General Education Board, David E. Cloyd, accused Davison of "insolence" and reported on one occasion that Gray was compelled "to throw Davison, bodily, out of his office at the Bank." Indeed, Davison was very assertive. Moreover, he insisted that black people should control their own educational institutions because "one learns to govern only by governing." "I have always thought," wrote Davison to Peabody, "that the colored man, when it comes to schools for his own people, should not only have considerable voice, but should be required to largely govern them, for the object of all education is to develop the power of self-government." Thus Davison appointed many blacks to Fort Valley's Board of Trustees and put them in charge of important committees. This disturbed the white trustees. As E. C. Branson complained to Peabody, "I shall discharge my duties as trustee to the very best of my ability, but with two Negroes with me on the committee to select teachers, they hold the reins, and at some critical juncture may run away with a most important department of our work."[29]

In contrast to their perceptions of Davison, the white philanthropists and trustees viewed Hunt as more accommodating to white authority. White trustees E. C. Branson and Gray were particularly pleased with Hunt. "Mr. Gray says that Hunt is a gentleman," Branson informed Buttrick, "and when Mr. Gray says a thing like that about a darky, he must be a wonderful darky." Branson saw Hunt as a "man of capability, common sense, and devotion, a useful man." Beyond the opinions, however, Hunt was clearly more accommodating to white intervention. "I believe we shall for sometime need not only the financial help, but the sympathetic cooperation and wise counsel of men, who like yourself, are interested in such work and who by reason of broader training are better able to give wholesome advice," said Hunt to Peabody. Under Hunt's principalship, the philanthropists had a firm voice in deciding Fort Valley's programs and policies.[30]

Increased philanthropic control significantly affected the role of black trustees and teachers in shaping Fort Valley's development. Against the onslaught of philanthropic intervention, Davison based his leadership on the support of the black staff and delegated much authority to them. According to W. T. B. Williams, under Davison the black trustees shared very largely in the immediate control of the school. "Their opinion was asked apparently, even if not followed, about every little thing." Hunt, however, generally did not consult the black trustees about the affairs of the school. Similarly, he hired and dismissed teachers without the advice of Fort Valley's Teachers' Committee. Even Torbert, Hunt's main supporter, complained that the principal was "getting rid of some of the best material available in the race without giving good reasons for the making of such changes." Yet as long as the philanthropists and white trustees did not complain, Hunt saw no need to consult the black staff. "I may be wrong," he said to Peabody, "but as I have seen and known colored schools it seems a necessity that one person should be in control, especially in the management of the teaching force." Hunt maintained that committees led invariably to "disaffection and discontent," which he proposed to remedy through one-man rule. This relationship to philanthropic power resulted in self-contradictory leadership that frequently characterized the black leaders of such institutions as Fort Valley. On one hand, they accommodated the interests of white philanthropists and trustees, and, on the other, they ruled their black staff, faculty, and students with an iron hand. This schizophrenic behavior made sense within the larger framework of black oppression. The white philanthropists and trustees searched for a principal who could efficiently put into practice their ideology of black education. The execution of their orders, however, required autocratic rule because black teachers in general were not inclined to impose upon black schoolchildren a model of industrial education designed to turn them into unskilled and semiskilled laborers.[31]

Fort Valley typified the widespread efforts by philanthropists and their allies to induce black high schools, normal schools, and colleges to establish industrial teacher training courses to produce teachers for the black common schools. The philanthropists found it impossible to cooperate with existing institutions because of fundamentally different conceptions of the purpose of black education in general and different philosophies of the nature and goals of industrial education in particular. Other organizations significantly involved in the development of black secondary and normal schools and colleges—Congregationalists, Baptists, Methodist Episcopalians, Presbyterians, African Methodist Episcopal, Colored Methodists, and African Methodist Zion—gave some attention to industrial education. Within the schools controlled by these organizations, however, industrial education remained in a secondary role, was used mainly to prepare select individuals for skilled occupations, and certainly was not advocated as a core curriculum for the training of teachers. Whereas most organizations and individuals involved in black education viewed the preparation of teachers as primarily academic training, the philanthropists saw industrial training as the very foundation of teacher education. From the philanthropists' standpoint, there was but one appropriate model of teacher education for blacks, that of Hampton and Tuskegee. Their extreme devotion to the Hampton-Tuskegee model of industrial normal education placed them at odds with the general flow of black teacher training and compelled them to attempt a major transformation of it as in the Fort Valley case.[32]

Conflict over the content and goals of black teacher training institutions emerged early in the twentieth century. Soon after the General Education Board was established in 1902, its agents undertook a careful inspection of the black private secondary schools, normal schools, and colleges. The board's inspectors started in 1903 with the schools operated by the American Baptist Home Mission Society. Then the society supported twelve colleges and fourteen secondary schools for black youth. In December 1903, Wallace Buttrick filed a preliminary report on eight of the society's black colleges and noted that their major problem was too much emphasis on classical and higher literary training. Jackson College in Mississippi taught Latin and Greek; Alabama Baptist University, aiming "to develop a classical school for negroes," offered Latin and Greek in the second year of "the so-called Normal Department"; and Shaw University in North Carolina emphasized "classical training." In 1904 Buttrick, with the help of school inspectors W. T. B. Williams and David Cloyd, continued his assessment of black private institutions. Buttrick himself visited scores of black private institutions, completing a journey of forty-five hundred miles between 5 and 22 October 1904. He found that Leland University in New Orleans, formerly under the Baptist

Home Mission Society, had an endowment of over $100,000 and "fine property of some 18 acres with two large buildings." Moreover, Leland exerted "a wide influence among the 75,000 colored Baptists of Louisiana." "It is my judgment, however," said Buttrick, "that it holds too strictly to classical ideals and that under the present president the school is not likely to take any active interest in training the negro for productive efficiency." Any black institution emphasizing classical liberal education was regarded by Buttrick as impractical and not geared to prepare black youth for useful citizenship and productive efficiency.[33]

Even those institutions offering a considerable amount of industrial education were viewed as misguided so long as the industrial training was not used primarily for the preparation of teachers. Bishop College in Marshall, Texas, for instance, had a fine and well-equipped building for men's industrial work, including blacksmithing, carpentry, machine work in wood and iron, and facilities for mechanical drawing. Buttrick described the teacher of men's industries as a man of "undoubted high character, general intelligence, and mechanical skill." Yet the fundamental flaw in this program, according to Buttrick, was that the instructor was not a trained teacher and did not know how to transform industrial training into a program of teacher education. Thus, said Buttrick, "He can supervise the erection of buildings, can train the young men in carpentry, iron work, etc., but he is not prepared to direct a manual training department or to train the students as teachers." Buttrick emphasized a point often misunderstood by his contemporaries and later historians. Many then and now believed that industrial education was advocated in the secondary schools, normal schools, and colleges to train individuals for industrial occupations. Industrial philanthropists, however, believed industrial education courses were central in the training of teachers. Buttrick was not the least bit concerned about the failure of such courses to produce skilled industrial workers. "The chief sign of weakness," said he, "is a failure to make the industrial courses educational and a lack of correlation between the industrial and literary work." In short, the industrial work at Bishop was not designed, as it was at Hampton and Tuskegee, to train industrial teachers for the black common schools.[34]

In October 1904, as Buttrick completed his inspection of black private schools and analyzed related observations recorded by the General Education Board's school inspectors, he reached very definite conclusions regarding the potential role of philanthropic foundations in shaping black teacher training institutions. At Houston and Hearne, Texas, he visited two schools established, controlled, and taught by black teachers. Both schools emphasized "the classical and so-called higher education." After this experience Buttrick had seen enough of black classical liberal schools under the leadership of black educators and trustees. "I am led to believe," he wrote, "that the negroes are not yet prepared to direct their own schools." He maintained that the really good schools for black youth had the counsel and advice of white people. More important, Buttrick had formed his own impression of what constituted a really good school for black youth. He recommended that all industrial philanthropy adjust its course to direct private and denominational schools toward "the true education of the negroes." In Buttrick's words:

> Denominational schools still have a mission and for many years will continue to have. But they should have well trained—modern trained—educators as principals, they should be "Hamptonized" as far as is practicable, they should largely eliminate Latin, Greek, etc., to say nothing of piano music and the like, they should teach agriculture and related industries with constant and growing appreciation of the educational values in such courses; in a word, they should "choose and object" and direct all efforts to the accomplishment of that clearly defined and clearly seen object, viz.—such training of the negro for the life that now is as shall make of him a producer—a servant—of his day and generation in the highest sense.

Black private institutions in general, as Fort Valley in particular, had to be transformed because the principals were not modern in that they held to the classical liberal curriculum. The schools were not "Hamptonized" as they taught Latin, Greek, piano music, and other academic subjects aside from the "three R's." The industrial courses, when offered, were designed to produce skilled workers and not to train industrial teachers who would socialize black children to be common laborers and servants in the South's caste economy. How could the black private institutions be changed? "Do not give them a dollar," advised Buttrick, "unless they accept supervision, do genuine work, and hold to a course of study in which there is orderly progress from the elementary to the secondary." His report and recommendations were read by John D. Rockefeller, Jr., and Frederick T. Gates and, according to Gates, "We have no doubt of the justice of your observations." Gates concluded that the philanthropists should use all their influence toward the ends set forth by Buttrick.[35]

In pursuing this course the philanthropists found moderate success and a great deal of opposition. Those institutions supported by the various religious denominations continued to regard academic or literary education as the most important facet of their work and strongly objected to the notion that academic subjects should be subordinated or correlated to industrial training. In 1900 the American Missionary Association supported five major black colleges—Fisk, Talladega, Tougaloo, Straight, and Tillotson—along with forty-three normal schools for black youth. The Methodist Episcopal church operated one theological seminary, ten colleges, and twelve secondary schools for blacks in the South. The Presbyterian church, U.S.A., maintained two colleges for men, five normal and graded schools for women, and eighteen coeducational graded and normal schools. The American Baptist Home Mission Society controlled twelve colleges and fourteen secondary schools. The African Methodist Episcopal church supported Wilberforce University in Ohio, Turner Normal School in Tennessee, Campbell College in Mississippi, Kittrell College in North Carolina, Allen University in South Carolina, and Central Park Normal and Industrial School, Payne College, and Morris Brown University in Georgia. The Colored Methodist Episcopal church established and sustained Miles College in Alabama, Lane College in Tennessee, Holsey Normal and Industrial Institute in Georgia, and the Mississippi Industrial College. These and other secondary and normal schools and colleges maintained by various religious denominations relegated industrial education to a separate and distinctly secondary role. As Thomas J. Morgan, corresponding secretary of the American Baptist Home Mission Society, wrote to Buttrick: "I feel very keenly the sense of responsibility for using what little influence I may have in developing our schools to a high grade, so that they may offer to the ambitious and competent young Negroes the best possible opportunities for self-culture, development, training and preparation, for life's duties." Although most of the denominations were in favor of annexing industrial training courses, they would not transform their institutions into either trade schools or industrial normal schools. The power and prestige of the great philanthropic foundations could not influence the denominations to abandon their primary commitment to classical liberal education, even though this commitment meant losing badly needed money such as the funds contributed by philanthropists to Hampton, Tuskegee, and Fort Valley.[36]

The philanthropists' campaigns to transform existing black secondary and normal schools into Hampton-Tuskegee-style industrial teacher training centers met with moderate success among the growing number of small, independent black private institutions. The leading nondenominational schools were Snow Hill Normal and Industrial Institute and Calhoun Colored School in Alabama, Robert Hungerford Normal and Industrial School in Florida, Utica Normal and Industrial Institute in Mississippi, Manassas Industrial School in Virginia, Penn Normal Industrial and Agricultural School and Voorhees Industrial School in South Carolina, the High Point Normal and Industrial School in North Carolina, and the Fort Valley High and Industrial School in Georgia. Such institutions depended for their support mainly on voluntary contributions recruited by their financial agents in the North from philanthropists. As the small, nondenominational, black private graded and normal schools multiplied early in the twentieth century, their principals and financial agents were forced to travel north for extended periods to raise funds just to meet annual expenditures. For most of them, successful northern fund-raising campaigns often meant the difference between financial life or death. The leaders of these institutions, whether committed to industrial education per se or to a pragmatic search for funds, were unique in their adherence to the Hampton-Tuskegee model of industrial normal education.[37]

For the advocates of the Hampton-Tuskegee model, obtaining the cooperation of a cadre of black industrial graded and normal schools was only a small conquest. These institutions in general did not have the physical facilities or teaching forces to accommodate a significant number of students at the high school or normal school grades. In 1917 Thomas Jesse Jones, in his popular survey of black private and higher education, demonstrated that the Hampton-Tuskegee offshoots and similar schools enrolled few or no students in their normal and secondary courses. For instance, Robert Hungerford, Snow Hill, and Penn Normal enrolled no students beyond the elementary grades, and Calhoun, Utica, Manassas, Voorhees, and High Point Normal were described as elementary schools "with a few pupils in secondary subjects." The secondary enrollments ranged from zero to thirty-four, and only a minority of those enrolled were expected to finish the tenth grade. Clearly, this population was not bound to make much impact on the black teacher shortage and would not go very far in spreading industrial education throughout the black common schools in the rural South.[38]

Meanwhile, the southern states were making little effort to provide public support for the training of black teachers. The annual output of graduates of both high school and normal courses from state normal schools and land-grant colleges was significantly less than the annual increase in new classrooms that the black public schools were providing, to say nothing of the replacement of teachers who left the profession. Moreover, not all of the graduates would teach. In a study made by Jackson Davis of the General Education Board in 1924, it was found that southern state normal schools and land-grant colleges between 1921 and 1928 produced 387 graduates from the normal departments, 33 graduates from the colleges, and 505 graduates from the high school departments. It was estimated that at least eight thousand new black teachers were needed that year just to fill the vacancies in the public schools. Hence, if the entire number of black high school, normal school, and college graduates from southern state-supported institutions had entered teaching in 1922, they would have constituted but 11.5 percent of the new black teachers required for the public schools for that year. The state schools could not supply enough black teachers to fill the jobs in the major cities and towns, and these were the most attractive teaching positions in the southern states. The common schools in the rural South, where the majority of black children lived, had little chance of securing normal school or high school graduates and virtually no chance of securing black college graduates. Black private schools continued to produce the vast majority of secondary, normal, and college graduates, but they could supply only a fraction of the yearly demands for new black teachers. Throughout the first third of the century there remained a large vacuum in the South's black teaching force, especially in the rural common schools.[39]

Northern philanthropists were acutely conscious of this vacuum and sought to fill it with a unique educational institution, the county training school. Beginning in 1911, the General Education Board, John F. Slater Fund, and Anna T. Jeanes Fund decided to pursue their interest in the development of industrial and manual training in black rural schools through state departments of education in general and particularly through the preparation of teachers in county training schools. The county training school system was made possible in large part because the General Education Board devised a plan to place its paid agents as official staff of southern state departments of education. The board offered in 1911 to assist the state department of education in each of the southern states to employ as a regular member of the department staff a state agent for black rural schools. Virginia had already done so in 1910. Kentucky, Alabama, and Arkansas responded at once and were closely followed by North Carolina, Georgia, Tennessee, and Louisiana. By 1918 there were state supervisors of Negro rural schools in Mississippi, South Carolina, Maryland, and Texas as well. They were all white men of considerable experience as county superintendents or in other positions of school management. The position was modeled on the work of Jackson Davis, the superintendent of schools in Henrico County, Virginia. H. B. Frissell, principal of Hampton Institute and trustee of the General Education Board, brought Davis's work to the attention of the General Education Board in 1909. Davis, having been converted to the Hampton Idea, kept close supervision over the black schools in his county to make certain that they offered the right kind of industrial training. Desiring to expand Davis's work statewide, the board approached the state of Virginia and proposed to attach to the state superintendent's office a school supervisor, an educational administrator who would be an official of the State Department of Education and who would have permanent tenure and authority to work out a program of education for black schools.[40]

In 1910 Davis was appointed state supervisor of Negro rural schools

for Virginia. His appointment was confirmed by the Virginia State Department of Education, but he was selected "on the nomination of the
State Superintendent of Education and the Secretary of the General Education Board." The board paid his salary, $2,500 a year, and travel
expenses, which amounted to $500 or as much as was required to cover
expenses each year. He was required to file monthly and annual reports
of his travel and administration of black rural schools with the board
and the Virginia State Department of Education. The same agreement
was made with other appointees as state supervisors. Although the state
supervisors of Negro rural schools were officially responsible to the state
superintendents of education, they took their assignments from the General Education Board. Upon accepting the position of state supervisor in
North Carolina, N. C. Newbold wrote to Wallace Buttrick in New York
to confirm the duties of his new position. Newbold understood his duties
to be as follows:

> The position which I am to fill is to be known as, "State Supervisor
> of Rural Elementary Schools." In broad terms its duties are: To give
> special attention and encouragement to the upbuilding of the negro
> rural schools by helping to introduce into them all kinds of useful
> and profitable industrial education and vocational subjects; to pro-
> mote better farming, better community conditions, better morals
> and cleaner home life; to endeavor in every possible way to make
> better workers, and better citizens of the negroes of North Carolina.

In short, Newbold's job was to spread the Hampton-Tuskegee program
of industrial education throughout the black common schools of North
Carolina. Advancing the Hampton-Tuskegee program was the primary
responsibility of all the state supervisors.[41]

Under the authority and supervision of the state agents the philanthropic foundations developed and expanded the county training schools.
The basic idea was to establish an industrial boarding school, centrally
located in the counties of southern states, with facilities and teachers to
operate seven elementary grades and three years of secondary and normal school courses to train industrial teachers for the little country
schools. The county training school movement began in 1911 with the
construction of the Tangipahoa Parish Training School for Colored Children of Louisiana. In the same year the General Education Board and
John F. Slater Fund supported three additional county training schools.
By March 1913, James H. Dillard, general agent of the Slater Fund, was
convinced of the value of the "county industrial schools." He therefore
wrote to the southern state superintendents describing this new institution for rural blacks and offering philanthropic funding to any county
interested in creating one. The state superintendents of Alabama, Flor-

*Tangipahoa Parish Training School of Louisiana was the first of its kind.
Courtesy of Fisk University Library.*

*Wharton Negro Training School of Wharton, Texas. Courtesy of Fisk
University Library.*

ida, North Carolina, Tennessee, Texas, and Virginia expressed interest and promised cooperation. By 1917, all the former slave states, except Missouri and West Virginia, had one or more county training schools. During the twenty-year period from 1911 to 1931, the number of county training schools supported in a given year grew from 4 to 390. This rapid increase indicated that the philanthropists saw great opportunities to spread industrial education through these schools. In its 1917–18 annual report, the board stated: "There is perhaps no more promising movement in Negro Education than the development of the County Training Schools, which offer seven years of elementary work, with suitable industrial courses, and in addition three years of high school work emphasizing the arts of home making and farm life; the last year includes a simple course in teacher training." Having failed or achieved only modest success in its attempts to "Hamptonize" existing black educational institutions, the philanthropists established their own unique structure of black education.[42]

For local authorities to receive county training schools, the board and the Slater Fund demanded that they meet certain minimum requirements. The school property must belong to the state, county, or district, and the county training school must be recognized as part of the local public school system. Further, the local school boards were required to make an annual appropriation for teachers' salaries of not less than $750. The board and the Slater Fund demanded a school term of at least eight months and required that the course work extend at least through the eighth grade. The philanthropists expected local school officials to add two years of high school and normal school courses for the training of industrial teachers. It was the policy of the board and Slater Fund to appropriate to each county training school $500 per year for teachers' salaries. This appropriation was made on a diminishing scale, in the hope that all costs would be absorbed eventually by local school authorities. The philanthropists also contributed funds to erect industrial shops, teachers' homes, and dormitories. Altogether, from 1911 to 1937, when the county training schools were finally integrated into the public school system of the South, the board contributed $1,488,678 to the schools, and the Slater Fund, by 1932, had contributed $1,208,475.[43]

The state superintendent of Negro rural schools was responsible for defining the county training schools at the local level and for selecting suitable locations for the schools, planning the course of study, and hiring industrial teachers and principals to staff them. The state supervisor for Alabama, James L. Sibley, defined the purpose of the county training school as threefold: "to give definite instruction in home economics to girls; in agriculture to boys; and in teacher training to both." The Georgia state supervisor, George D. Godard, viewed the county training school movement as an opportunity to spread industrial education in black common schools and "to make the Negro a more economical, industrious, and profitable citizen." Supervisor J. A. Presson of Arkansas emphasized the county training school as a vehicle to "prepare the girls and boys for more efficient work and happier lives in the home and on the farm." The state supervisor in Tennessee, S. L. Smith, equipped the Dyersburg County Training School with a kitchen, "as nearly like a well-ordered kitchen of the city as possible." "This will," Smith contended, "better prepare the girls to do cooking for the white people of the town." Before he could do this, however, he had to convert the president of the county Board of Education to the cause of industrial education. This man, a native white southerner, advocated, according to Smith, "that Negro children learn Latin, Greek, and Higher Mathematics." Leo M. Favrot, then state supervisor in Louisiana, saw the southern states' role in promoting the new industrial schools as analogous to the duties of the antebellum slaveholders: "Under the industrial system that prevailed in slavery times the Negroes were not left in ignorance, but were carefully trained along industrial lines. In those days the industrial slaveholder assumed a responsibility which in our day and time the state can ill-afford to shun. In those days it was to the interest of the slaveholder to train the slave Negro to become efficient. It is no less to the interest of the South today to train the Negro in industrial efficiency." Favrot eventually came to be regional director of the county training school movement, and he made a detailed study of the schools in 1923. He reported that all the county school officials in the South were "making the training schools distinctly industrial and agricultural all the way through the course offered."[44]

Although the philanthropists found it relatively easy to sell the idea of the county training school to the state supervisors, it was quite another task to sell it to the black people of the rural South. Publicly, the philanthropists and their agents claimed that the county training schools were a response to a general demand for industrial education arising from the southern black rural community. Moreover, the philanthropists stated publicly that the money contributed to support these schools was given with no strings attached and that each county was left to define and construct the curriculum. "No attempt has been made to dictate what shall be taught," said Jackson Davis in 1918, who was then head of the board's southern black education division. Similarly, Leo M. Favrot wrote: "There has never been a serious effort to make uniform the training school course of study." These public pronouncements stood in marked contrast to the philanthropists' private actions.[45]

In spite of this and other pronouncements, the state supervisors encountered opposition from rural black principals and teachers from the outset. In 1913 Favrot stated privately that rural black teachers' opposition to industrial training made it extremely difficult to introduce industrial education into the black rural schools of Arkansas. Four years later, John A. Presson, who succeeded Favrot as state supervisor of Arkansas, gained some insight into the underlying causes of the black teachers' resistance to industrial education. He visited the state's black colleges where a good portion of them had been educated. Presson discovered that the three black colleges—Philander Smith, Arkansas Baptist, and Shorter—were "not equipped at all, for teaching industrial subjects." Moreover, "They seem to pride themselves on their academic work, and take great credit to themselves for work offered in traditional courses, such as are given by leading colleges of the country." Because these colleges had in attendance "a considerable number of students who are planning to teach in the schools of the state," Presson was anxious to convert them to a more favorable view of industrial education. He was not very successful in this effort. Similarly, S. L. Smith visited the Haywood County, Tennessee, Training School in 1914 and discovered black teachers "attempting to teach four years of Latin, and neglecting a great deal of the [industrial] school work." Such matters reached the breaking point the following year, when James H. Dillard discovered a county training school in Georgia that had installed a classical liberal curriculum. The Ben Hill County Training School had changed its name to the Queensland Normal and Industrial Institute, and the principal had divided the institute into four departments embracing Greek, German, psychology, ethics, moral philosophy, economics, and evidences of Christianity. Dillard asked George Godard, state supervisor, to cut out the "objectionable part of this course."[46]

The philanthropic agents were particularly disturbed by what happened at Ben Hill. They recognized that many of the first teachers and principals in the county training schools were educated in liberal arts institutions. Hence the philanthropists paid for such principals and teachers to attend summer school at Hampton or Tuskegee so they would learn how to do industrial education the right way. In this instance, the attempted baptism failed. As Jackson Davis said of the Ben Hill principal, "I had hoped that this principal had received some inoculation of sound doctrine at Hampton this summer, but evidently it did not take." Davis understood, however, that the problem was much larger than one principal: "Many of the principals are not able to resist the popular demand of colored people for pretentious and high sounding courses." Both Davis and Dillard realized that such popular demands could be suppressed only by compulsion. "It is quite evident that we shall have to use more pressure in having the proper kind of work done in these schools," said Davis. Dillard thought that it was "high time" for

"Domestic science" class at Marion County, South Carolina, Training School. The young women were being prepared to work as cooks in the homes of whites in the county. Courtesy of Fisk University Library.

Ben Hill County Training School of Georgia. Here, black educators, by initially installing a classical liberal program, subverted the industrial education curriculum. Courtesy of Fisk University Library.

the philanthropic agents and state supervisors to get together, "where we could be perfectly quiet and could discuss and work out a good, sensible course of study for County Training Schools." In October 1915, Abraham Flexner, on behalf of the board, informed all the state supervisors that a meeting had been scheduled "in order to agree upon a program for the development of the county training schools and in order to discuss further the situation with which you all are dealing." In March 1916 Dillard convinced the southern state supervisors at a meeting in New York City to construct a uniform course of study for the county training schools.[47]

The New York City conference resulted in the appointment of Leo Favrot and Jackson Davis to write a course guide for the county training schools. This guide was published in 1917 under the deceptive title of *Suggested Course for County Training Schools.* It was much more than suggestive; it was a course of study to which all county training schools were expected to conform, and the state supervisors were charged with enforcing it. The course booklet outlined the typical Hampton-Tuskegee industrial education program, a knowledge of the three R's and a substantial amount of simple industrial and agricultural labor. It was recommended that the county training schools devote about one-half of their time to teaching the three R's and the other half to the theory and practice of gardening, cooking, woodwork, laundering, and routine manual labor. In addition to the industrial courses, it was recommended that each boy organize a "pig club" and each girl cultivate a home garden. The secondary courses were to emphasize observation and practice teaching, elementary principles of teaching, and school management. The teacher training course also included ample time for agriculture, gardening, cooking, sewing, housekeeping, canning, and similar tasks. The academic subjects in the teacher training course did not go beyond what was required for a first grade county teachers' license, which was very little beyond the subjects of the common school course. Studies of educational practices in the county training schools demonstrated that in general they conformed to the course of study developed by Dillard and Davis.[48]

At the time the county training school movement had its inception, relatively few of the black teachers in rural elementary schools had been trained in industrial education. As Favrot discovered in 1913, "Probably less than three percent of the public school teachers in Negro schools have normal training of any kind, and practically none of these are trained for industrial activities." The philanthropists and other supporters of the county training schools had hoped that the institutions would provide for black students a simple preparation for teaching industrial education in the rural schools of the county wherein the training school was located. But the teacher training function performed by county training schools was never of major importance. The proponents of the county training schools were unconscious of or underestimated the changes in education and certification that were occurring in the teaching profession. As teacher training programs at the normal school and college level developed, the opportunity for even four-year secondary schools, not to mention county training schools, to discharge this function rapidly diminished. With higher standards for certification paralleling the development of professional standards, the job opportunities in teaching for county training school graduates diminished proportionately. By 1932, except for Louisiana, all southern states had abolished teacher training work in the public black secondary schools. The enrollment in the teacher training courses in county training schools was never significant. A report completed in 1928 demonstrated that of the 35,000 students enrolled in these schools only 324 students were enrolled in teacher training departments. The low enrollment occurred in large part because blacks who aspired to be teachers searched for a higher quality of academic education than was offered in the county training schools.[49]

In the long run, the philanthropists and southern school reformers were unable to direct the course of black teacher preparatory programs along the lines of the Hampton-Tuskegee model. As southern states and localities required higher levels of education for entry-level teachers, the roles of small private normal schools and county training schools diminished. As illustrated in Table 4.2, in the academic year 1929–30 very few black students were enrolled in the small private teacher preparation institutions; the majority were enrolled in four-year private colleges and universities. At this time, although 75 percent of the black high school teachers in the South had at least a bachelor's degree, only about 9 percent of the black elementary school teachers had at least a bachelor's degree. The vast majority of southern black students were enrolled in the elementary grades, and thus the teachers of the masses were still more likely to receive training in private normal schools and county training schools. Yet state teacher certification requirements and student aspirations converged to shape long-run trends away from the industrial normal and county training school models.[50]

Nevertheless, black southerners were left to contend with a significant structure that had been built to reproduce them as contented common laborers in the South's caste economy. Because they filled a void in black education that normally would have been filled by public high schools, the county training schools became a far-reaching and dominant institution in southern black secondary education. In 293 of 912 counties in fifteen southern and border states, the county training school was, for blacks between the ages of fifteen and nineteen, the sole source of public

TABLE 4.2

Total College Enrollment and Enrollment of Graduates in Institutions
of Higher Learning for Blacks in the South, 1929–1930

Type of institutions	Total enrollment			Enrollment of graduates					
	Number of institutions	Regular session	Summer session, extension or correspondence courses	Number of institutions	4-year	3-year	2-year	1-year	Graduate degree
State teachers colleges	8	6,577	1,552	8	311	4	320	1	—
State normal schools	11	2,540	2,433	11	—	9	546	43	—
Private teacher-preparation institutions	2	577	—	2	388	—	—	—	—
Public universities	2	697	583	2	73	—	—	—	—
City teachers colleges	4	864	—	3	174	—	—	—	—
Private colleges and universities	59	14,025	8,219	39	1,563	—	—	—	15
Total	86	25,280	12,787	65	2,509	13	866	44	15

Source: Caliver, *Education of Negro Teachers*, p. 93.

secondary education in 1933. Further evidence of the centrality of the county training school in black education is that 44.2 percent of all southern black pupils of high school age were located in counties where county training schools were either the only secondary schools or the ones with the most number of grades. In states with large black populations, the county training school provided the only or most advanced secondary education for 64.9 percent of black youth in Mississippi, 59.2 percent in Virginia, 54 percent in Louisiana, 52.5 percent in Alabama, 48.4 percent in Florida, 47.9 percent in South Carolina, and 40.2 percent in Georgia. These percentages increase when rural schools are considered separately. In 1933, 66 percent of all rural southern black high school pupils were enrolled in county training schools. The legacy of the county training schools was not so much in what they prepared black students to become as in the ways they shut off alternative development. Most important, the students who were forced to attend these schools because they had no other access to educational opportunities were denied good academic training. A considerable amount of valuable classroom time was spent doing simple manual labor exercises, and the so-called academic component was watered down to the lowest level. The graduates of the county training schools were not prepared to undertake college-level work, they did not attain occupational skills that were salable in the job market, and in the long run they were denied the opportunity to teach in the little country schools. After 1935 these schools were rapidly phased out or in a few instances transformed into public high schools. The development of these county industrial schools rested on the assumption that good academic education was dysfunctional for the world in which black children were compelled to live. This conception of black education was reflected in the structure and content of the county training schools and pushed them heavily toward an emphasis on work and social adjustment. The intended purpose of these schools was to make black children think and feel that traditional, high-quality academic education was incongruent with their station in life. Their purpose was to adjust black southerners to a life of subordination, and they were oppressive in form and content, except when their intended purposes were subverted by local school officials.[51]

5

COMMON SCHOOLS FOR

BLACK CHILDREN

THE SECOND CRUSADE, 1900–1935

PUBLIC ELEMENTARY SCHOOLS became available to the majority of southern black children during the first third of the twentieth century, long after common schools had become universal for other American schoolchildren. For the nation outside of the South, the common school crusade occurred between 1830 and 1860. Ex-slaves, as explained in Chapter 1, waged the first crusade for state systems of common schools in the American South following the Civil War. Although they succeeded in instituting a public school system in a region where universal public education had been unknown, it was only partially developed when the planters returned to power in 1876 and promptly contained the expansion of common schools in general and particularly for black children. The planters' great conquest required the political support of white small farmers, and a virulent racism formed the cornerstone of this interclass bargain. By the late nineteenth century white small farmers were demanding a public school system which they expected to educate their children. This demand brought them to a point at which their own educational interests were at variance with the planters' traditional preferences for private academies which called for very limited state support for public education. But the political interests of the planters shaped their behavior in this instance more than did their traditional opposition to state-regulated, tax-supported, universal public education. They accommodated the white small farmers' demand for public education, but there were two important consequences of this bargain. Public school funds for black children were diverted to white children, and there was increased opposition to black education by both planters and white small farmers. Hence the planters' return to power in alliance with white small farmers suppressed the ex-slaves' campaign for universal public schooling. Consequently, black rural southerners, unlike working classes elsewhere in America, could expect little support for common schools from state and local governments. Thus following the planters' return to power in the late 1870s, black southerners began to turn inward and attempted to construct and maintain the semblance of a common school system from their own meager resources. Much was accomplished, but it was impossible for such an economically poor social class to finance a system of universal education. Black southerners therefore had to wage a second crusade to establish common schools for their children.[1]

The economic and social forces that were aligned against universal education for black children in the Reconstruction era still existed at the dawn of the twentieth century. For the profitable growing of cash crops, chiefly cotton and tobacco, planters considered a cheap labor supply as essential and regarded black agricultural laborers as the mainstay of their exploited work force. Many planters, believing that schooling actually spoiled a good field hand, preferred their laborers illiterate or at best semiliterate. Moreover, the labor needs for growing cash crops and the rhythms of economic life were inherently opposed to formal schooling. Nowhere was this clash between cotton production and formal schooling expressed more eloquently than in Richard Wright's *Twelve Million Black Voices*. Born and bred in Mississippi's cotton economy and speaking on behalf of the South's black agricultural laborers, Wright said:

> Sometimes there is a weather-worn, pine-built schoolhouse for our children, but even if the school were open for the full term our children would not have time to go. We cannot let them leave the fields when cotton is waiting to be picked. When time comes to break the sod, the sod must be broken; when the time comes to plant the seeds, the seeds must be planted, and when the time comes to loosen the red clay from about the bright green stalks of the cotton plants, that, too, must be done even if it is September and school is open. Hunger is the punishment if we violate the laws of Queen Cotton. The seasons of the year form the mold that shapes our lives, and who can change the seasons?[2]

In 1900 significant numbers of black children and their mothers were breaking sod, planting seeds, and harvesting crops. Of black children between the ages of ten and fifteen, inclusive, 49.3 percent of boys and 30.6 percent of girls were engaged in gainful occupations, and the overwhelming majority of them, 404,255 out of 516,276, were employed as unskilled agricultural laborers. The proportions of white boys and girls of the same ages engaged in gainful occupations were 22.5 and 7 percent respectively. Almost one-half, 46.6 percent, of black children aged ten to fifteen were gainfully employed in 1910. Black women also were a significant part of the South's agricultural labor force. Of the 665,791 females reported by the census of 1900 as engaged in agricultural labor,

509,687 or 76 percent were black. The number of black women working as farm laborers increased from 509,687 in 1900 to 970,060 in 1910; this increase of 460,337 was more than three times the corresponding increase for males. More than 40 percent of all black women in America over ten years of age were at work in 1900, as against 16 percent of all white women. Further, 26 percent of all the black married women were in the labor force, but only 3 percent of the white married women of the country were at work. The majority of black males gainfully employed were also engaged in agricultural labor. These estimates do not include unpaid family labor, which was high for blacks in the South.[3]

Despite the structure and work rhythms of the southern agricultural economy, black children did not voluntarily sacrifice formal schooling for gainful employment. Rather, there were no public or private schools available to the great majority of black children, and in the absence of school facilities employment seemed the next best opportunity. Both the heavy use of black children in the agricultural labor force and the limited availability of black public schools reflected the planters' domination of the rural South. Where public schools were available black parents in general accepted the loss of child labor and additional household income so that their children would attend school. The southern planters understood black attitudes toward formal schooling and thus regarded the establishment of black public schools as a powerful distraction for their school-age laborers. The planters, therefore, used what power and influence they had in local and state governments to restrict the availability of public schools to black children. The structure of the black public school system at the turn of the century, particularly in the rural South, seemed quite congruent with the planters' economic and political interest. As illustrated in Table 5.1, there were in the South in 1900 2,136,016 black children five to fourteen years of age. Yet only 36 percent of these children attended school. Of the 1,120,683 black children five to nine years of age, only 22 percent attended, and of the 1,015,333 black children ten to fourteen years of age, slightly over one-half attended school. Furthermore, a full 86 percent of all those children fortunate enough to go to school received less than six months of instruction per year. Even when schools were available, most of the children lived beyond a reasonable walking distance of one and a half miles from the schools in their area, and the region's rough topography made walking difficult. Unlike for white children, southern state and local governments refused to provide transportation for black children. This structure of schooling for black children had been solidified since 1875 and at the beginning of the twentieth century seemed fixed for a long time to come. Meanwhile, processes of migration and urbanization converged with school reform cam-

TABLE 5.1

Elementary School Attendance by Race and Age in Southern States, 1900

State	Number of children 5 to 9 years old, inclusive		Number attending school		Percent attending school		Number of children 10 to 14 years old, inclusive		Number attending school		Percent attending school	
	Black	White	Black	White	Black	White	Black	White	Black	White	Black	White
Alabama	118,403	138,291	16,274	36,001	14	26	105,926	122,759	43,810	80,917	41	66
Arkansas	51,793	135,628	12,715	47,321	25	35	46,714	119,767	25,419	84,881	54	71
Delaware	3,548	15,891	1,153	7,775	32	49	3,401	15,345	2,121	12,646	62	82
Florida	30,401	40,048	8,854	15,361	29	38	26,361	34,604	16,439	26,943	62	78
Georgia	151,516	161,648	33,070	58,855	22	36	134,540	143,325	61,290	100,298	46	70
Kentucky	31,972	241,287	9,785	94,543	31	39	33,155	218,498	22,594	170,721	68	78
Louisiana	93,447	98,428	12,792	28,315	14	29	82,803	86,582	28,751	56,705	35	65
Maryland	27,586	105,159	8,820	51,077	32	49	26,539	99,678	16,857	79,817	64	80
Mississippi	134,292	87,836	36,770	37,835	27	43	118,560	79,505	62,279	59,441	53	75
Missouri	16,837	353,927	7,008	179,566	42	51	17,328	329,937	12,697	276,777	73	84
North Carolina	89,833	173,531	21,405	58,126	24	33	81,296	154,029	44,783	103,892	55	67
South Carolina	119,669	74,594	21,288	22,644	18	30	106,982	67,435	47,853	42,959	45	64
Tennessee	63,022	201,783	15,395	72,135	24	36	59,343	184,430	33,522	133,177	56	72
Texas	92,492	339,863	17,339	80,501	19	24	82,697	300,480	55,867	241,086	66	80
Virginia	91,469	149,159	21,900	57,639	24	39	85,609	135,228	48,938	102,251	57	76
West Virginia	4,403	116,566	1,645	49,159	37	42	4,079	106,658	2,758	88,199	68	83
Totals	1,120,683	2,433,639	246,273	896,853	22	37	1,015,333	2,198,440	525,978	1,660,708	52	76

Source: U.S. Bureau of the Census, Twelfth Census of the United States: 1900, Population, pt. 2, pp. 6, 12, 20, 24, 26, 42, 44, 48, 56, 58, 74, 88, 94, 100, 104, 353, 359.

paigns by black southerners and northern philanthropists to point to a
new day for common schools for black children.[4]

One of the most significant factors contributing to the second crusade
for black common schools was the rapid rate at which black children
were withdrawn from the agricultural labor force after 1910. Although
nearly one-half of all black children aged ten to fifteen were gainfully
employed, primarily in agricultural pursuits, in 1910, by 1920 this percentage had dropped sharply to 21.8 and it decreased to 16.1 in 1930.
The migration of black laborers from the rural farm areas to the city was
central to this emancipation of black children from daily labor. The
migration, which started in full force in 1914, was also a key factor in
forcing the southern white agrarian classes to reconsider the idea of
universal schooling for black children. When the United States Department of Labor made an investigation of the black migration in 1917, its
researchers cited increased support for a viable system of black schools
as a means to "keep the Negroes in the South and make them satisfied
with their lot." As a means of checking the exodus of blacks to the city,
an insightful editor in the Jackson, Mississippi, *Daily News* made the
following observation:

> A Negro father, if he is honest, hard working, and industrious, has
> the same ambition for his children that a white man possesses. He
> wants to see his offspring receive an education in order that they
> may be properly equipped for the battle of life. But they are not
> getting this. Every person who is familiar with educational affairs in
> Mississippi knows this to be the case. And it forms one of the chief
> reasons why thrifty, industrious Negroes, who want to get ahead in
> the world, who have a desire to live decently, are following the lure
> of higher wages and better living conditions and moving to the
> northern states.

To be sure, not every white southerner shared this perspective. But the
Daily News's conclusion, that black agricultural laborers should "continue to desert our farms, leaving thousands of fertile acres untilled,"
unless they received a "square deal" in the matter of education, appealed
to the most stubborn planters.[5]

The migration opened the way for a second crusade for black common
schools in the rural South. This crusade, known by contemporary observers and later historians as the Rosenwald school building program,
was launched officially in 1914, the same year the migration started in
full force. By the mid-1930s, black elementary schools, though still far
from excellent, had been transformed into a viable system of universal
education. This transformation was effected by ordinary black men and
women, local white school officials, small numbers of southern white lay

people, and northern philanthropic agencies. Among the philanthropic agencies most influential in advancing common schools for rural black children was the Negro Rural School Fund, also called the Anna T. Jeanes Foundation. Beginning in 1909, the Jeanes Fund cooperated with southern public school authorities in employing supervisors of industrial teachers. These supervisors were appointed by the county superintendent, worked under his direction, and were considered members of his regular corps of teachers. The Jeanes Fund paid 84 percent of their salaries in the early years. The Jeanes teachers' work included a wide range of activities, including teaching and supervising elementary industrial work and the promotion of school and community clubs. Perhaps the largest proportion of supervisors' time was consumed in raising money for new schoolhouses and school equipment and in efforts to extend the school term. From 1913 to 1928, these Jeanes teachers raised an aggregate of approximately $5 million. Yet despite the significant contributions of the Anna T. Jeanes Foundation, it was the Rosenwald schools, financed in part by the Julius Rosenwald Fund, that came to symbolize the crusade for black common schools in the rural South during the first third of the twentieth century. The Rosenwald building program is crucial because it illustrates most clearly the general character and scope of black southerners' second crusade for common schools. It was black southerners' enduring beliefs in universal schooling and their collective social actions to achieve it that made possible and sustained the Rosenwald school building program.[6]

In the spring of 1914, the Loachopoka School in Lee County, Alabama, was completed as the first Rosenwald school. It was a one-teacher frame building erected at the modest cost of $942. Of this amount the local black citizens raised $150 in cash and gave an estimated $132 in free labor. Local white citizens donated $360, and Julius Rosenwald, the Chicago philanthropist and president of Sears, Roebuck, and Company, contributed $300. Lee County in 1910 was 60 percent black. This project launched one of the largest and most dramatic rural school construction programs of the era, resulting by 1932 in the building of 4,977 rural black schools with a pupil seating capacity of 663,615. The schoolhouses were located in 883 counties across fifteen southern states and together with teachers' homes and industrial shops cost in cash $28,408,520. Of this amount, as illustrated in Table 5.2, the Julius Rosenwald Fund gave 15.36 percent, rural black people contributed 16.64 percent, whites donated 4.27 percent, and 63.73 percent was appropriated from public tax funds, collected largely, if not wholly, from black taxpayers. These schools were called Rosenwald schools because of the contributions from the Rosenwald Fund, and that label led to the popular belief that they were paid for mainly by the fund. In actual practice, the fund never gave even one-half the cost of a schoolhouse, and it generally contributed an average of about one-sixth of the total monetary cost of the building, grounds, and equipment. Most of the cash, either through private contributions or public tax funds, came from rural black citizens. Their additional contributions in the form of land, labor, and building materials were also substantial.[7]

This alternative to state-financed public education was necessary because in the early twentieth century whites all over the South seized the school funds belonging to the disfranchised black citizens, gerrymandered school districts so as to exclude blacks from certain local tax benefits, and expounded a racist ideology to provide a moral justification of unequal treatment. Although in a few southern urban settings the degree of discrimination was less profound in the period after 1900, severe racial discrimination was especially pronounced in the southern countryside. The disparity in per capita expenditures between blacks and whites in the public schools was greater in 1910 than in 1900 and greater in 1900 than earlier, in every southern state. In the rural schools of North Carolina, for instance, black teachers as a class were paid less in 1908 than in 1907. In Alabama, the average length of the public school term for blacks was cut from ninety-five days in 1908 to ninety in 1910, and the average salary paid black school teachers was also reduced. In one Alabama county, the number of black schools decreased from thirty to three. W. E. B. DuBois, in his study *The Common School and the Negro American*, said in 1911: "Not only has the general enrollment and attendance of Negro children in the rural schools of the lower South and to a large extent the city schools been at a standstill in the last ten years, and in many cases actually decreased, but many of the school authorities have shown by their acts and in a few cases expressed declaration that it was their policy to eliminate the Negro school as far as possible." Hence the percentage of black children five to eighteen years old enrolled in the public schools of the South decreased during the first decade of the twentieth century.[8]

State actions to reduce the number of schools available to rural blacks were supported by the popular myth that black public schools were financed largely by money collected from white taxpayers. In 1909, however, Charles L. Coon, an agent of the Southern Education Board, disproved the frequent southern white charge that black education was a burden on the white taxpayer. Coon had demonstrated in the North Carolina state school report for 1905–6 that, counting indirect taxes, more money was collected from blacks than was appropriated to their schools. In 1909 he elaborated this argument and presented it to the Twelfth Conference for Education in the South. Coon's study was then published and disseminated in pamphlet form by the Committee of

TABLE 5.2

Summary of Completed Buildings and of Amounts and Percentages of Cash Contributions by Blacks, Whites, Public Taxation, and Rosenwald Fund, 10 June 1914–1 July 1932

State	Number of buildings				Capacity		Total cost: Buildings, grounds, and equipment	Contributions*			
	Total	Schools	Homes	Shop	Teacher	Pupil		Blacks	Whites	Taxation	Rosenwald
Alabama	407	389	7	11	898	40,410	$ 1,285,060	$ 452,968	$ 137,746	$ 445,526	$ 248,820
Arkansas	389	338	19	32	1,044	46,980	1,952,441	172,134	53,714	1,420,852	305,741
Florida	125	120	1	4	501	22,545	1,432,706	54,758	67,021	1,186,602	124,325
Georgia	261	242	12	7	829	37,305	1,378,859	253,852	118,456	759,002	247,569
Kentucky	158	155	2	1	402	18,090	1,081,710	88,897	13,475	848,748	130,590
Louisiana	435	393	31	9	1,139	51,255	1,721,506	457,318	70,407	855,781	338,000
Maryland	153	149	2	2	343	15,435	899,658	84,973	5,224	699,761	109,700
Mississippi	633	557	58	18	1,730	77,850	2,851,421	859,688	323,143	1,128,673	539,917
Missouri	4	3	—	1	28	1,260	257,959	500	6,000	237,609	13,850
North Carolina	813	787	18	8	2,538	114,210	5,167,042	666,736	75,140	3,707,740	717,426
Oklahoma	198	176	16	6	435	19,575	1,127,449	28,865	5,475	948,054	145,055
South Carolina	500	481	8	11	1,646	74,070	2,892,360	507,994	224,525	1,706,241	453,600
Tennessee	373	354	9	10	988	44,460	1,969,822	296,388	28,027	1,354,157	291,250
Texas	527	464	31	32	1,274	57,330	2,496,521	392,851	60,494	1,623,800	419,376
Virginia	381	367	3	11	952	42,840	1,894,006	407,969	23,128	1,183,259	279,650
Totals	5,357	4,977	217	163	14,747	663,615	$28,408,520	$4,725,891	$1,211,975	$18,105,805	$4,364,869

Source: Statistical Reports on Rural School Construction Program, Box 331, JRFP-FU.

*Percentages donated: blacks 16.64 percent; whites 4.27 percent; public 63.73 percent; Rosenwald Fund 15.36 percent.

Twelve for the Advancement of the Interests of the Negro Race. More recent studies demonstrate that during the period 1880 to 1900 the percentage of tax disbursements in North Carolina for black schools exceeded the proportion of direct taxes blacks paid. After 1900, however, the proportion of expenditures that went to black schools dropped sharply, and by 1910 the proportion of direct taxes blacks paid virtually equaled the percentage of school taxes they received. When the funding for the construction of school buildings is considered, the drop in per capita expenditure for blacks was even greater. During the period 1900 to 1920, every southern state sharply increased its tax appropriations for building schoolhouses, but virtually none of this money went for black schools. Booker T. Washington was on the mark when he said: "The money is actually being taken from the colored people and given to white schools." Rural blacks in particular were victims of taxation without representation, but none of this was new to them.[9]

Since the end of the Reconstruction era black southerners had adapted to a structure of oppressive education by practicing double taxation. They had no choice but to pay both direct and indirect taxes for public education. Southern public school authorities diverted school taxes largely to the development of white public education. Blacks then resorted to making private contributions to finance public schools. To have their privately financed schools recognized and even partially supported by state and local school authorities, black southerners had to deed to the state their contributions of money, land, and school equipment. In 1909 Monroe N. Work and Richard R. Wright, Jr., and then W. E. B. DuBois, in 1910, traced these traditions of "self-help" in black education. Wright documented the large amounts of property and labor contributed by southern blacks to the construction of schoolhouses. In a table illustrating the ownership of schoolhouses in 155 counties in thirteen southern states, Wright demonstrated that of 4,137 schoolhouses blacks owned 1,816 or 43.9 percent. Moreover, he discovered that many schoolhouses reported as public domain were paid for in large part by blacks through voluntary contributions. "The fact is," said Wright, "in most cases the Negroes, because of aid given them by the county fund, deeded them to the county." Significantly, this was the tradition out of which the second crusade for black common schools emerged and by which it was sustained. External support from philanthropic foundations was very helpful. But southern rural blacks absorbed the contributions of the Rosenwald and Jeanes funds into a long-standing tradition of "self-help" or double taxation that had developed among Afro-Americans decades before 1914.[10]

The events that led to the establishment of the Rosenwald rural schoolhouse construction program began in 1895, when Fisk University graduate Clinton J. Calloway joined Tuskegee Institute's staff as a member of the school's Department of Extension. He began his extension work in Kowalgia, Alabama, a small farming community about thirty-five miles from Tuskegee, by helping the residents build a modern community school. The existing school was "an old shanty belonging to one of the planters which was used to house the school children and their one teacher." Calloway assisted in the establishment of a new three-building, eleven-teacher school, built mainly from money and labor donated by Kowalgia's black residents. "My experience here gave me a working knowledge of how to organize communities and build schoolhouses," he recalled in 1927. In 1901 Calloway returned to Tuskegee's campus as director of extension. He and an assistant cooperated with Macon County, Alabama, black farmers to raise money to build schoolhouses and to negotiate with the local board of education in efforts to lengthen the school term for black children. In 1906 Calloway founded a monthly magazine, the *Messenger*, published at Tuskegee, to combine the growing campaign for school improvement with information on better farming methods.[11]

Calloway's rural school construction campaign received an unexpected boost when Julius Rosenwald celebrated his fiftieth birthday on 12 August 1912. Rosenwald commemorated the event in part by donating $25,000 to Booker T. Washington to support "Offshoots of Tuskegee." These "offshoots" were various normal schools throughout the South that had adopted the Hampton-Tuskegee model of industrial education as their basic curriculum for training teachers. Washington distributed all but $2,100 of Rosenwald's gift among such industrial normal schools as Snow Hill Normal and Industrial Institute ($4,000), Utica Normal and Industrial Institute ($4,000), Voorhees Industrial School ($3,000), Fort Valley High and Industrial School ($3,000), Robert Hungerford Industrial School ($1,000), and High Point Industrial School ($1,000). Calloway, realizing there was still money left, persuaded Washington to use some of the remaining $2,100 to aid rural schoolhouse construction programs in counties surrounding Tuskegee: "I suggested that Dr. Washington put my proposal through to Mr. Rosenwald. He did." Writing to Rosenwald in September 1912 about Calloway's idea, Washington said: "We are giving some careful, and I hope serious attention to the suggestion of making a plan for the helping of colored people in the direction of small country schoolhouses. In connection with this idea, I am wondering if you would permit us to make an experiment in the direction of building six schoolhouses at various points, preferably near here, so that we can watch the experiment closely, out of the special fund which you have set aside for small schools." Furthermore, Washington "found by investigation that many people who cannot give money, would give a half day or a day's work and others would give material in the way of nails, brick, lime, etc." He had learned much about these activities from Calloway, who had begun reporting such self-help activities to Monroe N. Work, editor of Tuskegee's *Negro Year Book*.[12]

Rosenwald granted Washington's request, and, in 1913, financial assistance for schoolhouse construction was given to six Alabama black communities in Macon, Lee, and Montgomery counties. To match the funds donated by Rosenwald, Calloway reported in April 1913 that black residents in all six communities contributed money, land, and free labor to the construction of schoolhouses. In Montgomery County, for instance, blacks in one community raised $95 during the first fundraising rally, planned to raise another $150 in two weeks' time, and had "already secured the land for the building."[13]

On 10 June 1914, after Washington had made his report on the construction of six experimental schools, Rosenwald expressed a willingness to enlarge the program, and in August 1914, he agreed to contribute $30,000 to aid in building one hundred small rural schoolhouses. The conditions were to be the same as those governing the building of the six experimental schools: black residents of the selected school district were required to raise enough money to match or exceed the amount requested from the Rosenwald Fund, which initially was a maximum of $350; the approval and cooperation of the state, county, or township school officers were required; all property, including the land, money, and other voluntary contributions by blacks, was to be deeded to the local public school authorities; the school building to be erected had to be approved by Tuskegee's Extension Department; and the efforts in each state were to be coordinated by the state agents of Negro education and the Jeanes Fund supervisors.[14]

By 22 February 1916, ninety-two schools had been completed; seventy-nine of them were built in Alabama, and the rest were constructed in other southern states, including four in Arkansas, three in Georgia, three in North Carolina, one in South Carolina, one in Mississippi, and one in Tennessee. The total amount contributed in cash by all parties was $103,783, of which public school authorities contributed $16,550, local white citizens $6,209, Julius Rosenwald $33,821, and rural black citizens $47,203. Of the total cash contributions, only 16 percent came from public tax funds, whereas rural blacks contributed 45.5 percent, whites 5.9 percent, and Rosenwald 32.6 percent. The average cost per school was $1,128, and the average contribution per school by rural blacks was $513 in cash, plus land, labor, and building materials that were not always counted as part of their total contributions. The monetary contributions of rural blacks were decisive in the formative years of the Rosenwald schoolhouse construction program. As shown when comparing Table 5.2 with Table 5.3, rural blacks accounted for 16.64 percent of the total cost of buildings, grounds, and equipment from 10 June 1914 to 1 July 1932, but 20.3 percent of the total cost up until 1 July 1927. Two factors account largely for the decline in cash contributions by blacks from 45.5 percent in 1916 to 33.9 percent in 1920, to 20.3 percent in 1927 and 16.64 percent in 1932. First, as the migration of blacks from the rural South to southern and northern cities accelerated, white landowners, fearful of losing a critical mass of cash tenants, sharecroppers, farm laborers, and domestic servants, returned larger shares of public tax funds to support the construction of rural schoolhouses for blacks, which whites felt would serve as an incentive to blacks to stay. This fear was well founded as almost half of Georgia's black males from fifteen to thirty-four years of age left the state during the 1920s. Second, as the rural schoolhouse construction campaign moved closer in time to the Great Depression, blacks gave proportionately less in cash and more in land, labor, and building materials. This was especially true after 1920, when the rules governing the distribution of Rosenwald aid specifically allowed that "labor, land and materials may be counted as cash at current market values."[15]

On 30 October 1917 Rosenwald incorporated the Julius Rosenwald Fund, "for the well-being of mankind." An important mission of the fund was to enlarge the southern rural schoolhouse construction program for black children. Between 1917 and 1920, several committees and individuals were assigned to evaluate the fund's impact on rural schoolhouse construction and to make recommendations for a more efficient and widespread program. In 1920 Rosenwald established a southern office in Nashville, Tennessee, and shifted the administration of the school construction program from Tuskegee Institute to the new headquarters. S. L. Smith, state agent of Negro education in Tennessee, was selected as director of the fund's southern branch, and Clinton J. Calloway was appointed assistant field agent. The regulations for distributing aid were updated, but two old rules remained. The regulations provided "that the sites and buildings of all schools aided by the Fund shall be the property of the public school authorities," and "that, in providing these buildings, it is a condition precedent to receiving the aid of the Fund that the people of the several communities shall secure, from other sources: to wit—from public school funds, private contributions, etc., an amount equal to or greater than that provided by the Fund." Both the Rosenwald agents and public school authorities knew that the new program, as did the old one, required rural blacks to deed their money, land, labor, and building materials to southern local school systems.[16]

Although the records of voluntary contributions in the forms of land, labor, and materials are too incomplete to determine their total worth in

TABLE 5.3

Summary of Completed Buildings and of Amounts and Percentages of Cash Contributions by Blacks, Whites, Public Taxation, and Rosenwald Fund, 10 June 1914–1 July 1927

State	Number of buildings		Capacity		Total cost: Buildings, grounds, and equipment	Contributions*			
	Schools	Homes	Teacher	Pupil		Blacks	Whites	Taxation	Rosenwald
Alabama	345	5	718	32,310	$ 905,545	$ 349,820	$ 68,391	$ 292,464	$ 194,870
Arkansas	238	9	665	29,925	1,202,415	107,771	35,834	862,399	196,411
Florida	38	1	158	7,110	394,136	28,143	32,565	293,878	39,550
Georgia	165	9	510	22,950	733,475	177,492	47,299	364,802	143,882
Kentucky	115	2	237	10,665	503,045	59,272	10,875	360,658	72,240
Louisiana	310	19	851	38,295	1,212,566	340,201	53,209	560,856	258,300
Maryland	107	0	223	10,035	512,485	58,834	4,174	376,577	72,900
Mississippi	432	41	1,289	58,005	2,026,044	657,989	208,691	746,464	412,900
North Carolina	636	16	1,829	82,305	3,394,049	569,261	68,615	2,226,737	529,436
Oklahoma	117	13	248	11,160	589,558	24,130	3,125	471,223	91,080
South Carolina	373	4	1,253	56,385	2,224,521	415,806	175,058	1,279,857	353,800
Tennessee	284	7	724	32,580	1,369,495	242,298	21,977	890,520	214,700
Texas	303	15	699	31,455	1,252,186	190,088	35,615	783,641	242,842
Virginia	306	2	727	32,715	1,322,144	329,658	19,433	766,453	209,600
Totals	3,769	143	10,131	455,895	$17,641,664	$3,550,763	$784,861	$10,276,529	$3,032,511

Source: Statistical Reports on Rural School Construction Program, Box 331, JRFP-FU.

*Percentages donated: blacks 20.13 percent; whites 4.45 percent; public 58.25 percent; Rosenwald Fund 17.18 percent.

cash at 1914–32 market values, sufficient evidence exists to indicate that such contributions constituted significant shares of the total resources expended for Rosenwald schoolhouses. In 1921, for example, rural blacks in Coffee County, Alabama, donated ten acres of land for a school site, $700 in cash, and a pledge for an additional $1,500, and they also pledged to furnish most of the materials and all of the labor with which to construct the building. Few first-person sources, particularly sources estimating labor time and building materials, were left by the black builders of these rural schoolhouses. But the state agents of Negro education, Rosenwald agents, Jeanes Fund teachers, and local public school authorities were so impressed by the resourcefulness, tenacity, and sacrifices of rural black people that they left a vast and vivid record of many noncash contributions. Their accounts provide further evidence that rural black southerners, living in a cash-short economy and virtually disfranchised by public school authorities, paid from their limited resources a tremendous private cost for their "public" education.[17]

M. H. Griffin, the black Rosenwald building agent of Alabama, launched his career in the rural school construction program in 1921 in Autauga County. He met with blacks in the town of Autaugaville and shared in their ambitious and successful campaign to establish the Autauga County Training School. County training schools were combined elementary and normal schools with physical plants costing much more than those of one- and two-room schoolhouses. The blacks in Autauga, constituting more than 50 percent of the county's total population of twenty thousand, were mostly tenant farmers, which meant that they were "only eking out a living." The day of Griffin's first fund-raising rally "was hot, in the early part of August, when money was at a real premium with farmers." He recorded several "hair-raising scenes" which unfolded as these tenant farmers gathered to pay from their scanty earnings the costs of building a school. "I remember one old lady," wrote Griffin, "who wanted a hand in the 'Big School,' who said 'I have only one copper cent, and it goes for the children of Autaugaville.' " Her sacrifice moved the people to collect over $200, about all the money they had among them and more than their average annual income per capita. These sacrifices, however, did not yield nearly enough to pay for the cost of a new schoolhouse.[18]

A month later, Griffin returned to Autaugaville for the second fund-raising rally. He discovered that fund-raising clubs had been formed in every black community in Autauga County. At the town meeting, following a number of rousing speeches regarding the importance of education and self-improvement, the second fund-raising campaign began in earnest. Griffin describes what happened:

I have never seen greater human sacrifices made for the cause of education. Children without shoes on their feet gave from fifty cents to one dollar and old men and old women, whose costumes represented several years of wear, gave from one to five dollars. The more progressive group gave from ten to twenty-five dollars. When the rally had closed we had the handsome sum of thirteen hundred dollars. Now we were at our rowes end, as we felt that the colored people had done all in the range of human limitation for the school, and yet we lacked more than a thousand dollars with which to qualify the project. Our next big question was "Where shall we get the rest of the money?" Colored men offered to pawn their cows and calves for the money and they did do just this thing. They made notes and gave for security pledges on their future crops, their cows and calves, and other belongings for the money. They raised in this way one thousand dollars, and we started out for a contractor.

The new Autauga County Training School was completed in the fall of 1921. It cost $12,000.[19]

Griffin, energized from this first successful project, then turned his attention to Hobson City, an all-black town in Calhoun County, Alabama. There the principal of the old backwoods country school had organized approximately 150 children into a "Snuff Box Brigade." These children were provided snuff boxes to raise pennies, nickels, and dimes, and by the end of their first fund-raising rally had more than $200. This effort inspired the adults, who were already deeply committed to building a decent school for the children. In Griffin's words, "Men began to vie with each other in giving, and when the rally finally closed we had one thousand and fifty dollars on the table." With additional contributions of labor and land by black citizens, Hobson City was able to erect a modern schoolhouse. Although the popular belief was that Julius Rosenwald paid for such schools, Griffin knew the whole truth. "It should be borne in mind," he said about the Hobson City school, "that funds with which this project was completed came from people who represented a poor working class, men who worked at furnaces, women who washed and ironed for white people, and children who chopped cotton in the heat of the day for money to go in their snuff boxes."[20]

In December 1923 Griffin went on to Bexar, Marion County, Alabama, to tell the people of the conditions under which they could receive Rosenwald aid to help build a new schoolhouse. He met with the black residents "in a little old dingy schoolhouse lighted with a kerosene brass lamp, with smoke ascending to the top of the building." This community was poorer than most Alabama black rural communities. "They were at a loss when we told them they would have to raise seven hundred dol-

The old Hunter Hill School of Autauga County, Alabama (top), was an example of the typical common school available to southern black children prior to the Rosenwald school construction campaigns. The new Hunter Hill School (bottom) represented the three- and four-teacher wooden frame schools that replaced the old schools. Courtesy of Fisk University Library.

The old Duncan School of Cass County, Texas (top), and the new Duncan School (bottom) built in the early 1920s. Courtesy of Fisk University Library.

lars. That sounded like a million to them," recalled Griffin, for in Bexar, $700 equaled the combined annual incomes of about seven black male adults. Having virtually no cash, the residents donated labor and materials. Griffin said: "Men went to the woods, cut down trees, hauled them to the saw mill and had them cut into lumber. Others cleared away the grounds, and even women worked carrying water, and feeding the men while they labored until enough material was placed on the grounds for the two-teacher building." Consequently, in this very poor community, where "food and clothing represented the most crude kind," and "not a house had a screen or a glass window," and where many other living conditions were intolerable, the people built a two-teacher school. Further, they were able to attract a young married couple to come as teachers.[21]

Griffin worked in Alabama from 1921 to 1925. In January of his last year as a Rosenwald school agent in that state, he met with rural blacks of Boligee in Greene County. They gathered in "a little old rickety building without any heat" to plan the construction of a consolidated school in a remote rural community. The majority of black people were tenant farmers, and they were hard hit that year because the boll weevil had caused tremendous damage to cotton crops. When the fund-raising rally began and the master of ceremonies introduced the guests, among the many points he made was the following: " 'We have never had a school in this vicinity, most of our children have grown into manhood and womanhood without the semblance of an opportunity to get an insight into life, etc." "As he spoke," Griffin remembered, "tears began to trickle down his face." At that moment, "one old man, who had seen slavery days, with all of his life's earnings in an old greasy sack, slowly drew it from his pocket, and emptied it on the table." Griffin recalled that the ex-slave said: " 'I want to see the children of my grandchildren have a chance, and so I am giving my all.' " The ex-slave's commitment to education for the children and his willingness to sacrifice his life's earnings inspired the larger audience. Though Griffin thought initially that these boll weevil–stricken sharecroppers would raise only $10, the rally closed with $1,365 on the table. "They shouted and they cried and applauded when the amount was announced." Their additional donations in labor and materials enabled them to complete a five-room county training school at a cost of $6,450.[22]

Dozens of such stories, said S. L. Smith, "might be told to show the fine spirit of cooperation and the willing sacrifices made to secure schools." Smith, first as state agent of Negro education in Tennessee from 1913 to 1920, and then as the Rosenwald Fund's director for southern schools from 1921 to 1937, was clearly in a position to observe such events. In the fall of 1914 he visited Tuskegee Institute and learned of the availability of Rosenwald aid for rural schoolhouse construction. As a result of this visit he helped the black residents of Fayette County build Tennessee's first Rosenwald-supported school in 1915. This fund-raising campaign was organized by a black principal who was teaching in "an old lodge" and his wife, a Jeanes teacher. Fayette County had a total population of slightly over thirty thousand residents, and more than twenty-two thousand of them were black. But there were no public schools for the overwhelming majority of black children in the county in 1915. Smith recalled his first visit to a black fund-raising rally: "I was notified that 1200 lodge members over the county had voted to give a dollar each and I was asked to be present at a county-wide meeting. Although it was a rainy day the committees of the lodges brought in and laid on the table 936 one-dollar bills and promised that the other lodges would report soon. Their interest grew in the project, their total contributions being more than $2,000." The Fayette County school building cost $3,500 in cash. Black citizens contributed $2,200 of this amount, plus additional resources in labor and materials. The Rosenwald Fund donated $500, and the county public school authorities appropriated $800. Efforts did not cease after the first schoolhouse was completed, for between 1915 and 1920, the black principal and his wife succeeded in building twenty Rosenwald schools throughout Fayette County.[23]

Examples of other successful grass-roots campaigns occurred in Tennessee, Arkansas, South Carolina, Virginia, Texas, and Mississippi. In Hardeman County, Tennessee, Smith offered Rosenwald aid to "the first community completing a brick building on the G-A Community School Plan." Moreover, he stated that he would recommend the building as a county training school. Such schools were eligible for $500 a year from the Slater Fund for teachers' salaries and about $1,000 from the General Education Board for equipment. Two communities, Whitehead and Bolivar, became interested and began raising the necessary funds. Smith described what happened in this rivalry for the new schoolhouse:

The Whitehead community after raising enough money to buy the brick began to negotiate with a Nashville firm, and the Bolivar community, not having the necessary money, bought a brick kiln and largely by free labor about 25,000 bricks were made, stacked in kiln form, and a house built over them. Just as they had started a fire for burning the brick there came a severe rain storm, blowing down the house and making of the brick kiln one large pile of mud. The other community kept at work and completed the brick building costing more than $14,000, of which $9,000 was paid in by the Negroes themselves. The Bolivar community was not discouraged by the loss of the brick but began immediately to raise funds, and

School construction fund-raising rally in rural Alabama in the 1920s.
Courtesy of Fisk University Library.

Greene County Training School of Boligee, Alabama, constructed in
1925. Courtesy of Fisk University Library.

shortly after I left the state, work on an excellent four-teacher building with an auditorium was completed.[24]

Describing a similar instance, Smith recalled that for two years the
black citizens near Cedar Hill, Tennessee, "put forth heroic efforts in
raising money to build a four-teacher Rosenwald school." They succeeded in raising $1,600 in cash, used $600 of it to buy a four-acre tract
of land and deposited $1,000 in the bank to help pay for the cost of
construction. Before the construction began, however, the bank failed
and the people "lost every dollar of their money." Undaunted by this
great loss, the people rallied a second time under the leadership of the
local Jeanes teacher. Although they could not raise another $1,000 in
cash, "they donated their time and enough rough lumber to satisfy the
requirement of $1,000 by the Board of Education." In another West
Tennessee county, Smith observed, "an elderly Negro woman [donated]
10 to 15 acres of land on which to build a school, and later on a Rosenwald county training school was built there."[25]

Smith was succeeded as state agent of Negro education by O. H.
Bernard, formerly superintendent of schools in Robertson County, Tennessee. Bernard had helped build a Rosenwald school in Robertson in
1917. He recalled that the pivotal moment came when "an old colored
woman agreed to deed to the county a desirable building site consisting
of two acres of ground." With this land as a beginning, a small cash
appropriation was secured from the county Board of Education, which,
with free labor from blacks and money from the Rosenwald Fund, was
sufficient to complete a one-room schoolhouse.[26]

The well-known southern educator Leo M. Favrot was then the state
agent of Negro education in Arkansas when the first Rosenwald school
was erected there in Hempstead County in 1915. It was called the Red-
land School and was located near McCaskill. Furnished but unpainted, it
cost $2,300, of which $350 was contributed by the Rosenwald Fund,
$150 by the public school authorities, and $1,800 by the black residents.
Times were more difficult in Cleveland County, Arkansas, however, because blacks could contribute only a small sum in cash, "two or three
hundred dollars at the most," recalled Favrot. Still, the black residents of
Cleveland County were determined to build a decent schoolhouse for
their children. They were fortunate in having one resident who knew the
logging business and could run a sawmill. In 1920, as the Cleveland
County superintendent of public schools told Favrot, this black man,
having obtained a Rosenwald school blueprint, spearheaded a successful
school construction campaign. "He called together the men and boys of
the district and they went out into their own pine-timbered lands and cut
and sawed the logs as needed." Further, "They stacked, dried and dressed

The six-teacher Hardeman County, Tennessee, Training School was one of the more expensive and better constructed Rosenwald schools. Courtesy of Fisk University Library.

Biedenhard School of Warren County, Mississippi, and the workers who donated their labor to build it. This three-teacher frame building was a typical Rosenwald school. Courtesy of Fisk University Library.

their lumber" and hauled the finished material two and one-half miles to the construction site. The black people donated the lumber, all of the labor, and the land, and built a two-room schoolhouse that cost the community less than $400 in cash.[27]

Near Marche, Arkansas, was the Round Hill School. For fifty-nine years, school was taught "in a crude building, poorly lighted, without desks," except for homemade wooden benches. In 1921, recorded the Arkansas Rosenwald school agent, T. L. Dorman, only two meetings were required for black residents to change this condition. "Some pledged labor, others donated trees to be cut and sawed into lumber. The women and children picked berries and muscadines; these were sold and the proceeds given to the building committee." Eighty-year-old Mr. Tetline, whose health prohibited his contribution in labor, "gave his wagon and team to be used in hauling material." When the new building was dedicated in 1921 with a barbecue dinner, Mr. Tetline donated the beef for this extraordinary occasion.[28]

"In a great many communities," said J. B. Fulton, state agent of Negro education in South Carolina, "men who have accumulated some money have been willing to give mortgages on their own property in order to secure the pledges of their neighbors who have been less fortunate." Regarding black monetary contributions to public schools in Virginia, Harris Hart, state superintendent of public schools, said: "In some instances, the county boards have been able to contribute but little money towards the erection of these schools, and yet in these cases the people have gone ahead and signed notes for enough money to put up their part and also to take care of that part which the boards would gladly have given, but were unable to do so because of an insufficiency of funds." Hart recalled three examples of this behavior. In one county, "About nine men of the community signed notes putting up their homes in order to secure enough money for a school." In another county, blacks built a six-teacher county training school which cost about $12,000; the school board gave "only $100." In a third county, "The people have a four-teacher building, which cost around $8,000, but were able to secure only about $500 from the school officials of the county because of the stringency." The pattern had been routinized; southern school authorities consistently cried financial insolvency when pressed to support the development of common schools for black children and offered blacks no alternative for establishing universal public education except through the practice of double taxation, hard work, and time.[29]

In Jones County, Texas, blacks had no public school before a Rosenwald building was erected in the early 1920s. G. T. Bludworth, assistant state agent for Negro education, reported that it had once been known "to whites and blacks alike, that the sun must not go down on a negro's head in Jones County." But the onetime cattle raisers became cotton growers and "discovered it was next to impossible to successfully raise and gather the fleecy staple without the aid of the negro." Soon there was a substantial black community in Jones County with a school-age population of about 140 children. The black community held a "mass meeting" to discuss probable ways and means by which a school building could be constructed. "They finally agreed to donate three hundred days work, either on the building itself during the time of its erection or to hire out wherever work could be found, the wages to be turned in to the Board to apply on the building." With minimal aid from the public school authorities, the black community of Jones County, according to Bludworth, succeeded in building a schoolhouse "valued at ten thousand dollars."[30]

The rural blacks of another Texas county wanted a new two-teacher schoolhouse. Their old school had been in use since the Civil War and was considerably dilapidated. Having very little cash, they resorted to means practiced by rural blacks throughout the American South. In the words of Bludworth:

> The Negroes held a conference among themselves and decided since they owned lands upon which the pine grew to donate the timber sufficient to purchase the lumber necessary. The proposition was accepted by the County superintendent. The negroes felled the trees and hauled the logs (after sawing them) to the sawmills nearby and exchanged the logs for seasoned lumber. With this lumber, labor donated and the money available, together with the aid of the Rosenwald Fund, they erected and equipped a new Rosenwald building and dedicated it with great elan.

Blacks in Wood County, Texas, turned to similar tactics when informed by the public school authorities that there was "no money for building purposes." "Not to be outdone," said Bludworth, "the negroes of the community met, elected one of their number as their leader and decided to plant a community crop of cotton, the proceeds to go into the building." The people cultivated and harvested enough cotton to purchase the land, lumber, and most of the equipment for the new schoolhouse. Wood County's black residents, with money from the Rosenwald Fund and their labor donated, constructed and equipped a "modern" school. Black Texans were not the only ones who grew a crop to finance a school. From Mrs. J. E. Johnson, president of the Parent-Teachers Association of Prentiss, Mississippi, comes a similar story. In that community "the farmers pledged an acre or less of cotton to be called 'The Rosenwald Patch' and the proceeds were to be used for the building."[31]

Nearly all of the philanthropic and public school officials who worked in the area of southern black education recognized that rural blacks paid a high price for "public" schooling that should have been financed by tax revenues. "The sacrifices made by the Negroes themselves," said D. L. Lewis, supervisor of rural schools in South Carolina, "bespeak for them the finest kind of interest in the education of their children." As he recalled: "In Jasper County, South Carolina, which is predominantly a Negro county, a young Negro man, who has been blind almost from birth and who has received some education, feeling the call of his people, gave ceaseless effort to the establishment of a Rosenwald school in his community. As a result of his self-sacrificing work a splendid four-room Rosenwald building was erected and equipped, and this blind Negro is now serving as one of the teachers." W. T. B. Williams, the black educator who in the 1920s was field director for the John F. Slater Fund and the Anna T. Jeanes Fund, seemed somewhat less surprised by the actions of rural blacks. "Usually it is not difficult to interest Negroes in the building of Rosenwald schools," he said. Nevertheless, even Williams noted some of their sacrifices: "I saw recently at the dedication of a fine Rosenwald school a colored man with no children who had mortgaged his farm to secure the money necessary to complete the building." "No sacrifice is too great for them to make," Williams concluded.[32]

Such testimony by Rosenwald school agents, Jeanes teachers, rural school supervisors, and state agents of Negro education across the South demonstrates convincingly that these school construction campaigns were not isolated incidents but examples of widespread grass-roots reforms that epitomized the educational beliefs and behavior of black southerners. J. B. Fulton, state agent for Negro schools in South Carolina, had witnessed the establishment of a Rosenwald school in every county in the state except three, "and one of these three has a building under construction." Fulton knew of "many human interest stories" in connection with the building of rural schools for black children. He seemed most impressed, however, with the selfless behavior of the more well-to-do black men: "In a great many communities men who have accumulated some money have been willing to give mortgages on their own property in order to secure the pledges of their neighbors who have been less fortunate." Similarly, Zela Fields, a Jeanes teacher in Colbert County, Alabama, recorded that the local blacksmith, Foster Nolen, deeded one acre of his land to the local school officials and gave the first timber toward the construction of a new school. Nolen, "a man about seventy-five or eighty years old," regretted deeply that he had no strength to help build the school with his own hands. Whether it was Colbert County, Alabama, or Jasper County, South Carolina, the beliefs and behavior of rural blacks in this crusade for common schools reflected and reinforced cumulative Afro-American traditions that had developed over time and spread over space. The common patterns of behavior among black men and women of diverse social environments evidence the educational and communal values blacks transmitted from generation to generation. Thus the behavior of blacks in the second crusade for universal common schooling was strikingly similar to the behavior of former slaves in their campaign for universal public education during the Reconstruction era.[33]

In addition to the money, land, labor, and building materials that rural blacks gave to pay for the costs of schoolhouse construction, they also contributed significant amounts of money and labor to the maintenance and improvement of school buildings. In the late 1920s, each of fourteen southern states established "Rosenwald School Day," an annual event that punctuated the year-long campaigns to raise money and contribute labor for school improvement activities. The money raised on Rosenwald Day and during the school term for the academic year 1930–31 is summarized in Table 5.4. It is significant that even during a year of the Great Depression rural blacks raised $81,377.13 during the academic year and $9,471.12 on Rosenwald Day, a combined total of $90,848.25. This practice continued beyond the Rosenwald Fund's termination of its contributions in 1932 to the black rural school building campaign. In 1933, for instance, black people in Tennessee contributed $803.99 in cash on Rosenwald Day and collected $7,507.71 during the 1932–33 academic year. During the same academic year blacks in Virginia contributed $5,220, in Mississippi they collected $1,965, and in North Carolina they raised $14,000. These practices continued through the 1930s. In 1937 the enterprising black residents of East Baton Rouge, Louisiana, showed a film of the Joe Louis–Max Schmeling boxing match as a means to raise funds for school improvement activities.[34]

It was particularly painful for black southerners to make private contributions for the maintenance of public schools during the late 1920s and 1930s because their already low incomes dropped sharply during these hard economic times. Various studies at the time revealed the extremely low incomes of these rural black families. Studies of black farm families who were chiefly tenants and sharecroppers showed that few were able to earn beyond what was required for bare subsistence. The average annual income in 1934 of a selected group of more than two thousand of these families was $105.43. Distributed among a family of five persons, this represented a monthly income of about $1.75 per person. Farm owners earned more, but they made up scarcely more than 20 percent of rural black families. A study of six hundred black families in an Alabama rural area in 1932 documented average annual earnings of $90. Arthur Raper, who examined two counties in Georgia in 1927, and again in 1934, found that the black families averaged $302 in 1927 in

TABLE 5.4
Summary of Rosenwald School Day Program by States for the Academic Year 1930–1931

State	Number reporting				Number attending Rosenwald School Day program	Money collected for school improvement	
	Counties	Schools	Teachers	Pupils enrolled		Rosenwald Day	During year
Alabama	39	113	375	15,653	13,584	$ 484.02	$ 6,739.80
Arkansas	25	79	*	*	3,215	2,415.00	*
Florida	25	86	276	11,996	2,184	411.68	2,433.10
Georgia	49	67	297	10,770	2,785	328.76	7,070.44
Kentucky	21	21	88	3,203	2,798	44.50	865.31
Louisiana	29	105	345	16,769	5,669	251.56	4,308.28
Mississippi	37	104	408	18,496	8,006	518.83	6,573.82
Missouri	7	38	64	3,105	473	546.32	836.22
North Carolina	81	565	1,851	75,631	22,268	1,052.33	19,114.02
Oklahoma	36	132	300	10,098	5,291	185.57	1,714.79
South Carolina	36	119	483	21,989	10,277	734.23	8,138.51
Tennessee	38	187	422	17,522	19,280	514.82	7,915.72
Texas	39	108	285	11,313	7,750	734.40	5,499.00
Virginia	51	244	415	16,243	8,972	1,249.10	10,168.12
Totals	513	1,968	5,609	232,788	112,552	$9,471.12	$81,377.13

Source: Statistical Reports on Rural School Construction Program, Box 331, JRFP-FU.
*Data not submitted.

Rosenwald School Day at Bethlehem School of Monroe County, Arkansas. The schoolchildren are displaying the cans they carried throughout the community to collect money for school maintenance and improvements. Courtesy of Fisk University Library.

Dublin School of Coahoma County, Mississippi. In 1935 this school won the statewide prize in the Rosenwald Day "Improvement and Beautification" contest. Courtesy of Fisk University Library.

the first county and $380 in the second; but in 1934 their annual earn-ings were $190 and $299, respectively. Black farm laborers earned as little as $86 annually. Some of these families spent half of their incomes for food alone. Detailed studies of diet made at various points indicated serious deviations from the standard in calories. Meanwhile, rural blacks were forced to take from their meager annual incomes and contribute money to the construction and maintenance of public schools for black children because southern state and local governments refused to accept responsibility for black public education.[35]

Of the resources contributed to sustain and improve rural black schools, particularly during the economically lean years of the late 1920s and 1930s, the free labor for maintenance and repair work probably constituted an even larger share than cash donations. A Rosenwald school maintenance report from Louisiana indicates the value of labor contributed to school improvement for the 1932–33 academic year. The formula used for estimating the market value of labor contributions al-lowed two dollars per day for men, one dollar for women, and one-half dollar for children. Therefore, it was estimated that for school mainte-nance, rural blacks in Louisiana contributed labor valued at $2,947.33. This contribution was the larger share of resources donated in Louisiana for the 1932–33 academic year. The school improvement activities per-formed included the beautification of grounds, protecting the drinking water, providing fuel sheds, painting school buildings every three years, and serving hot lunches. Studies of southern school finances for the period demonstrate that school officials, though very reluctant to appro-priate money for schoolhouses and teachers for black children, expended virtually no funds for school maintenance, repair, supplies, and transpor-tation. Black teachers, parents, and citizens taxed themselves for public school improvement costs, and this practice became increasingly difficult as poor rural communities experienced the Great Depression.[36]

The educational activities of southern rural blacks during the second crusade for universal common schooling permit us to see whether whole ranges of their behavior between 1860 and 1935 were accurate indica-tors of enduring cultural beliefs in education that were transmitted from generation to generation. Studying the black experience at a particular moment in time in contradistinction to studying it at different moments in time can be very misleading. Horace Mann Bond, for instance, wrote his classic study of the history and sociology of black education during the Great Depression. Disappointed with the progress of black education at that time, Bond maintained that "the Negro parent needs to become conscious in a greater measure of the values of education." Bond then pointed out that "during the Reconstruction Period, education was a passion with Negroes." Moreover, he recognized that the Rosenwald school campaigns had energized the collective will and educational ambitions of southern rural black communities. Yet, to Bond, these developments seemed fragmented and discontinuous, and he credited much of the black behavior to the external stimuli provided by northern philanthropic foundations. Bond failed to understand, however, that Afro-Americans did not have to be transformed into a new class of people who valued education, for they already did. It did not take the Civil War, emancipation, or northern philanthropic foundations to acculturate blacks because blacks carried within their culture enduring beliefs in the value of learning and self-improvement. The war and Reconstruction (1860–77) and the World War I migration and resulting common school crusade (1914–32) enlarged the arenas in which ordinary black men and women could make choices. During such periods they could do and say what often could not be done and said in more oppressive times. What southern rural blacks did during the second common school crusade only revealed what they had thought but could not act upon during the period following Reconstruction, when planters and white small farmers virtually excluded them from the benefits of public education.[37]

Moreover, what rural blacks did during the period 1914 to 1932 could not be done during the Great Depression. The cycles remind one of the words from the black spiritual, "Nobody Knows the Trouble I've Seen": "Sometimes I'm up; sometimes I'm down; sometimes I'm almost to the ground." By the mid-1930s rural black southerners were pressed to the ground. Their behavior of self-help and practice of double taxation, though not extinguished completely, became much less substantial than in the preceding decades. Many new schoolhouses had been built between 1914 and 1932, but the wooden frame one- and two-teacher buildings needed daily maintenance and repair work, and the schoolchildren needed transportation, equipment, books, and supplies. Traditionally, most of these "auxiliary" expenses had been borne by black teachers and parents. Yet examples from North Carolina, Virginia, and Maryland indicate that during the worst years of the depression not even the most committed black parents and teachers could continue to bear "auxiliary" expenses. In 1934 Geneva Holmes, a black teacher in Maxton, North Carolina, requested aid from the Rosenwald Fund for basic school supplies and equipment. Apologizing for having to make the request, she explained: "The teachers in the school use every means to try to secure equipment as individuals but our salaries have been cut so low that we are not able to use very much personal money for school equipment." In Bowling Green, Virginia, a black teacher named Nannie L. Craighead requested financial assistance to transport her students to a health clinic in Richmond. She reported that seventy-three of her seventy-six pupils had either enlarged tonsils, defective teeth, or defective vision. Blacks in

St. Inigoes, Maryland, needed funds to overhaul their dilapidated school buildings, but the local white school officials refused to make the repairs. According to the black Reverend E. P. Moon, the white public schools of St. Inigoes were "modern and teachers well paid." Yet the black public schools there were neglected. "We weep! We cry! We appeal to the authorities, but no attention is paid us," wrote Moon to the Rosenwald Fund. In New Bern, North Carolina, the black residents needed money to purchase a school bus because their children had to leave home at 6 A.M. to get to school on time and in the winter months they suffered frequently from overexposure to cold weather. The local school board would not provide a bus for black children. Such problems varied from town to town. In 1935 the black Parent-Teacher Association in Kelford, North Carolina, needed help with its project to install lights in the public school for black children. The local power company had stopped the power line about one mile from the school and refused to furnish service except at unreasonable expense. The Parent-Teacher Association decided to install a farm light plant and requested the Rosenwald Fund to assist in this endeavor.[38]

Before the Great Depression rural black southerners generally absorbed these expenses and much more out of their own resources. Their financial resources, however, had been drained thoroughly by the practice of double taxation during their second crusade for universal common schools. Then the Depression came and the passageways of earlier decades were momentarily shut off. In Columbia, North Carolina, the black school population was increasing rapidly in 1934, and the community needed badly to add two more classrooms to accommodate the new pupils. Despite deeply held beliefs in education and self-improvement, the black community had no money to act on its educational values. "We can't get much money, seemingly the people just can't get any money," wrote F. L. Blount, a black teacher in the elementary school for black children. Such conditions forced men like Blount to beg for money from private philanthropic foundations or, as he put it, "allow so many boys and girls to stay out of school because of conditions of which they are not responsible." Blount wrote reluctantly to Edwin Embree of the Rosenwald Fund:

> Mr. Embree, I know already that you have almost exhausted your funds on Negro Education and other good causes but we have just got to ask you for a little. Please if you can give us just a little money on our project here in this very humble community of good people. If you can't give us but a little that little will go a long way on our project. Please let me hear from you. If you don't have much money to give us you do have great advice that will go a long way in

pointing the way out for us. We do thank you for any thing that you
have to give us whether it be money, advice or encouragement.

Blount's letter reflected the spirit of a people who had been pressed to the
ground by the Great Depression. During the preceding two decades rural
black southerners had stood proudly on their own feet and pursued
universal schooling with a tenacity and determination unexcelled and
seldom, if ever, approached by their contemporary social classes. But
that was a different arena from the 1930s, and they could act on their
beliefs during the rural school crusade in ways that were impossible
during the succeeding decade. In maintaining their enduring beliefs in
education and self-improvement, however, they were fundamentally the
same people through both good and bad times.[39]

When the Rosenwald school building program ended in the early
1930s, rural black southerners had much to be proud of and much to
regret. On one hand, the process of double taxation and collective social
action enabled them to improve tremendously the material conditions of
their educational system; on the other, this same process was unjust and
oppressive, and their accommodation to double taxation helped extend
over them the power of their oppressors. Yet on the positive side, the
structure of black common schools was radically transformed by the
second crusade. In 1932 more than one-fourth of all the black schoolchildren in the South were taught in Rosenwald schools. As early as the
academic year 1925–26, 27.4 percent of southern rural black pupils and
29.7 percent of the rural black teachers were housed in Rosenwald
schools (see Table 5.5). Although the 3,464 Rosenwald schools erected
by 1926 constituted only 15.4 percent of the total 22,494 rural schools
for southern black children, their seating capacity was generally double
that of the average rural black school. Consequently, the average enrollment per rural black school in 1926 was 66 pupils; the average in Rosenwald schools was 120. In the fifteen southern states where the Rosenwald plan was in effect, Rosenwald schools were built in 880 or 66
percent of the 1,327 counties. Rosenwald schools were located in 95
percent of the counties in South Carolina, 90 percent of those in Alabama, 86 percent in Louisiana, Maryland, and North Carolina, and 75
percent in Virginia. These schools were spread throughout the South and
particularly in counties with large black populations.[40]

The second crusade for common schools resulted in a much more
developed elementary school system for black children. This significantly
improved structure of opportunity at the elementary level enabled black
southerners to alter radically their patterns of school enrollment and
attendance. During earlier decades they valued schooling but could not
act on their values because the opportunity to attend school was not

TABLE 5.5

Black Teachers and Student Enrollment in Southern States and Percentage of Rural Teachers and Students in Rosenwald Schools for the Academic Year 1925–1926

State	Teachers			Enrollment			Percentage of Rosenwald schools	
	Total	Rural	Urban	Total	Rural	Urban	Percentage of all rural black teachers	Percentage of all rural enrollment
Alabama	3,348	2,662	686	190,029	149,737	40,292	25.9	20.7
Arkansas	2,499	2,250	249	114,170	97,170	17,000	30.6	28.5
Florida	1,864	1,264	600	79,185	49,800	29,285	10.0	11.3
Georgia	4,444	3,312	1,132	257,674	167,488	90,186	13.4	12.0
Kentucky	1,337	789	548	45,854	26,531	19,323	28.7	38.5
Louisiana	2,500	1,600	900	137,000	100,000	37,000	48.7	35.1
Maryland	1,282	773	509	49,251	29,879	19,372	24.7	28.7
Mississippi	5,125	4,106	1,019	272,202	218,202	54,000	28.7	24.3
North Carolina	5,569	4,268	1,301	254,617	196,009	58,608	38.3	37.6
Oklahoma	1,213	705	508	43,761	26,610	17,151	30.9	36.8
South Carolina	4,228	2,967	1,261	234,707	162,844	71,863	38.3	31.4
Tennessee	2,556	1,708	848	116,535	75,335	41,200	40.2	41.0
Texas	4,436	3,388	1,048	198,763	99,069	99,694	18.9	29.2
Virginia	3,794	2,893	901	152,974	116,015	36,959	22.8	25.6
Totals	44,195	32,685	11,510	2,146,722	1,514,689	632,033	29.7	27.4

Source: Reports submitted by state supervisors of Negro education to S. L. Smith, director of the Rosenwald Fund's School Construction Program, Box 331, JRFP-FU.

available to the majority. By 1935, however, enough elementary schools had been built to accommodate the majority of black children. Indeed, there was a remarkable difference between black school enrollment patterns in 1900 and 1940. In 1900 the proportion of black children of elementary school age attending school was significantly lower than the corresponding proportion of whites. As illustrated in Table 5.1, in 1900 only 22 percent of blacks five to nine years of age and 52 percent of those ten to fourteen years of age were attending school. Of those black children aged five to fourteen, only 36 percent were in school. The proportion of white children aged five to fourteen attending school in the South in 1900 was markedly higher: 37 percent for whites aged five to nine, 76 percent for those aged ten to fourteen, and 55 percent for the entire age group. But the campaigns for black elementary schools in the rural South during the period 1900 to 1935 successfully transformed the structure of enrollment and attendance for younger black children. By 1940, as illustrated in Table 5.6, 66 percent of southern black children five to nine years of age were attending school compared to 65 percent of southern whites of the same age. Of blacks aged ten to fourteen, 90 percent were attending school in 1940, compared to 91 percent of the white children of the same ages. The school attendance rates of black children five to fourteen years of age increased from 36 percent in 1900 to 78 percent in 1940, and the corresponding rate for whites went from 55 percent in 1900 to 79 percent in 1940. Younger black children, whose rates of attendance were significantly lower than those of younger whites in 1900, had reached parity by 1940. This great transformation of the overall structure of black elementary schooling was in large part attributable to the school construction campaigns of the second crusade. To be sure, the overwhelming majority of younger black pupils attended wretched and inadequate one-teacher elementary schools. Their school terms were shorter than those for southern white pupils and their teachers were less well prepared and less well paid than white teachers. Still, there were school buildings, teachers, desks, and seats throughout the black South in 1940 that had not been available in 1900. This new access to common schooling allowed black southerners to act on enduring educational values in 1940 in ways that they could not in 1900. The remarkable transformation of black school attendance behavior reflected the intersection of enduring educational values with changing educational opportunities.

Nonetheless, it is important to consider the fundamental injustice and political costs of the system of double taxation that fueled the second crusade for black common schooling and enabled black southerners to have for the first time in their history at least the semblance of universal elementary education. First, the brunt of public taxation on real prop-

TABLE 5.6

Elementary School Attendance by Race and Age in Southern States, 1940

State	Number of children 5 to 9 years old, inclusive		Number attending school		Percent attending school		Number of children 10 to 14 years old, inclusive		Number attending school		Percent attending school	
	Black	White	Black	White	Black	White	Black	White	Black	White	Black	White
Alabama	114,289	190,209	70,566	123,833	62	65	113,310	201,031	100,414	189,483	89	94
Arkansas	50,896	149,377	33,877	99,460	67	67	51,089	155,251	45,679	136,949	89	88
Delaware	3,004	16,678	2,169	12,524	72	75	2,726	18,626	2,627	18,067	96	97
Florida	45,560	107,408	31,541	75,927	69	70	48,495	122,588	43,277	115,531	89	94
Georgia	122,083	196,973	81,711	137,019	67	70	120,045	204,964	104,714	189,197	87	92
Kentucky	17,411	268,588	11,124	112,980	64	42	19,073	274,785	16,148	172,632	85	63
Louisiana	84,488	143,488	56,741	97,808	67	68	90,586	153,250	79,105	145,125	87	95
Maryland	28,092	112,738	20,567	83,387	73	74	29,325	127,027	27,737	122,455	95	96
Mississippi	124,319	110,899	74,276	78,679	60	71	123,597	118,416	102,855	110,974	83	94
Missouri	18,746	271,242	14,947	208,682	80	77	19,737	296,447	18,477	281,587	94	95
North Carolina	115,375	268,466	78,089	176,437	68	66	118,097	283,283	109,643	268,921	93	95
South Carolina	103,500	110,536	65,834	76,677	64	69	101,607	114,382	92,019	109,957	91	96
Tennessee	46,572	237,235	31,091	152,451	67	64	48,630	245,454	44,720	221,439	92	90
Texas	92,450	501,032	63,607	319,333	69	64	94,988	532,417	90,196	501,003	95	94
Virginia	69,444	183,024	43,907	114,998	63	63	73,993	196,294	67,865	185,725	92	95
West Virginia	10,806	181,181	8,077	121,980	75	67	12,171	193,621	11,745	187,788	97	97
Totals	1,047,035	3,049,074	688,133	1,992,155	66	65	1,067,129	3,237,836	957,221	2,956,833	90	91

Source: U.S. Bureau of the Census, Sixteenth Census of the United States: 1940, Population, vol. 2, pt. 1, pp. 217, 399, 907; pt. 2, pp. 25, 197; pt. 3, pp. 185, 343, 517; pt. 4, p. 213; pt. 5, p. 277; pt. 6, pp. 357, 571, 773; pt. 7, pp. 145, 453.

erty, land, and business fell heavily on the region's black laborers. A good share of the taxes levied on southern planters and industrialists was transformed into lower wages paid to common laborers. Second, although this particular form of so-called "self-help" reinforced and taught sacrifice, it was terribly unjust. Black southerners paid their taxes as citizens, and while white taxpayers got a system of free public education, black taxpayers got virtually nothing except when they taxed themselves again. The Rosenwald school building campaign was the most visible component of a deeper and wider process of double taxation. Even before the Rosenwald projects began, southern state school officials recognized that black citizens were willing to tax themselves voluntarily to obtain school buildings, equipment, and teachers, and officials encouraged this voluntary taxation. Moreover, examples from some states indicate that school authorities viewed double taxation as a necessary and just burden to be borne by black citizens. N. C. Newbold, an eminent white state school official in North Carolina, became the state's first agent of Negro rural schools in June 1913, at least three years before there were Rosenwald projects in North Carolina. In his first annual report on the conditions of black rural education, Newbold stated: "The average negro rural schoolhouse is really a disgrace to an independent, civilized people. To one who does not know our history, these schoolhouses, though mute, would tell in unmistaken terms a story of injustice, inhumanity and neglect on the part of our white people." He attributed the wretched state of rural black schooling to two causes. It had taken "all our time, thought and money these latter years to rebuild and equip in even a modest way the schoolhouses for our own children." More important, "In the main the best, most tolerant minded, far reaching among us have regarded the negro schools as a liability rather than an asset." "Many have gone on the theory," Newbold continued, "that the poorer the school supplied to the Negroes, the better it would be for society and the state." Yet he was optimistic regarding progress in black rural education because the attitude of whites toward black education appeared to be changing for the better, and black citizens showed a willingness to impose upon themselves a voluntary tax to finance the construction of schoolhouses for their children. Newbold viewed this practice of double taxation among blacks as "only fair to the white people of the state" because blacks in the past had "depended upon the meagre school tax to do all for them." In other words, Newbold expected black citizens to depend heavily on their private resources to build a system of "public" schools for black children, while the school tax, which was paid by all the citizens of the state—black and white—was used disproportionately to build schools for white children.[41]

For the academic year 1913 to 1914, Newbold reported that the amount of money raised by rural blacks for new buildings was $9,396.37, and the value of labor given by them for new buildings was $6,384.89. Similarly, the first state supervisor of rural elementary schools in Virginia, Jackson Davis, began his new job in 1911 and quickly took note of and encouraged the practice of double taxation among Virginia's black citizens. He discovered the existence of black "school leagues" throughout Virginia, and accounts of their activities appeared regularly in his monthly reports. For the academic year 1914–15, at least two years before there were any Rosenwald projects in Virginia, Davis reported that "School Leagues were organized at 680 schools, and they contributed in cash for new schools, equipment, extensions of terms, and improvements $46,738.67." Clearly, Davis understood that those contributions represented a system of double taxation, but he thought it merited praise instead of condemnation. As he put it,

> It is sometimes said that negroes do not pay enough school taxes to run their own schools, but these facts indicate that they not only pay willingly according to the value of their property, but that many go beyond this with personal contributions to their schools, amounting in 35 counties to $46,738.67. This is, in reality, a voluntary school tax, and often means a sacrifice, but it speaks volumes of the desire of an increasing number of home-owning Negroes to give their children good schools at home, and to keep them in the country trained for useful citizenship.

Davis was succeeded as state supervisor of rural elementary schools by Arthur D. Wright, who reported that during the 1914–15 academic year Virginia's black school leagues raised "a total voluntary school tax of $33,689." As Richard R. Wright, Jr., demonstrated in *Self-Help in Negro Education*, such practices were common throughout the black South.[42]

Although we shall never know the precise amount in cash, land, and labor contributed by black southerners to public school authorities, a vast quantity of primary sources indicates that the double taxation of black southerners was a widespread and long-standing custom. We see a certain fineness or heroism in the sacrifices made by such poor and ordinary men and women. Indeed, as Davis said, their actions spoke volumes about their beliefs in learning and self-improvement. For black southerners, that particular way of living had been a common experience since slavery. Yet the traditions of double taxation and extraordinary sacrifice had distinct limits, beyond which they were both unjust and dangerous. One limit was the point at which "self-help" became unconscious submission to oppression. In vital respects, the regionwide process of double taxation was an accommodation to the oppressive nature of southern society. It made the regular process of excluding black children from the benefits of tax-supported public education easier and more bearable for both whites and blacks. It said much about blacks' desire for education and their willingness to sacrifice for it, but it also said much about their powerlessness, their taxation without representation, and their oppression. The process of double taxation also reflected the manner in which black southerners during the period 1900 to 1935 interpreted and dealt with their oppression. They submitted to the process because they felt that it was the only way they could secure an education for their children, a way to protect and develop their communities, a way to sustain passageways to better times.

6

THE BLACK PUBLIC

HIGH SCHOOL AND THE

REPRODUCTION OF CASTE

IN THE URBAN SOUTH,

1880–1935

DURING THE PERIOD from 1880 to the mid-1930s almost all of the few black high schools in the South were located in urban areas. Hence the study of the development of black secondary education necessitates an examination of the interrelationship between education and political economy in the urban South. The most oppressive feature of black secondary education was that southern local and state governments, though maintaining and expanding the benefits of public secondary education for white children, refused to provide public high school facilities for black children. Almost all of the southern rural communities with significantly large Afro-American populations and more than half of the major southern cities failed to provide any public high schools for black youth. The virtual absence of black public high schools reflected the opposition of the vast majority of white southerners, particularly in the rural communities and small towns, to black secondary education. Blacks in the rural South were excluded from the revolution in public secondary education that characterized the nation and the region during the period 1880 to 1935. Blacks in the urban South were not affected significantly by the marked extension of public secondary education until after 1920, when increased migration, changes in the labor market, and a growing population of black adolescents forced a new attentiveness to the need for black public secondary education. This movement, however, was quite different in character and content than the general expansion of both northern and southern public secondary education.

Both contemporary observers and later scholars agree that it was in the period 1880 to 1930 that the American high school was transformed from an elite, private institution into a public one attended by the children of the masses. At the beginning of this era less than 3 percent of the national high school age population—either those aged fourteen to seventeen or fifteen to nineteen—was enrolled in high school and even fewer attended regularly. The National Survey of Secondary Education reported that, in 1930, some 47 percent of the nation's children of high school age were enrolled in public secondary schools. This enrollment, in the words of the then commissioner of education, was so unusual for the secondary level that it attracted the attention of Europe, where only 8 to 10 percent of the high school age population attended high school. By 1934, the proportion of American children of high school age enrolled in public high schools had increased to 60 percent, and, including private school enrollments, it approximated 64 percent. Decades earlier, in 1880, American secondary education was mainly private and attended largely by children of well-to-do families. The relatively high increase in secondary school enrollment was caused by the expansion of public high school facilities. In the late 1880s, as more public school facilities were established, public secondary enrollment exceeded private for the first time. Over the next four decades public high schools were built in large numbers; city, state, and federal school reports, as well as reports by private philanthropic foundations, bulged with photographs and feature stories on the new fortresslike public high school buildings. State by state public high schools were made available to the masses, and enrollments in secondary education increased rapidly. By 1934, it had become the "people's college."[1]

The white South, in spite of its relatively impoverished economy, managed with the help of northern philanthropy to keep pace with the nation. In 1930 some 38 percent of the region's white children of high school age were enrolled in public secondary schools as compared with 47 percent for the nation as a whole. By 1934, for the nation as a whole, sixty pupils were enrolled in public high school for every one hundred children aged fourteen to seventeen, inclusive; for every hundred white southerners of the same ages, fifty-four pupils were enrolled in public secondary schools. Thus in the southern states the proportion of white children enrolled in public high school was 93 percent of that for the nation as a whole. In some southern states, notably Florida, Mississippi, Missouri, Delaware, North Carolina, and South Carolina, the proportion of white children enrolled was equal to or greater than the national proportion of 60 percent.[2]

The treatment accorded black children during the transformation of American secondary education helps to disentangle general class discrimination from its more specific form of racial oppression. By the early 1930s, state-sponsored and state-funded building campaigns had made public secondary schools available to all classes of white children. Afro-

Americans were generally excluded from the American and southern transformation of public secondary education. As illustrated in Table 6.1, in 1890 only .39 percent or 3,106 of the 804,522 black children of high school age were enrolled in high school and more than two-thirds of them were attending private high schools. The proportion of southern black children enrolled in secondary schools increased to 2.8 percent by 1910, as illustrated in Table 6.2, and the majority of these high school pupils were still enrolled in private schools. Although in 1910 black children represented 29 percent of the total secondary school population, they constituted only 5 percent of the pupils enrolled in the secondary grades of southern public schools. By 1930, the ratio of black public high school enrollment to school population reached 10.1 percent, and it jumped to 18 percent during the 1933–34 academic year. Even then it was 10 percent or less in Alabama, Arkansas, Georgia, and Mississippi. The proportion of children enrolled in high school in 1934 was nearly four times as great for the white population as for Afro-Americans in Alabama, between four and five times as great in Arkansas, Florida, and Louisiana, and slightly more than five times as great in Georgia and South Carolina. The disparity was greatest in Mississippi, where there were proportionately more than nine times as many white as black children enrolled in public high schools in 1934. Significantly, Mississippi was at that time the only state in America in which black children constituted the majority of the total secondary school population. By the early 1930s, therefore, when rural whites, urban working-class whites, and the children of European immigrants had been brought systematically into the "people's college," black children as a class were deliberately excluded. In 230 southern counties blacks constituted 12.5 percent or more of the total population, but no high school facilities were available for black youth, and 195 other counties, with a similar proportion of blacks, had elementary schools with one or two secondary grades attached but had no four-year high schools for black children.[3]

A major factor that shaped the discriminatory nature of black secondary education during the first three decades of the twentieth century was the United States Supreme Court's 1899 decision in the case of *Cumming v. School Board of Richmond County, Georgia*. This case reflected the unique oppression of Afro-American people and set their experience apart from the prejudice and ethnic discrimination encountered by European immigrants and the more general discrimination against working-class people. The case began in 1880, when the Richmond County School Board, after a long-standing demand by the local black community, established Ware High School in Augusta, Georgia. It was the only public high school for blacks in Georgia and one of perhaps four in the eleven former Confederate states. Ware High became a solid academic

TABLE 6.1

High School Enrollment by Age, Race, and Southern States, 1890

State	Total population 15 to 19 years of age		Number enrolled in public and private high schools				Percentage high school enrollment is of population 15 to 19 years of age	
			Black		White			
	Black	White	Public	Private	Public	Private	Black	White
Alabama	81,558	93,035	0	90	693	2,508	.11	3.4
Arkansas	37,241	95,122	56	29	1,106	640	.22	1.8
Delaware	3,091	14,173	0	0	1,255	297	.00	10.9
Florida	19,203	23,996	10	46	866	211	.29	4.4
Georgia*	100,241	108,946	0	316	2,330	9,764	.31	9.3
Kentucky	30,473	178,569	155	67	2,597	2,609	.72	2.9
Louisiana	62,012	62,042	0	111	778	1,280	.17	3.3
Maryland	23,673	86,764	0	68	1,255	1,695	.28	3.4
Mississippi	90,611	62,693	0	90	561	2,104	.09	4.3
Missouri	17,106	279,516	354	54	7,243	3,936	2.40	4.0
North Carolina	69,593	113,732	70	379	510	4,524	.64	4.4
South Carolina	80,609	50,890	22	355	669	1,532	.46	4.3
Tennessee	52,489	153,227	0	263	1,031	4,648	.50	3.7
Texas	55,893	189,361	209	190	3,693	4,041	.71	4.1
Virginia	76,702	112,447	62	90	2,122	3,081	.19	4.6
West Virginia	4,027	81,800	20	0	467	200	.49	.81
Totals	804,522	1,706,313	958	2,148	27,176	41,070	.39	4.0

Source: U.S. Commissioner of Education, Annual Report, 1890–91, 2:792, 1470–71; U.S. Bureau of the Census, Report on Population of the United States at the Eleventh Census, 1890, pt. 1, pp. 832–78.

*Report of the State School Commissioner of Georgia, 1890 (Atlanta, 1890), pp. 156–60.

TABLE 6.2
High School Enrollment by Age, Race, and Southern States, 1910

| State | Total population 15 to 19 years of age | | Number enrolled in public and private high schools | | | | Percentage high school enrollment is of population 15 to 19 years of age | |
| | | | Black | | White | | | |
	Black	White	Public	Private	Public	Private	Black	White
Alabama	99,130	130,280	1,680	1,290	14,025	2,012	2.9	12.3
Arkansas	50,309	123,518	366	606	6,227	1,304	1.9	6.1
Delaware	3,228	16,230	65	86	1,661	227	4.7	11.6
Florida	30,891	45,190	187	433	3,099	375	2.0	7.7
Georgia	129,923	150,446	648	1,528	19,833	3,063	1.7	15.2
Kentucky	28,163	213,423	1,342	563	6,874	24,537	6.7	14.7
Louisiana	76,868	98,251	98	1,101	4,778	864	1.6	5.7
Maryland	23,398	104,997	496	318	7,641	1,786	3.5	9.0
Mississippi	112,527	83,576	387	1,427	7,349	1,111	1.6	10.1
Missouri	14,765	319,266	1,183	363	31,705	3,237	10.5	10.9
North Carolina	80,253	161,587	880	2,224	13,470	4,347	3.9	11.0

South Carolina	99,118	73,519	198	919	7,964	488	1.1	11.5
Tennessee	54,363	183,283	538	1,296	9,094	5,728	3.4	8.1
Texas	77,329	345,830	1,363	1,488	29,096	3,600	3.7	9.5
Virginia	75,047	142,144	688	2,405	10,879	3,165	4.1	9.9
West Virginia	6,575	118,560	87	300	3,949	779	5.9	4.0
Totals	961,887	2,310,100	10,206	16,347	177,644	56,623	2.8	10.1

Sources: U.S. Bureau of the Census, *Negro Population, 1790–1915*, p. 192; U.S. Bureau of the Census, *Thirteenth Census of the United States, Population*, vol. 3, Table 7; U.S. Commissioner of Education, *Report for the Year 1909–10*, vol. 2, pp. 1142, 1153, 1261–62; Alabama State Department of Education, *Annual Report of the Department of Education*, 1912, pp. 307, 317; North Carolina State Department of Public Instruction, *Biennial Report of the Superintendent of Public Instruction, 1910–11*, pp. 17, 19; Georgia State Department of Education, *Thirty-Ninth Annual Report to the General Assembly of Georgia*, pp. 266–83; Kentucky State Department of Education, *Biennial Report of the Superintendent of Public Instruction, 1910–11*, pp. 11–16, 84–88, 118–22; South Carolina State Department of Education, *Forty-Third Annual Report of the State Superintendent of Education, 1911*, pp. 137–39, 161.

secondary school, a source of pride and an avenue of mobility for Augusta's striving black community. Yet on 10 July 1897, the school board, pointing to the need for more black elementary schools and claiming that the schools were financially hard-pressed, voted to terminate Ware High and to use its annual budget of $845 to hire four new teachers for the black elementary schools. This decision aroused a storm of protest in the local black community and set in motion a series of lawsuits that started in the local superior court and ended up in the U.S. Supreme Court.[4]

The lawyers for Augusta's black plaintiffs pointed out before the U.S. Supreme Court that the *Plessy* v. *Ferguson* case of 1896 allowed states to establish racial segregation only if the accommodations and facilities in public institutions were equal. In other words, even if the racial segregation of schoolchildren was constitutional, the opportunities offered students of each race had to be substantially the same, if courts followed the "equal, but separate" rule of *Plessy*. The vast majority of previous decisions in both southern and northern courts favored this interpretation of *Plessy*. Yet in his opinion for the U.S. Supreme Court, Justice John Marshall Harlan circumvented the question of whether *Plessy* required equal school facilities by simply not discussing the issue. Upon his belief that the school board would respond to a court injunction by closing the white high schools instead of reopening Ware, Harlan concluded that the black plaintiffs' demand for substantially equal facilities would damage white children without assisting blacks. This was a gross violation of the separate but equal principle established in *Plessy*. Harlan ruled that to sustain an equal protection claim, the plaintiffs had to show positively that it was race and race alone that led to the school board's action. In behalf of the Supreme Court, Harlan ruled that no such case was established. This ruling was issued even though the plaintiffs' lawyers demonstrated that the Richmond County School Board provided sufficient elementary schools for whites but not blacks, paid substantially higher salaries to white than to black teachers, and closed Ware, the only black public high school, while continuing two white public high schools. If this was not proof of racially discriminatory behavior, then blacks throughout the South had virtually no hope of sustaining an equal protection claim, and, consequently, both the equal protection clause of the Fourteenth Amendment and the "equal, but separate" rule of *Plessy* were meaningless.[5]

The U.S. Supreme Court ruling in *Cumming* transformed the promise of equal protection into "a derisive taunt." More specifically, the peculiar ruling meant that southern school boards did not have to offer public secondary education for black youth. This was the first time the U.S. Supreme Court confronted the problem of racial discrimination in education, and its decision was significant in the development of southern black secondary education. It was not until 1945 that a full four-year public high school, which was what Ware had been, was reestablished in Richmond County, Georgia. Indeed, black southerners in general, especially in rural areas, did not receive public secondary schools until after World War II. Even in the major urban areas little was done between the closing of Ware High in 1897 and 1930. A survey of black secondary education, as illustrated in Table 6.3, reveals that, in 1915, most major southern cities had no public high schools for black children. Twenty-three cities of twenty thousand or more inhabitants, with black high school age populations ranging from 18 to 59 percent of the total high school age populations, had no three- or four-year public secondary schools for black children. In 1915, there lived in these twenty-three cities 48,765 black and 76,708 white children between the ages of fifteen and nineteen, inclusive. In the same cities there were 17,814 white children and no black children enrolled in four- or three-year public high schools. Although they represented 39 percent of the total secondary school age population, black children constituted zero percent of the enrollment in public high schools.[6]

Having effectively restrained the development of public secondary education for black children, southern states proceeded with vigor to make public high schools available to white children. At the turn of the century, the public high school, as an essential part of an organized state education system, had not been developed in the South. During the years from 1865 to 1885 the need for elementary schools was so great that little attention was paid to public secondary education. As late as 1888, the United States commissioner of education reported only 67 public high schools in the southern states, and in 1898 only 796. Over the next two decades southern states, in partnership with the General Education Board, laid a solid foundation for universalizing white public secondary education. In 1905 the board initiated a reform campaign that in the long run proved extraordinarily successful. At that time many southern state departments of education did not have sufficient funds to quicken the pace of secondary school construction that had begun in the late nineteenth century. Because of the lack of money and personnel, local movements were making slow and irregular progress. At this juncture the board stated its willingness to make appropriations to the several southern state universities for the salaries and traveling expenses of a professor of secondary education. His primary work was to ascertain where conditions were favorable for the establishment of public high schools; to organize in such places public high schools in accordance with the laws of the state; and to foster in such communities a public sentiment conducive to sustaining public high schools. The board insisted that

TABLE 6.3
Southern Cities of 20,000 or More Inhabitants without Public High Schools for Blacks, 1915

| City | Distribution of secondary education | | | | High school age population (15–19) | | Percentages of blacks and whites in high school age population | | Total population | | Percentages of blacks and whites in total population | |
| | Number of public high schools | | Enrollment in public high schools | | | | | | | | | |
	Black	White	Black	White	Black	White	Black	White	Black	White	Black	White
Mobile	0	2	0	951	2,057	2,787	42	58	22,763	28,758	44	56
Montgomery	0	2	0	609	1,984	1,889	51	49	19,322	18,814	51	49
Atlanta	0	4	0	2,723	7,184	10,013	34	66	51,902	102,937	34	66
Augusta	0	2	0	549	1,968	2,212	47	53	18,344	22,696	45	55
Columbus	0	1	0	450	710	1,226	37	67	6,047	12,910	37	63
Macon	0	3	0	987	1,819	2,319	44	56	18,150	22,515	45	55
Savannah	0	1	0	657	3,059	2,970	51	49	33,246	31,818	51	49
New Orleans	0	4	0	2,895	8,755	25,088	26	74	89,262	249,813	26	74
Shreveport	0	1	0	702	1,403	1,213	54	46	13,896	14,119	50	50
Charlotte	0	1	0	623	1,311	2,247	37	63	11,752	22,262	35	65
Wilmington	0	1	0	406	1,439	995	59	41	12,107	13,641	47	53
Winston-Salem	0	1	0	414	2,693	3,277	45	55	20,735	27,660	43	57
Charleston	0	2	0	690	3,198	2,722	54	46	31,056	27,777	53	47
Columbia	0	2	0	622	1,211	1,314	48	52	11,546	14,773	44	56

Newport News	0	1	0	321	347	1,581	18	82	3,714	16,491	82	18
Portsmouth	0	1	0	594	1,088	2,304	32	68	11,617	21,573	35	65
Roanoke	0	1	0	846	936	2,753	25	75	7,924	26,950	23	77
Tampa	0	1	0	496	815	2,818	22	78	8,951	28,831	24	76
Pensacola	0	1	0	213	1,034	1,264	45	55	10,214	12,768	44	56
Jacksonville	0	1	0	576	2,738	2,514	52	48	29,293	28,406	51	49
Meridian	0	1	0	513	938	1,390	40	60	9,321	13,964	40	60
Jackson	0	1	0	517	970	943	51	49	10,544	10,718	50	50
Vicksburg	0	1	0	460	1,108	869	56	44	12,053	8,761	58	42
Totals	0	36	0	17,814	48,765	76,708	39	61	463,759	778,955	37	63

Source: Included are all public schools (except colleges) offering either a four-year or three-year course of secondary study. *Thirteenth Census of the United States, 1910, Population,* 2:44, 318, 370, 726; 3:292, 656, 742, 802, 954; *Fourteenth Census of the United States, 1920, Population,* 2:342; U.S. Bureau of Education, *Negro Education,* Bulletin, 1916, No. 39, vol. 2, pp. 27–668; U.S. Commissioner of Education, *Annual Report of Education for the Year Ended June 30, 1917,* pp. 116–33; Florida State Department of Public Instruction, *Biennial Report of the Superintendent of Public Instruction of the State of Florida,* p. 217.

these professors be state and university officials, answerable only to their state and university superiors. The board, claiming that it did not dictate or even suggest the lines along which the professors exerted themselves, paid the professors' salaries and expenses and required them to file with the board monthly reports of their activities.[7]

State by state the board pushed this plan across the South. The first contract was made in Virginia in 1905, and cooperative work was under way by 1910 in Alabama, Arkansas, Florida, Georgia, Kentucky, Louisiana, Tennessee, Mississippi, North Carolina, South Carolina, Virginia, and West Virginia. Some of the professors of secondary education, such as Bruce R. Payne of Virginia, went on to brilliant careers in southern education; all were educational crusaders, dedicated to the proposition that all white adolescents deserved access to a good public high school. Their reports contained detailed accounts of state statutes supporting the establishment of public high schools, the number and value of high school buildings, school equipment, cost, curriculum, teaching, and enrollment. Such information was diffused through special bulletins and the reports of state superintendents, so that white southerners were informed of their situation. These professors traveled extensively to address lay people, local school authorities, teachers, business organizations, and county and state conferences. Their investments soon paid high returns. By 1914, Virginia had 186 new high schools, Georgia had more than 200, Arkansas and South Carolina more than 100 each. Tennessee established 74 new public high schools; Alabama organized 60; Florida 45; Mississippi more than 30; and West Virginia, in spite of a late start, constructed 27 new public high schools. The location of these new schools was planned carefully so as to extend the benefits of secondary education to as many white youths as possible in the rural South. Of the 100 new four-year public high schools established in North Carolina between 1905 and 1914, 62 were rural and 48 were urban. This pattern was typical of the regionwide transformation of white secondary education. By 1935, the majority of southern white public high schools were located in rural areas. This distribution accounts in large part for the dramatic increases in southern white secondary enrollment and helps to explain how it reached virtual parity with the national enrollment by 1935.[8]

Black children were excluded from this emergent system of public secondary education. The number of four-year white public schools in Georgia, for instance, increased from 4 in 1904 to 122 in 1916. At that time Georgia had no four-year public high schools for its black children, who constituted 46 percent of the state's secondary school age population. This was not merely a condition of inequality but a process of racial oppression extending throughout the South. Similarly, in 1916, Mississippi, South Carolina, Louisiana, and North Carolina had no four-year public high schools for black children. Afro-American youth constituted 57 percent of Mississippi's secondary school age population, 57 percent of South Carolina's, 44 percent of Louisiana's, and 33 percent of North Carolina's. Florida, Maryland, and Delaware each had one public high school for black youth. In 1916 there were in all sixteen of the former slave states a total of only 58 public high schools for black children. Of this number 37 had four-year courses, 18 had three-year courses, and 3 had less than three-year courses. Over one-half (33 of the 58) of these public high schools were located in the border states of West Virginia, Tennessee, Texas, and Kentucky. Practically all the four-year and three-year black public high schools were located in large southern cities. Virtually no public high schools for black youth, even of two years, existed in southern rural communities, where more than two-thirds of the black children of high school age resided.[9]

Before 1920 southern black public secondary education was available primarily through private institutions. The total number of blacks enrolled in public and private secondary schools in 1916 was 20,872. Of these, 11,130 were enrolled in private high schools, 5,283 in public high schools, and 4,459 were in the secondary education departments of the twenty-eight land-grant and state normal schools and colleges. There were about 216 private black high schools in the South in 1916, and 106 of them offered four-year courses of study. Although black children throughout the former slave states depended heavily on the private system for the rare opportunity to attend high school, such dependence was greater in the deep South. Although scarcely a fourth of the black pupils enrolled in secondary grades in the border states were in private schools, slightly more than three-fourths of the pupils in Alabama, Arkansas, Florida, Georgia, Louisiana, Mississippi, North Carolina, and South Carolina combined were in private institutions. In 1916, fully 95 percent of the southern black secondary school age population was not enrolled in public institutions, and in the deep South the proportion not enrolled in public secondary schools was 97 percent. The few high schools that did exist were grossly overcrowded; there was literally no place to sit for those not enrolled. Black children had been bypassed by the southern revolution in public secondary educational opportunities.[10]

This state of affairs reflected in part the relative power and consciousness of different classes of white southerners as they interacted with different segments of the Afro-American South. One group—the planters and their white working-class allies—formed a large majority of the white southern people in most states and counties, particularly in the country districts and small towns. This coalition did not believe in the education of black children and accepted only the barest rudiments of a black elementary school system, which they conceded only after realizing that the masses of black farmers, sharecroppers, and day laborers could not be forced or persuaded to tolerate less. The planters bitterly opposed any education for black children beyond the elementary grades. They used their influence in state and local governments to exclude black youth from the system of public secondary education. During the period 1880 to 1920, they were successful except in a few cities. The few black public high schools that did exist in this era were the result of joint efforts of local black leaders and urban white southerners. A few urban white southerners believed that the solution to the "race problem" and political stability in the region lay in part in a reasonable implementation of the "equal but separate" principle. This class remained small, and in most cases it had little influence. But here and there the "good white folk," as they were known, helped local blacks to acquire fairly decent high schools. One such white southern educator was John Herbert Phillips, the school superintendent of Birmingham, Alabama. In the late 1890s, Birmingham's black leaders, led by Dr. W. R. Pettiford, launched a campaign for a black high school. They won the crucial support of the president of the school board, Samuel Ullman. Despite the political disfranchisement campaign going on at the time and the opposition of some important local white political leaders, blacks gained approval for a public high school. Phillips supported their efforts. The high school was established in 1901 under the principalship of Arthur H. Parker. Such outcomes reflected black leaders' negotiations with local white business and professional "progressives" in an era when public black high schools were extremely rare. Their achievements in some of the major southern cities are illustrated in Table 6.4. The high schools growing out of these interracial efforts were about the only public high schools available to black children, and they constituted a fragmented system of secondary education for a few urban poor children who could not afford to go to private schools.[11]

This system of black public secondary education, however limited, is a significant indication of educational alternatives for black children in the South during the age of Booker T. Washington, 1895 to 1915. Both contemporary observers and later historians have portrayed the white South as taking a monolithic view of black education. Indeed, we are told that Washington and northern philanthropists placed prime emphasis on nonacademic, industrial education because that was all the white South would tolerate. Hence, when Thomas Jesse Jones, an agent of northern industrial philanthropy, conducted a study of black secondary and higher education in 1916, he was startled to find "the large place given to foreign languages and especially to the ancient languages" in southern black public high schools. Because these schools were established, regulated, and funded by local white school boards, and southern whites were supposed to tolerate only industrial education for black youth, it made no sense to Jones that virtually all of the few black public high schools in the region were of the "classical or college preparatory" type.[12]

In 1916 Virginia maintained six black public high schools. All emphasized the classical liberal curriculum. Many required their students to take Greek, and nearly all made Latin the central subject. Interestingly, the black public high school in Lynchburg was headed by Helen D. Urghart, a southern white woman, and taught by four southern white female instructors. Three years of Latin and algebra were offered along with history, physics, and English. The industrial education amounted to an elective course in manual training for boys, taught by a teacher from another city school, and cooking and sewing for girls. The black public high schools at Danville, Norfolk, Petersburg, Mount Hermon, and Richmond also emphasized the college preparatory curriculum. Similarly, the five black public high schools in Tennessee were academic rather than industrial institutions. The black high school at Chattanooga required its students to take four years of Latin; three years of Latin were required by the black high schools in Nashville, Knoxville, and Memphis. Lincoln Public High School, less classical than the other four, demanded only one year of Latin. Texas, with more than thirty black public high schools, had more than three times as many as any other southern state. The black secondary schools in the larger cities of San Antonio, Houston, Fort Worth, Dallas, and Beaumont, as well as those in the smaller towns of Temple, Dennison, and Palestine, offered the classical liberal curriculum. The black public high schools in Louisville, Paris, Frankfort, Bowling Green, Owensboro, Paducah, and Lexington, Kentucky, were of similar orientation. The classical liberal curriculum also pervaded the black high schools in Birmingham, Little Rock, Baltimore, St. Louis, and Kansas City. Indeed, during the period 1880 to 1920, despite the widespread advocacy of industrial education for black children, the limited system of black public secondary education in the South remained classical or college preparatory. This was possible because of the activities of local black leaders and the cooperation of a small class of moderate southern whites who believed in academic education for black children.[13]

After 1920, a particular coalition of southern white school reformers and northern industrial philanthropists combined to create a marked expansion of black public secondary education. Unlike the planters who opposed black secondary education, or the white southerners who cooperated with black leaders to establish classical liberal public high schools, this coalition came reluctantly to support a brand of industrial secondary

TABLE 6.4

Southern Cities of 20,000 or More Inhabitants with Public High Schools for Blacks, 1915

| City | Distribution of secondary education | | | | | | Percentages of blacks and whites in high school age population | | Total population | | Percentages of blacks and whites in total population | |
| | Number of public high schools | | Enrollment in public high schools | | High school age population (15–19) | | | | | | | |
	Black	White	Black	White	Black	White	Black	White	Black	White	Black	White
Birmingham	1	2	343	1,924	4,878	7,578	39	61	52,305	80,369	39	61
Little Rock	1	1	100	1,175	1,586	2,883	36	44	14,539	31,402	32	68
Fort Smith	1	1	60	734	446	1,945	19	81	4,456	19,519	19	81
Covington	1	1	34	483	237	5,175	3	97	2,899	50,371	5	95
Lexington	1	1	111	537	1,028	2,158	32	68	11,011	24,088	29	71
Louisville	1	2	402	2,847	3,607	18,545	16	84	40,522	183,390	18	82
Baltimore	1	2	788	4,471	7,607	46,636	14	86	84,749	473,387	15	85
St. Louis	1	5	811	7,221	3,335	63,075	5	95	43,960	642,488	6	94
Kansas City	1	4	462	5,439	1,279	19,429	10	90	25,566	224,677	10	90
Springfield	1	1	52	1,057	229	3,466	6	94	1,995	33,206	6	94
Knoxville	1	1	253	788	872	3,262	21	79	7,638	28,708	21	79
Memphis	1	2	303	1,244	4,885	7,083	41	59	52,441	78,590	40	60
Nashville	1	1	281	1,479	4,016	7,586	35	65	36,523	73,831	33	67
Dallas	1	4	243	2,907	1,696	7,069	19	81	18,024	74,080	20	80
El Paso	1	1	26	625	122	3,370	3	97	1,452	37,827	4	96
Houston	1	2	199	2,167	2,262	5,252	30	70	23,929	55,508	30	70
Fort Worth	1	2	133	2,310	1,648	5,510	18	82	13,280	60,032	18	82
Waco	1	1	169	1,256	613	2,194	22	78	6,067	20,358	22	78
Lynchburg	1	1	144	633	1,114	2,166	34	66	9,466	20,028	32	68

Norfolk	1	1	181	1,313	2,307	3,779	38	62	25,039	42,413	37	63
Petersburg	1	1	175	320	1,211	1,300	48	52	11,014	13,113	46	54
Richmond	1	3	394	2,124	4,808	8,057	37	63	46,749	80,879	37	63
Totals	22	40	5,664	43,054	49,786	229,684	18	82	533,624	2,348,264	19	81

Source: Included are all public schools (except colleges) offering either a four-year or three-year course of secondary study. *Thirteenth Census of the United States, 1910, Population,* 1:132, 178–80, 272, 437–63; U.S. Bureau of Education, *Negro Education,* Bulletin, 1916, No. 39, vol. 2, pp. 128, 573–672; Virginia State Board of Education, *Annual Report of the Superintendent of Public Instruction, 1914–15,* pp. 289–308; Birmingham, Alabama, Board of Education, *Annual Report of the Birmingham Schools, 1915,* p. 9; Covington, Kentucky, Board of Education, *Report,* pp. 36–37; Louisville, Kentucky, Board of Education, *Fifth Report of the Board of Education of Louisville, Kentucky, 1915 to 1916,* p. 254; Baltimore, Maryland, Board of School Commissioners, *Eighty-Seventh Annual Report,* pp. 42, 69; Missouri State Department of Education, *Sixty-Seventh Report of the Public Schools,* pp. 286–88, 304; Houston, Texas, Board of School Trustees, *Annual Report of Public Schools, 1917–18,* pp. 119–21; El Paso, Texas, Board of School Trustees, *Report of the Public Schools: 1914–15,* p. 36; Nashville, Tennessee, Board of School Commissioners, *Annual Report of the Public Schools, 1915–16,* p. 21; Memphis, Tennessee, Board of Education, *Annual Report, 1914–15,* p. 62; Knoxville, Tennessee, Board of Education, *Forty-Third Annual Report,* p. 13; U.S. Commissioner of Education, *Annual Report of Education for 1917,* 2:116–33.

education designed to train black children as a docile, industrial caste
of unskilled and semiskilled urban workers. Before the 1920s, northern industrial philanthropists, though contributing millions of dollars to
Hampton-Tuskegee-style industrial schools, had resisted contributing to
the development of black high schools. This was in sharp contrast to
their contributions toward the development of southern white public
secondary education. Even Booker T. Washington, who certainly tended
to ignore the faults of northern philanthropists, expressed his unhappi-
ness with this situation. In 1910 he wrote anxiously to Wallace Buttrick
of the General Education Board: "I very much fear that if the General
Education Board continues to employ people to encourage white high
schools, and does nothing for Negro high schools, the southern white
people will take it for granted that the Negro is to have few if any high
schools." The board, citing the failure of southern state departments of
education to request such help for black secondary education, refused to
support black high schools. This argument, however, did not explain the
philanthropists' failure to support black public secondary education in
those southern cities willing to support black high schools. Basically, the
philanthropists, in concert with most southern urban school boards before 1920, did not view black secondary education as relevant to its
schemes for the social and economic development of the New South.
This situation soon changed.[14]

The significant shift of the black population from the rural to the
urban South during the period 1916 to 1930 forced a new attentiveness
to secondary education for black youth. As early as June 1916 the U.S.
Department of Labor called attention to a disturbing labor condition in
the South. A great migratory stream of black laborers was flowing out of
the rural South into the urban areas of southern and northern states.
Economic depression struck in full force in the rural sections of the
South early in the decade 1920–30, and an ever-increasing number of
rural black boys and girls were moving with and without their parents to
southern cities. Until 1929, most of the urban portions of the nation
enjoyed a high degree of prosperity, and not surprisingly this tremendous
flow of population from the farms to the cities took place, at a rate much
faster than could be absorbed by the urban labor markets. For black
southerners, the economic depression in the rural areas was only one
primary reason for migrating. The general social and political oppression
in the plantation South, including the absence of schools for black children, were long-standing causes of a steady stream of black migration
into southern and northern cities. The underlying discontent with the
plantation economy is one reason why the black migration from the
rural South to the urban South, in sharp contrast to the migration from

the South to northern cities, did not slow down during the Great Depression.[15]

City officials and public school authorities in the urban South were shocked and alarmed by the rapid increases in the black youth population. The cities, unlike the plantation economies, did not afford a smooth transition from the home to the labor market. Adolescents in the urban South, as elsewhere in urban America, could not be absorbed into the industrial labor market. If they were not in school, generally there was little else for them to do but roam the streets. This led invariably to intolerable numbers of juvenile delinquents and posed serious social crises for youth, families, and cities. In rural societies, especially in good economic periods, youth could be easily absorbed into the agricultural economy as farmhands or domestic helpers. The urban labor markets even in times of economic prosperity could not absorb major portions of its youth population. Hence, elsewhere in America and for white youth in the South, urban reformers championed prolonged schooling as the best method to keep teenagers off the streets, out of the already saturated labor markets, and to train them properly for their later roles as adults, wage earners, and citizens. Until the decade 1920–30, city and school authorities in most of the urban South resisted prolonged schooling for black youth. They feared the educational advancement of black youth more than the social problems caused by the absence of public secondary education. But as the region's urban black youth populations grew rapidly during the second and third decades of the twentieth century, the sheer magnitude of the problem forced a new attentiveness to the question of black public secondary education. Consequently, the same coalition that transformed white public secondary education—northern philanthropists and southern school officials—joined to forge a new system of urban black secondary education. But they did not build on the tradition or precedents of black public secondary education that had been hammered out in the urban South between 1880 and 1920. Indeed, they rejected the existing model of black public secondary education as inappropriate to the "needs of the Negro" and sought to translate their own conceptions of blacks' economic roles in the urban South into a new model of secondary black education.[16]

It was not northern philanthropy but the urban South's response to the post–World War I demographic, economic, and political changes that stimulated the growth in black public secondary education. No philanthropic foundation became actively involved in the development of black public high schools in the South until after 1926. By that time all of the larger cities in the South had already established at least one black secondary school. North Carolina, for instance, had no black public high

schools in 1917 but had established 21 accredited black high schools by
the 1924–25 academic year. Of these high schools 4 were departments of
state normal schools, 3 were rural schools, and 14 were city schools.
These schools followed the academic model. In 1926 the state's 49 accredited black four-year high schools (23 private and 26 public) sent out
1,220 graduates, of whom 627 or 51.3 percent continued their study
beyond the secondary level. Mississippi, which lagged behind North
Carolina and most of the southern states in the development of black
secondary education, had only 3 public high schools for black children in
1924. They were located at Vicksburg, Yazoo City, and Mound Bayou.
Barring the Mound Bayou school, which cost $115,000, entirely built
with money contributed by blacks, the facilities for secondary education
at the other two schools were quite limited. Over the next two years,
however, Jackson built a black high school at a cost of $125,000,
Natchez built one costing $115,000, and the state built an agricultural
high school at Coahoma County. This was virtually nothing compared to
the 1,020 public high schools for whites, valued at $13,338,623, but for
the first time even Mississippi built high schools for blacks in its larger
cities.[17]

These trends caught the attention of northern philanthropists in 1925.
In January of that year representatives of the General Education Board,
the Jeanes Fund, the Slater Fund, and the Rosenwald Fund, attending a
conference on southern education in Gulfport, Mississippi, set aside time
to discuss the development of black public high schools. At this meeting
the philanthropists heard several anecdotal accounts of the building of
black public high schools in major southern cities. Wanting more detailed and accurate information, they requested a report on the recent
development of black public high schools in the eleven former Confederate states. This report, prepared by Frances Mathis, secretary to Leo M.
Favrot of the General Education Board, circulated among the key philanthropic agents. Mathis demonstrated that in 1925, the former Confederate states maintained a combined total of 143 four-year public high
schools for black children. In 1915 these same states had had only 21
black public secondary schools. Mathis's report included statistics on the
cost of high school buildings established and equipment purchased from
1918 to 1925. Alabama had erected 14 new buildings at a total cost of
$785,807; they ranged in cost from $3,400 to $125,000. Between 1918
and 1924, Tennessee erected 22 new high school buildings for black
children, ranging in cost from $9,000 to $122,000. New buildings were
also erected in Louisiana, Mississippi, South Carolina, Georgia, Texas,
Virginia, Florida, and Arkansas.[18]

Northern philanthropists had avoided aiding the development of
black secondary education, and they seemed unaware of and surprised

by this growth. In January 1925 Julius Rosenwald wrote to Abraham Flexner of the General Education Board, asking his opinion regarding the "opportunity to do something for Negro education by way of stimulating the building of high schools in one or two southern states." Once the Mathis report reached the Rosenwald Fund, its members realized that substantial progress had been made already and apparently in some instances with a "fair spirit" of cooperation on the part of whites and blacks in the urban South. "Indeed," responded Francis W. Shepardson, acting director and secretary of the Rosenwald Fund, "the figures which have reached me have been rather surprising, so much so that I have wondered whether there was any need of a stimulus." Wallace Buttrick of the General Education Board, noting that "the larger cities have already expended hundreds of thousands of dollars each on high schools," reasoned that if there was any work left for philanthropy, it was in the smaller cities. Northern philanthropists, having convinced themselves that the main reason they did not support black secondary education was southern white opposition, found themselves in a predicament. The urban South, however prejudiced against secondary education for black children, was substantially ahead of the policies and practice of northern philanthropy. In view of this reality representatives of the General Education Board called a conference in April 1925, at their New York office to discuss black public secondary education in the southern states.[19]

When the philanthropists met to discuss the development of black public secondary education on 30 April 1925, most of the key agents were present. From the General Education Board were Wallace Buttrick, Wickliffe Rose, E. C. Sage, H. J. Thorkelson, Frank P. Bachman, Jackson Davis, and Leo M. Favrot. The Rosenwald Fund sent its chief school officers, S. L. Smith and Francis W. Shepardson. James H. Dillard, B. C. Caldwell, and W. T. B. Williams represented the Jeanes and Slater funds. Abraham Flexner of the General Education Board attended several sessions. The informal sessions touched various issues regarding southern black education but centered mostly on the development of black high schools. Many points were considered important enough to record. Yet three of them were most critical in shaping philanthropic involvement in the development of southern black secondary education. First, Favrot, arguing that many mistakes in curriculum planning and construction had attended the expansion of southern white secondary education, urged that similar mistakes be avoided in the development of black secondary education. Second, Buttrick, assuming that philanthropic agents would become involved in shaping black secondary education, stressed the need to downplay philanthropic intervention: "It should appear that people of the community themselves are doing the thing rather than agencies from the outside." Third, after recognizing that the southern black high school movement was going forward without any stimulus from northern philanthropic foundations, the agents concluded: "There is no need to stimulate it. The main thing is to control it and direct it into the right channels." Why did the philanthropic agents feel it was necessary to control the black secondary education movement and what were the "right channels" into which it was to be directed? These questions were answered as the philanthropists entered a series of black high school reform movements in several southern cities.[20]

Although all of the northern philanthropic agents contributed funds and personnel to shape the course of black public secondary education, the vanguard role was assumed by the Rosenwald Fund. By 1928, when the fund became actively involved in the development of an urban black high school, its trustees and agents had decided to promote secondary industrial education. Little Rock, Arkansas, was chosen as the city for the fund's first program. In November 1928 Alfred K. Stern, trustee of the Rosenwald Fund, wrote to R. C. Hall, Little Rock's superintendent of schools: "We have selected Little Rock as the first of the cities in which we are willing to participate in the experiment of providing an industrial high school for Negroes." Superintendent Hall was grateful and shared with the fund the hope that its experiment would be successful, "both for its usefulness in Little Rock and as a model for development in other cities." The city certainly needed financial assistance. It had just completed a new junior and senior white high school, and the black children's portion of the school fund had been diverted to create superior facilities for white children. The black school, Gibbs High, was near condemnation, and the Little Rock School Board authorized the construction of a new building for black pupils. Having spent nearly all of the city's school building fund on the construction of the new white high school, however, the School Board had insufficient funds to erect a black high school. Little Rock school officials saw the fund's interest in the development of black industrial secondary education as an opportunity to secure the additional money needed to finance a new black high school. The city secured from the fund a pledge to pay one-third of the total cost of the proposed building and thus authorized $200,000 to $250,000 to construct a building large enough to house a combined elementary and secondary school for black children.[21]

From the outset the Rosenwald Fund's representatives made it clear that their primary interest was in the development of black industrial education. They soon discovered, however, that the Little Rock school officials were concerned mainly with acquiring outside money to help finance their racially dual school system. In a conference between the fund's agents and the Little Rock School Board, held in October 1928, the philanthropists learned that the city did not intend initially to include industrial education courses in the proposed black high school. First, it was the city's view that rooms and equipment for trade courses would increase the total cost of the building beyond the amount of construction funds available to the School Board. Second, the black citizens of Little Rock expressed plainly to the School Board their opposition to increased emphasis on industrial education. "The School Board and I have given them as much industrial education as it is wise to give," said Hall to the philanthropists, "you will find the Negroes here wanting only the literary courses." Continued exchanges clarified further the differences between the Rosenwald agents and Little Rock's school officials. The fund's agents wanted the new black high school to align its industrial education curriculum with the occupations that black workers usually found in the Little Rock area. In view of this interest, the agents requested Hall to supply social and demographic data showing the number of children to be accommodated by the new school, projections of changes in the black population over the next decade, existing opportunities for blacks in the local industries and information about any industry expecting to increase its number of black workers, and the city's capacity to absorb potential black high school graduates into the local economy.[22]

Whereas the philanthropists' inquiry was based on the fundamental assumption that black secondary industrial education could train black youth for "Negro jobs," Hall's reply suggested strongly that in Little Rock there was no relationship between secondary education and the type of jobs held by black workers. Hall wrote to George R. Arthur, manager of the fund's "Negro Welfare" department:

> First, we have about nine hundred pupils available for the new school from seventh to twelfth grades, inclusive. Second, we cannot forecast now that there will be any material change in the industrial development of this community that will affect the negro population. Third, we have no large industries employing negro labor, and I hardly believe that such industries will come in the next ten years. Fourth, there is now very little [opportunity] for the pupils of vocational courses in high school, and there has been no demand from the negroes for such courses though we have tried hard to introduce some of them, especially laundry and vocational sewing.

Hall further informed Arthur that "most of the negro labor in this section is common day labor, janitors, porters, chauffeurs, and draymen," and "there is no industry where negro laborers are the main working force." Hall knew well that black workers in Little Rock were generally hired in jobs requiring no secondary education. In fact, most "negro jobs" required no schooling at all. Hall, therefore, showed little interest in the industrial features of black secondary education.[23]

President Embree of the Rosenwald Fund understood Hall's message. As he wrote in the margin of Hall's letter, "well, maybe they don't need a trade school in Arkansas." Indeed, blacks did not need the type of industrial high school the Rosenwald agents had in mind. It made little sense for black pupils to spend their time studying to become janitors, porters, chauffeurs, cooks, and laundry women when such jobs did not require even an elementary education, not to mention a high school education. The Rosenwald Fund did not intend, however, to develop black industrial high schools that would produce technically trained young men and women for skilled jobs or for occupational mobility. The fund sought to develop a secondary industrial education that rationalized and reproduced the existing structure of "Negro jobs." Hence the philanthropists brushed aside Hall's concerns and insights and pushed ahead with their plans to transform southern black secondary education into a system of training and socialization primarily for prospective unskilled and semi-skilled workers.[24]

To accomplish its goal the Rosenwald Fund adopted a new approach that came to characterize its reform campaigns in several southern cities. The fund hired its own team of experts on school architecture, industrial education curricula, and the social and economic characteristics of urban black communities. Walter R. McCornack of Cleveland, Ohio, one of America's finest school architects, was hired to make certain that each high school supported by the fund would be built with the appropriate rooms and the necessary equipment for secondary industrial education. The fund's experts on industrial education curricula were Frederick E. Clerk and Franklin J. Keller. Clerk was the principal of the New Trier High School in Illinois and Keller was principal of New York City's East Side Continuation School, which ten thousand students attended part time for vocational training. The well-known black sociologist Charles S. Johnson was contracted to supervise studies of the social and economic life of blacks in each southern city where the fund chose to help build a black industrial high school or establish an industrial department within an academic high school. Most of the field research was conducted by Mabel Byrd of Fisk University's Social Science Department. This team of consultants distinguished the Rosenwald approach to school reform. First, the social scientists would conduct a study of the black population, its occupational structure, and projections of its industrial future in selected southern cities. Then the curriculum experts would use these findings to develop an industrial education program unique to the Negro job structure of each city. The architect would design a school or department in which the rooms and equipment reflected the particular alignment between curricula and industrial opportunities or prescribed occupations for black youth.[25]

In late 1929 Byrd made a thorough survey of the white and Negro industrial and business communities of Little Rock, interviewed "leading citizens" of both communities, and visited twenty industrial establishments. She distributed questionnaires to students at Gibbs High School, to graduates of the school, and to local black mechanics. Byrd found that Afro-Americans made up 25 percent of Little Rock's total population. Practically all of the employed adults were engaged in common labor occupations. The black men were employed mainly as helpers in the various trades, or as cooks, gardeners or "yard boys," barbers, chauffeurs, truck drivers, laundry men, railroad workers, or agricultural laborers on farms just outside of the city. Black women worked as seamstresses, cooks, laundry women, and "fancy pressers." In the entire city of Little Rock there were only three black plasterers and five bricklayers carrying union cards. Black men worked as unskilled and semiskilled auto mechanics. Five hundred black men were employed in the Missouri Pacific railroad shop as helpers to white skilled operators. Byrd discovered that black men, "excepting in their own businesses," were employed as helpers in electrical work. Byrd concluded her survey by recommending, on the basis of the jobs held by the city's black adults, that the new black high school offer the following trades: household management, dressmaking, beauty culture, farming, plumbing, commercial cooking, building trades, auto mechanics, electricity, and machine shop.[26]

This investigation represented the best of the sociological and school survey movements of the era. Early twentieth-century school reformers borrowed the term "survey" from the field of sociology. By the late 1920s, it was a relatively new idea in education, though it was obviously an expansion of a standard idea and practice in sociology. The New York City School Survey of 1911 convinced school reformers that the survey method had great practical possibilities. Because the science of engineering was based on a thorough survey of conditions and problems, exact measurement, experimental control of process, and adjustment of procedures in light of facts, "educational engineers" viewed the survey method as a scientific way to adapt the aims and processes of education to the local political economy. It was a means of "educational diagnosis" based on the school population and community to be served. Byrd's survey of Little Rock furnished the sociological characteristics of black living and working conditions and recommended a program of studies that would train black youth for what were generally regarded as "Negro jobs."[27]

The survey of Little Rock was then submitted to the curricula experts, Keller and Clerk, for their analyses and recommendations. They visited Little Rock early in 1930, several months after the opening of the new black elementary and secondary school. Their task was to conduct a firsthand inspection of the school's curriculum in practice as it related to the sociological position of blacks in Little Rock. Keller and Clerk discovered that the proposed industrial curriculum had not been translated into instructional practices. Particularly, the equipment in the industrial shops was meager and not suited to the industrial training recommended by the Rosenwald agents. "The present administration frankly admits that the so-called industrial work has up to the present time been only manual training (except for the vocational sewing class) and is of value only as a cultural accompaniment to college preparatory subjects," stated Keller and Clerk. The best equipment for boys was in the mill room, but Keller and Clerk reported that "none of it is being used." Clearly, things were developing contrary to the philanthropists' plans. They had hoped to see an industrial training program that approximated the actual work situations of black adults and that deemphasized college preparatory subjects.[28]

This plan was thwarted in Little Rock largely because of the behavior of local black leaders. As early as December 1928, leaders of Little Rock's black community began protesting against the establishment of an industrial high school. Upon learning that the new high school would be named Negro Industrial High School, W. A. Booker, a local black attorney, wrote anxiously to Arthur of the Rosenwald Fund: "Our people here have been waiting patiently over a span of years for a real high school, one that would not be a subterfuge; one that would give a thorough educational training and literary background, and a curriculum upon which a college education could be well predicated." Booker informed Arthur that "serious objection" had "already gone forth on the part of our Negro taxpayers and citizens of the proposed change of the name from Gibbs High School to that of the 'Negro Industrial High School.'" Booker argued that the black taxpayers' objections were well grounded and should be sustained. It made no sense to Booker that black citizens should have to accept industrial training to attain for black children "what justice urges and what we as the taxpayers and the fathers ahead of us have long since earned." Almost a year later, in September 1929, Booker was still protesting the name of the new high school.[29]

By the time Little Rock's new black high school held its official opening ceremonies in the fall of 1929, Booker and the local black community had defeated the efforts to name the school Negro Industrial High. It was called Paul Laurence Dunbar High School. Hailed as "the finest high school building in the South for Negro boys and girls," Dunbar had a seating capacity of sixteen hundred, an auditorium, cafeteria, library, sixteen hundred lockers, forty classrooms, and seven industrial shops. The Rosenwald Fund contributed $67,500 and the General Education Board gave $30,000 toward the total cost of $400,000. The program of studies provided three routes to a diploma: a classical liberal academic course for college-bound students; a combination course that allowed students to graduate with enough credits for college entrance and at the same time earn special vocational certificates; and an industrial curriculum in which pupils could earn enough credits to attain a diploma but would not have enough academic credits to enter college. The influence of the industrial education philosophy on the overall curriculum was evidenced by the absence of a required academic core curriculum. In the tenth and eleventh grades, for example, only English and history (with special emphasis on auto mechanics) were required, and in the twelfth grade only English was required. Yet the academic electives included Latin, algebra, biology, world history, geography, plane geometry, American history, chemistry, physics, trigonometry, economics, biology, and fine arts.[30]

A report on the distribution of Dunbar's pupils in various courses revealed that in the fall of 1930, 1,106 of the school's 1,163 junior high and secondary students were enrolled in industrial courses. Of these 831 were females enrolled in Regular Sewing I (205), Regular Sewing II (237), Home Making I (115), Home Making II (174), Vocational Sewing (40), and Laundry (60). Most of the male pupils were enrolled in Manual Arts I (151) and Manual Arts II (134), with a few in Bricklaying (15), Carpentry (15), and Auto Mechanics (27). No classes were offered in sheet metal work, electrical work, plumbing, or printing. This occupational training was congruent with the domestic service, cooking, serving, laundry, and industrial helper jobs held by Little Rock's black adults. Few students, however, majored in the industrial curriculum, though many took a course or two. Black parents counseled their children to take the academic courses. In addition, Little Rock was home for three four-year degree-granting black colleges: Philander Smith, Arkansas Baptist, and Shorter. The state college for black students, Arkansas Agricultural, Mechanical, and Normal College, was located only forty-five miles away, in Pine Bluff. As Faustine Childress Jones has demonstrated, the proximity of these schools meant that Dunbar's graduates who had aspirations for higher education could attend college. In the short run, the philanthropists' efforts to redirect black secondary education in Little Rock into the "right channels" or industrial training had very limited success; in the long run Dunbar became a model of academic excellence. The black citizens, taxpayers, and educators outmaneuvered the philanthropists.[31]

The Rosenwald Fund's next major campaign to reform black secondary education took place in New Orleans and ended in failure, but it clarified, even more than did the Little Rock experiment, the philanthropists' perceptions of the "right channels" for black public high schools. On 30 March 1931, Nichols Bauer, the New Orleans superintendent

Paul Laurence Dunbar High School of Little Rock, Arkansas, 1930.
This was the first industrial-academic high school aided by the Julius
Rosenwald Fund. Courtesy of Fisk University Library.

of public schools, wrote optimistically to Alfred K. Stern: "As I see it, the negro trade school is a certainty." Bauer's insight was poor in this instance. In fact, the proposed trade school for black youth in New Orleans was never built, and the Rosenwald Fund, which authorized $125,000 toward the construction costs of an estimated $400,000 building, eventually withdrew the pledge as philanthropists became disappointed with the apathetic and obstructive behavior of Orleans Parish School Board members. Although the philanthropists' venture into New Orleans ended in failure and disappointment, it demonstrated more about their ideology of black public secondary education than did their involvement in more successful projects. After acquiring considerable experience in the Little Rock endeavor, the philanthropists had not only a clearer idea of what they wanted to achieve but more knowledge about methods and procedures to attain their goals. They also had observed that the Little Rock campaign strayed from their basic policies and were determined to avoid the same mistakes in New Orleans. The philanthropists were determined to do the job right and build a model program of black secondary industrial education in New Orleans.[32]

The New Orleans experiment enables us to rethink the larger process of philanthropic interest in black public high schools. By examining a

major reform campaign that was carefully articulated and, but for the resistance of local school authorities would have been translated into institutionalized behavior, we get a sharper portrait of the philanthropists' intended reforms versus their compromised achievements. When examining relationships between dominant and subordinate classes, it is important to describe and analyze unrealized movements. Such events give us a better understanding of what was intended in contradistinction to what was achieved. The Little Rock experiment demonstrates how the philanthropists' goals converged with those of white school authorities and black citizens in developing a compromised model of black secondary education; the New Orleans venture illustrates what the philanthropists might have done were they not forced to compromise.

In September 1930, the Rosenwald Fund authorized an appropriation of $125,000 toward a black secondary industrial school in New Orleans. This was the largest appropriation ever authorized by the fund for construction of a black public high school. The fund's agents hoped to establish the finest model of black public secondary education in New Orleans. "As I explained previously, we are very anxious to make this a model industrial high school in every respect; we feel that we can profit by our experience in other cities," Stern wrote to Isaac S. Heller, a member of the Orleans Parish School Board and friend of the Rosenwald family. Late in February 1931, in a letter to Superintendent Bauer, Rosenwald agent Stern explained why the fund was so concerned about the proposed new black high school. "It will be the first secondary school for Negroes built exclusively for trade instruction to which the fund has made an appropriation." The fund's agents had often expressed their desire to support black high schools devoted exclusively to training black youth for industrial jobs in the urban South. President Embree stated that the fund's agents had reservations about the usefulness of "the old manual training," which he believed was valuable as general instruction but did not train workers for specific jobs in the labor market. Indeed, the fund's members declined to assist Birmingham, Alabama, in the development of a black high school because its industrial education component represented the old manual training as opposed to more direct training for specific industrial jobs. The philanthropists saw in New Orleans the first real opportunity to shift the direction of black secondary education toward training for specific jobs.[33]

Isaac S. Heller, a close friend of Alfred K. Stern, played the key role in articulating the fund's proposal in Orleans Parish School Board meetings. From the outset, Heller encountered stiff resistance from several of his colleagues. In December 1929, Heller detailed his opponents' viewpoints regarding the proposed black industrial high school:

> According to the point of view of those members of the School Board who are opposed to the negro trade school, they feel that it would be wrong to provide school board funds to the education of any negro children as long as there are white children who cannot be provided for, and as long as no "school board funds" are being applied to the industrial education of white boys. They raised a further argument, specious though it is, that such a school would encourage the further encroachment of the negro on trades where the whites now predominate. The undersigned [Heller] argued at length against all of this with but little success, *stressing the point, first, that this school would interest itself only in trades obviously negro.*

In an effort to gain the support of the leader of the opposition, Edmund Garland, Heller arranged a private luncheon meeting to persuade him to reverse his stand against the proposed black industrial high school. Heller's efforts were not successful.[34]

To aid in the formulation and selling of the fund's educational program, Heller anxiously called for a sociological survey of the industrial conditions and the corresponding educational needs of blacks in New Orleans. In January 1930 he persuaded the School Board to allow Mabel

Byrd to conduct a survey of New Orleans. The Rosenwald Fund paid for the survey. He met with Byrd in early January 1930 and presented her with a letter, pursuant to a resolution passed by the School Board, authorizing the sociological and school survey. Heller informed Byrd that her survey should pay particular attention to the position of black workers in the local economy. "I have asked her not only to determine the present status and needs of the trades in New Orleans with respect to negroes, but also to emphasize those trades where there is little or no competition between the races," wrote Heller to Embree. This approach was consistent with the fund's goal to develop black secondary education that reinforced racial segmentation rather than competition in southern urban economies.[35]

Sociological data on black New Orleans were collected by Byrd during mid-January of 1930. She presented a preliminary report on methods of procedure and data sources to the Orleans Parish School Board in late January. She had collected data on the occupations of black workers in twenty-five industrial plants, including shipbuilding companies, construction companies, sheet metal companies, automobile firms, cotton mills, clothing industries, and hairdressing and barber shops. Byrd interviewed the managers of these industrial plants, the commissioner of labor, the business agents of the plasterers', bricklayers', and longshoremen's unions, the director of public service, and several individual leaders in education, industry, and the media. She distributed questionnaires to the black students attending McDonough elementary and secondary school and to fifty-one of the school's 1925 to 1929 graduates. Questionnaires were also given to selected black tradesmen. Finally, Byrd investigated the local market demands for black workers through the records of the employment bureaus and the want ads of the daily newspapers. With the board's approval Byrd proceeded to organize the data and write the final report.[36]

Two main points were emphasized in the final study, "Report of the Special Inquiry Undertaken in New Orleans into the Industrial Status of Negroes." First, Byrd argued that unless New Orleans established industrial high schools to improve the labor efficiency of its black population it would be outdistanced in economic prosperity by comparable cities, which had taken steps to increase the productive capacity of their laboring population. Second, Byrd assured the Orleans Parish School Board that black secondary industrial education as conceived by agents of the Rosenwald Fund was designed to keep black workers in "their place" and that the proposed black high school would deliberately and systematically prevent black youth from acquiring trade training that would enable them to compete with white workers for the more skilled and higher-paying industrial occupations. The report stated:

The industrial training that will presently be described does not have for its object the education of the negro element of the population, except where there is a demand, and where there will be a demand for a larger supply of colored skilled labor. In making this survey the investigators have given particular attention to the attitude of the white skilled labor and to the present status of the negro in industry today. We have borne this particularly in mind so that this school, when established, would not result in increasing competition between the races.

But how could a high school train "colored skilled labor" without increasing competition for the better skilled jobs? The Rosenwald Fund attempted to resolve this dilemma by defining skilled labor as practical knowledge, supplemented by industrial education, thereby resulting in increased labor efficiency and productivity. Under this definition, any unskilled work could be transformed by industrial education into skilled work, and workers could move from unskilled to skilled labor without changing occupations. Black housemaids without formal industrial education, for instance, were unskilled, and those with training in domestic science were defined as skilled laborers. Byrd's report pointed out that "the negro girl and woman occupies traditionally the field of domestic service in New Orleans." But the traditional method of training, the "mother to daughter variety," was "unscientific and wasteful," and it had led to an unfortunate situation in which "a well-trained, efficient, reliable houseworker is scarce and is becoming more scarce as the years pass." Byrd concluded that "thorough training in domestic science will correct this condition and put into the field a larger supply of competent houseworkers." This represented the fund's idea of how to increase black skilled labor without increasing competition between the races.[37]

From the philanthropists' viewpoint, it was the worker who was unskilled, not the occupation. Hence Byrd's report stated that secondary industrial education could produce scientifically trained and more efficient black caterers, laundry women, dressmakers, maids, gardeners, chefs and cooks, tailors, chauffeurs, auto mechanics, printers and bookbinders, bricklayers, plasterers, and sewing machine operators. These were the occupations held largely by black workers in New Orleans. Black women predominated in the occupations of laundry work, house service, and hairdressing. They constituted 96 percent of the laundry women, 79 percent of the hairdressers, and 86 percent of the house servants. Black women made up 75 to 80 percent of the labor force of many shops in the clothing industry. Black male workers were concentrated heavily in the building trades, railroads, personal service, and gardening. They were 80 percent of New Orleans' bricklayers, 95 percent of the plasterers, 50 percent of the cement workmen, and almost 100 percent of the slate roofers. On the basis of these findings, the Rosenwald Fund agents recommended to the Orleans Parish School Board that the proposed black high school offer the following trades: domestic science, dressmaking, power sewing machine operating, hair-dressing, maids in doctors' offices, gardening, barbering, commercial cooking, tailoring, bricklaying and plastering, chauffeuring/auto mechanics, and printing. The survey pointed out that for black youth printing was a "limited field," though "in certain printing establishments negro printers are used and negro girls employed as book binders." When the fund recommended the training of a limited number of black youth in printing and bookbinding, therefore, it was in keeping with its advocacy of racial segregation in the labor force.[38]

After completing its school survey and making its final report to the Orleans Parish School Board, the fund sent its school architect, Walter R. McCornack, to help the local architect draw up plans for the proposed industrial high school. His employment to help the local architect with the planning, construction, and equipment of the proposed black high school was a condition of the Rosenwald grant. McCornack's fee, 1 percent of the total cost of construction and equipment, was to be borne by the School Board. The fund thus had its first opportunity to design and equip a secondary school exclusively for industrial training in local "Negro jobs." The sketches drawn by McCornack and illustrated in figure 6.1 reflect the philanthropists' conception of how a true black industrial high school would be constructed. There were no rooms in the plans for academic education.[39]

In November 1930 Keller went to New Orleans to develop a curriculum for the proposed high school. On the basis of his own site inspections, Mabel Byrd's community and school survey, and consultation with McCornack, Keller produced a seventeen-page document which addressed all conceivable dimensions of black secondary industrial education, including purpose, method, relations to academic education, the qualifications of pupils, the design and equipment of buildings, curricula, and the general principles of vocational guidance. Consistent with the basic aims of the fund, Keller concluded: "The school should prepare boys and girls for vocations which are open to Negroes in New Orleans." Further, he recommended that academic education should not be an important part of the curriculum: "The school should accept all boys and girls who are qualified for instruction in the trades regardless of any specific academic attainment." Indeed, Keller proposed that students be admitted to secondary industrial education even without any prior formal education. He thought that the proposed high school should devote 75 percent of its classroom time to shop work and 25 percent to related

FIGURE 6.1

Architectural Sketch of an Industrial High School

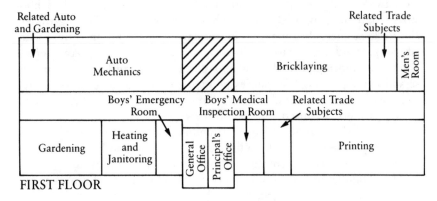

Related Auto
and Gardening

Related Trade
Subjects

Auto
Mechanics

Bricklaying

Men's
Room

Boys' Emergency
Room

Boys' Medical
Inspection Room

Related Trade
Subjects

Gardening

Heating
and
Janitoring

General
Office

Principal's
Office

Printing

FIRST FLOOR

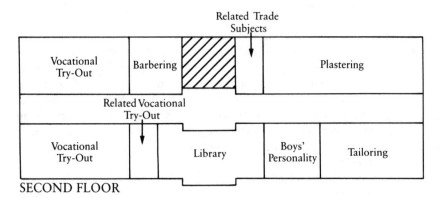

Related Trade
Subjects

Vocational
Try-Out

Barbering

Plastering

Related Vocational
Try-Out

Vocational
Try-Out

Library

Boys'
Personality

Tailoring

SECOND FLOOR

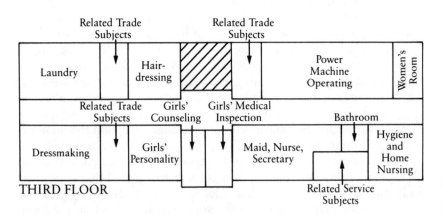

Related Trade
Subjects

Related Trade
Subjects

Laundry

Hair-
dressing

Power
Machine
Operating

Women's
Room

Related Trade
Subjects

Girls'
Counseling

Girls' Medical
Inspection

Bathroom

Dressmaking

Girls'
Personality

Maid, Nurse,
Secretary

Hygiene
and
Home
Nursing

THIRD FLOOR

Related Service
Subjects

Source: McCornack's sketches, Box 310, JRFP-FU

academic subjects, which would include English, mathematics, science, and drawing. The related subjects, said Keller, could be "taught incidentally by the shop teachers."[40]

By late 1930, the philanthropists were all set to build a model black industrial high school in New Orleans. There was only one major obstacle: the Orleans Parish School Board, reflecting the peculiar rationality of southern white racism, could not reach a decision to build the school. At a School Board meeting in February 1930, one member, August Schabel, opposed the plan on the ground that it would result in "all the negroes in the entire state coming to New Orleans." Schabel betrayed his awareness of the value of education among black families, and, knowing that there were no secondary schools for blacks in rural Louisiana, he could anticipate an unintended consequence not foreseen by the philanthropists. He also demonstrated another southern white viewpoint. Schabel perceived secondary education as an avenue of social advancement and could not appreciate fully the philanthropists' conception of a process of industrial education that would hold people within their racial or class position. Thus he viewed support for a black industrial high school as "advancing the negroes in our system more rapidly than we have advanced the whites." Isaac Heller quickly informed his fellow school board member of the real intent of the proposed black industrial high school:

> The establishment of this school does not in any way contemplate educating these negroes in the trade school into trades that will in any way affect the white labor or deprive the white men of their positions, and that it is not the intention of this Board to increase friction between the races or competition between the races. It is rather to educate the negroes in trades and positions to which negroes are best qualified, and under no circumstances to educate them to compete with white labor of this city.

Heller found support for his position from board members Henry O. Schaumburg and Phillip G. Ricks. "I believe there is a need in this community for a negro trade school and the trades that will be taught there, for colored boys and for colored girls, to make them housekeepers, maids, cooks, printers, gardeners, mechanics, yard boys," said Ricks. Heller, Schaumburg, and Ricks persuaded Schabel and other board members to support the Rosenwald Fund's proposal, and it was voted unanimously to authorize the construction of a new black industrial high school.[41]

The board's authorization of funds to build a new black high school became the subject of editorials in the local newspapers, and so did the findings and recommendations of the school survey and curriculum report. The northern philanthropists were then treated to another southern white custom, that of being open and straightforward regarding social schemes to keep blacks subordinate. The *New Orleans States*, summarizing the basic position of the board and the Rosenwald Fund, wrote: "They kept particularly in mind that, if the school is established, it must not result in increasing competition between the races." The *Times Picayune* concurred. "Trade school training will render the negro youth more efficient in their chosen tasks and lead them into settled and stable occupations." Such news coverage informed the New Orleans black community of the social and political purposes of the proposed black industrial high school. Heller informed Stern in early March 1930 that local black leaders had begun protesting the idea of a black trade school. Stern advised Heller to regard this protest as merely a reflex response by particular black elites: "It is natural to expect some opposition from the Negro group to a project of this kind. We have found in our work that a certain element among the Negroes is constantly pleading for purely academic rather than vocational education for colored people." According to Stern, the Rosenwald Fund did "not argue against the professional and cultural instruction for the minority of the Negro group." But "any man who has the interest of the masses at heart would not stand out against the other ninety percent." The structure of black secondary education in 1930 belies Stern's definition of the masses. In 1930 only 7.9 percent of the black high school age population in Louisiana was enrolled in school. Hence it was not a question of the education of the minority versus that of the masses but of what type of education would be provided for the 7.9 percent. The black leaders in New Orleans waged a legitimate protest. Because only a small fraction of high school age black youth was actually enrolled in secondary schools, it made no sense to channel that minority into low-level industrial training.[42]

By the spring of 1930, the Rosenwald Fund was ready to proceed with the construction of the proposed black industrial high school, but various problems in New Orleans prevented the start of construction. Finally, in January 1931, to clear the final hurdles, the fund agents called a conference with the Orleans Parish School Board. The fund was represented by its president, Embree, its director, Stern, its curriculum expert, Keller, and its school architect, McCornack. Superintendent Bauer reported on the progress of the proposed high school, revealing at every turn that the School Board was at best lukewarm toward the idea. The board had purchased a lot for the proposed high school, but it had used the $275,000 originally allocated for building a combined academic and industrial high school to purchase the School Board's administration building. This action expressed the board's lack of commitment to black secondary industrial education. Moreover, the philanthropists learned from Bauer that the board had not allocated any of the city's Smith-

Hughes funds to black pupils. Because there were no facilities for black industrial education, explained Bauer, the Smith-Hughes funds were distributed entirely to white trade education.[43]

The Rosenwald Fund's agents tried one more time to convince the Orleans Parish School Board of the economic and racial benefits of a black industrial high school. "At no time should the school be regarded as another academic high school for negroes," said Embree. "It should be an out and out trade school, the fundamental purpose of which would be trade training and preparing negroes as fast as possible for jobs." Heller explained once more that the proposed black industrial high school would "avoid as far as possible training negroes in highly competitive fields where white mechanics were highly organized." The purpose of the school, Heller maintained, was to train black youth for "trades that are really negro trades." To extend the point, Heller argued that there were few opportunities for blacks trained in commercial subjects and hence there was no need to include such courses in the proposed school. Significantly, the proposed curriculum as drawn up by Keller and approved by the fund did not include such commercial subjects as stenography, accounting, and bookkeeping. In these and other ways the philanthropists tried to convince the School Board that the proposed high school would increase the productivity of the city's black work force, help rationalize the racially segmented labor market, and establish an appropriate model of black secondary education.[44]

The New Orleans school officials could not be persuaded to build a black industrial high school. They could never see the need to expend $400,000 to build and equip a high school to train black youth for "negro jobs" because they had already accomplished this goal without the aid of formal schooling. With each passing month the philanthropists became increasingly isolated as the sole champions of the proposed black industrial high school, and local white southerners ranged from indifferent to resistant. As Embree wrote to Heller in September 1931, "It seems to us that the school officials are so indifferent, if not positively obstructive, that there is little likelihood of real success." Hence, as the year 1931 ended, the Rosenwald Fund withdrew from its New Orleans venture, promising its hearty support if in the near future the city renewed the campaign to build a black industrial high school but knowing that the project had failed. This reform campaign provides an understanding of what might have occurred in the absence of local indifference and resistance. The undistorted values and beliefs of the philanthropists and their ideological interests in southern black education are illuminated in this effort, which was no less real because it ended in failure.[45]

In other campaigns in Columbus, Georgia, Greenville, South Carolina, and Winston-Salem, North Carolina, the Rosenwald Fund found much greater success. One of its more successful endeavors took place in Columbus, Georgia. The William H. Spencer High School of Columbus was dedicated in January 1931. The out-of-town guests included George Foster Peabody, Keller, and Stern. The fund contributed $22,500 toward the building's total cost of $112,000. In Columbus, the fund acquired the enthusiastic support of the local school superintendent, Roland B. Daniel, and the principal of Spencer High, F. R. Lampkin. Daniel was fundamentally opposed to academic education for black high school pupils, particularly in college preparatory subjects. "It is my opinion that we should give little attention at this time to the preparation of pupils for college," he wrote to Stern in December 1930. Moreover, he continued, "we have more Negro doctors and preachers now than the Negro population can support comfortably and it is easy for Negroes to be misled along this line." Daniel made it clear to the fund that he was committed to denying Columbus's black youth the opportunity to pursue academic courses of study. He also informed them that the principal he had selected, F. R. Lampkin, measured up "to our expectations." Daniel's perspectives on black secondary education made the philanthropists eager to participate in the Columbus experiment.[46]

Keller developed the curriculum for Spencer High as he did for all of the urban black high schools aided by Rosenwald money. Having become aware of black aspirations for academic education, Keller faced squarely the question of classical liberal versus industrial education for black high school pupils. In Keller's words, "On a number of occasions during my contact with pupils, teachers and parents, the question has been asked, 'Will the Spencer High School prepare me for college?'" Keller did not favor leaving the choice of curricula to black teachers and their pupils. Indeed, he praised the Columbus school authorities for not including college preparatory courses in Spencer High's curriculum. "There is exhibited commendable courage in eliminating traditional subjects which have no value for the more hand-minded boys and girls and especially for the negroes whose opportunity to make use of such traditional subjects is much more limited." On many occasions Keller advanced the argument that because black people were denied access to occupations in which they could apply academic training, it was the duty of school officials to eliminate the traditional academic subjects from black high schools. In place of the traditional academic curriculum, Keller offered a curriculum for "hand-minded" Negro boys and girls whose economic opportunities were restricted.[47]

In Keller's educational philosophy, "the culture of the hand-minded person was not that of the scholar." Taking the bricklayer as an idealized "hand-minded" person, Keller distinguished the education suited to "hand-minded" people from that appropriate for the scholar. The bricklayer's English, he contended, should relate "almost entirely to its use by contractors in contracts, specifications, and business letters." Keller then articulated the mathematics, social studies, and chemistry that were fitting for the bricklayer. His philosophy merits quoting in full:

> It would appear that for boys preparing to be bricklayers, for instance, algebra and plane geometry would be too heavy mental fare. While they should have command of the elementary operations and certainly should be able to erect a perpendicular to a horizontal surface, they need not be able to prove the propositions of Euclid. It is therefore suggested for boys and girls of this type there be substituted for the more advanced subjects, such as mathematics, chemistry and history, two general subjects. History might well be replaced by that type of information known variously as social science, current events, vocational civics, and the like. All of this is designed to adjust the worker to the society in which he lives and therefore to make him a more desirable and worthy member of the community. Mathematics and chemistry might well be replaced by that type of information sometimes designated as related technical knowledge. For the bricklayer this includes such topics as kind of clay, sand, and lime from which bricks are made, methods of making bricks, various kinds of brick and the purpose for which they are used, the history of building materials, the theory of arches, etc.

Although this curriculum theory reflected a system of values and beliefs that subordinated the freedom and choices of black children to the interests of an unequal and unjust southern society, Keller chose to view his own educational philosophy as one which "met the needs of the child." Keller's view, however, equated the "needs" of black children with the "needs" of a racially segmented and repressive labor market.[48]

When the aspirations and educational choices of black students ran counter to the roles prescribed for them by the philanthropic reformers, Keller invariably concluded that blacks were making choices not on the basis of need but out of hunger for prestige and a tendency to imitate whites. For example, the sociological survey of Columbus, Georgia, included an examination of the career aspirations of Spencer High's tenth grade pupils and of their parents' vocations. Seven of the eighty-four tenth graders listed stenography as their desired vocation. Yet Keller recommended specifically that Spencer High's pupils not have the opportunity to take stenography or typing, bookkeeping, and other commercial courses. The basis for his recommendation was that the sociological survey of black industrial opportunities in Columbus did not discover careers in commercial work for black high school graduates. Thus, said Keller, "If commercial courses were offered in the negro school there would no doubt be tremendous pressure to get into them and the only result would be keen disappointment for nearly everyone." The reason for this disappointment would be that black pupils, once trained in commercial fields, would be denied jobs in those occupations. Keller's curricula recommendations were adopted by Columbus's school officials, and black pupils at Spencer High were denied the opportunity to take courses in commercial fields. This was Keller's idea of "meeting the needs of the children."[49]

Spencer High's tenth graders, largely children of working-class parents, aspired to occupations more prestigious and higher paying than those held by their fathers and mothers. Of the eighty-two parents, fifty-three, or 67 percent, were common laborers, fifteen, or 18 percent, were skilled laborers—carpenters, bricklayers, blacksmiths, tailors, plumbers, and the like—and twelve, or 15 percent, were professionals, for example, teachers, ministers, and merchants. Seventy-four of the eighty-four tenth graders aspired to occupations above those of their parents. The majority, forty-five, or 54 percent, desired professional careers, thirty-six, or 43 percent, aspired to skilled occupations, two were undecided, and only one pupil listed a semiskilled job as a desired vocation. These pupils held career aspirations that the philanthropists and local school officials sought to repress. Spencer High's curriculum, which emphasized careers for cooks, maids, laundresses, seamstresses, auto mechanics, carpenters, bricklayers, and the like, was well aligned with the parents' occupations and was thus structured to reproduce those vocations in the children. The philanthropists confronted this problem in city after city, and in each case they recommended the reproduction of the local racially segmented labor market.[50]

The Rosenwald-sponsored survey of Greenville, South Carolina, demonstrated that, in 1930, black men worked mainly as janitors, porters, waiters, bellmen, butlers, hospital orderlies, elevator operators, cooks, farmers, mechanics, bricklayers, carpenters, tailors, welders, stationary firemen, and barbers. The principal occupations of black women were home and child nursing, cooking, waiting, house service, beauty culture, and laundering; 92 percent of the high school pupils' mothers were employed in those occupations. The sociological survey of Greenville included a study of the occupations of 1,824 parents and a study of the vocational choices of black pupils in the upper grades of the high school. Eighty-three percent of the parents were engaged in unskilled or semiskilled jobs. The study of parents' occupations also presented data on the average years of schooling and average wage per week by occupational category. Black mechanics averaged five years of schooling and earned a weekly wage of $25; greasers and washers in the automobile industry averaged four years of schooling. Beauty culture workers averaged eight

The newly completed William Spencer Industrial High School in Columbus, Georgia, 1930. Courtesy of Fisk University Library.

years of schooling and $10 per week. Janitors, with a mean of three years of schooling, earned $10 per week, and porters averaged four years of schooling and $8 per week. Their children had already achieved higher levels of education and desired more skilled and better-paying jobs.[51]

Although the fund's researchers discovered and reported to the philanthropists and local school officials that Greenville's black high school pupils showed virtually no desire to follow in their parents' occupations, it was still recommended that the high school train and socialize black pupils for occupations similar to those of their parents. As the Rosenwald survey observed:

Studies of the occupations of parents show that there is no general tendency of pupils to follow the vocation of their parents, but a study of this type does show the occupations around which the vocational life of the Negroes of the community is built, and regardless of the expressed desires of pupils in the elementary school and even in the high school to enter vocations other than those engaged in by their parents, because of factors over which children have no control, many of them will finally fall into the "major vocations" of the community.

Such recommendations, shared and adopted by philanthropists and Greenville's school officials, show the extent to which the implementation of an oppressive educational process for black children was a self-conscious effort. In this context the school was defined as an institution to train black pupils for occupations prescribed as "negro jobs" and one to prevent them from studying for vocations that were closed to black workers because of racism.[52]

One area closed to black workers was the textile industry. Significantly, Greenville was known as the textile center of the South, but blacks, except as janitors, were barred from jobs in the textile mills. In the antebellum South, however, the textile labor force included a significant number of black workers. The movement away from black labor began just before the Civil War, and by the late nineteenth century almost all of the cotton mill workers were white. Mill owners advanced the idea of an Anglo-Saxon kinship between management and labor. The resulting reliance on white labor and the attendant ideology of white nationalism reinforced an economic structure in which white workers, as long as they recognized the legal and customary authority of their exalted benefactors, would not have to face the prospect of active competition from black workers. In 1930 the South's one characteristic industry, textiles, excluded black workers. Likewise, Greenville's black high school curriculum, primarily an industrial program, excluded the whole area of textiles.[53]

The Rosenwald report recommended for black high school pupils a course in "washing and greasing" to prepare Greenville's black high school pupils for jobs at automobile service stations. It also recommended training in "public service occupations such as those of janitor, waiter, bellman, cook, bootblack, etc." "A course in shoe shining would prove unpopular among certain classes of Negroes in any southern community," the report continued, "because they do not realize its economic worth, and the splendid possibilities for developing a real vocation." This argument was characteristic of the philanthropists' thinking. Rather than focus on the reality that black workers, solely because of their race, had been excluded from most decent jobs in Greenville, the philanthropists chose to emphasize the "splendid possibilities" of shoe shining.[54]

The Winston-Salem, North Carolina, experiment was unique in that it forced the philanthropists to recognize that occupations generally held by black adults did not require a high school education. The new high school for black pupils was dedicated on 2 April 1931. The buildings, equipment, and grounds cost $400,000, of which the Rosenwald Fund contributed $50,000. In Winston-Salem, the tobacco industries employed 33.3 percent of the black male adult workers and 48 percent of the black female adult workers. To the dismay of Rosenwald agents, a survey of the tobacco factories from the stemming process to the making of cigarettes showed no process that could be taught in school. Mabel Byrd reported that "the machinist who cared for the highly intricate machines, in every case, was white, and this policy has been established over a period of years." In addition to the state of the tobacco industry, "no Negroes save janitors are employed in the Hanes Cotton Mills." The vast majority of jobs held by black adults in Winston-Salem required virtually no formal schooling and certainly none beyond the elementary school grades. This finding provoked the fund's curriculum expert, Keller, to reassess the relationship between black labor and formal education. As he stated, "It seems to me that a thoroughgoing study of many of the jobs available to negro boys and girls would reveal the fact that the actual technical knowledge represents a very small body of skills easily obtained by an intelligent pupil in a very brief period of time." Therefore, Keller maintained, "If this is true the industrial training of many young people is not a matter of very serious importance in their formal education." What, then, was the great importance of black secondary industrial education? According to Keller, its great mission was to give "purpose and motive" to the process of education and to make black adolescents "fully appreciative of their social heritage." In short, the ideological functions of black industrial education were more important than the technical functions. The primary aim was to gain the consent of black pupils to the racially segmented economy imposed on them by the dominant white society.[55]

One of the formidable problems faced by the philanthropists and their agents was to reconcile their racially distinct philosophies of public secondary education. Nowhere was this issue better illustrated than in the thoughts and actions of Bruce R. Payne, a former professor of secondary education at the University of Virginia who was then president of Peabody College in Nashville, Tennessee. An ardent believer in "democratic" ideals, Payne promoted white public secondary education. He did so in opposition to the ideas held by most southern whites that education beyond the elementary grades was not necessary except for children of social position and wealth. There was no subject on which Payne was more passionately eloquent than the right of every white child to as much education as he could absorb. Indeed, said Payne, "It is high time that under a popular government like ours, the use of the word 'masses' . . . should cease. Who are these superior beings that presume to sit thus in judgment upon their fellows, to assign them to classes, according to their high pleasure, to set for them metes and bounds beyond which they shall not go?" Yet on the subject of education of black children, Payne became one of those superior beings, presuming to sit in judgment upon his black fellows, to assign them to classes, and especially to set for them metes and bounds beyond which they were not to pass. As he wrote to his colleague George R. James of the Federal Reserve Board in August 1930: "You are dead right in saying that the problems of the negro schools and the white schools are not the same. We have got to know definitely what objectives any school has; particularly is that true in negro education. If we train negroes to live a life which human society forbids them to live after we have educated them, then they have a right to reprimand us after they are educated. I should expect such educated persons to become Bolshevists, and it will be our fault if they do." Afro-Americans, then, were not educated beyond their social position. Throughout the period 1900 to 1935, the philanthropists and their agents pushed two philosophies of public secondary education, one for democracy and one for oppression.[56]

Between 1928 and 1932, the Rosenwald Fund contributed money to the building of industrial departments in black high schools in Little Rock, Arkansas; Columbus, Georgia; Maysville, Kentucky; Winston-Salem, North Carolina; Greenville, South Carolina; and Atlanta, Georgia. It considered projects in many other cities. At no time, however, did the fund persuade any southern city to build a black high school devoted exclusively to industrial education despite its official policy of paying one-third of the total cost of such high schools and only one-fifth toward the cost of combined academic and industrial high schools. The fund did not contribute any money to help build purely academic high schools for black children. Although the philanthropists achieved limited success, the overall outcomes were far from their larger goal of establishing in the urban South a system of black secondary education that would train black youth for racially prescribed occupations and socialize them to fit into a repressive social order. The white South was too indifferent to the idea, and the black South generally resisted the philanthropists' model of secondary industrial education.[57]

In late 1931 the Rosenwald Fund withdrew abruptly from its campaigns to direct black secondary education into industrial channels. In vital respects, the fund's campaigns were the last major efforts by northern philanthropists to impose upon black children of the American South a racially repressive model of industrial education. These campaigns ended because of the lessons the philanthropists learned about race and class in the southern urban economy as the country moved deeper into the national economic depression. Northern philanthropists increasingly realized how sharp were the differences between their ideology of industrial education as a formula for racial segmentation in the labor market and the material reality of black economic oppression in the urban South. Building an ideological bridge across such intolerable contradictions was virtually impossible. The philanthropists' ideology of black secondary industrial education rested on two fundamental assumptions about black economic opportunities in the urban South. First, they assumed that certain occupations were virtually fixed as "Negro jobs" in which black workers were allegedly immune from active competition by white workers. These were the jobs the industrial high schools would train black youth to hold. Second, the philanthropists believed that expanding industrialization in the urban South would increase the standard of living for all classes, thereby widening the occupational opportunities for those on the bottom. Yet, because of fundamental changes in the southern economy during the late 1920s, and the philanthropists' own investigation of those changes as they occurred, the ideology of black secondary industrial education came apart at the seams.

The philanthropists' conception of black education and work in the urban South started to unravel by accident. They had set out in late 1929 to investigate local industrial opportunities for black workers in selected southern cities with the intent of pointing out, as Stern said, "in what lines Negroes have openings at present and in what numbers, as well as new opportunities for trained men where positions may be available." These investigations were expected to identify the jobs open to black workers so as to develop a structure and process of secondary industrial training that would channel black youth into the racially prescribed occupations. The unintended result, however, was the philanthropists' discovery that there were no "Negro jobs" in the urban South, no racially hierarchical economy in which each constituent class held fixed occupational slots. Rather, "Negro jobs" were mostly those jobs left over after whites achieved full employment. In periods of economic prosperity this meant that about 75 percent of southern black workers were farm workers, day laborers, and laundry women. Another 20 percent formed the urban working class of semiskilled laborers, public servants, and skilled artisans. The other 5 percent, the most economically advanced group, were farm owners, professionals, and small merchants. In periods of economic regression, however, many of these workers, particularly in the urban South, were pushed downward, and long-standing "Negro jobs" became "white jobs."[58]

The decade 1920 to 1930 was one period in which "Negro jobs" were transformed into "white jobs." As the economic depression struck hard in the rural sections of the South early in the decade, whites and blacks accelerated their migration to the cities in search of better opportunities. This flow of population from the farms to the cities converged later in the decade with other factors, including rising unemployment, declining production, and normal population growth, which in turn produced a crisis in the region's urban economies. At just this time the Rosenwald Fund agents were conducting sociological surveys of southern cities for its educational reforms with particular concern for the industrial opportunities of black workers.

George R. Arthur was one of the first Rosenwald agents to understand the significant displacement of black workers in the urban South. In

October 1929, having heard rumors about displacement, Arthur wrote to Karl F. Phillips, commissioner of conciliation in the U.S. Department of Labor, to request factual information on "the replacement of colored workers by white workers throughout the country, especially in southern cities." He sent copies of the same letter to J. A. Jackson of the U.S. Department of Commerce, Albion W. Hosley of Tuskegee Institute, Jesse O. Thomas, southern field director of the Urban League, and H. J. DeYarmett, superintendent of the trade school at Hampton Institute. DeYarmett had only fragmented evidence concerning displacement of workers. He told of a large contractor in Washington, D.C., who had for years employed black brickmasons and plasterers but had been forced to change to white labor because of recent clauses in the contracts of all-white unions requiring him to use only union labor. "My own observation has been that where the unions have become stronger in southern communities, it has become more difficult for the colored mechanic to secure work," replied DeYarmett. The well-known black sociologist Ira De A. Reid responded in behalf of the National Urban League. As director of the Urban League's Department of Research and Investigation, Reid was already examining the question of black job displacement in the urban South and had in the process discovered many instances. In Charlotte, North Carolina, the heavy trucks and transfers were being manned by white workers where black workers had formerly been. Moreover, "White school boys are taking the place of Negro elevator girls," said Reid. In Kansas City, Missouri, black waitresses were dismissed from a large drugstore and replaced by white females. Reid found that "in Spartanburg, South Carolina, white men are taking many of the jobs formerly done by Negroes such as driving express wagons and portering." Similarly, in Columbia, South Carolina, white workers had replaced black workers as drivers of garbage and dirt wagons for the city. Black workers in the same city were "losing out in the building trades." In Atlanta, Georgia, there was a general feeling among black workers "that the jobs they were losing to whites resulted from premeditation and proscription."[59]

Reid discovered in Charleston, South Carolina, that black male laborers were "losing constantly in all lines of work, particularly in building trades." According to Reid,

> Union men, particularly carpenters, have been known to walk off jobs when Negroes come on. White men are driving wagons instead of Negroes who formerly performed all of this service. The streets are now being cleaned by whites, but the asphalt paving is done by Negroes. The longshoremen occupations have remained intact for Negro workers. White men, however, have taken over the scavenger

positions with the city. Three years ago Negroes are reported to have laughed when white men were seen digging streets for sewer pipes. It is now the usual thing to see white men doing this work.

Similar patterns emerged throughout the urban South. In Savannah, Georgia, laundry wagons were being driven by white men when once only black men drove them. Jesse O. Thomas found in Jacksonville, Florida, an organization known as the Blue Shirt, which he described as a "Chamber of Commerce for the white working man." Its leaders drove about the city demanding the displacement of black workers. Any white employer who failed to comply with the Blue Shirt's demand was assailed in the organization's newsletter as a "nigger lover." After observing incidents of displacement in several southern cities, Thomas concluded: "There has been a complete reversal of the white South toward menial labor. A white man at the present time has no fear of losing his social cast because he digs a ditch, drives a garbage or scavenger truck."[60]

Because the philanthropists' program of black secondary industrial education rested heavily on the assumption that certain industrial occupations in the urban South belonged predominantly, if not exclusively, to black workers, they were naturally concerned whether the reports of displacement were true. Reid and Thomas had fine reputations as social investigators for the Urban League. The philanthropists, however, always contracted their own social scientists to conduct important social research. Thus the Rosenwald Fund requested Charles S. Johnson, eminent sociologist and longtime associate of the fund, to conduct a detailed and systematic sociological study of the displacement of black workers in selected southern cities. Johnson conducted inquiries in ten southern cities between 20 October and 4 November 1929. The cities were Montgomery and Birmingham, Alabama; Memphis and Nashville, Tennessee; Shreveport and New Orleans, Louisiana; Atlanta, Georgia; Jackson, Mississippi; Little Rock, Arkansas; and Louisville, Kentucky. At the time Johnson completed his investigation the Rosenwald Fund was still contemplating monetary contributions toward the construction of secondary industrial high schools in all of the ten cities except Montgomery and Jackson.[61]

Johnson discovered that a cluster of economic changes "placed white and Negro workers more acutely in competition for the same jobs, with a result that white workers were frequently given preference, particularly on city, county, and state work where political influence can grant favors to voters and receive votes in return." Population growth, mechanization, the increasing number of white women in industrial occupations, and the influx of rural workers converged to heighten the competition between blacks and whites for a declining number of industrial jobs because of the post–World War I depression of such industries as coal, lumber, iron, and steel, and, intermittently, building construction. Moreover, skilled labor in southern cities came increasingly under the control of labor unions, which either restricted or discouraged black membership. The textile industry—the dominant and most rapidly growing industry in the South—generally excluded black workers from all but janitorial service. The new occupational opportunities that opened in southern cities, including those in radio, auto mechanics, trucking, taxicab driving, and the like, offered few opportunities to black workers, and certainly none in skilled positions except in those rare instances when the owners were black. The growing shortage of jobs and increasing rates of unemployment precipitated white organizations' insistence on the employment of white workers even if that meant discharging black workers en masse. Among such white groups were the Federation of Women's Clubs, Junior Leagues, Ku Klux Klan, Blue Shirt, and White Knights. Another factor effecting the displacement of black workers was the emerging militant racist reaction to interracial contact between servants and customers, which affected black workers in hotels as bellmen, as barbers when the fad of bobbing women's hair emerged, and in certain food industries.[62]

The character and details of the displacement varied from city to city, but structurally the process was similar across the urban South. White workers who felt compelled to take jobs formerly regarded as "Negro work" resolved their frustrations by excluding black workers and by securing an increase in wages to perform the same tasks, even though they had less experience than the black workers they displaced. In Montgomery, in 1924, most of the truck drivers for the lumber, coal, and ice companies, wholesale houses, and laundries were black. By 1929, from 60 to 90 percent were white. In 1924 there were fewer than ten white carpenters in Montgomery; by 1929, about 50 percent of the carpenters were white. The same was true for brickmasonry. Johnson found that construction companies, which had used only black carpenters and brick masons at the beginning of the 1920s, used all-white or majority-white work forces at the end of the decade. Even the new buildings under construction at the Alabama State Normal School for Negroes were being erected with no black mechanics. Similarly, barber shops, insurance companies, and hotels replaced black workers with white workers. The Alabama Power Company had used many black workers as wiremen, but in 1929 all of the company's wiremen were white. A pickle factory that once had a labor force that was 80 percent black had changed to "only white workers." Johnson learned of complaints by black workers that the Federation of Women's Clubs and the Junior Chamber of Commerce, in their campaigns to find jobs for the newly arrived whites from the rural sections, urged businesses to replace their black workers with white workers.[63]

In Jackson, Mississippi, black workers in the building trades were being displaced rapidly. From 1919 to 1925, blacks and whites were organized in the same unions, and blacks were four times as numerous as whites. The white unionists complained that their families objected to interracial meetings, and to resolve the tension the American Federation of Labor established separate locals for black unionists. Following this action the black mechanics quickly lost control of jobs in the building trades. The white foremen felt responsible only to the white locals. Consequently, in 1929, there were "practically no Negro apprentices in training." Black plasterers in Jackson lost about 50 percent of their work. Blacks had predominated as drivers of bread, grocery, and laundry wagons, but in 1929, about 95 percent of Jackson's drivers were white. Even the black street cleaners were displaced. Once blacks had done all the street cleaning in Jackson. In 1929 white workers drove the wagons and blacks lifted the garbage cans to the wagons. In the new Post Office the black mail handlers were replaced with white mail handlers. The Jitney Jingle stores replaced black porters with white porters. The displaced black workers in Jackson cited the Federation of Women's Clubs, the Chamber of Commerce, the mayor's office, and the White Knights as the key groups demanding that "the better paid jobs be given to white workers."[64]

In Atlanta, Georgia, as in many other places throughout the urban South, the economically rational principle of hiring the best-qualified workers at the cheapest wage was stood on its head. Atlanta's Sanitary Department discharged all of its black truck drivers and replaced them with white drivers. The experienced black drivers had been paid $60 per month; the new white drivers were hired at a minimum wage of $100 per month. Moreover, some of the displaced black workers were then re-hired as helpers to the white drivers and paid $50 per month. Such patterns were consistent with the Chamber of Commerce's campaign to boost Atlanta as a haven for "satisfied, intelligent, contented Anglo-Saxon labor." The Jacob Drug Company, a chain of 120 stores in Atlanta, had for thirty years employed black youth as messengers. On 15 July 1929, however, the 230 black messengers were discharged and the white youth hired to take their places were given an increase in pay of $3 per week, plus a regulation uniform. Similarly, between 1919 and 1929, black truck drivers for the Hormel Company, Swift Company, Cudahy Packing Company, Wilson and Company, and White Provision Company were replaced by white drivers. The Georgia Baptist Hospital, one of the South's largest private hospitals, discharged its entire black work force and gave an increase in pay to the new white workers. The white patients, however, complained about the inexperience and inefficiency of the white workers and, after two months of trial and error, the black workers were called back. The black workers were given the same salary as before they were discharged even though the whites who replaced them were paid more during their short tenure.[65]

There were very few black workers in Atlanta's automobile industry. J. H. Wilson, general manager of the Ford Motor Company, maintained that his black employees were discharged because the company did not have racially separate washroom and dressing room facilities. Wilson also stated that he saw no future for black workers in the southern automobile industry. The regional manager of the Chevrolet Motor Company reported that none of his black workers had been displaced, but he employed only eighteen blacks among eighteen hundred workers and they were janitors and "yard boys." In Memphis, Johnson discovered that black skilled and unskilled laborers were being displaced. Black linesmen and truck drivers were being replaced with white workers. The local May Brothers Sawmill had employed three hundred black workers in 1919 but had fewer than fifteen in 1929. Black employees in railroad shops were "definitely being replaced." Further, reported Johnson: "In public works it is very noticeable that large groups of white men are doing the common labor which was formerly considered Negro jobs. Such vocations may be mentioned as street cleaning, telephone company jobs, excavating, teamsters, street grading, and repair work for the street car company." Similarly, in New Orleans the excavating, garbage collection, and cleaning of railroad cars, once done by black workers, had been taken over by whites in 1929. "Shop workers, tinsmiths, hostlers' helpers, cabinet makers' helpers before the war were all Negroes," Johnson wrote of New Orleans, "now they are all white." All of this and more were included in the report Johnson submitted to the Rosenwald Fund in November 1929.[66]

The northern philanthropists, therefore, found themselves in the peculiar position of advocating and implementing secondary industrial education to train black youth in certain occupations just at the time when black workers were being pushed out of those jobs and replaced by white workers. The philanthropists assumed that in the urban South black workers held an economic position, which, even if not absolutely fixed and permanent, was at least permanent enough to train and socialize black children into it. This economic position, albeit at the bottom of the industrial ladder, was viewed as the basis for regional social stability and economic prosperity. Hence secondary school courses in carpentry, bricklaying, plastering, painting, metal work, plumbing, shoe repairing, chauffeuring, barbering, electrical work, auto mechanics, printing, cement finishing, furniture repair, truck driving, and mill work were introduced and taught. Meanwhile, unemployed white laborers, compelled under distressed economic conditions to accept any grade of work and almost any rate of pay, collaborated with owners, politicians, editors, ministers, auxiliary groups, and militant right-wing organizations to oust black workers from those occupations. The philanthropists saw that the practical objective of their model of black secondary industrial education could not be attained. The ultimate failure of their industrial education programs had come not because of the absence of capital and devoted effort but because of changes in the southern and national economy which they did not foresee, and which, even if they had foreseen, they could not have prevented. Moreover, once they became aware of patterns of displacement they had not the knowledge or means to adapt industrial education to this level of oppression. No class of laborers could be educated for displacement.

The philanthropists now faced a blank wall. The rampant displacement of black workers from even the lowest rung of the industrial ladder posed anew the question of what could be accomplished by the industrial education of black youth. The philanthropists' astonishing answer was to terminate their movement to industrialize black secondary education and to turn their wealth and power more fully toward shaping black collegiate education. During the late 1920s, Hampton and Tuskegee abandoned their industrial training programs and soon became the two best-endowed black colleges for liberal arts education. The black federal land-grant colleges, built to foster agriculture and industrial education, were also transformed into basically liberal arts institutions. A system of higher education, however, presupposed the existence of academic high schools with adequate courses of study taught during a definite series of years by competent instructors. Yet it was that system of education which the philanthropists, in cooperation with southern state and local governments, had used their wealth and power to subordinate to the perceived necessity of training blacks to fit into the South's caste-ridden economy. Without question, the great economic expenditures and reform crusades for black industrial education contributed directly and significantly to the underdevelopment of black secondary education.

Whereas the majority, 54 percent, of southern white children of high school age were enrolled in public high schools by the mid-1930s, more than eight out of every ten black children of high school age were not enrolled in secondary schools. Table 6.5 reveals that, in 1933–34, the 152,310 black students enrolled in high schools constituted only 18 percent of the 847,163 black children of high school age in the sixteen former slave states. This pattern of southern black high school enrollment held through the 1930s. In 1940, as illustrated in Table 6.6, only 23 percent of the black high school age population was enrolled in public

TABLE 6.5

High School Enrollment by Age, Race, and Southern States, 1933–1934

State	Number of children 14 to 17 years of age, inclusive, 1930		Enrollment in secondary grades, 1933–34		Percentage ratio of enrollment to number of children	
	White	Black	White	Black	White	Black
Alabama	152,937	90,654	60,821	9,162	40	10
Arkansas	122,944	41,655	51,066	4,038	42	10
Delaware	14,623	2,368	9,573	771	66	33
Florida	78,055	33,775	52,415	5,550	67	16
Georgia	162,865	107,158	89,470	10,927	55	10
Kentucky	196,547	16,751	83,812	7,079	43	42
Louisiana	109,951	65,304	62,836	8,832	57	14
Maryland	97,122	19,714	49,781	5,536	51	28
Mississippi	87,549	93,660	57,959	6,757	66	7
Missouri	248,199	13,490	154,059	6,033	62	45
North Carolina	203,852	93,578	124,281	24,725	61	26
South Carolina	85,722	87,493	51,616	10,377	60	12
Tennessee	181,106	40,233	77,565	10,751	43	27
Texas	408,230	72,725	239,887	25,505	59	35
Virginia	147,543	60,816	80,697	12,475	55	21
West Virginia	136,638	7,789	75,114	3,792	55	49
Totals	2,433,893	847,163	1,320,952	152,310	54	18

Source: Wilkerson, *Special Problems of Negro Education*, p. 36.

secondary schools. In Alabama, Arkansas, Georgia, Louisiana, Mississippi, and South Carolina, states with large black populations, less than 18 percent of the black high school age population was enrolled in public secondary schools in 1940. For the nation as a whole and the white South, the elite public high school of the late nineteenth century was transformed into the "people's college" during the first third of the twentieth century. For blacks in the South, the struggle to attain public high schools for the majority of their high school age children would continue beyond the post–World War II era. While American youth in general were being pushed into public high schools, southern black youth, a sizable minority of black high school age children in America, were being locked out of the nation's public high schools. This oppression of black schoolchildren during the critical stage of the transformation of Ameri-

TABLE 6.6

Secondary School Enrollment and Graduates in
Black Public Schools in Southern States, 1940

State	Population 15–19 years of age, inclusive	Secondary school enrollment	Percent of population enrolled	High school graduates
Alabama	104,757	17,181	16.4	2,056
Arkansas	49,534	7,304	14.7	909
Delaware	3,319	953	28.7	92
Florida	48,698	11,365	23.3	1,299
Georgia	118,155	18,938	16.0	1,991
Kentucky	19,941	6,707	33.6	898
Louisiana	86,881	15,360	17.6	1,444
Maryland	28,987	8,306	28.6	1,226
Mississippi	114,415	10,739	9.3	1,425
Missouri	19,514	9,102	46.6	1,209
North Carolina	118,716	39,550	33.3	4,504
South Carolina	102,278	17,263	16.8	1,881
Tennessee	49,952	12,918	25.8	1,670
Texas	93,908	37,285	39.7	4,227
Virginia	74,438	21,658	29.0	2,692
West Virginia	11,775	5,330	45.2	678
Total	1,046,167	240,049	22.9	28,201

Source: U.S. Bureau of the Census, *Sixteenth Census of the United States, 1940*
(Washington, D.C.: U.S. Government Printing Office, 1941), vol. 2, pt. 1, pp. 209, 391,
899; pt. 3, pp. 177, 335, 509; pt. 4, pp. 205, 315; pt. 5, p. 269; pt. 6, pp. 349, 563, 765;
pt. 7, pp. 137, 445; Blose and Caliver, *Statistics of the Education of Negroes.*

can secondary education seriously affected the long-term development of
education in the black community and was one of the fundamental reasons that the educational progress of black Americans lagged far behind
that of other Americans.

7

TRAINING THE APOSTLES

OF LIBERAL CULTURE

BLACK HIGHER EDUCATION, 1900–1935

FROM THE Reconstruction era through the Great Depression black higher education in the South existed essentially through a system of private liberal arts colleges. During this period, the federal government gave scant aid to black land-grant schools, and the southern states followed with a few funds for black normal schools and colleges. Between 1870 and 1890, nine federal black land-grant colleges were established in the South, and this number increased to sixteen by 1915. In that same year, there were also seven state-controlled black colleges in the South. These black federal land-grant and state schools, however, were colleges or normal schools in name only. According to the 1917 survey of black higher education conducted by Thomas Jesse Jones, only one of the sixteen black federal land-grant schools in the former slave states taught students at the collegiate level. The Florida Agricultural and Mechanical College enrolled 12 black college students. The seven black state colleges or normal schools had no black students enrolled in collegiate grades. Of the 7,513 students enrolled in the combined twenty-three black land-grant and state schools, 4,061 were classified as elementary level students, 3,400 were considered secondary level students and, as mentioned above, only 12 were actually enrolled in the collegiate curriculum. In 1915 there were 2,474 black students enrolled in collegiate grades in the southern states and the District of Columbia, and only 12 of them attended land-grant and state schools. Hence, as late as World War I virtually all of the black college students in the southern states were enrolled in privately owned colleges. This structure of black higher education, albeit significantly improved, persisted into the late 1920s. Arthur J. Klein's 1928 survey of black higher education demonstrated that the private black colleges were nearly all the sole promoters of higher education for Afro-American students. For the academic year 1926–27, there were 13,860 black college students in America, and approximately 75 percent of them were enrolled in private colleges. By the mid-1930s, this situation had changed and black college students in public institutions accounted for 43 percent of the total black college enrollment in the sixteen former slave states and District of Columbia. Until this time, however, private philanthropy largely determined the shape and even the survival of southern black higher education.[1]

In the South the history of black higher education from 1865 to 1935 involves largely a study of the interrelationship between philanthropy and black communities—or at least black leaders—in the development of colleges and professional schools for black youth. Three separate and distinct philanthropic groups formed the power structure in black higher education during this period. At the beginning of the Reconstruction era northern white benevolent societies and denominational bodies (missionary philanthropy) and black religious organizations (Negro philanthropy) established the beginnings of a system of higher education for black southerners. The third group of philanthropists was large corporate philanthropic foundations and wealthy individuals (industrial philanthropy). They had been involved in the development of black common schools and industrial normal schools since the Reconstruction era, but in 1914 they turned their attention to plans for the systematic development of a few select institutions of black higher education. From the late nineteenth century through the first third of the twentieth century these various groups of philanthropists debated the role of higher education in the overall scheme of black education and the relationship of classical liberal training to larger issues of black political and economic life. At the core of different educational ideologies and reform movements lay the central goal of preparing black leaders or "social guides," as they were sometimes called, for participation in the political economy of the New South. Each philanthropic group, therefore, took as its point of departure a particular view of the relationship of higher education to the "Negro's place" in the New South and shaped its educational policy and practices around that vision. The different philanthropic groups, particularly the missionary and industrial philanthropists, were in sharp disagreement over the ends and means of black education in general. Most visible were their divergent conceptions of the value and purpose of black higher education.

The northern mission societies, which were most prominent in the early crusade to establish institutions of higher education for the exslaves, were also largely responsible for sustaining the leading black colleges. The American Missionary Association (AMA) colleges for the freed people included Fisk University, Straight University (now Dillard), Talladega College, and Tougaloo College. The Freedmen's Aid Society of the Methodist Episcopal church founded Bennett College, Clark University, Claflin College, Meharry Medical College, Morgan College, Philander Smith College, Rust College, and Wiley College. The American Baptist Home Mission Society (ABHMS) administered Benedict College, Bishop College, Morehouse College, Shaw University, Spelman Seminary, and Virginia Union University. The Presbyterian Board of Missions for Freedmen maintained Biddle University (now Johnson C. Smith), Knoxville College, and Stillman Seminary. The major nondenominational colleges operated by independent boards of northern missionaries were Atlanta University, Howard University, and Leland University.[2]

The leading Negro philanthropic organization was the African Methodist Episcopal church, which paved the way for black religious denominations to establish and maintain colleges for black students. The leading AME colleges were Allen University, Morris Brown College, and Wilberforce College. Other AME schools were Paul Quinn College, Edward Waters College, Kittrell College, and Shorter College. The college work fostered by the African Methodist Episcopal Zion church was confined to one institution, Livingstone College. The Colored Methodist Episcopal church owned and operated four colleges: Lane, Paine, Texas, and Miles Memorial. The bulk of educational work on the college level promoted by black Baptist denominations was carried on in schools under the control of the American Baptist Home Mission Society. Still, several state conventions of black Baptists undertook to provide higher education for black youth in pressing areas not provided for by the ABHMS. Black colleges founded by the black Baptists included Arkansas Baptist College, Selma University, and Virginia College and Seminary. Most of the colleges financed by black religious organizations were small and inadequately equipped, but so were those administered by white religious organizations. According to Arthur Klein's 1928 survey of black colleges, black church organizations had been able to provide an average annual income for their colleges in excess of that for institutions operated by the northern white denominational boards. Black religious organizations owned so few of the total number of black colleges, however, that less than 15 percent of the total number of black college students were enrolled in institutions sponsored by those organizations. The black colleges supported and controlled by white missionary philanthropists enrolled a sizable majority of black college and professional students.[3]

The missionary philanthropists rallied their colleagues to support classical liberal education for black Americans as a means to achieve racial equality in civil and political life. They assumed that the newly emancipated blacks would move into mainstream national culture, largely free to do and become what they chose, limited only by their own intrinsic worth and effort. It was supposed axiomatically, in other words, that the former slaves would be active participants in the republic on an equal footing with all other citizens. Education, then, according to the more liberal and dominant segments of missionary philanthropists, was intended to prepare a college-bred black leadership to uplift the black masses from the legacy of slavery and the restraints of the postbellum caste system. The AMA's "civilizing mission" demanded permanent institutions of higher education that could educate exceptional black youth to become leaders of their people. Thus the missionary philanthropists valued the higher education of black leaders over all other forms of educational work. To these philanthropists, black leadership training meant, above all, higher classical liberal education. This view reflected, on one hand, their paternalistic tendencies to make unilateral decisions regarding the educational needs of blacks. On the other hand, such enthusiastic support for black higher education expressed—making due allowance for exceptions—the missionaries' principled liberalism, which was innocent of any inclination to doubt the intellectual potential of black Americans. As the Freedmen's Aid Society put it, "This society (in connection with similar organizations) has demonstrated to the South that the freedmen possess good intellectual abilities and are capable of becoming good scholars. Recognizing the brotherhood of mankind and knowing that intellect does not depend upon the color of the skin nor the curl of the hair, we never doubted the Negro's ability to acquire knowledge, and distinguish himself by scholarly attainments." It was the mission societies' primary duty, argued one philanthropist, "to educate . . . a number of blacks and send them forth to regenerate their own people."[4]

To be sure, missionary philanthropists were not proposing social changes that were revolutionary by national standards, but they were radical within the southern social order. Equality was carefully defined as political and legal equality. They consented to inequality in the economic structure, generally shied away from questions of racial integration, and were probably convinced that blacks' cultural and religious values were inferior to those of middle-class whites. Their liberalism on civil and political questions was matched by their conservatism on cultural, religious, and economic matters. Missionary philanthropists held that slavery had generated pathological religious and cultural practices in the black community. Slavery, not race, kept blacks from acquiring the important moral and social values of thrift, industry, frugality, and sobriety, all of which were necessary to live a sustained Christian life. In turn, these missing morals and values prevented the development of a stable family life among Afro-Americans. Therefore, missionaries argued, it was essential for education to introduce the ex-slaves to the values and rules of modern society. Without education, they concluded, blacks would rapidly degenerate and become a national menace to American civilization. In vital respects, such views are easily identified with the more conservative retrogressionist ideologies of the late nineteenth century. Generally, retrogressionist arguments, as George Fredrickson and Herbert Gutman have shown, supported the advocacy of various forms of external control over blacks, including disfranchisement and increasingly rigorous legal segregation.[5]

For the equalitarian missionaries, black economic and social conditions merely reflected the debasing effects of slavery and had nothing to do with racial characteristics. They saw no reason not to extend equal civil and political rights to black Americans. Moreover, because blacks were mentally capable and entitled to equal rights under the law, education was viewed as a means to liberate the former slaves from the effects of enslavement. In the words of the Freedmen's Aid Society, "Let us atone for our sins, as much as possible, by furnishing schools and the means of improvement for the children, upon whose parents we have inflicted such fearful evils. Let us lend a helping hand in their escape from the degradation into which we have forced them by our complicity with oppressors. Justice, stern justice, demands this at our hands. Let us pay the debt we owe this race before we complain of weariness in the trifling sums we have given for schools and churches." Consequently, the missionary philanthropists conducted a continual criticism of the political disfranchisement, civil inequality, mob violence, and poor educational opportunities that characterized black life in the American South. From this perspective, they supported the training of a black college-bred leadership to protect the masses from "wicked and designing men."[6]

The mission societies started their educational crusade by concentrating upon schools for elementary level training, but by the early 1870s their emphasis had shifted to the establishment and maintenance of higher educational institutions. In 1870, the AMA, for example, had 157 common schools. By 1874, that number had declined to 13. In the meantime, however, the number of AMA colleges, high schools, and normal schools increased from 5 in 1867 to 29 in 1872 with the primary objective of training black youth as teachers. The AMA and other missionary philanthropists believed that common school and eventually secondary education were a state and local responsibility to be shared by private societies only until it could be assumed by state governments. Their colleges, however, were to be permanent. From the outset, the missionaries named their key institutions "colleges" and "universities," although most of their students were scarcely literate and virtually all of them were enrolled at the subcollegiate level. These labels, as Horace Mann Bond stated, "tell us that the founders took emancipation seriously, believing that the Civil War had settled, indeed, the issue of human inequality in the nation; they also tell us that the founders were applying, to the newly freed population, the ancient faith in the efficacy of higher education to elevate a people." The missionary colleges did not, as was often charged, offer their black students collegiate studies before they were ready. For instance, classes opened at the AMA's Talladega College in November 1867. All 140 students were in the elementary grades. Officials did not begin planning college work until 1878, and no such courses were outlined in the catalog until 1890. The first bachelor's degree was not granted until 1895. Generally, the missionaries developed their institutions of higher education at a reasonable and responsible pace.[7]

Consistent with their view of the need for a well-trained black leadership, the missionaries made liberal culture rather than industrial training the chief aim of their curriculum. The courses in the black colleges controlled by missionaries were similar to those in a majority of contemporary liberal arts schools. Freshmen studied Latin, Greek, and mathematics. Sophomores were taught Greek, Latin, French, mathematics, and natural science. Juniors studied the same courses with additional work in German, natural philosophy, history, English, and astronomy. Mental and moral science and political science were added for the seniors. Regular studies were supplemented at stated times with required essays, debates, declamations, and original addresses. Missionary colleges offered at least a smattering of industrial courses—mainly agriculture, building trades, and domestic science—but normally these courses were offered in the secondary or grammar grades. Some college students took manual training courses because these courses were usually connected with student work programs that allowed them to work their way through school. Industrial training, however, had no major role in the missionaries' philosophy and program of training a leadership class to guide the ex-slaves in their social, economic, and political development. In 1896 Henry L. Morehouse became the first to use the words "talented tenth" to describe this philosophy and program of black education. W. E. B. DuBois would soon make the concept central to his writings on higher education. As Morehouse put it, "In all ages the mighty impulses that have propelled a people onward in their progressive career, have proceeded from a few gifted souls." The "talented tenth" should be "trained to analyze and to generalize" by an education that would produce "thoroughly disciplined minds." From the missionaries' vantage point, this could be accomplished only through a solid grounding in the classical liberal curriculum.[8]

Between 1865 and 1900, there were tensions between the denominational missionary societies and the black leadership, but generally not over the question of curriculum. Black leaders also believed that the "Negro problem" could be solved most quickly through the training of southern black youth—mostly males—in the best traditions of New England culture and by sending such college-bred persons among the

masses as scholars, ministers, doctors, lawyers, businessmen, and politicians. Colleges such as Fisk, Atlanta, and Howard were viewed as social
settlements that imparted the culture of New England to black boys and
girls along with the culture of the Greeks and Romans. During the first
third of the twentieth century blacks would begin to modify this philosophy of education to include the scientific study of black life and culture
as DuBois so successfully inaugurated at Atlanta University in 1900 and
as Carter G. Woodson initiated with the founding of the *Journal of
Negro History* in 1916. But until this time black leaders and missionary
philanthropists generally agreed that the transplanted New England college in southern soil was the proper way to educate the sons and daugh-
ters of ex-slaves. This shared conception of the appropriate education of
black leaders was reflected in the curriculum of colleges owned and
operated by black religious organizations. Languages and mathematics
received greater emphasis than the other courses in these colleges. The
required subjects usually included Latin, Greek, English, mathematics,
elementary sciences, history, and mental and moral philosophy. The
electives included Latin, French, German, chemistry, physics, and bi-
ology. Thus it was agreed that prospective black leaders could not be
properly educated for teaching and leadership positions through industrial education. When the time came that white students who planned
to become teachers, doctors, lawyers, ministers, and professors "should
learn to hoe and plow and lay bricks rather than go to literary and
classical schools," wrote President James G. Merrill of Fisk in 1901, "it
will be the right policy to shut off all our literary and classical schools for
negroes in the South." Consequently, despite sharp tensions between missionaries and black leaders over questions of black participation in the
administration and faculty of missionary colleges, the two groups shared
a common conception of the appropriate training of black leaders, and
this common ground kept relations fairly harmonious. Both groups believed in the "talented tenth" theory.[9]

How did the "talented tenth" theory work out in practice? Between
1865 and 1900, the positive accomplishments of black higher education
were impressive. Of all the evaluations that could be cited, the most
profound and most eloquent was penned by DuBois, who praised the
early missionary philanthropists as "men radical in their belief in Negro
possibility." By 1900, DuBois continued, the black colleges supported by
northern missionary and black religious organizations had "trained in
Greek and Latin and mathematics, 2,000 men; and these men trained
fully 50,000 others in morals and manners, and they in turn taught the
alphabet to nine millions of men." The black colleges were far from
perfect, concluded DuBois, but "above the sneers of critics" stood "one
crushing rejoinder: in a single generation they put thirty thousand black

teachers in the South" and "wiped out the illiteracy of the majority of the black people of the land."[10]

Yet in 1900, the mission societies and black religious organizations knew that their existing institutions had many defects, that they had nowhere near the amount of capital needed to correct those defects, and that the production of black college and professional students and graduates was minuscule compared to the number needed merely to fill the educational, medical, legal, and ministerial positions in a segregated black community. As illustrated in Table 7.1, in 1900 there were 3,880 black students in colleges and professional schools and fewer than 400 graduates of college and professional programs. These new graduates were added to the existing pool of about 3,000 other graduates in a total black population of nearly 10 million. A decade later less than one-third of 1 percent of college-age blacks were attending college compared with more than 5 percent among whites. The ratio of black physicians to the total black population was 1 to 3,194 compared to 1 to 553 among whites; for lawyers the black ratio was 1 to 12,315 compared with 1 to 718 among whites; for college professors, 1 to 40,611 among blacks and 1 to 5,301 among whites; and in the teaching profession there was 1 black teacher for every 334 black persons compared with a ratio of 1 to 145 for whites. The small number and percentage of blacks enrolled in colleges and professional schools demonstrated clearly that nowhere near 10 percent of the college-age black population benefitted from higher education. However aggressively missionary and black religious leaders defended the wisdom of providing classical liberal education for the "talented tenth," they admitted to themselves that they had fallen far short of their goal, and they saw no light at the end of the tunnel.[11]

Meanwhile, beginning in the 1880s, industrial philanthropy, which had paralleled the growth of missionary and black religious philanthropy, placed its emphasis almost exclusively on industrial training. Industrial philanthropy began in the postbellum South with the educational reforms of the northern-based Peabody Educational Fund, which was founded in 1867 and was boosted by the establishment of the John F. Slater Fund in 1882. From the outset, the leaders of the industrial philanthropic foundations favored racial inequality in the American South and attached themselves early on to the Hampton Idea. Encouraged by Hampton's success, the trustees of the Slater Fund decided to concentrate their grants on industrial education. After 1890, J. L. M. Curry, former slaveholder and congressman in the antebellum South, assumed the position of field agent for both the Peabody and Slater funds and advanced further the Hampton-Tuskegee program of industrial education. With so much emphasis on Negro industrial training by such wealthy and prominent organizations and individuals, the black colleges came in for a good

TABLE 7.1
Black College and Professional Students and Graduates in Southern States and the District of Columbia, by Sex, 1900

State or District of Columbia	College students		Professional students		College and professional students	College graduates		Professional graduates		College and professional graduates
	Male	Female	Male	Female	Total	Male	Female	Male	Female	Total
Alabama	23	10	206	35	274	3	1	6	7	17
Arkansas	49	21	66	0	136	3	1	0	0	4
Delaware	12	8	0	0	20	1	0	0	0	1
District of Columbia	357	125	326	32	840	3	0	47	11	61
Florida	1	0	16	0	17	0	0	0	0	0
Georgia	223	67	183	67	540	6	3	23	1	33
Kentucky	18	18	23	0	59	0	0	3	0	3
Louisiana	23	12	41	12	88	6	3	11	7	27
Maryland	10	1	19	0	30	0	0	5	0	5
Mississippi	46	6			52	13	2	0	0	15
Missouri	12	1	0	0	13	0	0	0	0	0
North Carolina	348	81	178	13	620	39	4	33	5	81
South Carolina	45	31	65	0	141	6	6	0	0	12
Tennessee	220	77	281	0	578	13	2	59	0	74
Texas	97	91	41	0	229	3	0	1	0	4
Virginia	47	6	108	0	161	9	0	18	0	27
West Virginia	0	0	0	0	0	0	0	0	0	0
Total	1,562	606	1,553	159	3,880	105	22	206	31	364

Source: U.S. Commissioner of Education, *Report, 1899–1900* (Washington, D.C.: U.S. Government Printing Office, 1901), 2:2506–7.

deal of direct and indirect criticism. Much was said of black share-croppers who sought to learn Latin and knew nothing of farming, of pianos in cabins, and of college-bred Afro-Americans unable to obtain jobs.[12]

The industrial philanthropic foundations established in the early twentieth century followed the same pattern at least until the post–World War I period. The General Education Board, Anna T. Jeanes Foundation, Phelps-Stokes Fund, Carnegie Foundation, Laura Spelman Rockefeller Memorial Fund, and Julius Rosenwald Fund, all established between 1902 and 1917, cooperated in behalf of the Hampton-Tuskegee program of black industrial training. Moreover, industrial philanthropists viewed the missionary program of black higher education as the futile and even dangerous work of misguided romantics. In 1899 Tuskegee trustee William H. Baldwin, Jr., expressed the industrial philanthropists' general disappointment with the missionary colleges. Summarizing the missionary educational work from the Reconstruction era to the end of the nineteenth century, Baldwin commented:

> The days of reconstruction were dark for all. Their sting has not yet gone. Then appeared from the North a new army—an army of white teachers, armed with the spelling-book and the Bible; and from their attack there were many casualties on both sides, the southern whites as well as the blacks. For, although the spelling-book and the Bible were necessary for the proper education of the negro race, yet, with a false point of view, the northern white teacher educated the negro to hope that through the books he might, like the white men, learn to live from the fruits of a literary education. How false that theory was, thirty long years of experience has proved. That was not their opportunity. Their opportunity was to be taught the dignity of manual labor and how to perform it. We began at the wrong end. Instead of educating the negro in the lines which were open to him, he was educated out of his natural environment and the opportunities which lay immediately about him.

Convinced that what Afro-Americans needed most to learn was the discipline of manual labor and the boundaries of their "natural environment," Baldwin, like other industrial philanthropists, generally opposed the development of black higher education. "Except in the rarest of instances," Baldwin proclaimed, "I am bitterly opposed to the so-called higher education of Negroes." To be sure, he recognized that racial segregation of necessity required the existence of limited black higher education and professional opportunities to train needed professionals such as doctors, nurses, and social workers. Explicit in Baldwin's statements was the philosophy that higher education ought to direct black boys and girls to places in life that were congruent with the South's racial caste system, as opposed to providing them with the knowledge and experiences that created a wide, if not unlimited, range of social and economic possibilities. Further, the needs of the South's racially segregated society were to determine the scope and purpose of black higher education, not the interests and aspirations of individual students or the collective interests of black communities. As the first chairman of the General Education Board and an influential voice among northern industrial philanthropists, Baldwin helped channel the funds of these philanthropic foundations into black industrial schools and white colleges. Yet, as demonstrated in Chapter 3, he was not alone in this effort. Industrial philanthropists in general were opposed to black higher education, except in the rarest of instances, and did not change their position until after World War I.[13]

Thus a convergence of circumstances—the lack of federal and state support for the development of black higher education, the opposition of industrial philanthropy, and the impoverishment of missionary and black religious philanthropy—combined to retard the development of black higher education during the first two decades of the twentieth century. Most important, the key promoters of black higher education, missionary and black religious societies, could not accumulate the large amounts of capital required to place black colleges on solid financial grounds. Though they plodded on persistently, preserving a modest system of black collegiate education, their nineteenth-century momentum declined sharply after 1900. By the turn of the century, the mission societies were virtually bankrupt, and their campaign to develop black higher education was rapidly diminishing in scope and activity. In looking at the future of their black colleges, the missionary philanthropists had many reasons to be downhearted. By any standard, the material and financial status of black higher education was bad. Black colleges were understaffed, meagerly equipped, and poorly financed. The combined efforts of the missionary and black organizations could not raise sufficient funds to meet annual operating expenses, increase teachers' salaries, expand the physical plant, improve libraries, or purchase new scientific and technical equipment. Indeed, almost all of the missionary black colleges lacked sufficient endowments to ensure their survival. Of the one hundred black colleges and normal schools in 1914–15, two-thirds had no endowment funds; and the remaining third had a combined total of only $8.4 million. Most of this sum belonged to Hampton and Tuskegee Institutes, which had attracted large gifts from industrial philanthropists in support of industrial education. In 1926 the total endowment of ninety-nine black colleges and normal schools had risen to $20.3 million, and more than $14 million of this belonged to Hampton and Tuskegee Institutes; the ninety-seven remaining institutions had a combined total of $6.1 million. As late as 1932, seventy-five black colleges had either a negligible endowment or none at all.[14]

The relative impoverishment of black "colleges" and "universities" made it difficult for them to increase their college-level enrollments, which were already extremely small. In the academic year 1899–1900, only fifty-eight of the ninety-nine black colleges had any collegiate students. The proportion of collegiate and professional students in these ninety-nine institutions was small in relation to their precollegiate enrollment, which amounted to 27,869. These precollegiate students constituted more than nine-tenths of the total number of students enrolled in black colleges. This pattern had not changed significantly by World War I. In 1915 only thirty-three black private institutions were "teaching any subjects of college grade." The lack of good academic elementary and secondary schools for southern black students forced the black colleges to provide training for pupils at lower levels to help meet the educational needs of local black communities. Of the 12,726 students attending these institutions in 1915, 79 percent were in the elementary and secondary grades. Many institutions were endeavoring to maintain college classes for less than 5 percent of their enrollment. Thus, lacking an adequate supply of high schoolers to enter the freshman course, the black colleges enrolled elementary and secondary students mainly as a means to feed their college departments. These enrollment patterns in black colleges differed significantly from the national pattern. In 1900 approximately one-quarter of all students enrolled in American colleges were in precollegiate programs. As late as the 1930s, the black precollegiate enrollment represented about 40 percent of the total enrollment in black institutions of higher learning.[15]

Another important development, which threatened the survival of the missionary colleges and black higher education in general, was the establishment of national and regional accrediting agencies. In the late nineteenth century regional accrediting agencies such as the Middle States Association of Colleges and Secondary Schools, the Southern Association of Colleges and Secondary Schools, and the New England Association of Colleges and Secondary Schools were formed to give more fixed meanings to the terms "high school," "college," and "university." In the early twentieth century these regional accrediting agencies were joined by national standardizing organizations such as the College Entrance Examination Board and the Carnegie Foundation for the Advancement of Teaching. Before 1913, accrediting agencies worked mainly to establish closer relations among institutions of higher learning, to standardize college admission requirements, and to improve the academic quality of

college and university education. Beginning in 1913, however, the North
Central Association of Colleges and Secondary Schools issued the first
list of regionally accredited colleges and universities, which signaled the
movement to define institutions of higher learning by specific, factual,
mechanical, and uniform standards. This movement, financed by foundations like Carnegie, increased the pressures on black colleges to become full-fledged institutions of higher learning.[16]

In one sense, standardization or accrediting was a voluntary action.
No institution was surveyed for the purpose of accreditation except upon
application. Nevertheless, it was virtually impossible for a college or
university to exist as an important institution without the approval of
these rating bodies. The nonattainment or removal of accreditation,
whether by a regional or national accrediting agency, was a serious detri-
ment to the welfare of an institution. The mere publication of accredited
schools had an adverse effect upon institutions that did not appear on
the lists. Whether students were graduates of accredited or nonaccred-
ited institutions figured significantly in job opportunities, acceptance to
graduate and professional schools, and the acquisition of required state
certificates to practice professions from teaching to medicine.[17]

Although no formal accrediting agency took black colleges seriously
until 1928, when the Southern Association of Colleges and Secondary
Schools decided to rate black institutions separately, there were several
evaluations of black higher education from 1900 to 1928. In 1900 and
1910 W. E. B. DuBois made the first attempts to evaluate and classify the
black colleges. In 1900 DuBois listed thirty-four institutions as "colleges" with a total collegiate enrollment of 726 students. He concluded,
however, that these 726 students could have been accommodated by the
ten institutions which he rated as first-grade colleges. In 1910 DuBois
made a second and more careful evaluation of black higher education in
which he attempted to classify thirty-two black colleges. Institutions like
Howard, Fisk, Atlanta, Morehouse, and Virginia Union were classified
as "First-Grade Colored Colleges." Lincoln, Talladega, and Wilberforce
were examples of the "Second-Grade Colored Colleges," and schools
such as Lane, Bishop, and Miles Memorial were included under the label
"other colored colleges." DuBois's evaluation was, on balance, a friendly
one designed to strengthen the black college system by concentrating
college-level work in about thirty-two of the better black institutions.
But in 1917, Thomas Jesse Jones, director of research for the Phelps-
Stokes Fund, published a critical attack upon black higher education that
questioned the legitimacy of nearly all black institutions of higher learning. From 1914 to 1916, Jones conducted a survey of black higher education for the Federal Bureau of Education that resulted in a two-volume
book. In the volume on black colleges he identified only two institutions

as capable of offering college-level work. These were Howard University and Fisk University. In Jones's words, "hardly a colored college meets the standards set by the Carnegie Foundation and the North Central Association." These rating agencies required, among other things, that accredited colleges maintain at least six departments or professorships with one professor giving full time to each department. The college's annual income had to be sufficient to maintain professors with advanced degrees and to supply adequate library and laboratory facilities. The rating agencies also held that the operation of a preparatory department at the high school level was undesirable, and in no case could it be under the same faculty and discipline as the college. Finally, the North Central Association of Colleges and Secondary Schools recommended that accredited colleges possess an endowment of at least $200,000. At that time, Hampton and Tuskegee were the only black institutions with substantial endowments, and these industrial normal schools did not offer collegiate courses. For Jones, his findings strongly suggested that only two or three black institutions were equipped to become accredited colleges. Hence he recommended that the remaining "colleges" convert to secondary, elementary, and normal schools. Undoubtedly his views were harsh and unwarranted, reflecting significantly his bias toward the Hampton-Tuskegee model of industrial education. Still, Jones's survey, backed by the Federal Bureau of Education and northern industrial philanthropic foundations, underscored a major crisis in black higher education. Black colleges, however segregated, could not exist apart from the power and control of white standardizing agencies. It had become apparent to missionary philanthropists and black educators that their institutions were compelled to seek admission to the society of standardized colleges and on terms defined by all-white regional and national rating agencies. Thus for black institutions of higher learning, rating by accrediting agencies was a primary goal in the post–World War I era.[18]

The crucial threats to the survival of black higher education could not be met effectively by missionary philanthropists or black organizations, and the black colleges were forced to seek help from industrial philanthropists. As early as 1901, Thomas J. Morgan, then corresponding secretary for the American Baptist Home Mission Society, requested fellow Baptist John D. Rockefeller to "assume the expense of fully equipping" eight of the society's leading colleges. Writing to Wallace Buttrick, Rockefeller's adviser in philanthropic affairs, Morgan suggested several ways to support black colleges: "(a) by endowing each school separately; (b) by placing in the hands of the ABHMS a lump endowment sum; (c) the creation of a fund placed in the hands of trustees especially selected for the purpose; or (d) the donation of Mr. Rockefeller annually of such a sum of money as may be essential to carry on the work." Between 1901 and 1908, the ABHMS's leading members, Morgan, Malcolm MacVicar, Henry L. Morehouse, George Sale, and George Rice Hovey, wrote to Wallace Buttrick pleading for grants to keep their black colleges financially solvent. In January 1908, George Sale made a specific request for funds to improve the ABHMS's Virginia Union University. He listed four important needs: a dormitory that would cost at least $40,000; two residences adjoining the campus for the accommodation of teachers that would cost $3,000 each; increases in the salaries of continuing instructors; and most urgently, to raise the quality of its instructional program by adding faculty positions in pedagogy, history, and social science. For these purposes, Sale asked the General Education Board to make appropriations as follows: $20,000 toward the cost of the dormitory; $3,000 toward the purchase of the two residences for teachers; and $3,000 for faculty salaries. All requests were denied. The missionaries' correspondence with Wallace Buttrick and the General Education Board reveals the growing impoverishment of their societies relative to the financial resources necessary to keep their colleges abreast of modern standards. In 1901 Morgan wrote: "Reflecting upon the future of our educational work it seems to me we have reached an actual crisis that demands very careful consideration. Suppose, for instance, that the Society is obliged to carry on the work as heretofore. What shall we do? It is exceedingly difficult to secure money to keep the schools up to their present degree of efficiency and it is uncertain whether the present interest in the schools can be kept up among the churches and individuals." In Morgan's view, black colleges simply could "not expect too much of the Society in the immediate future with reference to enlargement, improvement, and increased costs." Likewise, George Rice Hovey, president of the ABHMS's Virginia Union University, said to Buttrick: "We, I fear, can never accomplish the work that we ought to do if we rely solely on the missionary society." Hovey's assessment characterized the general state of northern missionary societies for by the turn of the century, they had become too weak financially to keep their colleges abreast of modern standards. Unfortunately, the missionaries became bankrupt at a time when black colleges depended almost exclusively upon private aid.[19]

Significantly, although some of the missionaries threw themselves upon the mercy of the General Education Board—knowing full well the board's practice of contributing funds only to industrial schools—they were unwilling to compromise their primary mission of sustaining classical liberal colleges for the training of the black "talented tenth." George Sale, though careful not to attack industrial education, informed Buttrick that "the wisest policy for Virginia Union University is to place emphasis on its college and college preparatory work." Thomas J. Morgan recalled that from the beginning the ABHMS's schools had incorporated a smattering of industrial courses. Although he was favorable to the engrafting upon missionary colleges courses in industrial training, Morgan believed it would be a great misfortune to convert them to the trade school mission. In his letters to Buttrick, he constantly reaffirmed the ABHMS's commitment to its traditional philosophy of black education. As he wrote in January 1901,

> The one all-important function of these institutions, the work to which they must give their strength for many years to come is that of raising up a competent leadership; men and women who can think; who are independent and self-reliant; who can persuade and lead their people; they should be men and women who are themselves models and examples of what their people can and ought to become, especially should they be persons capable of teaching and preaching. No modification of their curriculum or their spirit and purpose should be allowed to interfere in any manner with this as the supreme purpose of their existence.

A day later, lest Buttrick forget, Morgan repeated the same philosophy: "I feel very keenly the sense of responsibility for using what little influence I may have in developing our schools to a high grade, so that they may offer to the ambitious and competent young Negroes the best possible opportunities for self-culture, development, training and preparation for life's duties." What worried the industrial philanthropists was the probability that such ambitious and competent young college-bred Negroes would impart their knowledge and culture to secondary and normal school students who would in turn transmit classical liberal education to the common schools, leaving no central role in the basic structure of black education for the Hampton-Tuskegee model of industrial training.[20]

On the surface it appeared that the two camps might reach a compromise because one group emphasized college training and the other precollegiate education. Booker T. Washington, for example, publicly supported higher education for black elites. Washington stated: "In saying what I do in regard to industrial education, I do not wish to be understood as meaning that the education of the negro should be confined to that kind alone, because we need men and women well educated in other directions; but for the masses, industrial education is the supreme need." No compromise was practical, however, because both the supporters of classical liberal and industrial education looked to the same group to spread their ideas to the masses of black citizens. They both believed that the education of black teachers was most critical to the long-term training and development of the larger black community. If the teachers were to be, as Morgan said, "models and examples of what their people can and ought to be," there was little chance that the two camps could reach a compromise regarding the proper training of black teachers. Their conceptions of what black people could and ought to be in the American South were simply too divergent and conflicting to reach any sound agreement on the training of teachers of black southerners. In the pre–World War I period, therefore, industrial philanthropists could not bring themselves to support the expansion of black higher education because they viewed it as an infringement upon terrain they aspired to occupy and control. In 1914 Buttrick expressed a fundamental difference between the missionaries' and industrialists' view of the appropriate structure of black higher education. "I have long believed that there should be developed in the South two or three strong institutions of higher learning for the Negroes and, further, that something should be done to develop two, or possibly three, of the medical schools for Negroes," wrote Buttrick to John D. Rockefeller, Jr. "The difficulty in any attempt to promote institutions of higher learning," continued Buttrick, "is the fact that most of the Christian denominations have each founded several such schools." Indeed, altogether they had founded more than one hundred such schools. Buttrick wanted to reduce the number of black colleges and professional schools to six and thereby leave the larger field of teacher training to industrial normal and county training schools. The denominations wanted not only to maintain their more than one hundred "colleges" and professional schools but to improve and expand them. The missionaries' plans were diametrically opposed to the industrial philanthropists' conception of the proper scope and function of black higher education.[21]

Although the industrial philanthropists refused to support the missionaries' plans for the development of black higher education, they had no intentions of abandoning black collegiate and professional education. Because industrial philanthropists appropriated virtually no money for black higher education before 1920, they were often perceived as committed exclusively to the idea of Negro industrial education. This was a misperception. In 1907 Buttrick stated well his colleagues' attitude toward black higher education: "I am convinced that all members of the [General Education] Board believe that there should be a sufficient number of thoroughgoing colleges for colored people in the southern states." Further, he was inclined to agree with his fellow trustees "that the matter of collegiate education for the colored people should be taken up as a whole by this Board." In fact, as Buttrick informed George Sale, superintendent of Negro education for the ABHMS, the board had already designated one of its "School Inspectors" to make "a careful study of the whole question" of black higher education. This report, completed in May 1907 by W. T. B. Williams of Hampton Institute, set forth basic reasons to develop a small number of strong black colleges in the South. First, these institutions would produce college-bred leaders to accultur- ate black Americans into the values and mores of southern society. Sec- ond, it was very important that black leaders be trained in the South by institutions "in touch with the conditions to be faced by the young peo- ple in later life rather than in the North by institutions . . . out of touch with southern life." Third, and most important, the development of a few strong institutions was viewed as a strategic means to reduce the number of existing black colleges. Williams argued:

> If more strong men and good college courses, and better equipment both in the way of dormitories and apparatus could be added in a few places, and some scholarships or student aid in the college de- partment, could be provided, as is common in the great northern universities, the mass of Negro college students would congregate in these few institutions and their numbers would steadily increase. This would render impossible many of the weaker college courses and would make for strength in organization and economy in the management of college training, for it would minimize duplication.

Williams expressed an interesting and noteworthy effect of standardiza- tion which was not so marked and known. If a few outstanding black colleges were established, industrial philanthropists could use these insti- tutions to pressure the remaining ones into discontinuing their collegiate courses because of their inability to keep pace with the rising standards of college-level work. Buttrick regarded Williams's report as "so valuable that in my judgement all the members of the Board ought to read it just as it stands."[22]

Despite an apparent similarity in principle, there was a fundamental difference between Williams's and DuBois's proposals to reduce the num- ber of black colleges. DuBois believed that a smaller number of finan- cially solvent black colleges, about thirty-three, was preferable to the larger number (one hundred) of weaker schools in constant danger of folding. Further, starting from the position that the black college enroll- ment was much too small, he believed that a smaller number of sound institutions could both improve their academic quality and expand their physical capacity to increase the overall number and proportion of black college students. Williams's report, consistent with the philanthropists' interests, recommended the concentration of black higher education in a few institutions, about four or six, as a means to reduce dramatically the opportunities for black students to pursue higher education. This proposal reflected the philanthropists' belief that far too many black students aspired to attend college, a belief that would not change signifi- cantly until southern states began requiring all teachers to have bachelor's degrees. In short, DuBois recommended concentration and efficiency in black higher education to increase opportunities, whereas the Williams report to the General Education Board recommended concentration and efficiency to reduce the scope of black higher education. Though their means were similar, they envisioned very different ends.

Williams's report impressed the board's trustees and spurred them to develop a formal rationale for the support of black higher education. Wallace Buttrick and Abraham Flexner were primarily responsible for formulating the board's policy. In 1910 Flexner became nationally known for writing Carnegie Foundation Bulletin No. 4, a detailed study titled "Medical Education in the United States and Canada." This survey and the policies derived from it foreshadowed the board's approach to black higher education. Flexner inspected 155 medical schools and reported their "appalling deficiencies," which led him to conclude that all but 31 of them should discontinue. After this report appeared, the Council of Medical Education of the American Medical Association intensified its efforts to eliminate "inferior" medical colleges. Much of the financial support for the medical reform movement was provided by the General Education Board. In 1911 the board appropriated $1.5 million to Johns Hopkins Medical School for the purpose of setting standards in American medical education. Flexner was placed in charge of the board's medical reform program. His main goal was to develop a model of medical education that would force weaker institutions to shut down because of their inability to approximate the new standards. Clearly, this policy followed closely the suggestions contained in the Williams report, though there was no direct relation between the two.[23]

In 1914 Flexner became a trustee of the General Education Board and assistant secretary to Wallace Buttrick. In this capacity, he began to apply his medical model to the field of black higher education. Fortunately Flexner did not have to conduct a study of black higher education comparable to his investigation of American medical education. Both he and Buttrick were acutely aware of the survey of black higher education being conducted by Thomas Jesse Jones for the Federal Bureau of Education. They were in close contact with Jones and realized, early on, that they could rely upon his forthcoming survey as a "Flexner report" of black higher education. Buttrick informed John D. Rockefeller, Jr., in February 1914, that he was in "frequent conference" with Jones, and he assured Rockefeller that Jones's survey would "throw light" on the whole question of black education. Though Jones's survey was not published until 1917, by December 1914 Flexner was already convinced that it would sound the death knell for many black colleges as his medical report had done for the vast majority of American medical schools. Writing to Oswald Garrison Villard about the value of the Jones survey, Flexner proclaimed:

> Dr. Jones is a disinterested and competent outsider whose report will separate the wheat from the chaff. After its appearance the public will have a source of information the accuracy and impartiality of which cannot be discredited. The situation here is not different in principle from that which once existed in reference to medical schools. There was an association of American medical colleges that could enforce no standards just because it meant that the members, in order to do this, would have to legislate against one another. After, however, the Carnegie Foundation Bulletin appeared, an entirely new situation was created. Since then things have been run by the better schools and the others are rapidly disappearing.

Jones, however, was not a disinterested outsider. As a former member of Hampton's faculty, he had helped develop the Hampton-Tuskegee approach to black education and as the director of the Phelps-Stokes Fund played a critical role in adapting the Hampton-Tuskegee philosophy to Britain's African colonies. His two-volume survey of black education, published in 1917, espoused the Hampton-Tuskegee philosophy. Anticipating the impact of the Jones survey, the General Education Board held its first interracial conference on Negro education in November 1915. The invited participants represented both the major black industrial and liberal arts institutions. Presidents Fayette A. McKenzie of Fisk University and John Hope of Morehouse College represented two of the most outstanding black private colleges. Others included Principal R. R. Moton of Tuskegee Institute, Principal H. B. Frissell of Hampton Institute, Abraham Flexner of the General Education Board, Thomas Jesse Jones of the Phelps-Stokes Fund, W. T. B. Williams, field agent for the John F. Slater Fund, and James H. Dillard, president of the Anna T. Jeanes Foundation. This conference brought together the forces that represented the industrial philanthropists' overall approach to the development of black education. On one hand, Frissell, Moton, Williams, Jones, Flexner, and Dillard exemplified the movement to spread industrial education throughout the Afro-American South as the all-pervasive educational curriculum. On the other, McKenzie and Hope symbolized the industrial philanthropists' developing commitment to influence the direction of black higher education.[24]

The discussions at this conference illuminated fundamental flaws in the Hampton-Tuskegee movement that ultimately forced industrial philanthropists to reshape their approach to the promotion of industrial education for the masses of black children. The discussions also pointed to the pressing need for industrial philanthropists to become involved in the development of black colleges and professional schools if they were to be successful in redirecting the scope and function of black higher education. The original Hampton-Tuskegee Idea had run its course by 1915 and was rapidly falling behind modern educational standards. It was based largely on a program of unskilled and semiskilled agricultural and industrial training, the discouraging of college and even high-quality secondary work, and a heavy emphasis on moral development and ideological training. This program had broken down under its own weight. The extreme emphasis on routinized labor, or "learning by doing," produced graduates who found it increasingly difficult to meet state and local academic requirements for teacher certification. In certain respects, southern state and local school authorities wanted Hampton-Tuskegee graduates as teachers because they were advertised as young black men and women who "knew their place" and who were uncontaminated by the pompous ideals of classical liberal education. Yet the South, as the nation, was emphasizing and implementing certain required standards of education for teachers and even demanding college degrees to teach in public high schools and normal schools.

Such changes presented serious challenges to the traditional Hampton-Tuskegee program. Defending this tradition, Hampton principal H. B. Frissell said: "To us at Hampton the doing of the thing is the important thing, and what we might call the academic side is comparatively secondary. We have got to learn to do by doing . . . the academic training is really secondary to the actual doing of the thing." The fundamental flaw in this approach was pointed out to Frissell and the other members of the conference by two of Hampton's prominent graduates, Robert R. Moton and W. T. B. Williams. Moton said: "I am a Hampton man. I went to the summer school [for teachers] two or three summers, and took gymnastics, nothing else, only on the physical side pure and simple." Williams maintained that such a poor academic program caused Hampton graduates to fall down on the job: "Even when they go to teach the elementary subjects they cannot bring any fresh information to the children." The ultimate defeat and embarrassment, as Moton recalled, was that Hampton could not find one of its own graduates sufficiently qualified to fill a teaching position at the Whittier Elementary Lab School located on Hampton's campus. In Moton's words: "We had to go to Howard University to get a man to help Miss Walter. With all our 1,200 graduates, we should have had a man we could have put in that place. We had no one with sufficient academic training for the Whittier school. That is what Miss Walter thought, and she is very loyal to us, so you see that is at our own Hampton school; after twenty-five years or so we ought to have been able to pick out some Hampton man for that work." Moton, who was in the process of leaving the Hampton staff to become principal of Tuskegee Institute, admitted that Tuskegee had similar problems. Its graduates were being kept out of the teaching profession because of poor academic training. Bruce R. Payne, president of the George Peabody College for Teachers, asked the next logical question, "What is the use of the Hampton training if we are not allowed to use it?" Hampton and Tuskegee were thus compelled to meet more modern and higher academic standards or continue producing students with insufficient academic training to pass certification standards required of entry-level teachers.[25]

The conference then shifted to the question of black higher education. H. B. Frissell asked the central question: "What is sound policy in respect to the number, scope, support, and development of higher academic institutions for Negroes?" Only John Hope questioned the relevance of engrafting vocational education on the college curriculum and stated firmly that he stood for the "modern sort of education" for black and white children. Flexner, speaking for the industrial philanthropists, insisted that black collegiate work was "very pretentious, and not calculated to get anywhere." Having tested some black college students in Latin, physics, and literature, he concluded ironically that "if it had been Greek they could not have been more puzzled." Flexner then asked for Hope's reaction to the General Education Board's thoughts about means to reduce the number of existing black colleges: "Dr. Hope, what would be the effect of selecting four or five Negro colleges and building them up, making them good, honest, sincere, effective colleges so far as they went, and letting the others alone, not try to suppress them or consolidate them, but just let them 'sweat,' would that tend in the long run, to stigmatize the inferior institutions that they would give up, the way the poor medical schools are giving up?" Hope admitted that such a policy might pressure weaker colleges to discontinue, but he did not sanction this approach.[26]

Shortly after this conference, the General Education Board formed a Committee on Negro Education to review its overall policy for the development of black education, paying particular attention to the questions of supporting schools for the training of black teachers and the shaping of black higher education. The committee's report was submitted to the board on 27 January 1916. "A crying need in Negro education," the committee reported, "is the development of state supported schools for the training of Negro teachers." The committee realized, however, "that many decades will elapse before Negro education is adequately provided for through taxation." Therefore, the committee recommended that the board use its resources to strengthen private institutions that promised to render "important educational service." "It should perhaps be explained," the committee stated, "that in making this recommendation the Committee has in mind, first, industrial schools, such as those at Fort Valley, Manassas, Calhoun, and St. Helena—schools which, on a much smaller scale, are doing for their own vicinities the valuable work which Hampton and Tuskegee have done for the country at large." Second, the committee had in mind academic institutions. It observed:

> The Negro is determined to have some opportunity for higher education, and certain Negroes have made good use of such opportunities as are open to the race. Of course, there are far too many Negro colleges and universities; and of this large number, not one is well equipped and manned on a sensible, modest scale. Wise cooperation with one or two institutions would be the most effective way of bringing order out of chaos, of distinguishing the real from the imitation.

Finally, the committee recommended support for black medical education. "The Negro physician has, in our judgment, a place in the South." It was recommended that the board support one or two black medical schools. Thus, in time, with these recommendations, the committee formulated principles calling first for support of industrial normal schools, second, for assisting one or two black colleges, and, third, for aiding one or two black medical schools. The board moved immediately to provide financial support for the smaller industrial schools, but a few years passed before any major campaigns were launched to assist black colleges and professional schools.[27]

Meanwhile, a confluence of changing political and social developments in black America heightened the industrial philanthropists' interest in the scope and purpose of black higher education. Most important were the emergence of more militant post–World War I black leaders and the subsequent realization that the Hampton-Tuskegee coalition was rapidly losing political ground to the college-bred "New Negro." During the war blacks became increasingly intolerant of economic and social injustices, especially in the South, where white terrorist groups increased their brutal attacks upon black civilians while black soldiers fought on the battle front to "make the world safe for democracy." There developed in the South, and to a significant degree in other sections of the nation, a grave interracial crisis. Inflammatory rumors filled the air, suspicion and fear were rife, lynchings multiplied, race riots broke out in several northern and southern cities, and the embers of discontent smoldered in many more. The widespread racial repression in the South, coupled with labor shortages in the North, escalated the migration of blacks to northern urban areas. The white South, fearing the loss of a major proportion of its agricultural laborers, opposed the migration and used both legal and extralegal means to keep blacks from boarding the trains bound northward. Efforts to deprive blacks of even so basic a freedom as the right to migrate only served to exacerbate racial tensions. Robert R. Moton, then the leading black spokesperson for the Hampton-Tuskegee coalition, was awakened to the pervasive undercurrent of social unrest among black civilians when he toured the South in 1918. Indeed, Moton was so alarmed that he felt compelled to alert President Woodrow Wilson to the ever-present danger. In June 1918, Moton wrote a confidential letter to the president:

> There is more genuine restlessness and dissatisfaction on the part of the colored people than I have before known. I have just returned from trips in Alabama, Georgia, North Carolina, and South Carolina. It seems to me something ought to be done pretty definitely to change the attitudes of these millions of black people; and this attitude, anything but satisfactory, not to use a stronger word, is due very largely to recent lynchings and burnings of colored people. The recent lynching in Georgia of six people in connection with a murder, and among them a woman, who it is reported was a prospective mother, has intensified tremendously this attitude of the colored people.

In Moton's view, blacks en masse were on the brink of becoming "indifferent or antagonistic" or "quietly hostile."[28]

After the signing of the Armistice in 1918, race relations in America deteriorated further. The South and the nation were shaken by the "Red Summer" of 1919, when a series of major riots threatened to precipitate widespread race warfare. Significantly, the Hampton-Tuskegee moderates, who traditionally served as mediators in such crises, had little influence among the post–World War I black leaders. By 1920, there was no powerful segment of the black leadership that favored the Hampton-Tuskegee accommodationist approach to race relations and political conflict. In March 1920, the NAACP's *Crisis* published a revealing article by Harry H. Jones, which argued that, except for R. R. Moton, few black leaders accepted the Hampton-Tuskegee philosophy of racial accommodation. The liberal and radical wings of the black intelligentsia were the dominant political voices in the black community, and the philanthropists understood the impact of this influence on their own political program. Philanthropist George Peabody, having read the Jones article, informed Hampton's principal, James Gregg, of its implications: "It is clear to me, with the Negro people having found themselves in a general way, during the war excitement, there is some danger of sharp definitely conscious line of division. We must, I think, give great weight in the present temper of susceptibility to the advertising influence of the

Crisis and other publications, including James Weldon Johnson and The
New York *Age*." The problem, then, from the standpoint of the philanthropists, was how to secure an articulate black conservative wing with
sufficient status within the race to counter the influence of such men as
DuBois, Trotter, and Johnson.[29]

Peabody wanted a conservative black leader to "write the most effective reply, which I have in mind, to the article in the March issue of the
Crisis." But he did not believe that Moton or Fred Moore, the New York
Age's editor, who sympathized with Moton's accommodationist philosophy, had sufficient status to challenge Johnson and DuBois. In fact, Peabody could only think of Isaac Fisher as a potentially effective ideologue
of the industrial philanthropic view of black educational and social affairs. Interestingly, Fisher, a Tuskegee graduate who took his ideology
from Booker T. Washington, was appointed to the Fisk University administration shortly after McKenzie became president. When McKenzie
suspended the student-operated *Fisk Herald* in 1917, he established the
conservative *Fisk University News* and made Fisher its editor. Following
the bitter race riots of 1919, in a period of rising black militancy, Fisher
called for the return of the "conservative Negro." He castigated the liberal and radical segments of the existing black leadership, claiming that
they had "muzzled" the voice of the conservative Negro and taken away
his "mandate to speak for his race." Fisher defined the conservative
Negro leader as one who urges his people to lay a foundation in economic efficiency, submits willingly to the laws and customs of the South,
and works for better race relations through the guidance of the "best
white South." Toward this end, he instituted at Fisk in 1917 a seminar on
race relations and later became a member of the southern-white-domi-
nated Commission on Inter-racial Co-operation. Yet such conservatives
as Fisher and Moton could not really challenge the intellectual leadership
the liberals and radicals had achieved in the black community by 1919.
DuBois probably expressed the dominant black view of the conservative
wing when he informed the Commission on Inter-racial Co-operation
that "Isaac Fisher represents nothing but his own blubbering self. Major
Moton is a fine fellow, but weak in the presence of white folks." To
DuBois and many other black leaders who demanded full American
rights for blacks, Moton and Fisher were "the sort of Colored men that
we call 'White Folks' Niggers.'" Whether they were such accommodationists was less important than their lack of influence among the postwar black leaders and especially among the masses. The black leaders of
the postwar period reflected the self-determinist and militant character
of the larger Afro-American society. Marcus Garvey and his Universal
Negro Improvement Association epitomized some of the core values and

fundamental political thoughts of the masses of Afro-Americans. Garvey arrived in the United States from Jamaica in 1916 and by 1922 had several hundred thousand followers. He led the largest mass movement among Afro-Americans before the civil rights movement of the 1960s. The political thrust toward self-determination and militant demands for equality and racial justice were also manifested in the emergence of a more liberal black press and the literary tenor of the "Harlem Renaissance." Historian V. P. Franklin argues convincingly that the postwar self-determinist political and literary activities reflected values deeply embedded in black culture and tradition.[30]

These developments reaffirmed the industrial philanthropists' growing convictions of the necessity to take hold of black higher education and to influence more directly the training of black leaders. Hence, during the early 1920s they launched two national endowment campaigns that incorporated several of their major goals to shape postsecondary black education and develop the "right type" of black teachers and leaders. One campaign was to raise a million-dollar endowment for Fisk University. This campaign embodied the industrial philanthropists' plan to develop one or two black private colleges to the point that they would set new standards for black higher education and thus stigmatize the "inferior" or less fortunate ones, possibly pressuring them to discontinue or convert to secondary schools. The other endowment campaign aimed to raise at least $5 million to be split equally between Hampton and Tuskegee. This campaign reflected the industrial philanthropists' continuing commitment to the Hampton-Tuskegee Idea. They recognized, however, that Hampton and Tuskegee must meet higher educational standards if the graduates were to continue to obtain teaching jobs and other positions of leadership. Together these campaigns, conducted by the same group of industrial philanthropists, were also intended to develop sympathetic harmony between the liberal arts colleges and the industrial schools.

Not surprisingly, the industrial philanthropists selected Fisk University as the college to be developed into a model institution of black higher education. Fisk was at the financial crossroads that precipitated the transformation of the power structure in black private higher education from missionary to industrial philanthropy. President George A. Gates, who headed Fisk from 1909 to 1913, faced a drying up of the old missionary sources of revenue and, in turn, made a strong plea for southern white friendship and financial support. Booker T. Washington had been appointed to the Board of Trustees in 1909 with the hope that he would bring some of his sources of revenue to Fisk. Fisk was also selected because the industrial philanthropists regarded it as the "cap-

Fisk University, Nashville, Tennessee, 1914. In 1914 the campus consisted of thirty-five acres and eleven buildings. The value of the campus, buildings, and equipment exceeded $370,000. Courtesy of Fisk University Library.

stone" of black private higher education. Wallace Buttrick said: "Perhaps the most promising of the academic institutions for the higher education of the Negro is Fisk University." Outside of Howard University, Fisk had nearly 20 percent of the private black college students enumerated in Thomas Jesse Jones's 1917 survey of black higher education. Fisk enrolled 188 of the 737 college students in private black colleges (this figure excludes the 1,050 college students enrolled in Howard University); Virginia Union University, with 51, had the next largest enrollment. Thus when the General Education Board held its 1915 conference to discuss the reorganization of black higher education, Fisk University's newly appointed white president, Fayette Avery McKenzie, was invited as a key representative of black higher education. Convinced that McKenzie was sympathetic to the board's policy, the industrial philanthropists selected him and his institution to spearhead their campaign to reshape black higher education.[31]

McKenzie, a professor of sociology at the Ohio State University before coming to Fisk in 1915, came to Nashville as a representative of industrial philanthropy. He dedicated his presidency to modernizing the curriculum (that is, emphasizing physical and social sciences) and raising a sizable endowment for the university. Industrial philanthropists regarded him as a leader who would break with the missionary or egalitarian past and lead Fisk down a path of conciliation and cooperation with conservative northern and southern whites. More than any of his predecessors,

McKenzie sought to make Fisk acceptable to the white South and north-ern industrial philanthropists. He urged Fisk students and graduates to eschew political and social questions and concentrate on interracial co-operation and economic development. In his inaugural address, McKen-zie paid homage to Fisk's liberal arts tradition but emphasized the con-cept of education for "service." In this context he promised that the university would help restore the South to economic prosperity: "It was the function of Fisk to increase the material wealth of the nation. . . . Fisk University claims the right to say that it will be one of the chief factors in achieving larger prosperity for the South. Every dollar spent here in the creation of power may mean a thousand dollars of increase in wealth of the South within a single generation." In line with these goals and priorities, McKenzie favored autocratic rule over his students and faculty, sought personal associations mainly with the teachers and ad-ministrators of the white schools in Nashville, and cultivated the good-will of the city's white business community. These actions pleased the industrial philanthropists, and they regarded McKenzie's reign as a new and wise departure from the missionary tradition.[32]

From the outset, industrial philanthropists reinforced McKenzie's be-havior by contributing their economic and political support to his re-gime. Julius Rosenwald, who visited Fisk at McKenzie's installation, was initially ambivalent about the possibility of transforming the college into an accommodationist institution. In revealing his "mixed feelings" about

Fisk students to Abraham Flexner, Rosenwald stated, "There seemed to be an air of superiority among them and a desire to take on the spirit of the white university rather than the spirit which has always impressed me at Tuskegee." Rosenwald and other industrial philanthropists believed that Tuskegee was training black leaders to maintain a separate and subordinate Negro society. They were primarily interested in supporting black institutions committed to this mission. Thus Flexner assured Rosenwald that McKenzie, with the help of industrial philanthropy, was working to transform Fisk into an institution more acceptable to southern white society. Toward this end, the General Education Board began appropriating in 1916 about $12,000 annually to help Fisk pay its yearly operating expenses. In 1917 the board contributed $50,000 to Fisk for endowment and building purposes and persuaded the Carnegie Foundation to give the same amount. Still, Fisk had no substantial endowment, was deeply in debt, and suffered from a deteriorating physical plant and a poorly paid faculty. According to Hollingsworth Wood, vice-chairman of the Fisk Board of Trustees, "$1,600 has been the maximum salary of a professor at Fisk University. This has meant lack of food in some cases." Fisk authorities knew that the college could not survive without a sizable endowment, and the industrial philanthropists were the only source of sufficient money. These circumstances, however, required compromise. As McKenzie put it, "Intimation has been made to me from several sources that if we continue to behave ourselves, if we are efficient in teaching and administration and continue to hold the right relationship to our environment, we can expect large and highly valuable financial aid in carrying out a great program at Fisk."[33]

The philanthropists' financial assistance to Fisk University was accompanied by a new coalition of Negro accommodationists, southern whites, and northern industrialists who took control of the university's administration from the old alliance of black educators and northern white missionaries. McKenzie and the philanthropists restructured the Fisk Board of Trustees to reflect the new power structure. In October 1915 Thomas Jesse Jones informed Flexner of the changes: "The Board of Trustees is being strengthened. Governor Brumbaugh and two influential colored men have been added in the last few weeks. With Mr. Cravath and Dr. Washington as trustees and the constant attention which I can give to the institution, we have at least a guarantee of fairly sound educational policy." By 1919, Jones was executive secretary of the Fisk Board of Trustees and one of five members on the Executive Committee. In 1920 the philanthropists, acting through the General Education Board, agreed to spearhead a campaign to obtain for Fisk a $1 million endowment, and their strength on the university's Board of Trustees increased. William H. Baldwin, son of the General Education Board's first chairman, was appointed by the board to chair the endowment committee. He was immediately appointed to the Fisk Board of Trustees and became, in 1924, the chairman of the trustees' Executive Committee. Other conservatives were added as the philanthropists moved in a quiet and forceful manner to reorganize the school's administration. In May 1920, Hollingsworth Wood notified the president of the General Education Board that "Dr. Moton of Tuskegee is now on the Board; Miss Ella Sachs, daughter of Samuel Sachs, and a close friend of the Rosenwalds, is an eager new member; and Mrs. Beverly B. Mumford of Richmond, Virginia adds an excellent influence from the southern viewpoint." The traditional missionary equalitarians were gradually pushed off the Fisk Board of Trustees. They were replaced mainly by northern industrialists, southern whites, and a few Negro accommodationists who were virtually handpicked by industrial philanthropists. The philanthropists were raising an endowment for a new Fisk that was largely controlled by their agents and supporters.[34]

These philanthropists no doubt hoped that their economic and firm political hold on Fisk would squelch the school's equalitarian tradition and open the way for the development of a more conservative black leadership class. In 1923 the General Education Board generated a memorandum on the Fisk endowment campaign which emphasized the urgent need to train "the right type of colored leaders" who would help make the Negro "a capable workman and a good citizen." The industrial philanthropists, as the memorandum stated, aimed primarily at "helping the Negro to the sane and responsible leadership that the South wants him to have." To the white South, "sane" Negro leaders were those who encouraged blacks to "stay in their place." The philanthropists recognized that they were facing a new situation between the races. "How the Negro is going to get on in this country and what his relations are to be with the whites, are no longer problems of a single section; they are national," the memorandum stated. To the philanthropists, this new situation, in the context of growing racial friction, increased the necessity of training "the right kind" of black leaders. The report maintained:

Due to various experiences during and since the World War, there is a growing disposition among the Negroes to suspect all white men and their motives and therefore to break all contacts with them and go it alone. Because such a movement by ten percent of the population is obviously futile, is no reason to overlook the fact that ten percent is a large enough proportion to cause considerable harm if permitted to go off at a tangent from the general interest. This very real menace to the public welfare makes the strengthening of school facilities for Negroes a matter of national significance.

Both McKenzie and the industrial philanthropists shared the belief that the new type of black college should help curb and even extinguish the self-determinist and equalitarian character of the emergent black leadership.[35]

Toward this end McKenzie, as Raymond Wolters has shown, set out to convince the industrial philanthropists that "Fisk students were not radical egalitarians but young men and women who had learned to make peace with the reality of the caste system." Thus McKenzie disbanded the student government association, forbade student dissent, and suspended the *Fisk Herald*, the oldest student publication among black colleges. He would not allow a campus chapter of the NAACP and instructed the librarian to excise radical articles in the NAACP literature. Student discipline was rigorously enforced, special "Jim Crow" entertainments were arranged for the white benefactors of the university, and Paul D. Cravath, president of the Fisk Board of Trustees, endorsed complete racial separation as "the only solution to the Negro problem." McKenzie would not allow certain forms of social intercourse such as dancing and holding hands, and he justified his code of discipline on the grounds that black students were particularly sensuous beings who needed to be subjected to firm control. In short, McKenzie attempted to repress student initiative, undermine their equalitarian spirit, and control their thinking on race relations so as to produce a class of black intellectuals that would uncomplainingly accept the southern racial hierarchy. Historian Lester C. Lamon concluded that "McKenzie's autocratic policies took away means of self-expression, created second-class citizens, and relied upon fear instead of reason to bring societal control." Although discipline and repression of student initiative and self-expression were strict before McKenzie became president, they became harsher and more racist during his administration.[36]

By June 1924, the industrial philanthropists had successfully completed their campaign for Fisk's million-dollar endowment. The following pledges were then in hand: $500,000 from the General Education Board; $250,000 from the Carnegie Foundation; and $250,000 secured elsewhere, including sizable pledges from such philanthropists as Julius Rosenwald and George Peabody. This endowment fund was not, however, collectible until Fisk's accumulated deficits were met. The outstanding indebtedness at that time was $70,000. To solve that problem, a special campaign to raise $50,000 led by Nashville's white citizens was successfully completed by June 1924. This campaign was organized by

Nashville's Commercial Club, which included Tennessee's governor, Nashville's mayor, and many of the city's leading businessmen. From 1915 to 1924, Fisk had become so conservative that the Commercial Club was inspired to call Fisk the "key" to interracial cooperation and understanding in the South. "He came into our midst unknown," the Commercial Club said of McKenzie, "and by his wise administration and official methods won our hearty co-operation." With such backing, plans were perfected for raising the money to eliminate the school's deficits and thereby secure the endowment for Fisk's financial rehabilitation.[37]

At this juncture, however, McKenzie's conservative administration was attacked by black students, intellectuals, and community organizations. Led by W. E. B. DuBois, the Fisk alumni attacked McKenzie's Draconian code of student discipline and expressed outrage at the humiliation and insults perpetrated on the student body. DuBois openly challenged the school's administration in 1924, when he was invited to give the commencement address. He especially criticized the administration's campaign to suppress Fisk's equalitarian tradition so as to obtain economic support from industrial philanthropy. The students, long dissatisfied with McKenzie's regime, were reinforced by alumni support and escalated their protest against the school's repressive policies. In February 1925, the *New York Times* reported that Fisk's alumni were organizing in "all sections of the United States to agitate for the removal of Dr. Fayette McKenzie, the white president of the University." The following month the students went on strike against McKenzie's administration, and they were backed in their protest by the alumni, the black press, and the local black community. On the day following the student rebellion more than twenty-five hundred black citizens of Nashville convened and formally declared that McKenzie's "usefulness as president of Fisk is at an end." This protest forced McKenzie to resign in April 1925. Fisk University trustee Thomas Jesse Jones attributed McKenzie's problems to black self-determination, the very force that he and other industrial philanthropists were trying to counter. As he wrote to fellow trustee, Paul Cravath,

> The present unfortunate and unfair criticism of Dr. McKenzie's policies is partly the result of misunderstandings, but largely the result of an effort on the part of a few designing Negroes to obtain control of Fisk University for a policy of Negro self-determination, so extreme in extent as to undermine all cooperation between whites and Negroes. Such an extreme attitude has appeared within the last few years in many parts of the world. While it is natural and in its more reasonable forms desirable, self-determination, as advocated by those who oppose Dr. McKenzie, is dangerous not only to

the well-being of Fisk University, but to sound race-relationships throughout America.[38]

DuBois praised the students' victory over McKenzie and hailed them as a new breed of black intellectuals sorely needed to challenge the power of industrial philanthropy: "God speed the breed! Suppose we do lose Fisk; suppose we lose every cent that the entrenched millionaires have set aside to buy our freedom and stifle our complaints. They have the power, they have the wealth, but glory to God we still own our own souls and led by young men like these at Fisk, let us neither flinch nor falter, but fight, and fight and fight again." But many black intellectuals, especially those responsible for black colleges, could not easily afford to attack the policies of industrial philanthropy. After the Fisk rebellion, the General Education Board withheld the endowment pledges on the grounds that they were not collectible until Fisk eliminated all its deficits. The Nashville Commercial Club, which was expected to raise the capital to cover the deficits, withdrew from the campaign following McKenzie's resignation. Convinced that McKenzie's successor, Thomas Elsa Jones, did "not conceive himself to be a leader or an emancipator of the Negro group," the philanthropists eventually granted Fisk the endowment. Fisk, however, was still dependent on industrial philanthropy throughout the period and into the present.[39]

Although northern philanthropists sought to move Fisk and other black colleges closer to the philosophy and practice of racial accommodation throughout the first third of the twentieth century, they seemed comfortable only with Hampton, Tuskegee, and similar industrial normal schools. This attitude was revealed through their parallel involvement in the Hampton-Tuskegee endowment campaign. To be sure, they recognized that educational standards at these institutions had to change to keep abreast of minimum requirements for teacher certification, but they saw no need to modify the basic social philosophy of black accommodation to white authority. The campaign for $5 million was organized during the summer of 1924 by Clarence H. Kelsey, chairman of the Title Guarantee and Trust Company and vice-chairman of the Hampton Board of Trustees. Anson Phelps-Stokes was appointed from the Tuskegee Board of Trustees as chairman of the Special Gifts Committee. The John Price Jones Corporation was engaged to prepare the publicity for the campaign and to help with the organizational work. As a result of these efforts, the following subscriptions had been secured by the end of the first year: George Eastman, $4.3 million; General Education Board, $1 million; John D. Rockefeller, Jr., $1 million; Arthur Curtis James, $300,000; Edward H. Harkness, $250,000; Julius Rosenwald, $100,000.

Amounts equal to or greater than $25,000 were pledged by the Phelps-Stokes Fund (the largest contribution it ever made to any single object), Slater Fund, George Foster Peabody, William M. Scott, William G. Wilcox, and the Madame C. J. Walker Manufacturing Company. George Eastman, largely as a result of this campaign, became deeply impressed with the importance of the Hampton-Tuskegee Idea to the nation and on 8 December 1924 announced that in the distribution of the major portion of his estate, Hampton and Tuskegee would each obtain securities valued at $2 million. This pledge was conditional on his requirement that the Hampton-Tuskegee endowment campaign reach its $5 million goal by 31 December 1925. Eastman also contributed another $300,000 toward the goal of $5 million. Anson Phelps-Stokes believed that Eastman's gift resulted from a visit to his home by Julius Rosenwald, Clarence Kelsey, and Robert Moton in November 1924.[40]

The "Special Memorandum" to promote the Hampton-Tuskegee campaign was prepared for Kelsey by the Jones Corporation, and it detailed the reasons for the endowment campaign and the continuing importance of the Hampton-Tuskegee Idea. Part Two of the memorandum, "Our Most Grave and Perplexing Domestic Problem," was introduced with the following quotations:

"The Color line is the problem of the present century."

"The relation of Whites and Negroes in the United States is our most grave and perplexing domestic problem."

"The Negro problem is one of the greatest questions that has ever presented itself to the American people."

These quotations were attributed to J. W. Gregory, the Chicago Commission on Race Relations, and William Howard Taft, respectively. This problem, according to the memorandum, had been exacerbated because the "rise of world-wide race consciousness and ideal of self-determination has had special effect on the American Negro." Consequently, "a wide variety of leadership has sprung up to give them expression." This development was viewed largely as a crisis of leadership:

Some of this leadership, as is natural under the circumstances, is demogogical or otherwise self seeking. Some of it is patently visionary. But there are thousands of earnest, intelligent Negroes today who are fired with a belief in the possibilities within their race and with the ambition to help realize those possibilities sanely and constructively. This whole movement, in all its various forms, has taken deep root. It is not confined to the big city groups but permeates every part of the country. A remarkable Negro periodical and daily press has grown up within the past few years devoted, almost wholly, to advancing, directly or indirectly, these ideas.

The memorandum pointed out that it was "impossible, even if it were desirable, to stop this movement." The important thing was to assure its development in "a sound and constructive form."[41]

The industrial philanthropists believed that the right black leaders could direct the masses along "constructive" lines. "As the Negro progresses," the report stated, "the ideals of at least the sound thinking majority will be most influenced by those of advanced education and experience." Herein were the reasons to raise Hampton and Tuskegee to a level of "advanced education" and to influence the attitudes of emergent black leaders, whether they were trained in advanced industrial schools or academic colleges. From the philanthropists' standpoint, the solution to the race problem was self-evident. First, "The Negro problem has been happily and permanently solved by the application of the Hampton-Tuskegee method in many individual communities." Second, "The Hampton-Tuskegee Idea, therefore, of solving the race problem in America is to *multiply these local solutions and the national problem solves itself.*" Third, "The proposed method for doing this is to *multiply the number of Hampton and Tuskegee men and women adequately trained for present day leadership.*" Although Armstrong had died in 1893, Booker T. Washington in 1915, and H. B. Frissell in 1917, the industrial philanthropists remained steadfastly committed to the Hampton-Tuskegee methods as the fundamental solution to the race problem. Anson Phelps-Stokes said in a letter to John D. Rockefeller, Jr.: "Personally, I am increasingly convinced that Hampton and Tuskegee provide the most important contribution yet found towards the solution of the race problem in this country, and towards the development of the Negro people so as to make them fitted for the highest citizenship." Throughout the endowment campaign the industrial philanthropists reminded themselves and the larger society that the Hampton methods produced Booker T. Washington, "the outstanding Negro leader of the past," and that every president of the United States, from Grant to Calvin Coolidge, had supported the Hampton-Tuskegee Idea. President Garfield was a trustee of Hampton, President Roosevelt served for nine years as a trustee of Tuskegee, and William Howard Taft became a trustee of Hampton while president of the United States and was, in 1925, president of Hampton's Board of Trustees. For the industrial philanthropists, the Hampton-Tuskegee Idea had become a matter of tried and true methods, of tradition, and had congealed into a permanent policy.[42]

The basic social philosophy underlying the Hampton-Tuskegee program for the training of black leaders remained unchanged. It was still a program of interracial harmony predicated on a social foundation of political disfranchisement, civil inequality, racial segregation, and the training of black youth for certain racially prescribed economic positions. The central question was whether this social and educational philosophy could remain intact as Hampton and Tuskegee were transformed from normal schools to secondary schools with certain forms of collegiate work. Nearly one-half, or $2 million, of the Hampton endowment was earmarked for "teacher training of collegiate grade now required by southern States." Attached to the endowment campaign's "Special Memorandum" were regulations governing certificates for teachers in North Carolina and Alabama. In 1925 North Carolina required for a high school teacher's certificate graduation from a "standard A Grade college in academic or scientific courses, embracing 120 semester hours," 18 of which had to be in professional educational subjects. Alabama required three years of standard college work approved by the State Board of Education, including nine hours of professional study. Such requirements forced Hampton and Tuskegee into the world of collegiate education. They started by offering the Bachelor of Science in agriculture and teaching, trying hard to hold closely to their traditional emphasis, but were soon compelled to expand the collegiate departments to cover a range of liberal arts fields.[43]

This very yielding to the new educational standards changed the social composition of the institution's student population, and the question of whether the Armstrong-Washington philosophy could prevail at the collegiate level was answered in part by the Hampton student strike of 1927. Traditionally, the Hampton-Tuskegee Idea rested on a denigration of academic subjects, which was easier to maintain when the institutions were composed of half-grown elementary students, regimented to strict military discipline, and overworked in simple agricultural and industrial tasks. But the new collegiate programs attracted different students. Although the total number of students enrolled at Hampton remained at about a thousand throughout the 1920s, the number of students in the college division grew steadily, from 21 in 1920 to 417 in 1927. By 1929, no new high school students were admitted. The new college-level students repeatedly insisted that academic standards be raised. In 1924 Hampton's Student Council charged that the director of the trade school had so little formal education and used such poor English that he was not qualified to teach. Similar accusations were lodged in 1925 against several teachers in the school of agriculture. There were additional complaints that white teachers were less concerned with academic subjects than with teaching manners and morals. Indeed, five of Hampton's white teachers participated in a Ku Klux Klan parade in support of a law

requiring racial segregation on Hampton's campus, and other white instructors established a segregated club and openly opposed the employment of qualified black teachers. In response to Hampton's low academic
standards and repressive racial policies, the students went on strike in
October 1927. They demanded an end to racism and paternalism and
insisted that "our educational system be so revised that we shall no
longer be subjected to instructions from teachers whose apparent education is below that of the average student." The students' demands, breaking with tradition, called essentially for an abandonment of the Hampton-Tuskegee Idea. Such matters were not easily settled on a campus that
had devoted more than half a century to a philosophy of racial subordination and industrial training. Student unrest and contention between
the faculty and administration persisted into the spring of 1929. Confronted with this disorder, James E. Gregg, successor to H. B. Frissell,
was forced to resign his office. The Hampton Board of Trustees quickly
concurred. Thus both the principal of Hampton and the president of
Fisk University, men who presided over the institutions' first significant
endowments, were forced to resign their office because the students rejected the very policies and social philosophy that underlay the endowment campaigns.[44]

The Hampton students put the final nail in the coffin of the old Hampton-Tuskegee Idea. As Robert A. Coles, one of the leaders of the student
revolt, said, Hampton's new students possessed "a DuBois ambition"
that would not mix with "a Booker Washington education." Such attitudes reflected an increasing demand for collegiate education among
black youth of the 1920s. Despite the industrial philanthropists' efforts
to reduce the number of black colleges (through their scheme of making
one or two vastly superior to the others) and their attempt to transform
industrial training into a collegiate program, black youth and their parents pushed for and achieved more and better higher educational opportunities. The enrollment of college students in public colleges in the sixteen former slave states and the District of Columbia grew from 12 in
1915 to 12,631 in 1935, and, as illustrated in Table 7.2, the enrollment
in private colleges in 1935 was 16,638. In 1915 there were only 2,474
students enrolled in the black private colleges. These accomplishments
and the beliefs and behavior that brought them about specifically rejected the Hampton-Tuskegee Idea and its philosophy of manual training
and racial subordination. The industrial philanthropists, as evidenced
by their contributions of time, money, and effort during the Hampton-
Tuskegee endowment campaign, did not voluntarily abandon the Hampton-Tuskegee Idea. Rather, the philosophy was decisively rejected by the
black students and leaders of the 1920s, and the key institutions were
compelled by changing educational requirements and student demands

TABLE 7.2
Black College and Professional Students in Private and Public
Colleges in Southern States and the District of Columbia, by Sex, 1935

State or District of Columbia	Private college students		Public college students		Public and private college students
	Male	Female	Male	Female	Total
Alabama	793	676	325	554	2,348
Arkansas	138	203	173	172	686
Delaware	0	0	33	50	83
District of Columbia	1,069	894	148	587	2,698
Florida	132	142	267	241	782
Georgia	907	1,078	136	198	2,319
Kentucky	0	0	288	510	798
Louisiana	575	569	273	270	1,687
Maryland	163	298	66	188	715
Mississippi	184	297	127	79	687
Missouri	0	0	215	340	559
North Carolina	652	830	782	1,722	3,986
South Carolina	542	770	254	247	1,813
Tennessee	881	945	460	793	3,079
Texas	740	1,097	453	700	2,990
Virginia	960	1,103	495	523	3,081
West Virginia	0	0	464	494	958
Total	7,736	8,902	4,963	7,668	29,269

Source: Blose and Caliver, *Statistics of the Education of Negroes*, pp. 37–40.

to become standard institutions of higher learning. Thus was ushered in a new and different era in black higher education, and all concerned parties, blacks, missionaries, industrial philanthropists, and southern whites, had to adjust to this new departure. The battles for control and influence over the training of black leaders did not cease, but they were fought on a different terrain.[45]

The progress of black higher education during the 1930s was mixed. The northern missionaries and black educators who presided over the black colleges entered the 1920s extremely worried about the financial and material conditions of black colleges. Then, during the 1930s, northern industrial philanthropists presented black college educators with good opportunities for improving the material conditions of black higher education. To be sure, financial solvency was critical, but it was only a means to the more important and long-standing mission of black higher education. For the northern missionaries and black educators, the great mission of black colleges was that of training a competent leadership, men and women who could think, who were independent and self-reliant, and who could persuade and lead the black masses. This mission was contradicted by the wonderful material 'improvements in endowments, physical plants, and faculty salaries because the industrial philanthropists who provided these gifts pressed continuously for the spontaneous loyalty of the college-bred Negro. As black colleges became increasingly dependent on donations from northern industrial philanthropists, the missionaries and black educators found it extremely difficult, if not impossible, to accept philanthropic gifts and assert simultaneously that many of the political and economic aims of the philanthropists were at variance with the fundamental interests of the black masses. From 1915 to 1960, the General Education Board alone expended for black higher education (exclusive of grants for medical education) over $41 million. The board disbursed over $5 million to Atlanta University; $5 million to Fisk University; $3.8 million to Tuskegee Institute; $3.5 million to Spelman College; $2.15 million to Dillard University; $1.9 million to Morehouse College; and $1.1 million to Clark College. The board symbolized the central place that northern philanthropists had come to occupy in the development of black higher education in the South. Given the industrial philanthropists' demand for a conservative black leadership that would cooperate with instead of challenge the Jim Crow system, a certain amount of compromise, indifference, apathy, and even fear developed among black college educators and students.[46]

Observers of the black colleges during the 1930s were dismayed at the apparent shift in consciousness among black college educators and students which paralleled the colleges' increasing dependence on the purse strings of northern industrial philanthropy. As early as 1930, W. E. B. DuBois, in a commencement address at Howard University, chastised the black college male students for their nihilistic behavior:

> Our college man today is, on the average, a man untouched by real culture. He deliberately surrenders to selfish and even silly ideals, swarming into semiprofessional athletics and Greek letter societies, and affecting to despise scholarship and the hard grind of study and research. The greatest meetings of the Negro college year like those of the white college year have become vulgar exhibitions of liquor, extravagance, and fur coats. We have in our colleges a growing mass of stupidity and indifference.

DuBois and other prominent black intellectuals worried that black college students and educators had forsaken their obligation to become socially responsible leaders of their people. Historian and educator Carter G. Woodson argued in 1933 that the "mis-education" of black students had resulted in the creation of a highly educated bourgeois that was estranged from ordinary black people, "the very people upon whom they must eventually count for carrying out a program of progress." In 1934 writer and poet Langston Hughes denounced the "cowards from the colleges," the "meek professors and well-paid presidents," who submitted willingly to racism and the general subordination of black people. The following year, George Streator, business manager of the *Crisis*, proclaimed that black college faculty were much too conservative, "years behind the New Deal." "Further," said Streator, "Negro college students are not radical; they are reactionary." Such critics showed little sympathy for the black college educators' inability openly to protest against the system of racial caste and still expect to be well received in philanthropic circles.[47]

Some educators in black colleges, however, were also disturbed by the growing apathy and social irresponsibility of black college students. In 1937, Lafayette Harris, president of Philander Smith College in Little Rock, Arkansas, castigated black students for their general apathy and particular estrangement from common black folk: "Probably nothing gives one more concern than the frequently apparent fatalistic and nonchalant attitude of many a Negro college student and educated Negro. With him, very little seems to matter except meals, sleep, and folly. Community problems are never even recognized as existing. They know nothing of their less fortunate fellowmen and care less." The following year Randolph Edmonds, a professor at Dillard University, blamed black college educators for the attitudes of black students toward the masses. "The Negro youth is being educated to regard the race with contempt, not only by white teachers in mixed schools, but by Negro instructors in Negro colleges." The central contention of much of this criticism was that the college-bred Negroes, or "talented tenth," were not being educated to think and act in behalf of the interests of black people. Rather, they were internalizing a social ideology nearly indistinguishable from that of the philanthropists who helped finance black higher education. As one black student assessed the social consciousness of black educated leaders in 1938, "The American race problem has brought us many anomalies. But it may be some time before it equals the Negro leader, supported by workingmen's dollars, leading a working population, and yet enunciating a philosophy which would do credit to the original economic royalist or the most eloquent spokesman for America's 'sixty sinister families.' " In vital respects, the fate of black higher education during the 1930s was closely related to the attitudes and interests of the nation's wealthiest families. Only black college educators could appreciate fully the difficulty of depending on this wealth while being urged to articulate a philosophy that challenged the philanthropists' conceptions of proper race and social relations.[48]

Undoubtedly, the verbal attacks upon black college educators and students during the 1930s were engendered in part by the growing liberalism of the era. The social critics may have been excessively harsh and even off the mark in their judgments of the social consciousness of black college educators and students. Black college educators had to steer between two equally critical courses. On one hand, they were dependent on the benevolence of industrial philanthropists for the very survival of the private black colleges that formed the backbone of black higher education. On the other hand, it was their mission to represent the struggles and aspirations of black people and to articulate the very source of the masses' discomfort and oppression. One course propelled them into conflict with the other because the industrial philanthropists supported black subordination. Black college educators had no noble path out of this contradiction and sought to contain it by placating northern industrial philanthropists while training black intellectuals who would help lead black people toward greater freedom and justice. Indeed, it was a painful and difficult course to steer that frequently brought down upon black college educators the wrath of both sides. This was a moment in the history of black higher education when presidents and faculty could do little more than succeed in keeping their institutions together while maintaining themselves and their students with as great a sense of dignity as was possible. When their students helped launch the civil rights movement of the 1960s, the hard work of these educators seemed far more heroic in the hour of harvest than it did during the years of cultivation.

EPILOGUE

BLACK EDUCATION IN SOUTHERN HISTORY

THE EDUCATIONAL sphere in the postbellum South was, among other things, an ideological medium through which northerners and southerners posed and apprehended fundamental questions of class, culture, race, and democracy. Black education was one of the central arenas for that struggle to define social reality and shape the future direction of southern society. Without question, it was not as important as economics or politics, but, perhaps, it was a better lens through which to comprehend the separate and distinct social visions of a New South. For it was through differing forms of training the young that each class and race tried to shape its own future and translate its particular experiences, ideas, values, and norms into a legitimate projection of broader social relations. Inherent in the idea of universal education was the opportunity to engage in long-term, systemic, public discourse to make particular forms of experience and projections of social life dominant. The postbellum crusade for control over the educational process was indissolubly linked to the struggle to weld the separate elements of southern life into a single vision of the South's future. Hence not only questions involving the status and future of black southerners but also those involving relations among classes of northern and southern whites were drawn into the arena of black education.

Because each group believed that it was critical to educate the young in the values, norms, perceptions, sentiments, and customs that supported and defined the emergent New South, campaigns to control education often revealed complexities and differences that were less conspicuous in other areas. For instance, whites all over the South and many in the North supported efforts to disfranchise black voters. White consensus in these campaigns suggests a unity of belief in white supremacy that combined different classes of whites into a single ideology. The educational arena, however, revealed important ideological differences based on the social position, cultural beliefs, political strategies, and perceived common interests of their proponents. White planters who dominated local governments in the rural South generally resisted universal public education, particularly when it applied to rural blacks. White urban industrialists believed that blacks should be disfranchised and remain permanently in a lower-class status, but they also believed that a proper system of universal education would improve the economic productivity of rising generations. Moreover, they believed that universal schooling would socialize the young to the disciplines and values needed for efficient service within social roles prescribed along race and class lines. Thus one set of dominant-class white southerners believed that formal schooling inappropriately tended to raise blacks' aspirations and to ruin them as plantation laborers, while another group of dominant-class white southerners thought that education, when properly controlled, could make blacks an asset instead of a burden to the South. Behind these different beliefs about ways of training the young lay discrete social visions of the character and order of the New South.[1]

Similarly, basic agreement on some questions did not succeed in uniting white northerners around any common conception of black education. Neither the antislavery legacy nor the Civil War–born sentiment of justice could transcend basic questions of political dominance, economic order, and race relations. To be sure, northerners favored universal public education, but they did not agree on the purpose and function of schooling among the freedpeople. Northern white industrialists, beginning with the establishment of the Peabody Education Fund in 1867, saw universal schooling in much the same way as did southern white industrialists—as a means to make black southerners an efficient laboring force of the South and to prepare them for a fairly definite caste system. It was mainly through their differences with the southern white planters that northern white industrialists gained their reputations as liberal reformers and were perceived as promoting in the South more just race relations. The Yankee missionaries, despite their paternalism, were guided in significant part by a sense of democratic idealism. They held that poor and racially subjugated children had a right to the finest quality of public education and to political and civil equality. Class, ideology, race, and region all intersected in complex and conflicting ways to present the former slaves with contending conceptions of the meaning and purpose of education in the new social order. Southern planters, urban industrialists, Yankee missionaries, and northern industrialists sought to gain black consent to their respective social and educational ideologies, even when a particular social vision, as in the case of the planters, meant virtually no schooling at all for black children.[2]

The long struggle over the development of education in the postbellum South occurred in large part because no dominant class could convince the freedpeople that its conception of education reflected a natural and proper social order. There was nothing inevitable about the former slaves' ability to resist these competing ideologies of education and society and pursue their own course. They had spent much time preparing themselves for the moment when they could act in ways more consonant with beliefs sacred to them that could not be expressed before emancipation. Initially, all of the dominant white groups suspected that the ex-slaves were a docile and tractable people. But the actions of the freedmen during the Civil War and Reconstruction periods convinced all parties that blacks had their own ideas about learning and self-improvement. Blacks soon made it apparent that they were committed to training their young for futures that prefigured full equality and autonomy. Consequently, the assumption that blacks had no ideas about the meaning and purpose of education in a free society was quickly replaced with the belief that they held the wrong ideas about how and for what purpose they should be educated. The ex-slaves split with their closest allies, Yankee missionaries, over the question of who should control the educational institutions for black children. Black southerners entered emancipation with an alternative culture, a history that they could draw upon, one that contained enduring beliefs in learning and self-improvement. They convinced their compatriots that a perceived common interest in literacy and schooling did not depend for its existence upon dominant-class culture.[3]

There developed in the slave community a fundamental belief in learning and self-improvement and a shared belief in universal education as a necessary basis for freedom and citizenship. The freedpeople carried with them into emancipation the distinctive orientation toward learning that developed in slave quarters during the decades preceding the Civil War. "On Sundays," recalled ex-slave Charity Bowery, "I have seen the negroes up in the country going away under large oaks, and in secret places, sitting in the woods with spelling books." The testimony of former slaves reveals their strong motivation for literacy and book learning. According to one description of a secret school of slaves, "every window and door was carefully closed to prevent discovery. In that little school hundreds of slaves learned to read and write a legible hand. After toiling all day for their masters they crept stealthily into this back alley, each with a bundle of pitch-pine splinters for lights." Yet the typical slave never attended school or a secret literacy session a day in his or her life. As one former slave remembered, "Why, we were no more than dogs! If they caught us with a piece of paper in our pockets, they'd whip us. They were afraid we'd learn to read and write, but I never got a chance." But their lack of a chance to learn did not mean that they had no desire for learning and self-improvement. Even the slavemasters' legal and customary repression of literacy among slaves betrayed the masters' respect for their slaves' capacity and desire for book learning. As the masters increased efforts to stifle the slaves' desire for literacy, the slaves seemed more convinced that education was fundamentally linked to freedom and dignity. This distinctive orientation toward learning was transmitted over time.[4]

This legacy helps us to understand in large part why the choices ex-slaves made during the war and Reconstruction included the building of a free school system. A large number of blacks who held leadership positions in the ministry, government, and education during the immediate postwar period had learned to read and write as slaves. They took the lead in shaping the various elements of black culture into a vision of education and social order at variance with the South's traditional views of public education. The slaves' educational values, nourished but often barely articulated before the Civil War, found expression during and especially after that conflict. Northern observers during these times noted that the former slaves considered book learning almost a sacred act. The Union army officers were the first to be shocked by black soldiers' desire to read and write. A chaplain of a Louisiana black regiment wrote: "I am sure I never witnessed greater eagerness for study; and all, who have examined the writing books and listened to the recitations in the schools, have expressed their astonishment and admiration. A majority of the men seem to regard their books as an indispensable portion of their equipments, and the cartridge box and spelling book are attached to the same belt." Such behavior caused friends and foes to reexamine their preconceived notions about black cultural beliefs on learning and self-improvement. The Warrenton, North Carolina, *Gazette* observed in 1882 that "relatively speaking" the Negroes were "taking more interest in education and surpassing us [whites] in gaining the rudiments of an education. They go to school every chance they get and shell out their money freely to pay the teachers." A survey of North Carolina white landlords, tenants, and laborers in 1886–87 found similar opinions. A Vance County white man proclaimed: "The colored take more interest in education than the whites." Whether southern blacks took more interest in education than southern whites was not the meaningful point of his observation. Most important was that white landlords, tenants, and laborers, who tended to attribute negative values to black people, were forced to recognize blacks' deep-rooted belief in education.[5]

These beliefs spread over time and space and were expressed in even the most backward little rural communities. In the summer of 1886, at age eighteen, W. E. B. DuBois taught school in the hills of Tennessee. He was a Fisk University student then, and it was common for "Fisk men" to venture into rural Tennessee during summer vacations to gain practical experience in teaching. In a rural black community that seemed least removed from slavery DuBois found a school. He was informed that but once since the Civil War had a teacher been there. The school, as DuBois described it, was not worthy of the name:

> The schoolhouse was a log hut, where Colonel Wheeler used to shelter his corn. It sat in a lot behind a rail fence and thorn bushes, near the sweetest of springs. There was an entrance where a door once was, and within, a massive rickety fireplace; great chinks between the logs served as windows. Furniture was scarce. A pale blackboard crouched in the corner. My desk was made of three boards, reinforced at critical points, and my chair, borrowed from the landlady, had to be returned every night. Seats for the children—these puzzled me much. I was haunted by a New England vision of neat little desks and chairs, but, alas! The reality was rough plank benches without backs, and at times without legs.

Yet, undaunted by their poverty and sustained by a distinctive orientation toward learning, the parents saw to it when school opened in late July that their children attended. In the early morning, DuBois heard "the patter of little feet down the dusty road," and soon he faced a "room of dark solemn faces and bright eager eyes." "There they sat," DuBois recalled, "nearly thirty of them, on the rough benches, their faces shading from a pale cream to a deep brown, the little feet bare and swinging, the eyes full of mischief, and the hands grasping Webster's blue-back spelling book." Those children were not in school because of compulsory school attendance laws; there were none in Tennessee at this time. Nor were they there because of any external stimuli from missionaries, industrialists, or planters. Instead they remind us of their ancestors who sat in the woods in secret places with spelling books. They further illuminate the cumulative Afro-American beliefs in learning and self-improvement that were transmitted from the slaves to the freedpeople.[6]

Blacks' motivation for intellectual achievement, which lay deep in the slave and ex-slave past, persisted into the twentieth century and into our own present. Observers of blacks' educational development have been virtually uniform in their recognition of this enduring cultural belief. In his early twentieth-century classic, *Following the Color Line*, Ray Stannard Baker wrote: "The eagerness of the coloured people for a chance to send their children to schools is something astonishing and pathetic. They will submit to all sorts of inconveniences in order that their children may get an education." Clearly, his observation was borne out by blacks' contributions to the development of a common school system in the rural South during the first third of the twentieth century. In 1941, reflecting on blacks' precious regard for education in his seminal folk history of Afro-America, *Twelve Million Black Voices*, Richard Wright

Eutaw School of Eutaw, Alabama, built during the 1920s, symbolized the better school facilities that southern blacks achieved during the second crusade (1900–1935) for universal common schools. Courtesy of Fisk University Library.

Blacks in Gee's Bend, Alabama, conduct school in their church in the mid-1930s. As late as the thirties, school conditions in some areas were little improved over Reconstruction era conditions. Courtesy of the Library of Congress.

wrote: "Any black man who can read a book is a hero to us. And we are joyful when we hear a black man speak like a book." Only several years had elapsed when Gunnar Myrdal, the Swedish social scientist, published his monumental book on the condition of blacks in America, entitled *An American Dilemma*. Unable to appreciate fully the culmination of blacks' educational values that had started decades before the Civil War, Myrdal concluded that they possessed "a naive, almost religious faith in education." But there was nothing naive about a belief in learning and self-improvement as a means to individual and collective dignity. It was not the end of their struggle for freedom and justice; only a means toward that end.[7]

Thus it is ironic that in time a body of historical and social science literature was built up which tended to interpret blacks' relatively lower levels of educational attainment in the twentieth century as the product of initial differences in attitude or cultural orientation toward learning and self-improvement. Even recent studies argue that black dialect, oral traditions, and cultural separatism prevented blacks from being more successful in school during the Reconstruction era. Further, it is maintained that the difference in historic patterns of school achievement between blacks and immigrant groups is mainly the result of long-standing attitudes toward learning and self-improvement. A careful examination of blacks' enduring beliefs in education and their historic struggle to acquire decent educational opportunities against almost overwhelming odds leaves little room to attribute their relatively low levels of educational attainment to uncongenial cultural values or educational norms. That more was not achieved means little, for the conditions have been appallingly difficult. Cultural values were hardly relevant in a society in which opportunities for education were unavailable. The slaves understood this reality, and so did their descendants. For the majority of black children in the South during most of the period under study (1860 to 1935), not even public elementary schools were available. High schools were virtually nonexistent, and the general unavailability of secondary education precluded even the opportunity to prepare for college. The education of blacks in the South reveals that various contending forces sought either to repress the development of black education or to shape it in ways that contradicted blacks' interests in intellectual development. The educational outcomes demonstrate that blacks got some but not much of what they wanted. They entered emancipation with fairly definite ideas about how to integrate education into their broader struggle for freedom and prosperity, but they were largely unable to shape their future in accordance with their social vision.[8]

NOTES

ABBREVIATIONS

GEB Papers   General Education Board Papers,
                      Rockefeller Archive Center
HIA   Hampton Institute Archives
Home Mission Monthly *American Baptist Home Mission Monthly*
JRFP-FU   Julius Rosenwald Fund Papers,
                      Fisk University Library

CHAPTER I

1. Webber, *Deep Like the Rivers*, pp. 136–37; Stowe, "Education of the Freedmen," p. 128; Nordhoff quoted in Blassingame, *Black New Orleans*, p. 108; Washington quoted in DuBois, *Black Reconstruction in America*, pp. 641–42; Blassingame, "Union Army as an Educational Institution"; Butchart, "Educating for Freedom"; Sweat, "Some Notes on the Role of Negroes"; Hornsby, "Freedmen's Bureau Schools in Texas," pp. 397–417; Duncan, *Freedom's Shore*, pp. 23–25; Berlin, Reidy, and Rowland, eds., *Freedom*, pp. 28, 32, 420, 615–30.

2. Franklin, *Black Self-Determination*, pp. 168–69; Gutman, "Observations on Selected Trends in American Working-Class Historiography"; DuBois, *Black Reconstruction in America*, pp. 641–49.

3. Alvord, *Inspector's Report*, pp. 9–10.

4. Bullock, *History of Negro Education in the South*, p. 26; Butchart, "Educating for Freedom," pp. 2, 25; *New Orleans Union*, 12 July 1864; Gutman, "Observations on Selected Trends in American Working-Class Historiography"; Alvord, *Fifth Semi-Annual Report on Schools for the Freedmen*, p. 29.

5. Gutman, "Observations on Selected Trends in American Working-Class Historiography."

6. *New Orleans Union*, 12 July 1864; Blassingame, "Union Army as an Educational Institution," p. 154; Blassingame, *Black New Orleans*, pp. 108–9; White, *Freedmen's Bureau in Louisiana*, pp. 167, 172, 175; *New Orleans Tri-*

bune, 22 Sept., 23 July 1864; Alvord, *Inspector's Report*, pp. 14–15; Howard, *Black Liberation in Kentucky*, pp. 160–61.

7. White, *Freedmen's Bureau in Louisiana*, pp. 172–75; Alvord, *Inspector's Report*, pp. 9–10, 14–15.

8. *New Orleans Tribune*, 5 Sept., 31 Oct., 6 Nov. 1866; White, *Freedmen's Bureau in Louisiana*, pp. 177–79; Blassingame, *Black New Orleans*, pp. 111–12.

9. Wright, "Development of Education for Blacks in Georgia," pp. 71–72; *Loyal Georgian*, 3 Feb. 1866; Alvord, *Fifth Semi-Annual Report*, p. 28; Alvord, *Third Semi-Annual Report*, p. 12; Jones, *Soldiers of Light and Love*, pp. 61, 73–74; Drago, *Black Politicians and Reconstruction in Georgia*, p. 27.

10. *Loyal Georgian*, 19, 16 May 1867, 3 Feb., 10 Mar. 1866; Jones, *Soldiers of Light and Love*, p. 84; Butchart, "Educating for Freedom," pp. 418–23; Duncan, *Freedom's Shore*, p. 45.

11. Horst, "Education for Manhood," p. 18; Alvord, *Inspector's Report*, pp. 9, 12; Blassingame, *Black New Orleans*, p. 113; Alvord, *Fifth Semi-Annual Report*, p. 5; Alvord, *Third Semi-Annual Report*, p. 30.

12. Alvord, *Ninth Semi-Annual Report*, p. 49; Alvord, *Eighth Semi-Annual Report*, p. 82; Butchart, "Educating for Freedom," p. 430; McPherson, *Struggle for Equality*, p. 406; Weinberg, *A Chance to Learn*, p. 43; Alvord, *Sixth Semi-Annual Report*, p. 74; Bass and Roberts, eds., *Proceedings of the 46 Indiana Annual Conference of the African Methodist Episcopal Church*, pp. 22, 31; Washington quoted in DuBois, *Black Reconstruction*, p. 642; Williams, "A.M.E. Christian Recorder"; Montgomery, "Negro Churches in the South."

13. DuBois, *Black Reconstruction*, pp. 649–56; Sweat, "Some Notes on the Role of Negroes"; Alvord, *Inspector's Report*, pp. 10, 20.

14. Blassingame, ed., *Slave Testimony*, pp. 173, 234, 267, 336, 382, 417, 544, 565, 620, 622, 643, 689, 710–12, 740–42; Heard, *From Slavery to the Bishopric in the A.M.E. Church*, p. 31; Jones, *The Experience of Thomas H. Jones*, pp. 14–21; Rawick, ed., *American Slave*, p. iii; Yetman, *Life under the "Peculiar Institution,"* pp. 257, 299; Feldstein, *Once a Slave*, pp. 62–63; Webber, *Deep Like the Rivers*, pp. 131–38; Cornelius, " 'We Slipped and Learned to Read.' "

15. Gutman, *The Black Family in Slavery and Freedom*, p. 431; Butchart, "Educating for Freedom," p. 429; Alvord, *Fourth Semi-Annual Report*; Alvord, *Inspector's Report*, p. 15; Cohen, "Negro Involuntary Servitude in the South," p. 47; Litwack, *Been in the Storm So Long*, p. 489; Jones, *Soldiers of Light and Love*, p. 59.

16. *New Orleans Black Republican*, 29 Apr. 1865; *Loyal Georgian*, 19, 16 May 1867; Butchart, "Educating for Freedom," pp. 430–31; Alvord, *Fifth Semi-Annual Report*, p. 47; Blassingame, *Black New Orleans*, pp. 39, 72, 129, 157–58.

17. Bullock, *History of Negro Education in the South*, p. 29; Alvord, *Inspector's Report*, pp. 2, 13; Butchart, "Educating for Freedom," p. 418; Butchart, *Northern Schools, Southern Blacks, and Reconstruction*, pp. 13–21; DuBois,

Black Reconstruction, pp. 649–56; Sweat, "Some Notes on the Role of Negroes"; Brown, *Education and Economic Development of the Negro in Virginia*, pp. 46–48; Weinberg, *A Chance to Learn*, p. 46.

18. Tyack and Lowe, "Constitutional Moment."

19. Ransom and Sutch, *One Kind of Freedom*; Mandle, *Roots of Black Poverty*; Wiener, *Social Origins of the New South*; Billings, *Planters and the Making of a "New South"*; Woodman, "Sequel to Slavery."

20. Wiener, "Planter Persistence and Social Change," p. 257; Katz, "Origins of Public Education," p. 392; Alvord, *Inspector's Report*, p. 12; Southern writer and Schurz quoted in Butchart, "Educating for Freedom," pp. 458, 460.

21. Ransom and Sutch, *One Kind of Freedom*, pp. 44–47, 57, 67; Mandle, *Roots of Black Poverty*, p. 17; Billings, *Planters and the Making of a "New South*," pp. 35–39.

22. Alvord, *Inspector's Report*, p. 13; Alvord, *Fourth Semi-Annual Report*, pp. 83–84; Chase quoted in ibid., p. 49.

23. White, *Freedmen's Bureau in Louisiana*, p. 186; Butchart, "Educating for Freedom," p. 474; Alvord, *Third Semi-Annual Report*, pp. 30–31; *New Orleans Tribune*, 23 July 1864; Bullock, *History of Negro Education in the South*, p. 43; Alvord, *Ninth Semi-Annual Report*, p. 42; Ransom and Sutch, *One Kind of Freedom*, p. 26.

24. Alvord, *Ninth Semi-Annual Report*, p. 33; Weinberg, *A Chance to Learn*, p. 52; Eaton quoted in Pinchbeck, *Virginia Negro Artisan and Tradesman*, p. 71.

25. Ransom and Sutch, *One Kind of Freedom*, p. 67; Butchart, "Educating for Freedom," pp. 455–57; Weinberg, *A Chance to Learn*, pp. 46–47; Bullock, *History of Negro Education in the South*, pp. 44–52; Billington, *American South*, pp. 189–96; Bond, *Education of the Negro in the American Social Order*, p. 115.

26. Cohen, "Negro Involuntary Servitude in the South"; Daniel, *Shadow of Slavery*; Wiener, "Planter-Merchant Conflict in Reconstruction Alabama," pp. 87–89.

27. Billings, *Planters and the Making of a "New South*," pp. 37, 206–8; Louisiana superintendent quoted in Alvord, *Seventh Semi-Annual Report*, pp. 33 35; Alvord, *Inspector's Report*, p. 21; Harlan, *Separate and Unequal*, p. 37; Jones, *Soldiers of Light and Love*, p. 81.

28. DuBois, *Black Reconstruction*, p. 641; Alvord, *Inspector's Report*, p. 12; Lusher quoted in Blassingame, *Black New Orleans*, p. 113; Butchart, "Educating for Freedom," p. 461.

29. Logan, "Opposition in the South to the Free-School System"; for a discussion of southern white industrialists' views of black education, see chapter 2 of Anderson, "Education for Servitude," pp. 41–80; Anderson, "Education as a Vehicle for the Manipulation of Black Workers," pp. 21–26; for industrialists' original testimony, see U.S. Senate Committee on Education and Labor, *Report upon the Relations between Labor and Capital*; for an analysis of the South's middle-class educational campaign, see Harlan, *Separate and Unequal*.

30. Jones, *Soldiers of Light and Love*, p. 109; Morris, *Reading, 'Riting, and Reconstruction*, p. 211; Butchart, *Northern Schools, Southern Blacks, and Reconstruction*, p. 135; McPherson, *Abolitionist Legacy*, pp. 203–5; Richardson, *Christian Reconstruction*, p. 125; Sherer, *Subordination or Liberation*, p. 65.

31. Jones, *Soldiers of Light and Love*, p. 127; Patton, "Major Richard Robert Wright, Sr.," pp. 139–46; U.S. Senate, *Report upon Relations between Labor and Capital*, pp. 813–14.

32. Butchart, *Northern Schools, Southern Blacks, and Reconstruction*, pp. 131–68; Richardson, *Christian Reconstruction*, p. 113.

33. Webber, *Deep Like the Rivers*, pp. 131–38; Franklin, *Black Self-Determination*, p. 175.

34. For a discussion of the southern and northern whites who favored a redirection of the social purpose of black education, see Anderson, "Education for Servitude," chaps. 1–3.

CHAPTER 2

1. For traditional interpretations of black industrial education, see Meier, *Negro Thought in America*, pp. 85–99; McPherson, *Abolitionist Legacy*, pp. 210–18; Enck, "Burden Borne"; Wright, "Development of the Hampton-Tuskegee Pattern of Higher Education," p. 337.

2. Hopkins, *Annual Report upon the Hampton Normal and Agricultural Institute*, p. 8; Armstrong, *Principal's Annual Report, 1887*, p. 6; for Hampton's first twenty classes, 604 of 723 graduates reported teaching in 1890. See Armstrong, *Twenty-Two Years' Work*, p. 293; for enrollment in trades and agriculture, see Hampton Normal and Agricultural Institute, *Catalogue*, pp. 109, 114.

3. Walker, "Industrial Education"; Fisher, *Industrial Education*; Powell, *Movement of Industrial Education*; Woodward, "Results of the St. Louis Manual Training School."

4. John F. Slater Fund, *Third Proceedings*, p. 14.

5. Armstrong to Ogden, 24 Jan. 1878, Ogden Papers; *Southern Workman* 11 (Jan. 1882): 3; ibid. 3 (Dec. 1874): 90.

6. *Southern Workman* 5 (Nov. 1876): 82; ibid. (Oct. 1876): 74; ibid. 3 (Oct. 1874): 74; ibid. (Dec. 1874): 90; ibid. 6 (Apr. 1877): 26–27; ibid. 8 (1879): 39; ibid. 1 (July 1872): 2.

7. *Southern Workman* 5 (Nov. 1876): 82; ibid. 8 (Apr. 1879): 39; ibid. 9 (Jan. 1880): 3; ibid. 6 (Dec. 1877): 90; Armstrong, "Normal School Work among the Freedmen," paper in HIA.

8. Armstrong, "Normal School Work among the Freedmen," pp. 58–61; Peabody, *Education for Life*, pp. 57–58, 83, 90–91, 54; Talbot, *Samuel Chapman Armstrong*, p. 155, quotations pp. 137, 170–71; *Southern Workman* 10 (Jan. 1881): 3; Armstrong, "Founding of Hampton Institute," pp. 6–7.

9. *Southern Workman* 6 (Dec. 1877): 94; ibid. 8 (Sept. 1879): 91; ibid. 10 (Apr. 1881): 39; Armstrong, "Normal School Work among the Freedmen," p. 4; *Southern Workman* 14 (Apr. 1885): 38; Bullock, *History of Negro Education in the South*, p. 76; Harlan, *Booker T. Washington: The Making of a Black Leader*, p. 58.

10. *Southern Workman* 10 (June 1881): 63; ibid. 6 (Dec. 1877): 90; ibid. 1 (July 1872): 2; ibid. 3 (Dec. 1874): 90; ibid. 10 (June 1881): 63; ibid. 14 (Apr. 1885): 38.

11. Armstrong, "A.M.A. Paper on the Negro Question," p. 94; Armstrong, "Normal School Work among the Freedmen," pp. 4–5.

12. *Southern Workman* 6 (May 1877): 34; ibid. 6 (Dec. 1877): 2; ibid. 7 (Apr. 1878): 25; ibid. 4 (Jan. 1875): 2; ibid. 9 (Jan. 1880): 3; ibid. 5 (Oct. 1876): 74; ibid. 6 (Mar. 1877): 18; ibid. 8 (1879): 39.

13. Armstrong to Ogden, 7 Oct. 1878, Whiting to Armstrong, 28 Dec. 1878, Ogden Papers; *Southern Workman* 9 (June 1880): 63; Barrows, ed., *First and Second Mohonk Conferences on the Negro Question*, p. 15; see Armstrong, *Principal's Annual Report*, June 1885; *Southern Workman* 6 (Mar. 1877): 18; ibid. 1 (Jan. 1872): 2; ibid. 4 (Jan. 1875): 2.

14. *Southern Workman* 8 (Sept. 1879): 102; ibid. (June 1879): 63; ibid. (Aug. 1879): 87; ibid. 10 (July 1881): 75; ibid. 8 (Nov. 1879): 98; ibid. (June 1879): 63; ibid. 9 (Apr. 1880): 45; Church, *Education in the United States*, p. 194.

15. *Southern Workman* 5 (Dec. 1876); ibid. 10 (June 1879); Washington, "Industry and Education," and Washington, "The Progress of the Negro," in Washington Papers; Washington, "The Educational Outlook in the South," p. 127.

16. Armstrong, Address before the 1877 Anniversary Meeting of the American Missionary Association, p. 94, in HIA; Harlan, *Booker T. Washington: The Making of a Black Leader*, p. 61; *Southern Workman* 3 (Nov. 1874): 44; ibid. 6 (Dec. 1877): 94.

17. *Southern Workman* 9 (Jan. 1880): 3; Armstrong, *Principal's Annual Report, 1874*; *Southern Workman* 7 (June 1878): 41; Armstrong, "Normal School Work among the Freedmen," p. 10.

18. *Southern Workman* 10 (Sept. 1881): 91; ibid. 7 (Jan. 1878): 2; ibid. 11 (Feb. 1882): 16; ibid. 6 (Dec. 1877): 94; Armstrong, "Normal School Work among the Freedmen," p. 4.

19. Meier, *Negro Thought in America*, p. 93; Hampton Normal and Agricultural Institute, *Catalogue, 1876*, pp. 35–37; *Southern Workman* 3 (Apr. 1874): 26; ibid. 6 (Dec. 1877): 94; ibid. 10 (Sept. 1881): 91.

20. Armstrong, "Normal School Work among the Freedmen," p. 4; *Southern Workman* 3 (Apr. 1874): 26; ibid. 6 (Dec. 1877): 94; ibid. 10 (Sept. 1881): 91.

21. *Southern Workman* 11 (June 1882): 67; ibid. 12 (June 1883): 71; ibid. 13 (June 1884): 72; ibid. 14 (June 1885): 75; ibid. 17 (June 1888): 68; Armstrong, *Principal's Annual Report, 1876*, p. 37.

22. For the paper as classroom reader, see *Southern Workman* 8 (Sept. 1879):

90; Bryce, *Economic Crumbs*; for series of Bryce's articles, see *Southern Workman* 7 (Sept. 1878): "Rights and Duties of Citizens," p. 69; "Labor," pp. 76–78; "Capital," p. 85; "Wages," p. 16; "Strikes and Lock-Outs," p. 57.

23. Bryce, "Capital," p. 85; Harlan, *Booker T. Washington: The Making of a Black Leader*, p. 74.

24. Bryce, "Labor," pp. 76–78; Bryce, "Wages," p. 16; in addition to Bryce's textbook *Economic Crumbs* and the *Southern Workman*, the students also used Bowker, *Economics for the People*, and Macy, *Our Government*.

25. Jones, *Social Studies in the Hampton Curriculum*, pp. 1–7; see Washington's address in Harlan and Smock, eds., *Booker T. Washington Papers*, 5: 532, 539.

26. Jones, *Social Studies in the Hampton Curriculum*, pp. 5–7.

27. Armstrong, *Principal's Annual Report, 1885*, p. 42; *Southern Workman* 11 (June 1882): 67; ibid. (Aug. 1882): 84. The sixty seniors of the 1882 class received the following percentages of correct answers: mathematics, 34.8; history, 66.5; chemistry, 62.1; English literature, 62.5; political economy, 78.5. Harlan, *Booker T. Washington: The Making of a Black Leader*, pp. 52–71, 76.

28. Armstrong, *Principal's Annual Report, 1886*, pp. 28–29; *Southern Workman* 6 (Dec. 1877): 94.

29. Armstrong, "Normal School Work among the Freedmen," p. 9; *Southern Workman* 6 (Dec. 1877): 94; ibid. 20 (June 1891): 207; ibid. 6 (June 1877): 73.

30. Armstrong, *Principal's Annual Report, 1874*, p. 9; ibid., *1887*, p. 5; *Southern Workman* 8 (June 1879): 63; ibid. 10 (Sept. 1881): 91; ibid. 17 (June 1888): 65–66, 70–71; Harlan, *Booker T. Washington: The Making of a Black Leader*, p. 72.

31. Armstrong, "Normal School Work among the Freedmen," p. 9; Hopkins, *Annual Report upon Hampton Institute*, pp. 5–6; for a catalog of significant changes in the Hampton curriculum, see *Hampton Bulletin* 14 (May 1918): Appendix; see also Peabody, *Education for Life*, pp. 366–67.

32. *Southern Workman* 21 (June 1893): 93; ibid. 9 (Nov. 1880): 112; Armstrong, *Principal's Annual Report, 1887*, p. 3.

33. "Industries," *Southern Workman* 19 (June 1890): 71–73.

34. *Southern Workman* 14 (June 1885): 90; ibid. 11 (June 1882): 64–67; Hampton Normal and Agricultural Institute, *Catalogue*, June 1886, pp. 25–30; *Southern Workman* 9 (Nov. 1880): 112.

35. Hampton Normal and Agricultural Institute, *Catalogue*, June 1886, p. 28; *Southern Workman* 14 (June 1885): 85.

36. Harlan, *Booker T. Washington: The Making of a Black Leader*, p. 63; Armstrong to Jackson, Letterbook (1879), p. 257, Armstrong to Walker, Letterbook (1879), p. 257, Armstrong to Bolding, Letterbook (1879), to Dennis, Letterbook (1879), to Clark, Letterbook (1879), to Bolden, Letterbook (1879), to Harris, Letterbook (1876), to Strong, Letterbook (1876), to White, Letterbook

(1874), HIA; see also student Discipline Books, HIA; Armstrong, *Principal's Annual Report, 1878*, p. 10; ibid., *1880*, p. 13.

37. Adams to Armstrong, 6 Mar. 1878, Mann to Armstrong, 12 Jan. 1888, HIA.

38. Alexander to Armstrong, 9 Jan. 1888, Boothe to Armstrong, 10 Jan. 1888, Satterwhite to Armstrong, 9 Jan. 1888, Marshall to Armstrong, 9 Jan. 1888, HIA.

39. Kiffie to Armstrong, 10 Jan. 1890, Colbert to Armstrong, 6 Jan. 1888, Shields to Armstrong, 11 Jan. 1888, Hawkins to Armstrong, 12 Jan. 1888, Mundy to Armstrong, 12 Jan. 1888, Johnson to Armstrong, 9 Jan. 1888, HIA.

40. Shields to Armstrong, 11 Jan. 1888, Boothe to Armstrong, 10 Jan. 1888, Hawkins to Armstrong, 12 Jan. 1888, Johnson to Armstrong, 9 Jan. 1888, Scott to Armstrong, 6 Jan. 1888, HIA.

41. Whiting to Frissell, 11 Nov. 1894, Rollins to Armstrong, 19 July 1877, Elks to Armstrong, 9 Jan. 1890, Spraggins to Armstrong, 10 Jan. 1890, Ruth to Armstrong, 9 Jan. 1890, Johnson to Armstrong, 9 Jan. 1888, Satterwhite to Armstrong, 9 Jan. 1888, HIA.

42. *Southern Workman* 8 (June 1879): 63; Tucker to Armstrong, 6 Jan. 1888, Hawkins to Armstrong, 12 Jan. 1888, David to Armstrong, 9 Jan. 1888, HIA; Armstrong quoted in Barrows, ed., *First and Second Mohonk Conferences on the Negro Question*, p. 15; Shields to Armstrong, 11 Jan. 1888, HIA.

43. Article on the creation of the Alumni Association in *Southern Workman* 7 (Mar. 1878): 19 (Clark was elected chairman and McAdoo secretary); Alumni Association of Hampton Normal and Agricultural Institute to the Faculty of Hampton Institute, 22 May 1878, HIA.

44. *Southern Workman* 8 (May 1879): 52; ibid. 17 (June 1888): 64; Frissell, "Progress of Negro Education," p. 39; *Southern Workman* 7 (May 1878): 33, quoting *Virginia Star*; ibid. 4 (Dec. 1875): 90, quoting *Christian Recorder*.

45. *People's Advocate*, 1, 8 July 1876.

46. Turner, "Wayside Dots and Jots," *Christian Recorder*, 2 May 1878.

47. *Virginia Star* (Richmond), 11 May 1878; *Louisianian* (New Orleans), 10 May 1879; diary of John M. Gregory, Gregory Papers, Ser. 2/1/1, Box No. 5, University of Illinois Archives, Urbana.

48. Crummell, "The Attitude of the American Mind toward the Negro Intellect"; see "Review of Crummell's *Common Sense in Common Schooling*"; Crummell to Miller, 28 July 1898, Crummell Papers.

49. *Cleveland Gazette*, 27 June 1890, 17 Nov. 1900; *Washington Bee*, 19, 26 Oct. 1895, 28 Mar. 1896.

50. Anderson, "Historical Development of Black Vocational Education," pp. 181–85.

51. *Southern Workman* 14 (Mar. 1885): 25; ibid. 17 (June 1888): 64; McPherson, *Abolitionist Legacy*, p. 213; *Freedmen's Aid Society, Twenty-Fifth An-*

nual *Report*, 1891, pp. 151, 164, 210; *Quadrennial Report of the Freedmen's Aid and Southern Education Society*, p. 6; "Industries Taught in Our Schools," pp. 189–92; Sherer, *Subordination or Liberation*, pp. 64, 133.

52. Meier, *Negro Thought in America*, p. 99; McPherson, *Abolitionist Legacy*, pp. 203–23; Sherer, *Subordination or Liberation*, p. 146.

53. *Southern Workman* 14 (Mar. 1885): 25.

54. McPherson, *Abolitionist Legacy*.

55. "Limiting Negro Education," *Home Mission Monthly* 18 (Mar. 1896): 98–100, 205–9; *New York Independent*, 26 Sept., 17 Oct. 1895; Morgan, "Education of the Negroes"; Morgan, "Negro Education"; Morgan, "Defects of Industrial Education."

56. Ward, "Higher Education," p. 322; *Home Mission Monthly* 18 (Apr. 1896): 123; Morgan, "Negro Preparation for Citizenship"; "The Higher Education of Colored Women," *Home Mission Monthly* 18 (May 1896): 160; also see Morgan, *Negro in America*.

57. DeForest, "Does Higher Education Befit the Negro," p. 73; *American Missionary* 47 (July 1894): 288; Sale, "Education of the Negro"; "Education in Our Home Mission Schools," *Home Mission Monthly* 18 (June 1896): 222–23; as quoted in Brawley, *History of Morehouse College*, p. 68; Mitchell, "Higher Education and the Negro"; Meserve, "Shaw University"; Genung, "Richmond Theological Seminary."

58. Osborn, "Benedict College"; Barrett, "Jackson College," pp. 319, 327; Ward, "Higher Education," p. 322. The Freedmen's Aid Society was more conservative than the American Missionary Association and the Home Mission Society. Thus it gave industrial training a higher place in the schools under its control. See Freedmen's Aid and Southern Education Society, *Report of the Board of Managers to the General Committee at the Annual Meeting, Held in Philadelphia* (13 and 14 Nov. 1899), p. 2. Of the 5,383 black students enrolled in the society's schools, 2,640 were in manual training courses, but none of the 3,997 whites were enrolled in such courses.

59. *Southern Workman* 19 (May 1890): 49; ibid. (July 1890): 84; McPherson, *Abolitionist Legacy*, p. 137; Barrows, ed., *First and Second Mohonk Conferences on the Negro Question*, p. 68; Roy, "The Higher Education of the Negroes, No Mistake," p. 91; Harris, "Normal School Training for the Negroes," p. 84.

60. Wayland to Ogden, 21 July 1896, Ogden Papers; Wayland, "Instruction of the Colored Citizens," pp. 78, 83; Wayland to Ogden, 10 Sept. 1896, Ogden Papers; *New York Independent*, 26 Sept., 17 Oct. 1895, 22 Dec. 1898; "Limiting Negro Education," *Home Mission Monthly* 18 (Mar. 1896): 98; Brawley, *Morehouse College*, p. 67; McKinley's address, 18 Dec. 1898, in John F. Slater Fund, *Proceedings*, 1899, pp. 41–44; McPherson, *Abolitionist Legacy*, p. 219.

61. "Eighteen Distinguished Men: Their Opinion of the Hampton-Tuskegee Idea," Box 17, Folder 6, Rosenwald Papers.

62. Harlan, Kaufman, and Smock, eds., *Booker T. Washington Papers*, 3:578–85.

63. Bruce, Address in New Old South Church, Boston, 3 Dec. 1904, Box 6, GEB Papers; Harlan, *Booker T. Washington: The Wizard*, pp. 148, 170.

64. Bruce, Address in New Old South Church, Boston, 3 Dec. 1904, Box 6, GEB Papers, p. 7; Harlan, *Booker T. Washington: The Wizard*, p. 148.

65. Bruce, Address in New Old South Church, Boston, 3 Dec. 1904, Box 6, GEB Papers, p. 8; Harlan, *Booker T. Washington: The Wizard*, p. 151; Sherer, *Subordination or Liberation*, p. 147.

66. Smith to Baldwin, 23 July 1903, Report by Park, 1 Jan. 1906, Washington Papers.

67. Washington quoted in *Southern Workman* 22 (June 1893):v–vi.

68. Frissell to Potter, 22 Feb. 1899, HIA; Ogden quoted in Enck, "Burden Borne," p. 52; Harlan, Kaufman, Kraft, and Smock, eds., *Booker T. Washington Papers*, 4:499, 526.

CHAPTER 3

1. Harlan, *Separate and Unequal*, pp. 75–78, 80–81, 89, 92, 97, 268; Bullock, *History of Negro Education in the South*, pp. 50, 89, 93; Wolters, *New Negro on Campus*, p. 139; McPherson, *Abolitionist Legacy*, pp. 210–12; Anderson, "Education as a Vehicle for the Manipulation of Black Workers," pp. 15–19; Dabney, *Universal Education in the South*, 1:vii–ix.

2. Harlan, *Separate and Unequal*, pp. 75–78, 80–81, 89, 92, 97, 268; Bullock, *History of Negro Education in the South*, pp. 50, 89, 93; Wolters, *New Negro on Campus*, p. 139; Dabney, *Universal Education in the South*, 1:vii–ix.

3. Billings, *Planters and the Making of a "New South,"* pp. 206–9.

4. Harris, "Stability and Change," p. 388; Baldwin, "Present Problem of Negro Education in the South"; Anderson, "Education as a Vehicle for the Manipulation of Black Workers," pp. 31–37; Enck, "Burden Borne," pp. 170–80; Harlan, *Separate and Unequal*, pp. 37, 77–78; McPherson, *Abolitionist Legacy*, p. 367.

5. Harlan, *Separate and Unequal*, pp. 75–85.

6. Frissell, "A Survey of the Field," pp. 3–6; Curry, "Education in the Southern States," p. 38; Baldwin quoted in Harlan, *Separate and Unequal*, p. 78.

7. Harlan, *Separate and Unequal*, p. 79; Dabney, "The Public School Problem in the South," pp. 1009–21; Winston, "Industrial Training in Relation to the Negro Problem," pp. 103, 105; Galloway, "The South and the Negro," pp. 206–8, 213–17; Winston, "Industrial Education and the New South," p. 510.

8. U.S. Commissioner of Education, *Report, 1900–1901*, p. 1009; Harlan, *Separate and Unequal*, pp. 84, 89; Anderson, "Northern Foundations and Southern Rural Black Education," pp. 378–80.

9. Woodward, *Origins of the New South*, pp. 395–401; Ogden, *Samuel Chapman Armstrong*; Mitchell, "Robert Curtis Ogden: A Leader in the Educational Renaissance of the South," Ogden Papers; Enck, "Burden Borne," pp. 47–60.

10. Enck, "Burden Borne," pp. 41, 51, 50; Harlan, *Separate and Unequal*, pp. 75–76, 79–82, 85–87; Ogden to Gilman, 12 May 1903, Ogden Papers; Harlan, *Booker T. Washington: The Making of a Black Leader*, pp. 62, 284.

11. Ware, *George Foster Peabody*, pp. 162, 170, 215; Enck, "Burden Borne," pp. 72–81.

12. Enck, "Burden Borne," pp. 77–78; Ware, *George Foster Peabody*, p. 214; Harlan, *Separate and Unequal*, pp. 75–76; Harlan, *Booker T. Washington: The Making of a Black Leader*, p. 238.

13. Brooks, *An American Citizen*, pp. 33–38, 53–54, 80, 191, 204–15; Dabney, *Universal Education in the South*, 2:145–49; Enck, "Burden Borne," pp. 60–71; Harlan, *Separate and Unequal*, pp. 76–78; Anderson, "Education for Servitude," chap. 5, for an extended discussion of the Baldwin-Washington relationship.

14. For the philanthropists' investment in the southern cotton economy, see Enck, "Burden Borne," pp. 152–64; Anderson, "Southern Improvement Company." For an excellent treatment of urban interest in organizing American agriculture, see Danbom, "The Industrialization of Agriculture, 1900–1930"; Ogden to Gilman, 12 May 1903, "Speech on Negro Education" (1900), Ogden to McKinney, 30 Apr. 1898, Ogden Papers; Anderson, "Education for Servitude," p. 217; Anderson, "Southern Improvement Company."

15. Peabody to Goetchius, 30 Jan. 1911, Peabody Papers.

16. Peabody to Goetchius, 30 Jan. 1911, to Jordan, 18 Dec. 1907, to Smith, 20 Mar. 1906, to Wilson, 20 May 1918, Peabody Papers; Anderson, "Education for Servitude," p. 217.

17. Baldwin, "Present Problem of Negro Education in the South," pp. 104–6; Baldwin to Bassett, 27 May 1904, Washington Papers.

18. Baldwin to Thompson, 15 Apr. 1900, Washington Papers; Baldwin, "Present Problem of Negro Education in the South," pp. 105–7; Anderson, "Education for Servitude," pp. 206–10.

19. See Carnegie, "The Work and Influence of Hampton," 12 Feb. 1904, p. 7; Dillard as quoted in Enck, "Burden Borne," p. 156; Page as quoted in Rusnak, "Walter Hines Page and *The World's Work*," p. 260; Wilcox, *Builder of Tuskegee*, p. 18.

20. Harlan, *Separate and Unequal*, pp. 80–81; Wolters, *New Negro on Campus*, p. 139; Bullock, *History of Negro Education in the South*, p. 93; Meier, *Negro Thought in America*, pp. 85–89; Peabody to Murphy, 14 Oct. 1911, Peabody Papers; Buttrick, "Proceedings of Tennessee School Superintendents' Conference," 8 Apr. 1903, Box 209, GEB Papers; Ogden to Gilman, 12 May 1903, Box 6, Ogden Papers; see esp. Enck, "Burden Borne," chap. 3; Rusnak,

"Walter Hines Page," chap. 7; Baldwin, "Present Problem of Negro Education in the South," pp. 94–100; Baldwin to Howell, 21 Apr. 1900, in Harlan and Smock, eds., *Booker T. Washington, Papers, Volume 5*, p. 489; Anderson, "Education for Servitude," pp. 227–37.

21. For an excellent treatment of black and white press criticisms of the philanthropic movement, see Enck, "Burden Borne," chap. 10; Pringle, "A History of the General Education Board," pp. 50–52, Buse Notes, both in Box 338, GEB Papers; Fosdick, *Adventure in Giving*, p. 23; Candler quoted in *New York World*, 24 Apr. 1901; *Memphis Commercial Appeal*, 1 Nov. 1900; Harlan, *Separate and Unequal*, pp. 98, 184, 215; Woodward, *Origins of the New South*, pp. 144–45; "Alive to a Menace," *Manufacturer's Record*, 13 Sept. 1906, p. 202; "Self-Help in the South," ibid., 4 Oct. 1906, p. 277; for some of the frequent attacks on northern philanthropists, see ibid., 30 Jan. 1902; 23 Jan. 1902, p. 17; 17 Apr. 1902, p. 1; 5 June 1902, pp. 217, 259; 2 Apr. 1903, p. 355; 16 Apr. 1903, p. 210; 30 Apr. 1903, p. 250; 16 July 1903, p. 290; 19 Nov. 1903, p. 517; 3 Dec. 1903, p. 336; 14 July 1904, p. 378; 23 Aug. 1906, p. 575; 13 Dec. 1906, p. 127; 27 Dec. 1906, p. 541.

22. Pringle, "A History of the General Education Board," pp. 50–52; "Southern Education Again," *Manufacturer's Record*, 24 July 1902, p. 1; "Two Sides of the Southern Educational Scheme," ibid., 10 July 1902, p. 447; Harlan, *Separate and Unequal*, pp. 184–85; Woodward, *Origins of the New South*, p. 352.

23. *New Orleans Picayune*, 10 May 1908; Pringle, "A History of the General Education Board," pp. 50–52; Harlan, *Separate and Unequal*, pp. 107, 125, 128, 139, 222; North Carolina labor commissioner quoted in New York *Herald*, 19 July 1905; Virginia landowner quoted in *Richmond Times-Dispatch*, 29 May 1904.

24. Barringer, "Negro Education in the South," pp. 231–43; Barringer, Curtis, and *Richmond Dispatch* quoted in Alexander, "Black Protest in the New South," pp. 61–62; Harlan, *Separate and Unequal*, p. 138.

25. Peabody to Goetchius, 20 Dec. 1911, Box 57, Peabody Papers; for the black public high schools, see Jones, ed., *Negro Education*, pp. 15–16; Baldwin to Adams, 1 Sept. 1903, Murphy to Ogden, 8 Mar. 1904, Box 6, Ogden Papers; Ogden to Baldwin, 26 Feb. 1904, Box 18, Baldwin to Washington, 21 Nov. 1901, Box 792, Washington Papers.

26. Burton, "Race and Reconstruction."

27. Baldwin to Adams, 1 Sept. 1903, Hill to Ogden, 21 Apr. 1905, Box 8, Murphy to Ogden, 8 Mar. 1904, Box 6, Ogden Papers; Woodward, *Origins of the New South*, pp. 142–49; Harlan, *Separate and Unequal*, chaps. 4–7.

28. Ogden to Washington, 14 June 1904, Washington Papers; for southern press support of philanthropists, see *Atlanta Constitution*, 22, 23, 24 Apr. 1901; *Birmingham News*, 5 Oct., 9 Nov. 1901; *Nashville Banner*, 9 Nov. 1901; *Chattanooga News*, 9 Nov. 1901; *Raleigh News and Observer*, 15 Nov. 1901; *Richmond Times*, 12 Nov. 1901; *Birmingham News*, 9 Nov. 1901; Hoyt to Ogden,

18 Apr. 1905, Powell to Ogden, 25 Apr. 1905, Kaufman to Ogden, 15 May 1905, Box 8, Ogden Papers; Gilreath to Frissell, 14 Feb., 5 Nov. 1909, 16 Mar. 1910, HIA; Anderson, "Education for Servitude," p. 221; Harris, "Stability and Change in Discrimination against Black Public Schools," pp. 387–89.

29. Harlan, *Separate and Unequal*, pp. 38, 116, 137, 184–87, 190, 233, 269; Baldwin to Edmonds, 26 Mar. 1900, Washington Papers; *Raleigh Morning Post*, 28 Apr. 1901; *Atlanta Constitution*, 22 Apr. 1901; Bond, *Negro Education in Alabama*, chap. 11; Bullock, *History of Negro Education in the South*, chap. 7.

30. Ogden to Baldwin, 27 May 1903, Ogden Papers; Ogden quoted in Enck, "Burden Borne," p. 387.

31. Harlan, *Booker T. Washington: The Wizard of Tuskegee*, p. 110; Washington, "Industry and Education," 5 June 1903, Washington, "Progress of the Negro," 16 Jan. 1893; Washington, Address Delivered at Old South Meeting House, Boston, 15 Dec. 1891, Washington Papers; Anderson, "Education for Servitude," chap. 5.

32. For some of the feature stories on Washington and Tuskegee Institute during the late nineteenth century, see "Booker T. Washington," p. 798; "Tuskegee Normal School," p. 430; "Educational Progress among the Negroes," *Montgomery Daily Advertiser*, 1 June 1888, p. 2; "Hope of Two Races," *Chicago Inter-Ocean*, 29 May 1892, p. 25; "Tuskegee and the Negro," *Charlotte Observer*, 31 Mar. 1898, p. 421; "Slave Boy and Leader of His Race," *New Voice*, 27 June 1899; "The Representation of the Colored South," *Illustrated American*, 19 Sept. 1896, p. 404; "A Colored Man on the Race Problem," *Leslie's Weekly*, 9 Dec. 1899, p. 462; "Washington: The Moses of His Race," *Volunteer Gazette*, 23 Oct. 1897, p. 6; "Booker T. Washington," *Weekly*, 31 Dec. 1898, p. 1284; "From Slave Kitchen to a College Presidency," *Christian Herald*, 17 Nov. 1877, p. 874; "A Washington of To-Day," *Christian Endeavor World*, 20 Apr. 1899, p. 589; "Booker T. Washington," *Boston Zion's Herald*, 10 Aug. 1898; "Booker T. Washington," *Christian Work*, 21 Dec. 1899, p. 1015; Washington, *My Larger Education*, p. 192; Baldwin to Washington, 18 Feb. 1899, Washington Papers; Brooks, *An American Citizen*, p. 192; Carnegie to Baldwin, 17 Apr. 1903, Baldwin to Washington, 25 May 1903, Resolution from Tuskegee Endowment Committee, 7 May 1903, Baldwin to Rockefeller, 9 Mar. 1904, Washington Papers.

33. Washington, *My Larger Education*, p. 15; Taylor, "We Only Want Our Rights as Citizens," in *Philadelphia Standard-Echo*, 21 Dec. 1895; Hope's address in Meltzer, ed., *In Their Own Words*, 2:125; Bruce, "Booker T. Washington"; Baldwin to Washington, 4 Dec. 1898, in Harlan, *Booker T. Washington Papers*, 4:526.

34. Harlan, *Booker T. Washington: The Making of a Black Leader*, p. 2 in preface; Aptheker, ed., *Correspondence of W. E. B. DuBois*, p. 53; DuBois, *Souls of Black Folk*, chap. 6; Washington quoted in *Philadelphia Standard-Echo*, 23 Nov. 1895; Washington repeated the emphasis on leadership training in an ad-

dress before the faculty and members of the Theological Department of Vanderbilt University, 29 Mar. 1907, Washington Papers; Ogden to McKinney, 30 Apr. 1898, Ogden Papers.

35. Fox, *Guardian of Boston*, pp. 35–40; Rudwick, *W. E. B. DuBois*, pp. 94–100, 117; Enck, "Burden Borne," pp. 389–403; Trotter, "The Top or the Bottom," in *Chicago Broad Ax*, 19 Apr. 1902, p. 1.

36. Enck, "Black Self-Help in the Progressive Era"; Meier, "Booker T. Washington and the Negro Press"; Washington to Baldwin, 17 Jan. 1904, Washington Papers; Washington to Garrison, in Fox, *Guardian of Boston*, p. 38; Rudwick, *W. E. B. DuBois*, pp. 90–91.

37. Fox, *Guardian of Boston*, pp. 42–45, 82–86; Fortune to Washington, 28 Mar. 1904, 11 Sept. 1891, Washington to Scott, 11 Nov. 1903, Washington to Ogden, 20 Oct. 1903, Washington Papers; Aptheker, ed., *Correspondence of W. E. B. DuBois*, pp. 46, 52, 105–6; Aptheker, "Washington-DuBois Conference of 1904," p. 345; DuBois to Peabody, 28 Dec. 1903, Box 1, Ogden Papers; Washington to Baldwin, 22 Jan. 1904, Washington Papers; McPherson, *Abolitionist Legacy*, pp. 368–93.

38. Harlan in Rudwick, *W. E. B. DuBois*, p. 8 of preface; for an excellent treatment of the neoabolitionists' break with the Tuskegee machine, see McPherson, *Abolitionist Legacy*, chap. 20; William Baldwin to George Baldwin, 14 Sept. 1903, Box 792, Washington Papers; Peabody to Murphy, 14 Oct. 1911, Box 1, Peabody Papers; Enck, "Burden Borne," p. 389.

39. Fisher to Washington, 6 Apr., 29 Oct. 1904, to Logan, 31 Aug. 1904, Box 21, Washington Papers; Wheeler, "Isaac Fisher," p. 17.

CHAPTER 4

1. U.S. Commissioner of Education, *Report, 1899–1900*, 2:2502–3; Bond, *Education of the Negro in the American Social Order*, pp. 264–68; Jackson Davis, "State Normal Schools and Agriculture and Mechanical Colleges for Negroes, 1912–13 to 1921–23," Sept. 1924, Box 313, Folder 3267, GEB Papers; McCuiston, *The South's Negro Teaching Force*, pp. 18–24.

2. Bellamy, "Henry A. Hunt," pp. 465–67; Torbert to Peabody, 6 Sept. 1906, Box 56, Peabody Papers.

3. Enck, "Black Self-Help in the Progressive Era," pp. 76–78.

4. Torbert to Peabody, 6 Sept. 1906, Box 56, Peabody Papers.

5. Boyd, *Philadelphia Blue Book*, pp. 495, 547; Hale to Buttrick, 28 Jan. 1911, Peabody to Buttrick, 9 July 1902, Box 45, GEB Papers; Ware, *George Foster Peabody*.

6. Bellamy, "Henry A. Hunt," p. 467; Torbert to Peabody, 6 Sept. 1906, Box 56, Peabody Papers; Davison to Peabody, 6 May 1902, Box 45, GEB Papers.

7. Frissell quoted in Enck, "Black Self-Help in the Progressive Era," pp. 410–

12; Baldwin, "Present Problem of Negro Education in the South"; Buttrick, "To Whom It May Concern," 29 Dec. 1903, Buttrick to Gates, 18 June 1904, Box 200, GEB Papers; Anderson, "Education as a Vehicle for the Manipulation of Black Workers," pp. 37–38.

8. Peabody to Buttrick, 12 Nov. 1902, Box 717, Peabody to Buttrick, 9 July 1902, Buttrick to Gould, Apr. 1903, Box 45, Buttrick to Peabody, 25 Sept. 1902, Box 717, GEB Papers.

9. Gray to Cloyd, 19 June 1902, to Peabody, 2 July 1902, Box 45, GEB Papers.

10. Buttrick to Peabody, 20 Sept. 1902, to Branson, Sept. 1902, Gray to Torbert, 21 Nov. 1902, to Peabody, 27 Jan. 1903, Cloyd to Buttrick, 3 Apr. 1903, Box 45, GEB Papers.

11. Peabody quoted in Gray to Buttrick, 21 Apr. 1903, Buttrick to Schenck, 22 May 1903, Schenck to Buttrick, 25 May 1903, Lewis to Gray, 5 June 1903, Box 45, GEB Papers.

12. Davison to Buttrick, 9 June 1903 (Fort Valley's annual report to trustees enclosed), Davison to Peabody, 8 June 1903, to Buttrick, 2 Oct. 1902, Box 45, GEB Papers.

13. Gray to Peabody, 8 June 1903, to Buttrick, 15, 25 June 1903, Davison to Buttrick, 25 June 1903, Buttrick to Davison, 30 June 1903, Box 45, GEB Papers.

14. Curti and Nash, *Philanthropy in the Shaping of American Higher Education*, pp. 175–76; Harlan, *Separate and Unequal* (1968 ed.), pp. 75–78, 80–81, 89, 92, 97, 268; Wolters, *New Negro on Campus*, p. 139; Bullock, *History of Negro Education in the South*, pp. 50, 89, 93.

15. Carethy to Buttrick, 3 July 1903, Scroggs to Buttrick, 28 May 1903, Culpepper to Peabody, 13 June 1903, Box 45, GEB Papers.

16. Anderson, "Hampton Model of Normal School Industrial Training"; Anderson, "Northern Foundations."

17. Baldwin to Baldwin, Jr., 2 Feb. 1903, Baldwin, Jr., to Baldwin, 6 Feb. 1903, Baldwin to Baldwin, Jr., Feb. 1903, Box 44, GEB Papers; Haynes, *Black Boy of Atlanta*, p. 90.

18. Buttrick to Branson, 18 July 1903, Washington to Peabody, 20 July 1903, Buttrick to Peabody, 10 Nov. 1903, Fisher to Branson, 31 July 1903, Branson to Buttrick, 9 Nov. 1903, Box 45, GEB Papers.

19. Buttrick to Branson, 18 July 1903, Box 45, Buttrick to Peabody, 5 Nov. 1903, Box 717, Hunt to Branson, 7 Aug. 1903, Buttrick to Peabody, 17 Aug. 1903, Hunt to Buttrick, 5 Apr. 1904, Box 45, GEB Papers.

20. Hill to Peabody, 15, 20 Dec. 1904, Box 45, GEB Papers.

21. Peabody to Hunt, 4 Jan. 1905, to Buttrick, 4 Jan. 1905, Hunt to Peabody, 10 Jan. 1905, Box 45, GEB Papers.

22. Buttrick to Hunt, 13 Jan. 1905, Hunt to Sage, 8 Feb. 1916, Godard to Sage, 10 Oct. 1916, Sage to Hunt, 29 Jan., 7 Dec. 1917, 27 Feb. 1920, Brierly to

Hunt, 29 Feb. 1924, Agreement between the General Education Board and Fort Valley High and Industrial School, 23 Jan. 1928, Box 45, GEB Papers.

23. Report of Williams on Fort Valley High and Industrial School, 19 Nov. 1906, Box 56, Peabody Papers.

24. Torbert to Peabody, 16 Apr., 6 June 1907, Hunt to Peabody, 9 May 1907, Box 56, Peabody Papers.

25. Torbert to Peabody, 6, 17 June, 1 July 1907, Schenck to Peabody, 1 May 1907, O'Neal to Peabody, 29 June 1907, Box 56, Peabody Papers.

26. Report of Williams on Fort Valley High and Industrial School, 19 Nov. 1906, Watts to the Board of Trustees of Fort Valley High and Industrial School, 9 May 1906, Nelson to Torbert, 7 Feb. 1907, Bowles to Peabody, 8 Feb. 1907, Grant to Peabody, 11 July 1907, Box 56, Peabody Papers.

27. Davison to Buttrick, 9 June 1903, Buttrick to Hunt, 17 May 1905, Hunt to Buttrick, 12 Feb. 1907, Nixon to Peabody, 4 Nov. 1903, Box 45, GEB Papers; Torbert to Peabody, 6 Sept. 1906, Nelson to Torbert, 7 Feb. 1907, Box 56, Peabody Papers.

28. Hunt to the General Education Board, 9 Apr. 1910, Williams to Buttrick, 24 Dec. 1914, Box 45, GEB Papers; Bellamy, "Henry A. Hunt," pp. 467–69; Hunt to Sage, 22 Dec. 1915, Box 45, GEB Papers; Peabody to Burnham, 11 Apr. 1921, Box 56, Peabody Papers; Buttrick to Hunt, 22 Apr. 1922, Box 45, GEB Papers.

29. Gray to Peabody, 19 Sept., 2 July 1902, Buttrick to Peabody, 20 Sept. 1902, Lloyd to Buttrick, 3 Apr. 1903, Davison to Peabody, 21 May 1902, Branson to Peabody, 25 Aug. 1902, Box 45, GEB Papers.

30. Branson quoted in Buttrick to Schenck, 19 Mar. 1904, Box 45, GEB Papers; Hunt to Peabody, 9 May 1907, Box 56, Peabody Papers.

31. Report of Williams on Fort Valley High and Industrial School, 19 Nov. 1906, Nixon et al. to Hunt, 20 Apr. 1906, Torbert to Peabody, 13 Apr. 1907, Box 56, Peabody Papers; Hunt to Buttrick, 5 May 1906, Box 45, GEB Papers.

32. Sherer, *Subordination or Liberation*.

33. Buttrick to Gates, 21 Dec. 1903, pp. 4, 5, 8, 11, Box 716, Itinerary of Buttrick, 5–22 Oct. 1904, p. 4, GEB Papers.

34. Itinerary of Buttrick, 5–22 Oct. 1904, p. 8, GEB Papers.

35. Itinerary of Buttrick, 5–22 Oct. 1904, p. 9, Buttrick to Gates, 14 Oct. 1904, Gates to Buttrick, 20 Oct. 1904, Box 716, Confidential Report by Buttrick to the Trustees of the John F. Slater Fund, Oct. 1903, pp. 1–40, Confidential Report by Buttrick to John F. Slater Fund, 7 Oct. 1903, Box 260, GEB Papers.

36. McPherson, *Abolitionist Legacy*, pp. 203–24; Morgan to Buttrick, 1 Feb. 1901, Box 717, GEB Papers.

37. Enck, "Burden Borne," pp. 404–7.

38. Jones, *Negro Education*, 2:94, 174, 348, 417, 654.

39. Davis, "State Normal Schools and Agricultural and Mechanical Colleges

for Negroes, 1912–13 to 1921–22," Sept. 1924, pp. 42–44, Box 313, Folder 3267, GEB Papers.

40. Report of the Special Committee on the Education of the Negro, 25 May 1911, Box 722, Buttrick to Rockefeller, 5 Feb. 1914, Box 203, "Complete List of State Agents for Negro Rural Schools with Date of Appointment," Box 286, Davis to Flexner, 29 July 1919, Box 36, GEB Papers; Smith, *Builders of Goodwill*, pp. 10–20.

41. Smith, *Builders of Goodwill*, pp. 11, 17–18; Report of the Special Committee on the Education of the Negro, 25 May 1911, Swearigin to Sage, 6 June 1919, Box 131, Newbold to Buttrick, 27 Feb. 1913, Box 115, Folder 1038, GEB Papers. For information on the educational activities of the state supervisors there are hundreds of reports in the GEB Papers: Mississippi, Box 98; Virginia, Boxes 187 and 188; Arkansas, Box 25; North Carolina, Box 115; South Carolina, Box 131; Tennessee, Box 158; Georgia, Box 67; Alabama, Box 17; Louisiana, Box 88. See also Fosdick, *Adventure in Giving*, pp. 66–69, 72–74.

42. Redcay, *County Training Schools*, pp. 24–45; Favrot, *Study of County Training Schools*, pp. 8–26; Presson, *Annual Report of Educational Activities in Negro Schools*, pp. 22–23; General Education Board, *Annual Report*, p. 51.

43. Redcay, *County Training Schools*, pp. 34–42; Fosdick, *Adventure in Giving*, p. 334; Favrot, *Study of County Training Schools*, pp. 12, 31–32.

44. Redcay, *County Training Schools*, p. 38; Sibley to Flexner, 16 Jan. 1915, Box 17, Favrot, "The Industrial Movement in Negro Schools," 9 June 1913, Box 25, Godard, "Report of Georgia State Supervisor of Negro Rural Schools for February 1914," 2 Mar. 1914, Box 67, Smith, "Report of Tennessee State Supervisor of Negro Rural Schools for September 1914," 5 Oct. 1914, Box 158, GEB Papers; Presson, *Report of Educational Activities in Negro Schools*, p. 21; Smith, "Report of Tennessee State Supervisor of Negro Rural Schools for October 1914," 5 Nov. 1914, Box 158, GEB Papers; Fosdick, *Adventure in Giving*, p. 101; Favrot, *Study of County Training Schools*, p. 9.

45. Davis, *County Training Schools*, p. 8; Favrot, *Study of County Training Schools*, p. 27.

46. Favrot, "The Industrial Movement in Negro Schools," 9 June 1913, Presson, "Report of Arkansas State Supervisor of Negro Rural Schools for January 1917," 5 Feb. 1917, Box 25, Smith, "Report of Tennessee State Supervisor of Negro Rural Schools for October 1915," 5 Nov. 1915, Box 158, Dillard to Newbold, 25 Sept. 1915, Box 286, Davis to Flexner, 2 Oct. 1915, Box 286, GEB Papers.

47. Davis to Flexner, 2, 14 Oct. 1915, to Dillard, 28 Sept. 1915, Godard to Flexner, 15 Oct. 1915, Wright to Flexner, 16 Oct. 1915, Flexner to Davis, Godard, and Wright, 8 Oct. 1915, Davis to Sage, 11 Mar. 1916, Box 286, GEB Papers.

48. John F. Slater Fund, *Suggested Course for County Training Schools*; Favrot, *Study of County Training Schools*, pp. 36–38; Redcay, *County Training*

Schools, pp. 33–37; Favrot, "The Industrial Movement in Negro Schools," 9 June 1913, Box 25, GEB Papers. For detailed information on subjects taught in the training schools, see Summary Reports from County Training Schools, Box 294, GEB Papers.

49. Redcay, *County Training Schools*, pp. 38–39; "Teacher Training Departments in County Training Schools Aided by the General Education Board, 1927–1928," Box 294, GEB Papers.

50. Caliver, *Education of Negro Teachers*, pp. 14, 32.

51. Redcay, *County Training Schools*, pp. 77–84, 100.

CHAPTER 5

1. Bond, *Education of the Negro*, p. 115.

2. Wright, *Twelve Million Black Voices*, p. 64.

3. Wright, "The Negro in Unskilled Labor"; Bond, *Education of the Negro*, pp. 216–17.

4. Caliver, *Availability of Education to Negroes in Rural Communities*, pp. 18–33; Bond, *Education of the Negro*, pp. 191–202.

5. Bond, *Education of the Negro*, pp. 216–17; U.S. Department of Labor, *Negro Migration in 1916–17*, pp. 111–12.

6. Caliver, *Rural Elementary Education among Negroes under Jeanes Supervising Teachers*, pp. 2–3.

7. Smith, *Builders of Goodwill*, pp. 20, 68, 119; McPherson, *Abolitionist Legacy*, p. 367.

8. Harlan, *Booker T. Washington: The Wizard of Tuskegee*, p. 192; DuBois and Dill, eds., *The Common School and the Negro American*, pp. 28, 117; Kousser, "Progressivism—For Middle Class Whites Only," p. 168; Margo, "Race Differences in Public School Expenditures"; Harris, "Stability and Change."

9. Coon, *Public Taxation and Negro Schools*; Work, ed., *Negro Year Book*, p. 223; Washington quoted in Harlan, *Booker T. Washington: The Wizard*, p. 193; Kousser, "Progressivism—For Middle Class Whites Only," pp. 170–75; Harris, "Stability and Change," pp. 379–81.

10. Wright, *Self-Help in Negro Education*, pp. 18–19; DuBois, *Negro Common School*, pp. 135, 158; DuBois, "Negro Philanthropists" (1910), Box 18, Folder 8, DuBois Papers; Work, "Self-Help among Negroes," pp. 616–18; Anderson, "Ex-slaves and the Rise of Universal Education."

11. Calloway, "The Birth of the Rosenwald Schools," 9 June 1927, Box 76, Folder 2, JRFP-FU; Harlan, *Booker T. Washington: The Wizard*, pp. 212, 214.

12. Washington to Graves, 12 Sept. 1912, to Rosenwald, 12 Sept. 1912, Box 336, JRFP-FU; Calloway to Work, 28 Apr. 1914, Box 5, Park Papers.

13. Calloway to Washington, 3 Apr. 1913, Box 336, JRFP-FU.

14. Smith, "Evolution of the Schoolhouse Construction Program by the Julius

Rosenwald Fund" (1928), Box 331, Folder 1, JRFP-FU; Woodson, "The Story of the Fund," pp. 3–4, Box 33, Folder 1, Rosenwald Papers.

15. The total cost of the 640 buildings erected from 10 June 1914 to 4 September 1920 was $1,343,509. Of this amount, blacks contributed $456,597 (33.9 percent), Rosenwald $263,515 (19.9 percent), local white citizens $61,326 (4.6 percent), and public school authorities $562,071 (41.9 percent); Smith, "Evolution of the Schoolhouse Construction Program by the Julius Rosenwald Fund," pp. 11, 94, 106, Box 331, Folder 1, JRFP-FU; Sowell, *Ethnic America*, p. 229; Woodson, "Story of the Fund," chap. 6, p. 14; "Plan for the Distribution of Aid from the Julius Rosenwald Fund for Building Rural School Houses in the South," 6 June 1920, signed by Buttrick, Flexner, Moton, Mrs. Washington, Calloway, Dresslar, Davis, Smith, Favrot, and Lambert, Box 33, Folder 1, JRFP-FU.

16. Smith, *Builders of Goodwill*, pp. 65–67; Woodson, "Story of the Fund," chap. 4, p. 19; "Plan for Distribution of Rosenwald Fund Aid," pp. 1–2.

17. Woodson, "Story of the Fund," chap. 5, p. 6; Griffin to Smith, Sept. 1921, Box 76, Folder 2, JRFP-FU; extensive correspondence regarding blacks' role in the building of Rosenwald schools is in Box 76, JRFP-FU.

18. Griffin to Smith, undated, Box 76, Folder 2, JRFP-FU; Woodson, "Story of the Fund," chap. 1, p. 8.

19. Griffin to Smith, undated, Box 76, Folder 2, JRFP-FU.

20. Griffin to Smith, undated, ibid.

21. Griffin to Smith, undated, ibid.

22. Griffin to Smith, undated, ibid.

23. Smith, "A Story of the Julius Rosenwald Fund in Tennessee from the Beginning to July 1, 1920," undated, ibid.

24. Smith quoted in Woodson, "Story of the Fund," chap. 7, p. 21.

25. Smith quoted in ibid., chap. 7, pp. 7, 22.

26. Bernard, "The Julius Rosenwald Fund in Tennessee," undated, Box 76, Folder 2, JRFP-FU.

27. Favrot, "The First Rosenwald Buildings in Arkansas and Louisiana," undated, ibid.; Woodson, "Story of the Fund," chap. 7, p. 4.

28. Dorman to Smith, 16 Sept. 1921, Box 76, Folder 2, JRFP-FU.

29. Woodson, "Story of the Fund," chap. 7, p. 9; Fulton, "The Rosenwald Building Program in South Carolina," undated, Box 76, Folder 2, JRFP-FU.

30. Bludworth, "Number One," 17 May 1927, Box 76, Folder 2, JRFP-FU.

31. Bludworth, "Number Three," 17 May 1927, Bludworth, "Number Two," 17 May 1927, ibid.; Woodson, "Story of the Fund," chap. 5, p. 14.

32. Lewis, "The Growth of Negro Education in South Carolina," 1927, Box 76, Folder 2; Williams, "The Rosenwald Fund in Negro Education," Box 76, Folder 2, JRFP-FU; Woodson, "Story of the Fund," chap. 7, p. 6.

33. Fulton, "The Rosenwald Building Program in South Carolina"; Fields, "Rosenwald School in Colbert County," Box 76, Folder 2, JRFP-FU.

34. See Annual Reports on Rosenwald School Day for Tennessee (1930–33),

Virginia (1929–33), Mississippi (1929–33), North Carolina (1929–33), Louisiana (1929–33), Kentucky (1929–33), and South Carolina (1929–33), respectively in Box 343, Folder 3, Box 343, Folder 9, Box 340, Folder 6, Box 341, Folder 7, Box 339, Folder 6, Box 339, Folder 3, and Box 342, Folder 6; "Foreman Rosenwald School Day—East Baton Rouge Parish, Louisiana," Box 339, Folder 7, JRFP-FU.

35. Johnson, *Shadow of the Plantation*, p. 124; Raper, *Preface to Peasantry*, pp. 33–45.

36. "Foreman Rosenwald School Day—East Baton Rouge Parish, Louisiana," Box 339, Folder 7, JRFP-FU; Bond, *Education of the Negro*, pp. 225–59.

37. Bond, *Education of the Negro*, pp. 292–94.

38. Holmes to the Trustees of the Rosenwald Fund, 26 Nov. 1934, King to Embree, 16 Nov. 1934, Craighead to Rosenwald Fund, 24 Nov. 1934, Riley to Embree, 23 Nov. 1934, Lawson to Embree, 18 Sept. 1934, Hawkins to Embree, 23 Nov. 1934, Moon to Embree, 27 Nov. 1934, Mann to Embree, 29 Nov. 1934, Bond to Embree, 5 Mar. 1935, Pruit to Embree, 30 Mar. 1935, Dickinson to Embree, 3 July 1935, Britton to Embree, 25 July 1935, Porter to Rosenwald Fund, 7 Nov. 1935, Box 331, Folders 3–5, JRFP-FU.

39. Blount to Embree, 27 Dec. 1934, Box 331, Folder 3, JRFP-FU.

40. Smith, "A Short Survey of Negro Schools in the Fourteen Southern States," 27 Feb. 1927, Box 548, Folder 4; Report on Completed Buildings by Type, 1932, Box 331, Folder 3, JRFP-FU.

41. Newbold, "Annual Report of State Agent of Negro Rural Schools for North Carolina, 1913 to 1914," 13 Dec. 1914, Box 115, Folder 1042, GEB Papers.

42. Newbold, "Annual Report of State Agent of Negro Rural Schools for North Carolina, 1913 to 1914," 13 Dec. 1914, pp. 13–14, Box 115, Folder 1042; Davis, Monthly and Annual Reports of Virginia Supervisor of Rural Elementary Schools, 1910 to 1915; Wright, "Annual Report of Virginia State School Inspector for Year Ending June 30, 1916," Box 188, Folder 1758, Box 187, Folder 1757; for similar accounts by other state supervisors, see reports by Godard of Georgia, 23 Dec. 1913, 23 Mar. 1914, Box 167, Folder 585; Sibley of Alabama, 1912–14, Box 17, Folder 145; Brooks of North Carolina, 1912–16, Box 131, Folder 1204, and Brannon of South Carolina (1917–19), Box 131, Folder 1204, all in GEB Papers; Wright, *Self-Help in Negro Education*.

CHAPTER 6

1. Krug, *Shaping of the American High School*, pp. 1–18; U.S. Office of Education, *Biennial Survey of Education in the United States*, chap. 2, p. 1; Sizer, *Secondary Schools at the Turn of the Century*, p. 35.

2. Wilkerson, *Special Problems of Negro Education*, pp. 36–37.

3. Wilkerson, *Special Problems of Negro Education*, p. 40; Frazier, *Negro in the United States*, pp. 436–37; Knox, "Historical Sketch of Secondary Education for Negroes."

4. Kousser, "Separate but Not Equal"; Patton, "Black Community of Augusta."

5. Kousser, "Separate but Not Equal," pp. 38–39.

6. Ibid., pp. 39, 43; Frazier, *Negro in the United States*, pp. 432–37; Redcay, *County Training Schools*, pp. 54–73.

7. Frost, "Development of Rural Secondary Education in the South"; Fosdick, *Adventure in Giving*, pp. 25–28; General Education Board, *General Education Board*, pp. 80–90.

8. Fosdick, *Adventure in Giving*, p. 34; General Education Board, *General Education Board*, p. 90; Frazier, *Negro in the United States*, p. 436.

9. *Forty-Fourth Annual Report of the Georgia State Department of Education*, p. 241; Jones, *Negro Education*, 1:42.

10. Jones, *Negro Education*, 1:41–42, 2:16, 140, 171, 319, 336, 475.

11. Kousser, "Separate but Not Equal," p. 18; Harris, "Stability and Change," p. 405.

12. Fosdick, *Adventure in Giving*, p. 107; Jones, *Negro Education*, 1:42–43.

13. Jones, *Negro Education*, 2:50, 128, 264–81, 331–32, 386, 535, 547–49, 553–608, 617, 622, 644–55.

14. Washington quoted in Fosdick, *Adventure in Giving*, pp. 99–100.

15. Smith, "Redistribution of the Negro Population."

16. Jones, "Negro Population in the United States."

17. "The Negro Common School in North Carolina," *Crisis* 34 (June 1927): 117–18; "The Negro Common School, Mississippi," *Crisis* 33 (Dec. 1926): 96–97.

18. Rosenwald to Flexner, 28 Jan. 1925, Mathis to Shepardson, 6 Feb. 1925, Dillard to Shepardson, 7 Feb. 1925, Shepardson to Smith, 28 Jan. 1925, to Dillard, 10 Feb. 1925, Box 129, Folder 8, JRFP-FU.

19. Rosenwald to Flexner, 28 Jan. 1925, Shepardson, "Negro High Schools in the South," 28 Jan. 1925, Dillard to Shepardson, 7 Feb. 1925, Box 129, Folder 8, "Conference on High Schools for Negroes," 30 Apr. 1925, Box 128, Folder 8, JRFP-FU.

20. "Conference on High Schools for Negroes," 30 Apr. 1925, Box 128, Folder 8, JRFP-FU.

21. Stern to Hall, 20 Nov. 1928, Hall to Embree, 22 June 1928, to Stern, 24 Nov. 1928, to Arthur, 2 Oct. 1928, Box 294, Folder 8, JRFP-FU.

22. Hall to Arthur, 2 Oct. 1928, Box 294, Folder 8, Embree to Powell, 1 Sept. 1928, Box 171, Folder 1, Arthur, "Minutes of Trip to Little Rock and Pine Bluff, Arkansas," 11–13 Oct. 1928, Box 294, Folder 8, JRFP-FU.

23. Hall to Arthur, 2 Oct. 1928, Box 294, Folder 9, JRFP-FU.

24. Embree's comments were written in margin of Hall to Arthur, 28 Sept. 1928.

25. Stern to Williams, 22 Nov., 2 Dec. 1929, Box 202, Folder 1, Minutes of the Julius Rosenwald Fund, 18 Dec. 1929, p. 231, Box 77, Folder 6, JRFP-FU.

26. Byrd, "Special Inquiry into the Industrial Status of the Negro (Little Rock, Arkansas)," Box 294, Folder 9, JRFP-FU.

27. Wells, "First School Survey"; Sears, *School Survey*.

28. Keller and Clerk, "Comments on the Little Rock Program of Studies and Curriculums," Summer 1930, Box 294, Folder 9, JRFP-FU.

29. Booker to Arthur, 10 Dec. 1928, 30 Sept. 1929, Box 294, Folder 8, JRFP-FU; Jones, *Traditional Model of Educational Excellence*, p. 4.

30. "Program of Studies and Curriculums of Dunbar High School," 1 Sept. 1930, Box 294, Folder 8, JRFP-FU.

31. Hamilton to Stern, 7 Oct. 1930; "Little Rock Public Schools, Negro Department," Feb. 1931, p. 24, Box 294, Folder 8, JRFP-FU; Jones, *Traditional Model of Educational Excellence*, pp. 4–10.

32. Bauer to Stern, 30 Mar. 1931, Box 310, Folder 3, JRFP-FU.

33. Stern to Heller, 2 Sept. 1930, Box 310, Folder 8, Stern to Bauer, 2 Feb. 1931, Box 310, Folder 3, Embree to Smith, 18 Oct. 1928, Box 174, Folder 10, JRFP-FU.

34. Stern to Favrot, 12 Mar. 1930; Stern said in this letter that Heller was due most of the credit for carrying the New Orleans project. Heller to Stern, 21 Dec. 1929 (emphasis added), Box 310, Folder 3, JRFP-FU.

35. Heller to Embree, 9 Jan. 1930, Box 310, Folder 3, JRFP-FU.

36. "Method of Procedure and Supporting Material of the Report Made for the New Orleans School Board," Jan. 1930, Box 310, Folder 3, JRFP-FU.

37. Byrd, "Report of the Special Inquiry Undertaken in New Orleans into the Industrial Status of Negroes," pp. 2–4, Box 310, Folder 3, JRFP-FU.

38. Ibid., pp. 4–11.

39. Ibid., p. 10.

40. Stern to Heller, 11 Nov. 1930, Keller, "New Orleans Trade School for Negroes: Some Standards Which Should Apply to the Construction, Maintenance and Administration of the School," pp. 1–3, 8, Box 310, Folder 3, JRFP-FU.

41. Heller to Stern, 13 Feb. 1930, "Orleans Parish School Board Meeting Held February 12, 1930" (stenographic notes of meeting), Box 310, Folder 3, JRFP-FU.

42. "Negro Industrial School," *New Orleans States*, 14 Feb. 1930; "Trade School for Negroes," *New Orleans Times Picayune*, 14 Feb. 1930; Stern to Heller, 4 Mar. 1930, Box 310, Folder 3, JRFP-FU; Caliver, *Secondary Education for Negroes*, pp. 14–15.

43. "Conference of Representatives of the Rosenwald Fund and of the Orleans

Parish School Board," 29 Jan. 1931, Box 310, Folder 3, JRFP-FU.

44. Ibid.

45. Embree to Heller, 29 Sept., 9 Nov. 1931, Box 310, Folder 3, JRFP-FU.

46. "Dedication of the William H. Spencer High School," vol. 1, Jan. 1931, Daniel to Stern, 5 Dec. 1930, Box 185, Folder 8, JRFP-FU.

47. Keller, "Report on the New William H. Spencer High School, Columbus, Georgia," Dec. 1930, pp. 2–3, 6, Box 185, Folder 8, JRFP-FU.

48. Ibid., pp. 3–4, 6–7.

49. Ibid., pp. 6–7; Lampkin to Stern, 15 Apr. 1931, survey of the 10th grade enclosed, Box 185, Folder 8, JRFP-FU.

50. Lampkin to Stern, 15 Apr. 1931, Box 185, Folder 8, JRFP-FU.

51. Johnson, "Vocational Survey—Greenville Negro City School System," 11 Jan. 1930, pp. 2, 3, 7, Box 546, Folder 15, JRFP-FU.

52. Ibid., pp. 2, 6–7.

53. Stokes, "Black and White Labor and the Development of the Southern Textile Industry, 1800–1920."

54. Johnson, "Vocational Survey," p. 7.

55. "Dedication: Winston-Salem's New High School for Negro Children," 2 Apr. 1931; "Supporting Data of the Special Inquiry into the Industrial Status of the Negro in Winston-Salem"; Byrd, "Report to the Board of Education of the Special Inquiry into the Vocational Opportunities and Needs of the Negro Youth in Winston-Salem"; Byrd, "Some Facts and Figures Relating to Negro Education in Winston-Salem, North Carolina, 1928–1929," pp. 13–14, Box 370, Folder 3, Keller and Meader, "Proposed Program for the New Negro Industrial High School at Winston-Salem, North Carolina," 5 Jan. 1931, Box 546, Folder 8, JRFP-FU.

56. Fosdick, *Adventure in Giving*, p. 30; Payne to James, 30 Aug. 1930, Box 138, Folder 6; Byrd, "Report to the Rosenwald Fund on Survey in Birmingham, Alabama, to Determine Vocational Opportunities for Negro Youth," Jan. 1930, pp. 1–20; Byrd, "Supporting Data of the Special Inquiry in Birmingham, Alabama, Concerning Vocational Opportunities for Negroes and Possible Adjustment to the Local Situation," 1930; Byrd, "Supporting Data of the Special Inquiry in Richmond, Virginia, Concerning Vocational Opportunities for Negroes and Possible Adjustment to the Local Industrial Situation," 1930; Byrd, "Report of the Special Inquiry Undertaken in Memphis into the Industrial Status of Negroes," 1930; Byrd, "Special Inquiry Undertaken in Salisbury, North Carolina, into the Industrial Status of Negroes," 1930; Byrd and Davis, "Report of the Special Inquiry Undertaken in Wilmington, North Carolina, into the Industrial Status of Negroes," 1929, Box 546, Folders 4, 5, 14, 15, 17, JRFP-FU.

57. "Industrial High Schools, Larger Projects," Box 253, Folder 2, Stern to Williams, 12 Nov. 1929, Box 202, Folder 1, Stern to Barnes, 3 Dec. 1929, Box 548, Folder 3, JRFP-FU.

58. Stern to Glenn, 15 Oct. 1929, Box 174, Folder 10, JRFP-FU.

59. Arthur to Phillips, 15 Oct. 1929, DeYarmett to Arthur, 19 Oct. 1929, Reid to Arthur, 21 Oct. 1929, Box 547, Folder 4, JRFP-FU.

60. Reid to Arthur, 21 Oct. 1929, Thomas to Arthur, 22 Oct. 1929, Box 547, Folder 4, JRFP-FU.

61. Johnson to Arthur, 7 Nov. 1929, Box 547, Folder 4, JRFP-FU.

62. Johnson, "Memorandum on Displacement of Negro Labor in Certain Southern Cities: Embodying the Results of Inquiries in Ten Southern Cities by Members of the Research Staff," Nov. 1929, pp. 1–9, Box 547, Folder 4, JRFP-FU.

63. Ibid., pp. 9–13.

64. Ibid., pp. 14–19.

65. Ibid., pp. 30–32.

66. Ibid., pp. 24–28; see also Johnson, "Present Trends in the Employment of Negro Labor," pp. 146–48; Thomas, "Forces in Race Conflict," pp. 314–15; Reid, "Lily-White Labor," pp. 170–73; National Urban League, News Release, Sept. 1929, Bulletin No. 31, Box 547, Folder 4, JRFP-FU.

CHAPTER 7

1. Logan, "Evolution of Private Colleges for Negroes," p. 216; Jones, *Negro Education,* 2:310; Klein, *Survey of Negro Colleges and Universities*; Holmes, *Evolution of the Negro College,* p. 201.

2. Holmes, *Evolution of the Negro College,* pp. 163–77.

3. Ibid., p. 216; Klein, *Survey of Negro Colleges and Universities,* pp. 5–33.

4. Richardson, *Christian Reconstruction,* p. 173; missionary philanthropists quoted from Holmes, *Evolution of the Negro College,* p. 69; Wright, "Development of Education for Blacks in Georgia," p. 31.

5. Butchart, "Educating for Freedom," p. 353; Fredrickson, *The Black Image in the White Mind,* p. 244, Gutman, *The Black Family in Slavery and Freedom,* p. 532.

6. Freedmen's Aid Society quoted from Holmes, *Evolution of the Negro College,* p. 69; Bond, "Century of Negro Higher Education," p. 187; Butchart, "Educating for Freedom," pp. 453–90; Wright, "Development of Education for Blacks in Georgia," p. 29; Logan, "Evolution of Private Colleges for Negroes," p. 216.

7. Richardson, *Christian Reconstruction,* pp. 113, 123, 128; Bond, "Century of Negro Higher Education," pp. 187–88.

8. Richardson, *Christian Reconstruction,* p. 125; McPherson, *Abolitionist Legacy,* pp. 213, 222; Morehouse quoted in ibid., p. 222.

9. Richardson, *Christian Reconstruction,* p. 125; Merrill quoted in McPherson, *Abolitionist Legacy,* p. 220.

10. DuBois quoted in McPherson, *Abolitionist Legacy,* p. 223.

11. Ibid.

12. Ibid., p. 213.

13. Baldwin, "Present Problem of Negro Education," pp. 52–60; Anderson, "Education for Servitude," pp. 208–16.

14. Weinberg, *A Chance to Learn*, p. 280.

15. Ibid., pp. 267, 280; Badger, "Negro Colleges and Universities"; Jones, *Negro Education*, 1:59.

16. Selden, *Accreditation*, pp. 32–37; Green, "Higher Standards for the Negro College"; Cozart, *History of the Association of Colleges and Secondary Schools*.

17. Selden, *Accreditation*, pp. 35–37.

18. DuBois, *College-Bred Negro*; DuBois and Dill, eds., *College-Bred Negro American*; Jones, *Negro Education*, 1:58, 64; Green, "Higher Standards for the Negro College"; Cozart, *History of the Association of Colleges and Secondary Schools*. Hampton and Tuskegee, the two black educational institutions most favored by industrial philanthropists, were excluded from consideration because they were normal schools and it was their mission to provide precollegiate education for the training of common school teachers.

19. Morgan to Buttrick, 25, 29, 31 Jan. 1901, Sale to Buttrick, 23 Dec. 1909, 8 Jan. 1908, Box 716, Sale to Buttrick, 1 Jan. 1908, MacVicar to Buttrick, 7 June, 12 Aug. 1902, Buttrick to MacVicar, 18 Aug. 1902, Hovey to Buttrick, 30 Mar. 1908, Box 170, GEB Papers; Jones, *Negro Education*, 1: 7–8.

20. Sale to Buttrick, 8 Jan. 1908, Box 170, Morgan to Buttrick, 31 Jan., 1 Feb. 1901, Box 717, GEB Papers.

21. Harlan and Smock, eds., *Booker T. Washington Papers*, 3:620; Buttrick to Rockefeller, 5 Feb. 1914, Box 203, GEB Papers.

22. Buttrick to Sale, 29 May 1907, Box 59, Report of Williams to Buttrick, 22 May 1907, Buttrick to the General Education Board, 22 May 1907, Box 716, GEB Papers.

23. Fosdick, *Adventure in Giving*, pp. 151–55; Hine, "Pursuit of Professional Equality," pp. 176–77.

24. Buttrick to Rockefeller, 5 Feb. 1914, Flexner to Villard, 1 Dec. 1914, Box 203, "General Education Board's Conference on Negro Education," 19 Nov. 1915, GEB Papers; DuBois, "Thomas Jesse Jones," p. 253; Berman, "Educational Colonialism in Africa," pp. 183–94; King, *Pan-Africanism and Education*, pp. 43–57.

25. "General Education Board's Conference on Negro Education," 29 Nov. 1915, pp. 133–34.

26. Ibid., pp. 130–38, 149–52, 162–64.

27. Report of Committee on Negro Education, 24 Jan. 1916, Box 722, GEB Papers.

28. Logan, *The Negro in the United States*, pp. 74–83; Moton to Wilson, 15 June 1918, Box 303, GEB Papers.

29. Jones, "Crisis in Negro Leadership"; Peabody to Gregg, 5 Apr. 1920, Box 58, Peabody Papers.

30. Peabody to Gregg, 5 Apr. 1920, Box 58, Peabody Papers; *Fisk University News*, Sept. 1919, pp. 2–4; DuBois to Eleazer, 12 Mar. 1926, Commission on Inter-racial Co-operation Collection; Franklin, *Black Self-Determination*.

31. Jones, *Negro Education*, 1:310, 314–15; "General Education Board's Conference on Negro Education," 29 Nov. 1915, GEB Papers; Lamon, "Black Community in Nashville," p. 231.

32. McKenzie, *Ideals of Fisk*, p. 7; Aptheker, ed., *W. E. B. DuBois*, pp. 52–57; DuBois, "Fisk"; Wolters, *New Negro on Campus*, pp. 35–39.

33. Rosenwald to Flexner, 15 Jan. 1917, Flexner to Rosenwald, 17 Jan. 1917, Box 138, Flexner to Swift, 2 Apr. 1917, Appleget to Thorkelson, 12 June 1928, "Appropriations Made by the General Education Board to Fisk University"; for endowment contributions, see Baldwin to General Education Board, 6 Oct. 1924, Wood to General Education Board, 6 May 1920, Box 128, GEB Papers; *Fisk University News*, Dec. 1924, p. 20.

34. *Fisk University News*, Apr. 1923, p. 7; ibid., Oct. 1920, p. 21; Jones to Flexner, 4 Oct. 1915, Wood to Buttrick, 6 May 1920, Thorkelson to Wood, 5 Nov. 1926, Box 138, GEB Papers. For the philanthropists' role in actively recruiting trustees, see Flexner to Rosenwald, 8, 17 Jan. 1917, Rosenwald to Flexner, 13 Jan. 1917, Flexner to Swift, 2 Apr. 1917, Flexner to Judson, 27 Mar. 1917, Judson to Flexner, 30 Mar., 13 Apr. 1917, Box 138, GEB Papers.

35. Flexner, Memorandum on the Fisk Endowment Campaign, 25 May 1923, Box 23, GEB Papers.

36. The most thorough accounts of McKenzie's repressive educational practices are Wolters, *New Negro on Campus*, pp. 26–69; Lamon, "Fisk University Student Strike"; Richardson, *History of Fisk University*, chaps. 6 and 7.

37. "Fisk University," a 1926 memorandum, Box 138, GEB Papers; "Fisk Endowment Drive in Nashville," *Fisk University News*, May 1924, pp. 31–32; "First Million-Dollar Endowment for College Education of the Negro in the History of America," ibid., Oct. 1924, pp. 1–13; Commercial Club of Nashville to General Education Board, 24 Jan. 1920, Box 138, GEB Papers; Jones, *Negro Education*, 1:314–15, 320–21.

38. Wolters, *New Negro on Campus*, pp. 34–40; *New York Times*, 8 Feb. 1925, sec. 2, p. 1; Jones to Cravath, 20 Sept. 1924, Box 3, Folder 20, McKenzie Papers.

39. DuBois quoted in Wolters, *New Negro on Campus*, pp. 62–63; "Fisk University," a 1926 memorandum, Box 138, GEB Papers. For General Education Board contributions, see Fosdick, *Adventure in Giving*, pp. 329–32; "Fisk University," Report by Jones to the General Education Board, 27, 28 Sept. 1928, Box 138, GEB Papers.

40. Stokes to Rockefeller, 8 Jan. 1925, Box 17, Folder 8, "Special Memoran-

dum Prepared for Clarence H. Kelsey, Esq.," 24 Oct. 1924, Box 17, Folder 5, Stokes to Rosenwald, 9 Dec. 1924, Box 17, Folder 6, Rosenwald Papers.

41. "Special Memorandum," 24 Oct. 1924, pp. 8, 23, 31–33, Box 17, Folder 5, Rosenwald Papers.

42. Ibid., pp. 10, 20; Stokes to Rockefeller, 8 Jan. 1925, Box 17, Folder 8, Rosenwald Papers.

43. "Special Memorandum," 24 Oct. 1924, p. 32, Appendix C, Box 17, Folder 5, Rosenwald Papers.

44. Wolters, *New Negro on Campus*, pp. 233, 248, 258, 273; DuBois, "The Hampton Strike," *Nation* 125 (2 Nov. 1927): 471–72.

45. Wolters, *New Negro on Campus*, p. 267.

46. Fosdick, *Adventure in Giving*, pp. 328–29.

47. Franklin, "Whatever Happened to the College-Bred Negro?" (DuBois, Woodson, and Hughes are quoted in Franklin's article); Hughes, "Cowards from the Colleges"; Streator, "Negro College Radicals."

48. Harris, "Problems before the College Negro"; Edmonds, "Education in Self-Contempt"; Allen, "Selling Out the Workers."

EPILOGUE

1. Anderson, "Education for Servitude," chap. 2; Harris, "Stability and Change," pp. 387–89.

2. Anderson, "Education for Servitude," chap. 1.

3. On the differences between northern missionaries and southern blacks, see McPherson, *Abolitionist Legacy*, pp. 262–95; Butchart, *Northern Schools, Southern Blacks, and Reconstruction*, pp. 169–79.

4. Blassingame, ed., *Slave Testimony*, pp. 267, 586; Morris, *Reading, 'Riting and Reconstruction*, p. 96.

5. Cornelius, " 'We Slipped and Learned to Read,' " p. 175; Berlin, Reidy, and Rowland, eds., *Freedom*, p. 618; Anderson, *Race and Politics in North Carolina*, p. 326.

6. DuBois, *Souls of Black Folk*, pp. 57–58.

7. Baker, *Following the Color Line*, p. 53; Wright, *Twelve Million Black Voices*, p. 65; Myrdal, *American Dilemma*, 2:884; Anderson, "Schooling and Achievement of Black Children," pp. 105–6.

8. Wyatt-Brown, "Black Schooling during Reconstruction," pp. 152–59; Sowell, *Ethnic America*, pp. 184, 203, 280.

BIBLIOGRAPHY

Manuscript and Archival Material

Atlanta, Georgia
  Atlanta University, Trevor Arnett Library
    Commission on Inter-racial Co-operation Collection
Chicago, Illinois
  University of Chicago
    Julius Rosenwald Fund Papers
Hampton, Virginia
  Hampton Institute Archives
Nashville, Tennessee
  Fisk University Archives
    W. E. B. DuBois Papers
    Charles S. Johnson Papers
    Fayette A. McKenzie Papers
    Robert E. Park Papers
    Julius Rosenwald Fund Papers
New York, New York
  Schomberg Center for Research in Black Culture
    Alexander Crummell Papers
Pocantico Hills, New York
  Rockefeller Archive Center
    General Education Board Papers
    Anna T. Jeanes Foundation Papers
    John F. Slater Fund Papers
    Laura Spellman Rockefeller Memorial Fund Papers
Washington, D.C.
  Library of Congress
    Andrew Carnegie Papers
    Jabez L. M. Curry Papers
    Abraham Flexner Papers
    Robert C. Ogden Papers
    George Foster Peabody Papers
    Booker T. Washington Papers

Government Publications

Alabama State Department of Education. *Annual Report of Department of Education, 1912.* Montgomery: Brown Printing Company, 1912.

Alvord, John W. *Inspector's Report of Schools and Finances.* U.S. Bureau of Refugees, Freedmen and Abandoned Lands. Washington, D.C.: U.S. Government Printing Office, 1866.

_____. *Semi-Annual Report on Schools for Freedmen, Third through Ninth.* Washington, D.C.: U.S. Government Printing Office, 1868–70.

Baltimore, Maryland, Board of School Commissioners. *Eighty-Seventh Annual Report to the Mayor and City Council of Baltimore.* Baltimore: Meyer and Thalheimer, City Printer, 1917.

Barringer, Paul B. "Negro Education in the South." In *Report of the U.S. Commissioner of Education, 1900–1901.* Washington, D.C.: U.S. Government Printing Office, 1901.

Birmingham, Alabama, Board of Education. *Annual Report of the Birmingham Schools, 1915.* Birmingham: Birmingham Printing Company, 1915.

Blose, David T., and Caliver, Ambrose. *Statistics of the Education of Negroes, 1929–30, and 1931–32.* U.S. Department of Interior, Office of Education. Bulletin 13, 1938. Washington, D.C.: U.S. Government Printing Office, 1936.

_____. *Statistics of the Education of Negroes, 1933–34 and 1935–36.* U.S. Department of Interior, Office of Education. Bulletin 13, 1935. Washington, D.C.: U.S. Government Printing Office, 1939.

_____. *Statistics of Education of the Negro Race, 1924–1926.* U.S. Department of Interior, Bureau of Education. Bulletin 19, pp. 1–42. Washington, D.C.: U.S. Government Printing Office, 1928.

Buck, James L. Blair. *The Development of Public Schools in Virginia, 1607–1952.* Richmond: Commonwealth of Virginia State Board of Education, 1952.

Caliver, Ambrose. *Availability of Education to Negroes in Rural Communities.* Washington, D.C.: U.S. Government Printing Office, 1936.

_____. *Education of Negro Teachers.* U.S. Department of Interior, Bulletin 10, Vol. 4. Washington, D.C.: U.S. Government Printing Office, 1933.

_____. *Rural Education among Negroes under Jeanes Supervising Teachers.* Washington, D.C.: U.S. Government Printing Office, 1933.

_____. *Secondary Education for Negroes.* Washington, D.C.: U.S. Government Printing Office, 1933.

_____, ed. *Fundamentals in the Education of Negroes.* Washington, D.C.: U.S. Government Printing Office, 1935.

Conway, Thomas W. *The Freedmen of Louisiana: Final Report of the Bureau of Free Labor, Department of the Gulf, to Major General E. R. S. Canby, Commanding, by Thomas W. Conway, General Superintendent of Freedmen.* New Orleans: Times, 1865.

Covington, Kentucky, Board of Education. *Report of the Board of Education from July 1, 1913 to June 30, 1916.* Covington: Board of Education, 1916.

Curry, J. L. M. "Difficulties, Complications, and Limitations Connected with the Education of the Negro." In *Report of the Commissioner of Education for the Year 1894–95,* 2:1367–74. Washington, D.C.: U.S. Government Printing Office, 1896.

———. "National Aid to Education." *Circulars of Information of the Bureau of Education,* No. 3. Washington, D.C.: U.S. Government Printing Office, 1884.

Dabney, Charles W. "The Public School Problem in the South." In *Report of the U.S. Commissioner of Education, 1900–1901,* 1:1009–26. Washington, D.C.: U.S. Government Printing Office, 1901.

Dickerman, G. S. "The Conference for Education in the South and the Southern Education Board." In *Report of the U.S. Commissioner of Education for the Year 1907,* 1:291–327. Washington, D.C.: U.S. Government Printing Office, 1908.

Eliot, T. D. *Report of Hon. T. D. Eliot, Chairman of the Committee on Freedmen's Affairs, to the House of Representatives, March 10, 1868.* Washington, D.C.: U.S. Government Printing Office, 1868.

El Paso, Texas, Board of School Trustees. *Report of the Public Schools of the City of El Paso, Texas, 1914–15.* El Paso: Industrial Arts Print Shop, 1915.

Florida State Department of Public Instruction. *Biennial Report of the Superintendent of Public Instruction.* Tallahassee: T. J. Appleyard, State Printer, 1916.

Forty-Fourth Annual Report of the Georgia State Department of Education for School Year Ending December 31, 1915. Atlanta: Charles P. Byrd, 1916.

Georgia State Department of Education. *Thirty-Ninth Annual Report to the General Assembly of Georgia.* Atlanta: Charles P. Byrd, State Printer, 1910.

Houston, Texas, Board of School Trustees. *Annual Report of the Public Schools of the Independent School District of the City of Houston, 1917–18.* Houston: Southwest Publishing Company, 1918.

Howard, Oliver Otis. *Report of Brevet Major General O. O. Howard, Commissioner, Bureau of Refugees, Freedmen, and Abandoned Lands, to the Secretary of War, October 20, 1869.* Washington, D.C.: U.S. Government Printing Office, 1869.

Jones, Thomas Jesse. *Negro Education: A Study of the Private and Higher Schools for Colored People in the United States.* 2 vols. U.S. Department of the Interior, Bureau of Education, Bulletins 38 and 39. Washington, D.C.: U.S. Government Printing Office, 1917.

Kentucky State Department of Education. *Biennial Report of the Superintendent of Public Instruction, 1910–11.* Frankfort: Kentucky State Journal Publishing Company, 1911.

Klein, Arthur J. *Survey of Negro Colleges and Universities.* U.S. Department of Interior, Bureau of Education, Bulletin 7. Washington, D.C.: U.S. Government Printing Office, 1929.

Knoxville, Tennessee, Board of Education. *Forty-Third Annual Report of the City Schools of Knoxville, Tennessee.* Knoxville: Stubly Printing Company, 1914.

Louisville, Kentucky, Board of Education. *Fifth Report of the Board of Education of Louisville, Kentucky, 1915 to 1916.* Louisville: C. T. Dearing Printing Company, 1916.

Mayo, Amory D. "Common School Education in the South from the Beginning of the Civil War to 1870–1876." In *Report of the U.S. Commissioner of Education for the Years 1900–1901,* 1:403–90. Washington, D.C.: U.S. Government Printing Office, 1902.

————. "The Final Establishment of the American Common School System in North Carolina, South Carolina, and Georgia, 1863–1900." *Report of the U.S. Commissioner of Education for the Year Ending June 30, 1904,* 1:999–1090. Washington, D.C.: U.S. Government Printing Office, 1905.

————. *Industrial Education in the South.* U.S. Department of Interior, Bureau of Education, Circular of Information 5. Washington, D.C.: U.S. Government Printing Office, 1888.

————. "Services of Doctor Curry in Connection with the Peabody Fund." In *Report of the Commissioner of Education for the Year 1903,* 1:524–25. Washington, D.C.: U.S. Government Printing Office, 1905.

————. "Work of Certain Northern Churches in the Education of the Freedmen, 1861–1900." In *Report of the United States Commissioner of Education for 1901–1902,* 1:285–314. Washington, D.C.: U.S. Government Printing Office, 1902.

Memphis, Tennessee, Board of Education. *Annual Report of Memphis City Schools, 1914–15.* Memphis: Board of Education, 1915.

Miller, Kelly. "The Education of the Negro." In *Report of the U.S. Commissioner of Education for the Year 1900–1901.* 1:731–859. Washington, D.C.: U.S. Government Printing Office, 1902.

Missouri State Department of Education. *Sixty-Seventh Report of the Public Schools.* Jefferson: Department of Education, 1916.

Nashville, Tennessee, Board of School Commissioners. *Annual Report of the Public Schools, 1915–16.* Nashville: Baird-Ward Printing Company, 1916.

North Carolina State Department of Public Instruction. *Biennial Report of the Superintendent of Public Instruction, 1910–11 and 1911–12.* Raleigh: Edwards and Broughton, 1912.

Parmalee, Julius H. "Freedmen's Aid Societies, 1861–1871." In *Negro Education: A Study of the Private and Higher Schools for Colored People in the United States.* U.S. Department of Interior, Bureau of Education, Bulletin 38, pp. 268–94. Washington, D.C.: U.S. Government Printing Office, 1917.

Sears, Jesse Brundage. *Philanthropy in the History of American Higher Education.* U.S. Department of Interior, Bureau of Education, Bulletin 26. Washington, D.C.: U.S. Government Printing Office, 1922.

South Carolina State Department of Education. *Annual Report of the State Superintendent of Education, 1911.* Columbia: R. L. Bryan Company, 1911.

U.S. Army. *Report of the Board of Education for Freedmen, Department of the Gulf.* New Orleans: True Delta, 1865.

U.S. Bureau of the Census. *Fourteenth Census of the United States, 1920.* Vol. 3, Population. Washington, D.C.: U.S. Government Printing Office, 1922.

————. *Negro Population in the United States, 1790–1915.* Washington, D.C.: U.S. Government Printing Office, 1918.

————. *Report on Population of the United States at the Eleventh Census, 1890.* Part 1. Washington, D.C.: U.S. Government Printing Office, 1895.

————. *Thirteenth Census of the United States, 1910.* Vols. 2 and 3, Population. Washington, D.C.: U.S. Government Printing Office, 1913.

————. *Twelfth Census of the United States, 1900.* Vol. 2, *Population.* Washington, D.C.: U.S. Government Printing Office, 1902.

U.S. Commissioner of Education. *Reports.* 1884–1902. Washington, D.C.: U.S. Government Printing Office, 1888–1903.

U.S. Congress. Joint Committee on Reconstruction. *Journal of the Joint Committee on Reconstruction at the First Session of the Thirty-Ninth Congress.* Washington, D.C.: U.S. Government Printing Office, 1866.

U.S. Congress. Joint Select Committee to Inquire into the Condition of Affairs in the Late Insurrectionary States. *Ku-Klux Conspiracy: Testimony.* Vols. 3, 4, 5. Washington, D.C.: U.S. Government Printing Office, 1872.

U.S. Congress, Senate. Committee on Education and Labor. *Report of the Committee of the Senate upon the Relations between Labor and Capital, and Testimony Taken by the Committee.* Vol. 4. Washington, D.C.: U.S. Government Printing Office, 1883.

U.S. Congress, Senate. *Report of Carl Schurz on the States of South Carolina, Georgia, Alabama, Mississippi, and Louisiana.* Executive Document 2, 39th Cong., 1st sess., 1865.

U.S. Department of Labor. *Negro Migration in 1916–17.* Washington, D.C.: U.S. Government Printing Office, 1919.

U.S. Department of War. Bureau of Refugees, Freedmen and Abandoned Lands. *Annual Report of the Assistant Commissioner, for the District of Columbia and West Virginia, for the Year Ending October 22, 1867.* Washington, D.C.: U.S. Government Printing Office, 1867.

U.S. Office of Education. *Biennial Survey of Education in the United States.* Bulletin 1937, No. 2, Vol. 1, chap. 2. Washington, D.C.: U.S. Government Printing Office, 1937.

Virginia State Board of Education. *Annual Report of the Superintendent of Public Instruction of Virginia, 1914–15.* Richmond: Superintendent of Public Printing, 1916.

Wilkerson, Doxey A. *Special Problems of Negro Education.* Washington, D.C.: U.S. Government Printing Office, 1939.

Winston, George T. "Industrial Education and the New South." In *Report of the U.S. Commissioner of Education, 1900–1901*, p. 510. Washington, D.C.: U.S. Government Printing Office, 1901.

Newspapers

Atlanta Constitution
Atlanta News
Boston Guardian
Charleston News and Courier
Charlotte Observer
Chattanooga News
Chicago Broad Ax
Chicago Inter-Ocean
Cleveland Gazette
Columbia State
Fisk University News (Nashville)
Loyal Georgian (Augusta)
Manufacturer's Record (Baltimore)
Memphis Commercial Appeal
Montgomery Daily Advertiser
Nashville Banner
New Orleans Black Republican
New Orleans Louisianian
New Orleans States
New Orleans Times Picayune
New Orleans Tribune
New Orleans Union

New Voice (Chester, Pennsylvania)
New York Age
New York Independent
New York Observer
New York Times
Norfolk Journal and Guide
People's Advocate (Alexandria, Virginia)
Philadelphia Christian Recorder
Philadelphia Standard-Echo
Philadelphia Tribune
Picayune (New Orleans)
Raleigh Morning Post
Raleigh News and Observer
Richmond Times
Richmond Times-Dispatch
Savannah Echo
Southern Workman (Hampton)
Virginia Star (Richmond)
Washington Bee
Zion's Herald (Boston)

Books and Pamphlets

Abbott, Martin. *The Freedmen's Bureau in South Carolina, 1865–1872*. Chapel Hill: University of North Carolina Press, 1967.

Adams, Myron W. *A History of Atlanta University, 1865–1929*. Atlanta: Atlanta University Press, 1930.

Adler, Cyrus. *Jacob H. Schiff: His Life and Letters*. Garden City, N.Y.: Doubleday, Doran, 1928.

_____. *Jacob Henry Schiff: A Biographical Sketch*. New York: American Jewish Committee, 1921.

Alderman, Edwin A., and Gordon, Armistead C. *J. L. M. Curry: A Biography*. New York: Macmillan, 1911.

Alvord, John W. *Letters from the South Relating to the Condition of the Freedmen, Addressed to Major General O. O. Howard, Commissioner, Bureau of Refugees, Freedmen, and Abandoned Lands.* Washington, D.C.: Howard University Press, 1870.

Anderson, Eric. *Race and Politics in North Carolina, 1872–1901: The Black Second.* Baton Rouge: Louisiana State University Press, 1981.

Aptheker, Herbert, ed. *The Correspondence of W. E. B. DuBois.* Vol. 1. Amherst: University of Massachusetts, 1973.

———, ed. *W. E. B. DuBois: The Education of Black People.* Amherst, University of Massachusetts Press, 1973.

Armstrong Association. *The Aim and Methods of Hampton.* New York: Armstrong Association, 1904.

Armstrong, Byron K. *Factors in the Formulation of Collegiate Programs for Negroes.* Ann Arbor: Edwards Brothers, 1939.

Armstrong, Edith Talbot. *Samuel Chapman Armstrong: A Biographical Study.* New York: Doubleday, Page, 1904.

Armstrong, M. F., and Ludlow, Helen W. *Hampton and Its Students.* New York: G. P. Putnam's Sons, 1874.

Armstrong, Samuel C. *Armstrong's Ideas on Education for Life.* Hampton: Hampton Institute Press, 1940.

———. *Ideas on Education Expressed by Samuel Chapman Armstrong.* Hampton: Hampton Institute Press, 1908.

———. *Principal's Annual Report of Hampton Institute.* 1874, 1876, 1886, 1887. Hampton: Normal School Press, 1874, 1876, 1886, 1887.

———. *Report of Hampton Institute.* Richmond: William Jones, 1880.

———. *Report of Hampton Normal and Agricultural Institute.* Richmond: Clemmitt and Jones, 1878.

Bacon, Alice M. *The Negro and the Atlanta Exposition.* John F. Slater Fund, Occasional Paper 7. Baltimore: John F. Slater Fund, 1896.

Bacote, Clarence A. *The Story of Atlanta University: A Century of Service, 1865–1965.* Atlanta: Atlanta University Press, 1969.

Baker, Ray Stannard. *Following the Color Line: American Negro Citizenship in the Progressive Era.* New York: Doubleday, Page, 1908.

Bardolph, Richard, ed. *The Civil Rights Record: Black Americans and the Law, 1849–1970.* New York: Thomas Y. Crowell, 1970.

Barringer, Paul B. *The American Negro: His Past and Future.* Raleigh: Edwards and Broughton, 1900.

Barrows, Isabel C., ed. *First and Second Mohonk Conferences on the Negro Question.* 1890–91. Reprint. New York: Negro Universities Press, 1969.

Bass, Jesse, and Roberts, D. P., eds. *Proceedings of the 46th Indiana Annual Conference of the African Methodist Episcopal Church, Held in Terre Haute, Indiana, August 26, 1885.* Philadelphia: Christian Recorder Print, 1885.

Beard, Augustus Field. *A Crusade of Brotherhood: A History of the American Missionary Association*. Boston: Pilgrim Press, 1909.

Bentley, George R. *A History of the Freedmen's Bureau*. Philadelphia: University of Pennsylvania Press, 1955.

Berlin, Ira; Reidy, Joseph P.; and Rowland, Leslie S., eds. *Freedom: A Documentary History of Emancipation, 1861–1867*. Ser. 2. Cambridge: Cambridge University Press, 1982.

Berwanger, Eugene H. *The Frontier against Slavery*. Urbana: University of Illinois Press, 1971.

Billings, Dwight B., Jr. *Planters and the Making of a "New South": Class, Politics, and Development in North Carolina, 1865–1900*. Chapel Hill: University of North Carolina Press, 1979.

Billington, Monroe Lee. *The American South: A Brief History*. New York: Charles Scribner's Sons, 1971.

Blassingame, John W. *Black New Orleans, 1860–1880*. Chicago: University of Chicago Press, 1973.

————, ed. *Slave Testimony: Two Centuries of Letters, Speeches, Interviews, and Autobiographies*. Baton Rouge: Louisiana State University Press, 1977.

Bond, Horace Mann. *The Educaton of the Negro in the American Social Order*. New York: Prentice-Hall, 1934.

————. *Negro Education in Alabama: A Study in Cotton and Steel*. Washington, D.C.: Associated Publishers, 1939.

Bowker, Richard R. *Economics for the People, Being Plain Talks on Economics, Especially for Use in Business, in Schools, and in Women's Reading Classes*. New York: Harper and Brothers, 1886.

Bowles, Samuel, and Gintis, Herbert. *Schooling in Capitalist America: Educational Reform and the Contradictions of Economic Life*. New York: Basic Books, 1976.

Boyd, Sibbald P. *The Philadelphia Blue Book*. Philadelphia: C. E. Howe, 1897.

Bratton, Theodore DuBose. *The Christian South and Negro Education*. Sewanee, Tenn.: University of the South Press, 1908.

Brawley, Benjamin. *Doctor Dillard of the Jeanes Fund*. New York: Fleming H. Revell, 1930.

————. *Early Effort for Industrial Education*. John F. Slater Fund, Occasional Paper 22. New York: John F. Slater Fund, 1923.

————. *History of Morehouse College*. Atlanta: Morehouse College, 1917.

Broderick, Francis L. *W. E. B. DuBois: Negro Leader in a Time of Crisis*. Stanford: Stanford University Press, 1959.

Brooks, John Graham. *An American Citizen: The Life of William Henry Baldwin, Jr*. Boston: Houghton Mifflin, 1910.

Brown, Hugh Victor. *A History of the Education of Negroes in North Carolina*. Goldsboro, N.C.: Irving Swain Press, 1961.

Brown, Ira V. *Lymon Abbott, Christian Evolutionist: A Study in Religious Lib-
eralism.* Cambridge, Mass.: Harvard University Press, 1967.
Brown, William Adams. *Morris Ketchum Jesup, A Character Sketch.* New York:
Charles Scribner's Sons, 1910.
Brown, William Henry. *The Education and Economic Development of the Ne-
gro in Virginia.* Charlottesville: University of Virginia Press, 1923.
Bryce, Tileston T. *Economic Crumbs, or Plain Talks for the People about Labor,
Capital, Money, Tariff, etc.* Hampton: Normal School Press, 1879.
Bullock, Henry Allen. *A History of Negro Education in the South from 1619 to
the Present.* Cambridge, Mass.: Harvard University Press, 1967.
Butchart, Ronald E. *Northern Schools, Southern Blacks, and Reconstruction:
Freedmen's Education, 1862–1875.* Westport, Conn.: Greenwood Press,
1980.
Campbell, Thomas Monroe. *The Movable School Goes to the Negro Farmer.*
Tuskegee: Tuskegee Institute Press, 1936.
Carnegie, Andrew. *The Autobiography of Andrew Carnegie.* Boston: Houghton
Mifflin, 1920.
Carpenter, John A. *Sword and Olive Branch: Oliver Otis Howard.* Pittsburgh:
University of Pittsburgh Press, 1964.
Cash, W. J. *The Mind of the South.* New York: Knopf, 1941.
Chase, Lucy, and Chase, Sarah. *Dear Ones at Home: Letters from Contraband
Camps.* Edited by Henry L. Swint. Nashville: Vanderbilt University Press,
1966.
Church, Robert L. *Education in the United States: An Interpretive History.*
New York: Free Press, 1976.
Coleman, Dr. J. F. B. *Tuskegee to Voorhees: The Booker T. Washington Idea
Projected by Elizabeth Evelyn Wright.* Columbia, S.C.: R. L. Bryan, 1922.
Coon, Charles Lee. *Public Taxation and Negro Schools.* Paper read before the
Twelfth Annual Conference for Education in the South, held at Atlanta, Geor-
gia, 14, 15, and 16 April 1909. Cheyney, Pa.: Committee of Twelve for the
Advancement of the Interests of the Negro Race, 1909.
Cornish, Dudley Taylor. *The Sable Arm: Negro Troops in the Union Army,
1861–1865.* New York: Longmans, Green, 1956.
Cozart, Leland Stanford. *A History of the Association of Colleges and Second-
ary Schools, 1934–1965.* Charlotte, N.C.: Heritage Press, 1967.
Cromwell, John W. *Address on the Difficulties of the Colored Youth in Obtain-
ing an Education in the Virginias, before the Colored Educational Conven-
tion Held at Richmond, Va., August 23d, 1875.* Philadelphia: G. T. Stockdale,
Printer, 1875.
Cronon, E. David. *Black Moses: The Story of Marcus Garvey and the Universal
Negro Improvement Association.* Madison: University of Wisconsin Press,
1955.

Crummell, Alexander. *The Attitude of the American Mind toward the Negro Intellect.* American Negro Academy Occasional Paper 3 (1898).

Curry, J. L. M. *A Brief Sketch of George Peabody, and a History of the Peabody Educational Fund through Thirty Years.* 1898. Reprint. New York: Negro Universities Press, 1969.

——. *The Southern States of the American Union.* New York: G. P. Putnam's Sons, 1894.

Curti, Merle. *The Social Ideas of American Educators.* New York: Charles Scribner's Sons, 1935.

Curti, Merle, and Nash, Roderick. *Philanthropy in the Shaping of American Higher Education.* New Brunswick: Rutgers University Press, 1965.

Dabney, Charles W. *The Problem in the South.* New York: General Education Board, 1903.

——. *Universal Education in the South.* 2 vols. Chapel Hill: University of North Carolina Press, 1936.

Dabney, Lillian G. *The History of Schools for Negroes in the District of Columbia, 1807–1947.* Washington, D.C.: Catholic University of America Press, 1949.

Danbom, David B. *The Resisted Revolution: Urban America and the Industrialization of Agriculture, 1900–1930.* Ames: Iowa State University Press, 1979.

Daniel, Pete. *The Shadow of Slavery: Peonage in the South, 1901–1969.* Urbana: University of Illinois Press, 1972.

Davis, Jackson. *County Training Schools.* Hampton: Hampton Institute Press, 1918.

——. *The Jeanes Visiting Teachers: An Address Given at the Inter-Territorial Jeanes Conference, Salisbury, Southern Rhodesia, May 27, 1935.* New York: Carnegie Corporation, 1936.

Davis, Ronald L. F. *Good and Faithful Labor: From Slavery to Sharecropping in the Natchez District, 1860–1890.* Westport, Conn.: Greenwood Press, 1982.

Davis, William Watson. *The Civil War and Reconstruction in Florida.* Gainesville: University of Florida Press, 1964.

Dean, Jennie. *The Beginning of the Manassas Industrial School for Colored Youth and Its Growth, 1888–1900.* Manassas, Va.: Manassas Industrial School Press, 1900.

Dittmer, John. *Black Georgia in the Progressive Era, 1900–1920.* Urbana: University of Illinois Press, 1977.

Donald, Henderson H. *The Negro Freedman: Life Conditions of the American Negro in the Early Years after Emancipation.* New York: Henry Schuman, 1952.

Drago, Edmund L. *Black Politicians and Reconstruction in Georgia: A Splendid Failure.* Baton Rouge: Louisiana State University Press, 1982.

DuBois, W. E. B. *The Autobiography of W. E. B. DuBois: A Soliloquy on View-*

ing My Life from the Last Decade of Its First Century. New York: International Publishers, 1968.

———. *Black Reconstruction in America: An Essay toward a History of the Part Which Black Folk Played in the Attempt to Reconstruct Democracy in America, 1860–1880*. 1935. Reprint. Cleveland: World, Meridian Books, 1962.

———. *The College-Bred Negro*. Atlanta: Atlanta University Press, 1900.

———. *Dusk of Dawn: An Essay toward an Autobiography of a Race Concept*. 1940. Reprint. New York: Schocken Books, 1968.

———. *The Souls of Black Folk: Essays and Sketches*. 1903. Reprint. Greenwich, Conn.: Fawcett, 1968.

———, ed. *The Negro Artisan*. Atlanta: Atlanta University Press, 1902.

———. *The Negro Common School*. Atlanta: Atlanta University Press, 1901.

DuBois, W. E. B., and Dill, Augustus G., eds. *The College-Bred Negro American*. Atlanta: Atlanta University Press, 1910.

———. *The Common School and the Negro American*. Atlanta: Atlanta University Press, 1911.

Duncan, Russell. *Freedom's Shore: Tunis Campbell and the Georgia Freedmen*. Athens: University of Georgia Press, 1986.

Edwards, William J. *Twenty-five Years in the Black Belt*. Boston: Cornhill, 1918.

Ellison, Ralph. *Invisible Man*. New York: Signet Books, 1947.

Embree, Edwin R., and Waxman, Julia. *Investment in People: The Story of the Julius Rosenwald Fund*. New York: Harper and Brothers, 1949.

———. *Julius Rosenwald Fund: A Review to June 30, 1928*. Chicago: Julius Rosenwald Fund, 1928.

Engs, Robert F. *Freedom's First Generation: Black Hampton, Virginia, 1861–1890*. Philadelphia: University of Pennsylvania Press, 1979.

Favrot, Leo M. *A Study of County Training Schools for Negroes in the South*. John F. Slater Fund Occasional Paper 23. Charlottesville: John F. Slater Fund, 1923.

Fee, John G. *Autobiography of John G. Fee*. Chicago: National Christian Association, 1891.

Feldstein, Stanley. *Once a Slave: The Slaves' View of Slavery*. New York: William Morrow, 1970.

Fischer, Roger A. *The Segregation Struggle in Louisiana, 1862–1877*. Urbana: University of Illinois Press, 1974.

Fisher, Berneice M. *Industrial Education: American Ideas and Institutions*. Madison: University of Wisconsin Press, 1967.

Fisher, John E. *The John F. Slater Fund: A Nineteenth Century Affirmative Action for Negro Education*. Lanham, Md.: University Press of America, 1986.

Fisk, Clinton B. *Plain Counsels for Freedmen: In Sixteen Brief Lectures*. Boston:

American Tract Society, 1866.

Flexner, Abraham, with the collaboration of Esther S. Bailey. *Funds and Foundations: Their Policies Past and Present.* New York: Harper and Brothers, 1952.

Flynn, Charles L., Jr. *White Land, Black Labor: Caste and Class in Late Nineteenth-Century Georgia.* Baton Rouge: Louisiana State University Press, 1983.

Foner, Eric, ed. *America's Black Past.* New York: Harper & Row, 1970.

Forten, Charlotte L. *The Journal of Charlotte L. Forten, A Free Negro in the Slave Era.* Edited by Ray Allen Billington. New York: Collier Books, 1961.

Fosdick, Raymond B. *Adventure in Giving: The Story of the General Education Board, A Foundation Established by John D. Rockefeller.* New York: Harper & Row, 1962.

Fox, Stephen R. *The Guardian of Boston: William Monroe Trotter.* New York: Atheneum, 1970.

Franklin, John Hope. *From Slavery to Freedom: A History of Negro Americans.* 3d ed. New York: Knopf, 1967.

———. *Reconstruction: After the Civil War.* Chicago: University of Chicago Press, 1961.

Franklin, V. P. *Black Self-Determination: A Cultural History of the Faith of the Fathers.* Westport, Conn.: Lawrence Hill and Company, 1984.

Franklin, V. P. and Anderson, James D., eds. *New Perspectives on Black Educational History.* Boston: G. K. Hall, 1978.

Frazier, E. Franklin. *The Negro in the United States.* 1949. Rev. ed. New York: Macmillan, 1957.

Fredrickson, George M. *The Black Image in the White Mind: The Debate on Afro-American Character and Destiny, 1817–1914.* New York: Harper & Row, 1971.

Freedmen's Aid and Southern Education Society. *Report of the Board of Managers to the General Committee at the Annual Meeting, Held in Philadelphia.* Cincinnati: Freedmen's Aid Society of the Methodist Episcopal Church, 1900.

Freedmen's Aid Society, Twenty-Fifth Annual Report. Cincinnati: Freedmen's Aid Society of the Methodist Episcopal Church, 1891.

General Education Board. *Annual Report of the General Education Board.* New York: General Education Board, 1918.

———. *The General Education Board: An Account of Its Activities, 1902–1914.* New York: General Education Board, 1915.

Genovese, Eugene D. *In Red and Black.* New York: Pantheon Books, 1971.

Gerteis, Louis S. *From Contraband to Freedman: Federal Policy toward Southern Blacks, 1861–1865.* Westport, Conn.: Greenwood Press, 1973.

Grantham, Dewey W. *Hoke Smith and the Politics of the New South.* Baton Rouge: Louisiana State University Press, 1958.

Gutman, Herbert G. *The Black Family in Slavery and Freedom, 1750–1925.* New York: Pantheon Books, 1976.

———. *Power and Culture: Essays on the American Working Class.* New York: Pantheon Books, 1987.

Hampton Normal and Agricultural Institute. *Catalogue of Hampton Normal and Agricultural Institute.* Hampton: Hampton Institute Press, 1886.

———. *Catalogue of the Hampton Normal and Agricultural Institute.* Hampton: Hampton Institute Press, 1900.

———. *A Life Well Lived: In Memory of Robert Curtis Ogden.* Hampton: Hampton Institute Press, 1914.

———. *Twenty-two Years' Work of the Hampton Normal and Agricultural Institute at Hampton, Virginia.* Hampton: Normal School Press, 1893.

———. *What Hampton Graduates Are Doing, 1878–1904.* Hampton: Hampton Institute Press, 1904.

Harding, Samuel B. *Select Orations.* New York: Macmillan, 1909.

Harlan, Louis R. *Booker T. Washington: The Making of a Black Leader, 1856–1901.* London: Oxford University Press, 1972.

———. *Booker T. Washington: The Wizard of Tuskegee, 1901–1915.* New York: Oxford University Press, 1983.

———. *Separate and Unequal: Public School Campaigns and Racism in the Southern Seaboard States, 1901–1915.* 1958. Reprint. New York: Atheneum, 1968.

Harlan, Louis R.; Kaufman, Stuart B.; Kraft, Barbara S.; and Smock, Raymond W., eds. *The Booker T. Washington Papers.* Vol. 4, *1896–1898.* Urbana: University of Illinois Press, 1975.

Harlan, Louis R.; Kaufman, Stuart B.; and Smock, Raymond W., eds. *The Booker T. Washington Papers.* Vol. 3, *1889–1895.* Urbana: University of Illinois Press, 1974.

Harlan, Louis R., and Smock, Raymond W., eds. *The Booker T. Washington Papers.* Vol. 5, *1899–1900.* Urbana: University of Illinois Press, 1976.

Harris, Abram, and Spero, Sterling. *The Black Worker.* New York: Columbia University Press, 1931.

Harris, Joel Chandler. *Life of Henry W. Grady: Including His Writings and Speeches.* New York: Cassel, 1890.

Haynes, Elizabeth Ross. *The Black Boy of Atlanta.* Boston: House of Edinboro, 1952.

Heard, William H. *From Slavery to the Bishopric in the A.M.E. Church.* New York: Arno Press, 1969.

Higginson, Thomas Wentworth. *Army Life in a Black Regiment.* Boston: Fields, Osgood, 1870.

Hine, Darlene Clark. *Black Victory: The Rise and Fall of the White Primary in Texas.* Millwood, N.Y.: KTO Press, 1979.

Holley, J. W. *Education and the Segregation Issue.* New York: William Fredrick Press, 1955.

Holmes, Dwight Oliver. *The Evolution of the Negro College.* College Park, Md.: McGrath, 1934.

Holt, Thomas. *Black over White: Negro Political Leadership in South Carolina during Reconstruction.* Urbana: University of Illinois Press, 1977.

Holtzclaw, William H. *The Black Man's Burden.* New York: Neale, 1915.

Hopkins, Mark. *Annual Report upon the Hampton Normal and Agricultural Institute* (June 1870). Hampton: Normal School Press, 1870.

Howard, Oliver Otis. *Autobiography of Oliver Otis Howard, Major General, United States Army.* 2 vols. New York: Baker & Taylor, 1907.

Howard, Victor B. *Black Liberation in Kentucky: Emancipation and Freedom, 1862–1884.* Lexington: University Press of Kentucky, 1983.

Huggins, Nathan I.; Kilson, Martin; and Fox, Daniel M., eds. *Key Issues in the Afro-American Experience.* New York: Harcourt Brace Jovanovich, 1971.

Hughes, William Hardin, and Patterson, Frederick D., eds. *Robert Russa Moton of Hampton and Tuskegee.* Chapel Hill: University of North Carolina Press, 1956.

Hundley, Mary Gibson. *The Dunbar Story, 1870–1955.* New York: Vantage Press, 1965.

Hyman, Harold M., ed. *The Radical Republicans and Reconstruction, 1861–1870.* Indianapolis: Bobbs-Merrill, 1967.

Ingle, Edward. *The Ogden Movement: An Educational Monopoly in the Making.* Baltimore: Manufacturer's Record Publishing Company, 1908.

John F. Slater Fund. *Suggested Course for County Training Schools.* John F. Slater Fund Occasional Paper 18. Lynchburg, Va.: John F. Slater Fund, 1917.

———. *Third Proceedings of the Trustees of the John F. Slater Fund for the Education of Freedmen.* Baltimore: John Murphy, 1883.

Johnson, Charles S. *Shadow of the Plantation.* Chicago: University of Chicago Press, 1934.

Jones, Faustine Childress. *A Traditional Model of Educational Excellence: Dunbar High School of Little Rock, Arkansas.* Washington, D.C.: Howard University Press, 1981.

Jones, Jacqueline. *Soldiers of Light and Love: Northern Teachers and Georgia Blacks, 1865–1873.* Chapel Hill: University of North Carolina Press, 1980.

Jones, Lance G. E. *The Jeanes Teacher in the United States, 1908–1933.* Chapel Hill: University of North Carolina Press, 1937.

———. *Negro Schools in the Southern States.* Oxford: Clarendon Press, 1928.

Jones, Thomas H. *The Experience of Thomas H. Jones, Who Was a Slave for Forty-Three Years.* 1862. Reprint. Philadelphia: Historic Publications, 1969.

Jones, Thomas Jesse. *Educational Adaptations: Report of Ten Years' Work of the Phelps-Stokes Fund, 1910–1920.* New York: Phelps-Stokes Fund, 1920.

———. *Social Studies in the Hampton Curriculum.* Hampton: Hampton Institute Press, 1908.

Jorgenson, Lloyd P. *The State and the Non-Public School, 1825–1925.* Columbia: University of Missouri Press, 1987.

Katz, Michael B. *The Irony of Early School Reform: Educational Innovation in Mid-Nineteenth Century Massachusetts.* Boston: Beacon Press, 1968.

King, Kenneth J. *Pan-Africanism and Education: A Study of Race, Philanthropy and Education in the Southern States of America and East Africa.* Oxford: Clarendon Press, 1971.

Knight, Edgar W. *The Influence of Reconstruction on Education in the South.* New York: Teachers College, Columbia University, 1913.

———. *Public Education in the South.* Boston: Ginn, 1922.

Kolchin, Peter. *First Freedom: The Response of Alabama's Blacks to Emancipation and Reconstruction.* Westport, Conn.: Greenwood Press, 1972.

Krishnayaja, Stephen G. *The Rural Community and the School: The Message of Negro and Other American Schools for India.* Calcutta: Association Press, 1934.

Krug, Edward A. *The Shaping of the American High School, 1880–1920.* Madison: University of Wisconsin Press, 1964.

Lamon, Lester C. *Black Tennesseans, 1900–1930.* Knoxville: University of Tennessee Press, 1977.

Leavell, Ullin Whitney. *Philanthropy in Negro Education.* 1930. Reprint. New York: Negro Universities Press, 1970.

Lee, Gordon C. *The Struggle for Federal Aid.* New York: Columbia University Press, 1949.

Lewis, Charles Lee. *Philander Priestley Claxton: Crusader for Public Education.* Knoxville: University of Tennessee Press, 1948.

Lieberson, Stanley. *A Piece of the Pie: Blacks and White Immigrants since 1880.* Berkeley and Los Angeles: University of California Press, 1980.

Link, William A. *A Hard Country and a Lonely Place: Schooling, Society and Reform in Rural Virginia, 1870–1920.* Chapel Hill: University of North Carolina Press, 1986.

Litwack, Leon F. *Been in the Storm So Long: The Aftermath of Slavery.* New York: Knopf, 1979.

———. *North of Slavery.* Chicago: University of Chicago Press, 1961.

Lockwood, Lewis C. *Mary S. Peake: The Colored Teacher at Fortress Monroe.* Boston: American Tract Society, 1863.

Logan, Frenise A. *The Negro in North Carolina, 1876–1894.* Chapel Hill: University of North Carolina Press, 1964.

Logan, Rayford W. *The Betrayal of the Negro: From Rutherford B. Hayes to Woodrow Wilson.* London: Collier, 1965.

———. *Howard University, 1867–1967.* New York: New York University Press, 1969.

———. *The Negro in the United States.* Vol. 1, *A History to 1945—From Slav-*

ery to Second-Class Citizenship. New York: Van Nostrand Reinhold, 1957.

Loram, Charles Templeman. *Adoption of the Penn School Methods to Education in South Africa.* New York: Phelps-Stokes Fund, 1927.

Macy, Jesse. *Our Government: How It Grew, What It Does, and How It Does It.* Boston: Ginn, 1886.

Mandle, Jay R. *The Roots of Black Poverty: The Southern Plantation Economy after the Civil War.* Durham: Duke University Press, 1978.

Martin, Tony. *Race First: The Ideological and Organizational Struggles of Marcus Garvey and the Universal Negro Improvement Association.* Westport, Conn.: Greenwood Press, 1976.

Mays, Benjamin Elijah. *Born to Rebel: An Autobiography.* New York: Scribner's, 1971.

McCuistion, Fred. *The South's Negro Teaching Force.* Nashville: Julius Rosenwald Fund, 1931.

McFeely, William S. *Yankee Stepfather: General O. O. Howard and the Freedmen.* New Haven: Yale University Press, 1968.

McKenzie, Fayette A. *Ideals of Fisk.* Nashville: Fisk University Press, 1915.

McKinney, Richard I. *Religion in Higher Education among Negroes.* New Haven: Yale University Press, 1945.

McKinney, Theophilus E., ed. *Higher Education among Negroes.* Charlotte: Johnson C. Smith University, 1932.

McMillan, Lewis K. *Negro Higher Education in the State of South Carolina.* Orangeburg: Privately printed by the author at South Carolina State A&M College, 1952.

McPherson, James. M. *The Abolitionist Legacy, from Reconstruction to the NAACP.* Princeton: Princeton University Press, 1975.

———. *The Struggle for Equality: Abolitionists and the Negro in the Civil War and Reconstruction.* Princeton: Princeton University Press, 1964.

Meier, August. *Negro Thought in America, 1880–1915: Racial Ideologies in the Age of Booker T. Washington.* Ann Arbor: University of Michigan Press, 1963.

Meier, August, and Rudwick, Elliott. *From Plantation to Ghetto: An Interpretive History of American Negroes.* American Century Series. New York: Hill & Wang, 1966.

Meltzer, Milton, ed. *In Their Own Words: A History of the American Negro.* 3 vols. New York: Thomas Y. Crowell, 1965.

Montgomery, David. *Beyond Equality: Labor and the Radical Republicans, 1862–1872.* New York: Vintage, 1967.

Morgan, Thomas J. *The Negro in America and the Ideal American Republic.* Philadelphia: American Baptist Publication Society, 1898.

Morris, Robert C. *Reading, 'Riting, and Reconstruction: The Education of Freedmen in the South, 1861–1870.* Chicago: University of Chicago Press, 1981.

Morrow, Ralph E. *Northern Methodism and Reconstruction.* East Lansing: Michigan State University Press, 1956.

Moton, Robert Russa. *What the Negro Thinks.* Garden City, N.Y.: Doubleday, 1929.

Murphy, Edgar Gardner. *The Basis of Ascendancy: A Discussion of Certain Principles of Public Policy Involved in the Development of the Southern States.* New York: Longmans, Green, 1909.

_____. *Problems of the Present South: A Discussion of Certain of the Educational, Industrial and Political Issues in the Southern States.* New York: Longmans, Green, 1910.

Murray, Andrew E. *Presbyterians and the Negro: A History.* Philadelphia: Presbyterian Historical Society, 1966.

Myrdal, Gunnar. *An American Dilemma: The Negro Problem and Modern Democracy.* Vol. 2. New York: McGraw-Hill, 1944.

National Negro Conference. *Proceedings, 1901.* New York: Arno Press, 1969.

Nevins, Allan. *Study in Power: John D. Rockefeller, Industrialist and Philanthropist.* 2 vols. New York: Charles Scribner's Sons, 1953.

Neyland, Leedell W., and Riley, John W. *The History of Florida Agricultural and Mechanical University.* Gainesville: University of Florida Press, 1963.

Nixon, Raymond Blalock. *Henry W. Grady: Spokesman of the New South.* New York: Knopf, 1943.

Noble, Stuart G. *Forty Years of the Public Schools in Mississippi with Special Reference to the Education of the Negro.* New York: Teachers College Press, 1918.

Ogden, Robert C. *Samuel Chapman Armstrong: A Sketch.* New York: Fleming H. Revell, 1894.

Payne, Daniel Alexander. *A History of the African Methodist Episcopal Church.* Nashville: A.M.E. Sunday School Union, 1891.

_____. *Recollections of Seventy Years.* Compiled and arranged by Sarah C. Bierce Scarborough, edited by Rev. C. S. Smith. Nashville: A.M.E. Sunday School Union, 1888.

Peabody, Francis G. *Education for Life: The Story of Hampton Institute.* Garden City, N.Y.: Doubleday, Page, 1918.

Pearson, Elizabeth Ware, ed. *Letters from Port Royal, Written at the Time of the Civil War.* Boston: W. B. Clarke, 1906.

Perdue, Robert E. *The Negro in Savannah, 1865–1900.* New York: Exposition Press, 1973.

Perman, Michael. *Reunion without Compromise: The South and Reconstruction, 1865–1868.* Cambridge: Cambridge University Press, 1973.

Phelps-Stokes, Anson, and Jones, Thomas Jesse. *Progress in Negro Status and Race Relations, 1911–1946.* New York: Phelps-Stokes Fund, 1948.

Pinchbeck, Raymond B. *The Virginia Negro Artisan and Tradesman.* Phelps-Stokes Fellowship Paper 7. Richmond: William Byrd Press, 1926.

Ponton, Mungo Melanchton. *Life and Times of Henry M. Turner: The Antecedent and Preliminary History of the Life and Times of Bishop H. M. Turner, His Boyhood, Education and Public Career, and His Relation to His Associates, Colleagues and Contemporaries.* Atlanta: A. B. Caldwell, 1917.

Powell, Burt. *The Movement of Industrial Education and the Establishment of the University, 1840–1870.* Urbana: University of Illinois Press, 1918.

Presson, John A. *Annual Report of Educational Activities in Negro Schools.* Little Rock: State Department of Education, 1922.

Quadrennial Report of the Freedmen's Aid and Southern Education Society to the General Conference of the Methodist Church. Cincinnati: Freedmen's Aid Society of the Methodist Episcopal Church, 1892.

Rabinowitz, Howard N. *Race Relations in the Urban South, 1865–1890.* Urban Life in America Series. New York: Oxford University Press, 1978.

Range, Willard. *The Rise and Progress of Negro Colleges in Georgia, 1865–1949.* Athens: University of Georgia Press, 1951.

Ransom, Roger L., and Sutch, Richard. *One Kind of Freedom: The Economic Consequences of Emancipation.* Cambridge: Cambridge University Press, 1977.

Raper, Arthur F. *Preface to Peasantry.* Chapel Hill: University of North Carolina Press, 1936.

Rawick, George P., ed. *The American Slave: A Composite Autobiography.* Vol. 2, pt. 2. Westport, Conn.: Greenwood Press, 1972.

Read, Florence Matilda. *The Story of Spelman College.* Princeton: Princeton University Press, 1961.

Redcay, Edward E. *County Training Schools and Public Secondary Education for Negroes in the South.* Washington, D.C.: John F. Slater Fund, 1935.

Redkey, Edwin S. *Black Exodus: Black Nationalist and Back-to-Africa Movements, 1890–1910.* New Haven: Yale University Press, 1969.

Rice, Jessie Pearl. *J. L. M. Curry: Southerner, Statesman, and Educator.* New York: King's Crown Press, 1949.

Richardson, Joe M. *Christian Reconstruction: The American Missionary Association and Southern Blacks, 1861–1890.* Athens: University of Georgia Press, 1986.

———. *A History of Fisk University, 1865–1946.* University, Ala.: University of Alabama Press, 1980.

———. *The Negro in the Reconstruction of Florida, 1865–1877.* Florida State University Studies 46. Tallahassee: Florida State University, 1965.

Rockefeller, John D. *Random Reminiscences of Men and Events.* New York: Doubleday, Page, 1909.

Rose, Willie Lee. *Rehearsal for Reconstruction: The Port Royal Experiment.* 1964. Reprint. New York: Random House, Vintage Books, 1967.

Rubin, Louis D., ed. *Teach the Freeman: The Correspondence of Rutherford B.*

Hayes and the Slater Fund for Negro Education, 1881–1887. 2 vols. Baton Rouge: Louisiana State University Press, 1959.

Rudwick, Elliott M. *W. E. B. DuBois: Propagandist of the Negro Protest.* 1960. Reprint. New York: Atheneum, 1968.

Scott, Emmett J., and Stowe, Lyman Beecher. *Booker T. Washington: Builder of a Civilization.* Garden City, N.Y.: Doubleday, 1916.

Scott, Mingo, Jr. *The Negro in Tennessee Politics and Governmental Affairs, 1865–1965.* Nashville: Rich, 1964.

Sears, Jesse B. *The School Survey.* Boston: Houghton Mifflin, 1925.

Selden, William K. *Accreditation: A Struggle over Standards in Higher Education.* New York: Harper and Brothers, 1960.

Sherer, Robert G. *Subordination or Liberation? The Development and Conflicting Theories of Black Education in Nineteenth Century Alabama.* University, Ala.: University of Alabama Press, 1977.

Simkins, Francis Butler, and Woody, Robert Hilliard. *South Carolina during Reconstruction.* Chapel Hill: University of North Carolina Press, 1932.

Simmons, William J. *Men of Mark: Eminent, Progressive and Rising.* Cleveland: Geo. M. Rewell, 1887.

Sizer, Theodore R. *Secondary Schools at the Turn of the Century.* New Haven: Yale University Press, 1964.

Slaughter, Linda Warfel. *The Freedmen of the South.* Cincinnati: Elm Street Printing Co., 1869.

Smith, Samuel L. *Builders of Goodwill: The Story of the State Agents of Negro Education in the South, 1910–1950.* Nashville: Tennessee Book Company, 1950.

Sowell, Thomas. *Ethnic America: A History.* New York: Basic Books, 1981.

Starobin, Robert S. *Industrial Slavery in the Old South.* New York: Oxford University Press, 1970.

Swint, Henry L. *The Northern Teacher in the South, 1862–1870.* Nashville: Vanderbilt University Press, 1941.

Talbot, Edith Armstrong. *Samuel Chapman Armstrong: A Biographical Study.* New York: Doubleday, Page, 1904.

Taylor, Alrutheus Ambush. *The Negro in Tennessee, 1865–1880.* Washington, D.C.: Associated Publishers, 1941.

———. *The Negro in the Reconstruction of Virginia.* Washington, D.C.: Association for the Study of Negro Life and History, 1926.

Taylor, Joe Gray. *Louisiana Reconstructed, 1863–1877.* Baton Rouge: Louisiana State University Press, 1974.

Thornbrough, Emma L., ed. *Booker T. Washington.* Englewood Cliffs, N.J.: Prentice-Hall, 1969.

Tindall, George Brown. *The Emergence of the New South, 1913–1945.* Baton Rouge: Louisiana State University Press, 1967.

————. *South Carolina Negroes, 1877–1900*. Columbia: University of South Carolina Press, 1952.

Tourgée, Albion W. *Bricks without Straw*. New York: Fords, Howard & Hulbert, 1880.

Trustees of the John F. Slater Fund. *County Teacher Training Schools for Negroes*. John F. Slater Fund Occasional Paper 14. New York: John F. Slater Fund, 1913.

Tuskegee Institute. *Unveiling of the Memorial Tablet in Memory of the Late William H. Baldwin, Jr., Sunday, April 14, 1909, Tuskegee Institute, Alabama*. Tuskegee: Tuskegee Institute Press, 1909.

Vaughn, William P. *Schools for All: The Blacks and Public Education in the South, 1865–1877*. Lexington: University Press of Kentucky, 1974.

Villard, Oswald Garrison. *Prophets True and False*. New York: Knopf, 1927.

Vincent, Theodore G. *Black Power and the Garvey Movement*. Berkeley, Calif.: Ramparts Press, 1971.

Ware, Louise. *George Foster Peabody: Banker, Philanthropist, Publicist*. Athens: University of Georgia Press, 1951.

Warren, Robert Penn. *Who Speaks for the Negro*. New York: Knopf, 1965.

Washington, Booker T. *The Future of the American Negro*. Boston: Small, Maynard, 1902.

————. *My Larger Education: Being Chapters from My Experience*. Garden City, N.Y.: Doubleday, Page, 1911.

————. *The Story of My Life and Work*. Atlanta: J. L. Nichols, 1900.

————. *The Story of the Negro*. New York: Doubleday, Page, 1909.

————. *Up from Slavery: An Autobiography*. New York: Doubleday, Page, 1902.

Wayne, Michael. *The Reshaping of Plantation Society: The Natchez District, 1860–1880*. Baton Rouge: Louisiana State University Press, 1983.

Webber, Thomas L. *Deep Like the Rivers: Education in the Slave Quarter Community, 1831–1865*. New York: Norton, 1978.

Weinberg, Meyer. *A Chance to Learn: A History of Race and Education in the United States*. Cambridge: Cambridge University Press, 1977.

Weiss, Nancy J. *The National Urban League, 1900–1940*. New York: Oxford University Press, 1974.

Wells-Barnett, Ida. *Crusade for Justice: The Autobiography of Ida B. Wells*. Edited by Alfreda Duster. Chicago: University of Chicago Press, 1970.

Werner, M. R. *Julius Rosenwald: The Life of a Practical Humanitarian*. New York: Harper and Brothers, 1939.

Wesley, Charles H. *Negro Labor in the United States, 1850–1925: A Study in American Economic History*. New York: Russell & Russell, 1927.

Wharton, Vernon Lane. *The Negro in Mississippi, 1865–1890*. 1947. Reprint. New York: Harper & Row, 1965.

White, Howard A. *The Freedmen's Bureau in Louisiana.* Baton Rouge: Louisiana State University Press, 1970.

Wiener, Jonathan M. *Social Origins of the New South: Alabama, 1865–1885.* Baton Rouge: Louisiana State University Press, 1979.

Wikramanayake, Marina. *A World in Shadow: The Free Black in Antebellum South Carolina.* Columbia: University of South Carolina Press, 1973.

Wilcox, William G. *The Builder of Tuskegee.* John F. Slater Fund Occasional Paper 17. Lynchburg, Va.: John F. Slater Fund, 1916.

Williams, W. T. B. *Duplication of Schools for Negro Youth.* John F. Slater Fund Occasional Paper 15. New York: John F. Slater Fund, 1914.

Williamson, Joel. *After Slavery: The Negro in South Carolina during Reconstruction, 1861–1877.* Chapel Hill: University of North Carolina Press, 1965.

Wolters, Raymond. *The New Negro on Campus: Black College Rebellions of the 1920s.* Princeton: Princeton University Press, 1975.

Wood, Forrest G. *Black Scare: The Racist Response to Emancipation and Reconstruction.* Berkeley and Los Angeles: University of California Press, 1970.

Woodson, Carter G. *The History of the Negro Church.* Washington, D.C.: Associated Publishers, 1921.

Woodward, C. Vann. *Origins of the New South, 1877–1913.* Baton Rouge: Louisiana State University Press, 1951.

Woolfolk, George Rublee. *Prairie View: A Study in Public Conscience, 1878–1946.* New York: Pageant Press, 1962.

Wooster, James W., Jr. *Edward Stephen Harkness, 1870–1940.* New York: William E. Rudge's Sons, 1949.

Work, Monroe N., ed. *Negro Year Book: An Annual Encyclopedia of the Negro.* Tuskegee: Negro Year Book Publishing Company, 1914.

Wright, Arthur D. *The Negro Rural School Fund, Inc., 1907–1933.* Washington, D.C.: Negro Rural School Fund, 1933.

Wright, Richard. *Black Boy.* New York: Harper & Row, 1937.

––––––. *Twelve Million Black Voices: A Folk History of the Negro in the United States.* New York: Viking, 1941.

Wright, Richard R., Jr. *Self-Help in Negro Education.* Cheyney, Pa.: Committee of Twelve, 1909.

Yetman, Norman R. *Life under the "Peculiar Institution": Selections from the Slave Narrative Collection.* New York: Holt, Rinehart and Winston, 1970.

Articles

Abbott, Lyman. "The South and Education." *Outlook* 27 (July 1907): 634–39.

Abbott, Martin. "The Freedmen's Bureau and Negro Schooling in South Carolina." *South Carolina Historical Magazine* 57 (Apr. 1956): 65–81.

Alderman, Edwin A. "Education for White and Black." *Independent* 53 (7 Nov. 1901): 2647–49.

Alderson, William T., Jr. "The Freedmen's Bureau and Negro Education in Virginia." *North Carolina Historical Review* 29 (Jan. 1952): 64–90.

Alexander, Roberta Sue. "Hostility and Hope: Black Education in North Carolina during Presidential Reconstruction, 1865–1867." *North Carolina Historical Review* 53 (Apr. 1976): 113–32.

Allen, J. Allen. "Selling Out the Workers." *Crisis* 45 (Mar. 1938): 80.

American Missionary Association. "Industries Taught in Our Schools." *American Missionary* 47 (May 1894): 189–92.

Anderson, James D. "Education as a Vehicle for the Manipulation of Black Workers." In *Work, Technology and Education: Dissenting Essays in the Intellectual Foundations of American Education*, edited by Walter Feinberg and Henry Rosemont, Jr., pp. 15–40. Urbana: University of Illinois Press, 1975.

———. "Ex-slaves and the Rise of Universal Education in the New South." In *Education and the Rise of the New South*, edited by Ronald K. Goodenow and Arthur O. White, pp. 1–25. Boston: G. K. Hall, 1981.

———. "The Hampton Model of Normal School Industrial Training, 1868–1900." In *New Perspectives on Black Educational History*, edited by V. P. Franklin and James D. Anderson, pp. 61–96. Boston: G. K. Hall, 1978.

———. "The Historical Development of Black Vocational Education." In *Work, Youth, and Schooling: Historical Perspectives on Vocationalism in American Education*, edited by Harvey Kantor and David B. Tyack, pp. 180–222. Stanford: Stanford University Press, 1982.

———. "Northern Foundations and Southern Rural Black Education, 1902–1935." *History of Education Quarterly* 18 (Winter 1978): 371–96.

———. "The Schooling and Achievement of Black Children: Before and after *Brown v. Topeka*, 1900–1980." In *The Effects of School Desegregation on Motivation and Achievement*, edited by Martin L. Maehr and David E. Bartz, pp. 103–21. Greenwich, Conn.: JAI Press, 1984.

———. "The Southern Improvement Company: Northern Reformers' Investment in Negro Cotton Tenancy, 1900–1920." *Agricultural History* 52 (Jan. 1978): 111–31.

Aptheker, Herbert. "The Negro College Student in the 1920s—Years of Preparation and Protest: An Introduction." *Science and Society* 33 (Spring 1969): 150–67.

———. "The Washington-DuBois Conference of 1904." *Science and Society* 13 (Fall 1949): 344–51.

Armstrong, Samuel C. "The Founding of Hampton Institute." *Old South Leaflets*, General Series, Vol. 6, no. 149 (1904): 6–7.

Armstrong, Warren B. "Union Chaplains and the Education of the Freedmen." *Journal of Negro History* 52 (Apr. 1967): 104–15.

Badger, Henry C. "Negro Colleges and Universities, 1900–1950." *Journal of*

Negro Education 21 (Winter 1952): 89–93.

Baldwin, William H., Jr. "The Present Problem of Negro Education." *Journal of Social Science* 37 (Dec. 1899): 52–63.

———. "The Present Problem of Negro Education in the South." *Proceedings of the Second Capon Springs Conference for Education in the South*, pp. 94–107. Raleigh: Edwards and Broughton, 1899.

———. "Publicity as a Means of Social Reform." *North American Review* 173 (Dec. 1901): 845–53.

Barrett, L. G. "Jackson College." *American Baptist Home Mission Monthly* 16 (Aug. 1889): 319, 327.

Barringer, Paul B. "Negro Education in the South." *Educational Review* 21 (Mar. 1901): 231–43.

Bell, John L., Jr. "Baptists and the Negro in North Carolina during Reconstruction." *North Carolina Historical Review* 42 (Oct. 1965): 391–409.

Bellamy, Donnie D. "Henry A. Hunt and Black Agricultural Leadership in the New South." *Journal of Negro History* 60 (Oct. 1975): 465–72.

Berman, Edward H. "Educational Colonialism in Africa: The Role of American Foundations, 1910–1945." In *Philanthropy and Cultural Imperialism: The Foundations at Home and Abroad*, edited by Robert F. Arnove, pp. 179–201. Boston: G. K. Hall, 1980.

Berry, Mary Frances. "Twentieth-Century Black Women in Education." *Journal of Negro Education* 51 (Summer 1982): 288–300.

Bethel, Elizabeth. "The Freedmen's Bureau in Alabama." *Journal of Southern History* 14 (Feb. 1948): 49–92.

Blanchard, F. Q. "A Quarter Century of the American Missionary Association." *Journal of Negro Education* 6 (Apr. 1937): 152–56.

Blassingame, John W. "The Union Army as an Educational Institution for Negroes, 1862–1865." *Journal of Negro Education* 34 (1965): 152–59.

Bond, Horace Mann. "A Century of Negro Higher Education." In *A Century of Higher Education: Classical Citadel to Collegiate Colossus*, edited by William W. Brickman and Stanley Lehrer, pp. 187–97. New York: Society for the Advancement of Education, 1962.

———. "Negro Education: A Debate in the Alabama Constitutional Convention of 1901." *Journal of Negro Education* 1 (Apr. 1932): 49–59.

"Booker T. Washington." *Christian Work*, Dec. 1899, p. 1015.

"Booker T. Washington." *Harper's Weekly*, Dec. 1898, p. 1284.

"Booker T. Washington." *Advance* 29 (Mar. 1895): 798.

Brigham, R. I. "Negro Education in Ante Bellum Missouri." *Journal of Negro History* 30 (Oct. 1945): 405–20.

Bruce, John E. "Booker T. Washington." *Philadelphia Tribune*. 16 Sept. 1899.

Bumstead, Horace. "The Freedmen's Children at School." *Andover Review* 4 (Dec. 1885): 550–60.

Burton, Orville Vernon. "Race and Reconstruction: Edgefield County, South

Carolina." *Journal of Social History* 12 (Fall 1978): 31–56.

Buttrick, Wallace. "The General Education Board." *Independent* 65 (6 Aug. 1908): 291–94.

Caldwell, B. C. "The Work of the Jeanes and Slater Funds." *Annals of the American Academy of Political and Social Science* 59 (Sept. 1913): 173–77.

Calloway, Thomas J. "Booker T. Washington and the Tuskegee Institute." *New England Magazine*, n.s. 17 (Oct. 1897): 131–46.

Carnegie, Andrew. "How Men Get Rich, and the Right View of Wealth." *World's Work* 17 (Dec. 1908): 1047–53.

———. "The Work and Influence of Hampton." *Proceedings of Armstrong Association Meeting*. New York: Armstrong Association, 1904.

Christensen, Lawrence O. "Schools for Blacks: J. Milton Turner in Reconstruction Missouri." *Missouri Historical Review* 76 (Jan. 1982): 121–35.

Clement, Rufus E. "The Church School as a Social Factor in Negro Life." *Journal of Negro History* 12 (Jan. 1927): 5–12.

Cohen, William. "Negro Involuntary Servitude in the South, 1865–1940: A Preliminary Analysis." *Journal of Southern History* 42 (Feb. 1976): 31–60.

"A Colored Man on the Race Problem." *Leslie's Weekly*, Dec. 1899, p. 462.

Connor, R. W. D. "The Peabody Education Fund." *South Atlantic Quarterly* 4 (Apr. 1905): 169–81.

Cornelius, Janet. " 'We Slipped and Learned to Read': Slave Accounts of the Literacy Process, 1830–1865." *Phylon* 44 (Sept. 1983): 171–86.

Coulter, E. Merton. "Henry M. Turner: Georgia Negro Preacher-Politician during the Reconstruction Era." *Georgia Historical Quarterly* 48 (Dec. 1964): 371–410.

Curry, J. L. M. "The Classes against the Masses." *Baptist Quarterly Review* 10 (Apr. 1889): 141–50.

———. "Education at the South." *Education* 2 (Jan. 1882): 278–83.

———. "Education in the Southern States." *Proceedings of the Second Capon Springs Conference for Education in the South*, pp. 33–43. Raleigh: Edwards and Broughton, 1899.

———. "Industrial Education for Everybody." *Independent* 52 (8 Feb. 1900): 357–58.

———. "The Peabody Education Fund." *Educational Review* 13 (Mar. 1897): 226–31.

———. "A Study in Community Life." *New England Magazine* 18 (Apr. 1898): 177–81.

Curti, Merle. "The History of American Philanthropy as a Field of Research." *American Historical Review* 62 (Jan. 1957): 352–63.

Davis, Jackson. "Negro Training and Racial Good-Will." *American Monthly Review of Reviews* 53 (Nov. 1918): 521–28.

———. "Practical Training in Negro Rural Schools." Southern Educational Association, *Proceedings and Addresses of the Twenty-fourth Annual Meeting, 1913* 24 (1913): 160–68.

Davis, Thomas E. "Some Racial Attitudes of Negro College and Grade School Students." *Journal of Negro Education* 6 (Apr. 1937): 157–65.

———. "A Study of Fisk University Freshmen from 1928 to 1930." *Journal of Negro Education* 2 (Oct. 1933): 477–83.

"Dedication of the William H. Spencer High School." *Spehisco* 1 (Jan. 1931): 1–4.

DeForest, Henry S. "Does Higher Education Benefit the Negro?" *American Missionary* 41 (Mar. 1887): 71–73.

———. "Talladega College, Talladega, Alabama." *American Missionary* 48 (July 1894): 287–89.

DeForest, John W. "The Man and Brother." *Atlantic Monthly* 22 (Oct. 1868): 414–25.

Doyle, Elizabeth J. "Nurseries of Treason: Schools in Occupied New Orleans." *Journal of Southern History* 26 (May 1960): 161–79.

DuBois, W. E. B. "Does the Negro Need Separate Schools?" *Journal of Negro Education* 4 (July 1935): 328–35.

———. "Fisk." *Crisis* 28 (Oct. 1924): 251–52.

———. "The Hampton Strike." *Nation* 125 (2 Nov. 1927): 471–72.

———. "Reconstruction and Its Benefits." *American Historical Review* 15 (July 1910): 781–99.

———. "Thomas Jesse Jones." *Crisis* 12 (Oct. 1921): 253.

Edmonds, Randolph. "Education in Self-Contempt." *Crisis* 45 (Aug. 1938): 262.

Eggleston, G. K. "The Freedmen's Bureau in Louisiana." *Louisiana Historical Quarterly* 32 (1949): 145–224.

Eliot, Charles W. "Farm Training for Negroes: Essential Factor in Colored Education in the South." *Survey* 38 (23 June 1917): 267–68.

Elliott, Claude. "The Freedmen's Bureau in Texas." *Southwestern Historical Quarterly* 56 (1952): 1–24.

Enck, Henry S. "Black Self-Help in the Progressive Era: The Northern Campaigns of Smaller Southern Black Industrial Schools, 1900–1915." *Journal of Negro History* 61 (Jan. 1976): 73–87.

———. "Tuskegee Institute and Northern White Philanthropy: A Case Study in Fund Raising, 1900–1915." *Journal of Negro History* 65 (Fall 1980): 336–48.

Favrot, Leo M. "County Training Schools for Negroes in the South: Summary of Findings and Recommendation." *Journal of Rural Education* 3 (Nov. 1923): 133–34.

———. "Negro Education in the South." National Education Association, *Proceedings of the Sixty-seventh Annual Meeting* 67 (1929): 472–77.

Fen, Sing Nan. "Notes on the Education of Negroes in North Carolina during the Civil War." *Journal of Negro Education* 36 (Winter 1967): 24–31.

Finkelstein, Barbara L. "Pedagogy as Intrusion: Teaching Values in Popular Primary Schools in Nineteenth-Century America." *History of Childhood Quarterly* 1 (Winter 1974): 349–78.

Fleming, Cynthia Griggs. "The Effect of Higher Education on Black Tennesseans after the Civil War." *Phylon* 44 (Sept. 1983): 204–16.

————. "A Survey of the Beginnings of Tennessee's Black Colleges and Universities, 1865–1920." *Tennessee Historical Quarterly* 39 (Summer 1980): 195–207.

Flexner, Abraham. "Upbuilding American Education: The National Work of the General Education Board." *Independent* 83 (9 Aug. 1915): 188–91.

Franklin, John Hope. "Jim Crow Goes to School: The Genesis of Legal Segregation in Southern Schools." *South Atlantic Quarterly* 58 (Spring 1959): 225–35.

Franklin, V. P. "Whatever Happened to the College-Bred Negro?" *History of Education Quarterly* 24 (Fall 1984): 411–18.

Fraser, Walter J., Jr. "William Henry Ruffner and the Establishment of Virginia's Public School System, 1870–1874." *Virginia Magazine of History and Biography* 79 (July 1971): 259–79.

Frazier, E. Franklin. "Negro in the Industrial South." *Nation* 125 (27 July 1927): 83–84.

Friedman, Lawrence J. "The Search for Docility: Racial Thought in the White South, 1861–1917." *Phylon* 31 (Fall 1970): 313–23.

Frissell, H. B. "The Progress of Negro Education." *South Atlantic Quarterly* 6 (Jan. 1907): 39.

————. "A Survey of the Field." *Proceedings of the First Capon Springs Conference for Christian Education in the South*, pp. 3–6. Raleigh: Capitol Printing Company, 1898.

"From Slave Kitchen to a College Presidency." *Christian Herald*, Nov. 1877, p. 874.

Frost, Norman. "The Development of Rural Secondary Education in the South." In *Secondary Education in the South*, edited by W. Carson Ryan, J. Minor Gwyn, and Arnold K. King, pp. 64–65. Chapel Hill: University of North Carolina Press, 1946.

Fuke, Richard Paul. "The Baltimore Association for the Moral and Educational Improvement of the Colored People, 1864–1870." *Maryland Historical Magazine* 66 (Winter 1971): 369–404.

Galloway, Charles B. "The South and the Negro." *Proceedings of the Seventh Conference for Education in the South*, pp. 206–17. New York: Committee on Publication, 1904.

[Gannett, William Channing, and Hale, Edward Everett]. "The Education of the Freedmen." *North American Review* 101 (Oct. 1865): 528–49.

Gara, Larry. "Teaching Negro Freedmen in the Post-War South: A Document." *Journal of Negro History* 40 (July 1955): 274–76.

Genung, George F. "Richmond Theological Seminary." *American Baptist Home Mission Monthly* 21 (Aug. 1889): 309–11.

Gilman, Daniel C. "Five Great Trusts." *Outlook* 83 (27 July 1907): 648–57.

———. "Thirty Years of the Peabody Education Fund." *Atlantic Monthly* 79 (Feb. 1897): 161–66.

Graham, Edward K. "The Hampton Institute Strike of 1927: A Case Study in Student Protest." *American Scholar* 38 (Autumn 1969): 668–83.

Green, Harry Washington. "Higher Standards for the Negro College." *Opportunity* 9 (Jan. 1931): 8–11.

Griggs, A. C. "Lucy Craft Laney." *Journal of Negro History* 19 (Jan. 1934): 97–102.

Gutman, Herbert G. "Observations on Selected Trends in American Working-Class Historiography Together with Some New Data that Might Affect Some of the Questions Asked by Historians of American Education Interested in the Relationship between Education and Work." Paper presented at the Conference on the Historiography of Education and Work, Stanford University, 17–18 Aug. 1979.

Guy-Sheftall, Beverly. "Black Women and Higher Education: Spelman and Bennett Colleges Revisited." *Journal of Negro Education* 51 (Summer 1982): 278–87.

Hampton Normal and Agricultural Institute. "Some Facts Relating to Hampton's Growth in Fifty Years." *Hampton Bulletin* 14 (May 1918): Appendix.

Harlan, Louis R. "Desegregation in New Orleans Public Schools during Reconstruction." *American Historical Review* 67 (Apr. 1962): 663–75.

———. "The Southern Education Board and the Race Issue in Public Education." *Journal of Southern History* 23 (May 1957): 189–202.

Harley, Sharon. "Beyond the Classroom: The Organizational Lives of Black Female Educators in the District of Columbia, 1890–1930." *Journal of Negro Education* 51 (Summer 1982): 254–65.

Harris, Carl V. "Stability and Change in Discrimination against Black Public Schools: Birmingham, Alabama, 1871–1931." *Journal of Southern History* 51 (Aug. 1985): 375–416.

Harris, J. John, III; Figgures, Cleopatra; and Carter, David G. "A Historical Perspective of the Emergence of Higher Education in Black Colleges." *Journal of Black Studies* 6 (Sept. 1975): 55–68.

Harris, Lafayette. "Problems before the College Negro." *Crisis* 44 (Aug. 1937): 234–36.

Harris, William T. "Normal School Training for Negroes." In *First and Second Mohonk Conferences on the Negro Question, 1890–91*, edited by Isabel C. Barrows, pp. 84–90. Reprint. New York: Negro Universities Press, 1969.

Heck, William H. "The Educational Uplift in the South." *World's Work* 8 (July 1904): 5026–29.

———. "A Unique Investigation: Methods of the General Education Board." *American Monthly Review of Reviews* 30 (Sept. 1904): 327–28.

Hine, Darlene Clark. "From Hospital to College: Black Nurse Leaders and the Rise of Collegiate Nursing Schools." *Journal of Negro Education* 51 (Summer 1982): 222–37.

———. "The Pursuit of Professional Equality: Meharry Medical College, 1921–1938, A Case Study." In *New Perspectives of Black Educational History*, edited by V. P. Franklin and James D. Anderson, pp. 173–92. Boston: G. K. Hall, 1978.

Holmes, D. O. W. "Beginnings of the Negro College." *Journal of Negro Education* 3 (Apr. 1934): 168–93.

———. "The Negro College Faces the Depression." *Journal of Negro Education* 2 (Jan. 1933): 16–25.

Hornsby, Alton, Jr. "The Freedmen's Bureau Schools in Texas, 1865–1870." *Southwestern Historical Quarterly* 76 (Apr. 1973): 397–417.

Hughes, Langston. "Cowards from the Colleges." *Crisis* 41 (Aug. 1934): 226–28.

Jackameit, William P. "A Short History of Negro Public Higher Education in West Virginia, 1890–1965." *West Virginia History* 37 (July 1976): 302–24.

Jackson, Luther Porter. "The Educational Efforts of the Freedmen's Bureau and Freedmen's Aid Societies in South Carolina, 1862–1872." *Journal of Negro History* 8 (Jan. 1923): 1–40.

———. "The Origin of Hampton Institute." *Journal of Negro History* 10 (Apr. 1925): 131–49.

Jenkins, Martin D. "Enrollment in Negro Colleges and Universities, 1937–38." *Journal of Negro Education* 7 (Apr. 1938): 118–23.

Johnson, Charles S. "Present Trends in the Employment of Negro Labor." *Opportunity: A Journal of Negro Life* 7 (Apr. 1929): 146–48.

Johnson, Guion Griffis. "The Ideology of White Supremacy, 1876–1910." In *Essays in Southern History*, edited by Fletcher M. Green, pp. 124–56. Chapel Hill: University of North Carolina Press, 1949.

Johnson, Kenneth R. "The Peabody Fund: Its Role in Alabama." *Alabama Review* 27 (Apr. 1974): 101–26.

Johnston, James Hugo, Jr. "The Participation of Negroes in the Government of Virginia from 1877 to 1888." *Journal of Negro History* 14 (July 1925): 251–71.

Jones, Allen W. "The Role of Tuskegee Institute in the Education of Black Farmers." *Journal of Negro History* 60 (Apr. 1975): 252–67.

Jones, Harry H. "The Crisis in Negro Leadership." *Crisis* 19 (Mar. 1920): 256–59.

Jones, Jacqueline. "Women Who Were More Than Men: Sex and Status in Freedmen's Teaching." *History of Education Quarterly* 19 (Spring 1979): 47–59.

Jones, Thomas Jesse. "Negro Population in the United States." *Annals of the American Academy of Political and Social Science* 49 (Sept. 1913): 1–9.

Jordan, Laylon Wayne. "Education for Community: C. G. Memminger and the Origination of Common Schools in Antebellum Charleston." *South Carolina Historical Magazine* 82 (Apr. 1982): 99–115.

Kassel, Charles. "Educating the Slave—A Forgotten Chapter of Civil War History." *Open Court* 41 (Apr. 1927): 239–56.

Katz, Michael B. "The Origins of Public Education: A Reassessment." *History of Education Quarterly* 16 (Winter 1976): 392.

Kelley, Alfred H. "The Congressional Controversy over School Segregation, 1865–1875." *American Historical Review* 64 (Apr. 1959): 537–63.

Kelley, Don Quinn. "Ideology and Education: Uplifting the Masses in Nineteenth Century Alabama." *Phylon* 40 (June 1979): 147–58.

Kessler, Sidney H. "The Organization of Negroes by the Knights of Labor." *Journal of Negro History* 32 (July 1952): 248–76.

King, Andrew A. "Booker T. Washington and the Myth of Heroic Materialism." *Quarterly Journal of Speech* 60 (Oct. 1974): 323–27.

Knight, Edgar W. "Reconstruction and Education in South Carolina." *South Atlantic Quarterly* 18 (1919): 350–64; 19 (1920): 55–66.

Knox, Ellis O. "A Historical Sketch of Secondary Education for Negroes." *Journal of Negro Education* 9 (July 1940): 440–53.

Kousser, J. Morgan. "Making Separate Equal: Integration of Black and White School Funds in Kentucky." *Journal of Interdisciplinary History* 11 (Winter 1980): 399–428.

———. "Progressivism—For Middle Class Whites Only: North Carolina Education, 1880–1910." *Journal of Southern History* 46 (May 1980): 168–94.

———. "Separate but Not Equal: The Supreme Court's First Decision on Racial Discrimination in Schools." *Journal of Southern History* 46 (Feb. 1980): 17–44.

Lamon, Lester C. "The Black Community in Nashville and the Fisk University Student Strike of 1924–1925." *Journal of Southern History* 40 (May 1974): 224–44.

———. "The Tennessee Agricultural and Industrial Normal School: Public Higher Education for Black Tennesseans." *Tennessee Historical Quarterly* 32 (Spring 1973): 42–58.

Leavell, Ullin Whitney. "Trends of Philanthropy in Negro Education: A Survey." *Journal of Negro Education* 2 (Jan. 1933): 38–52.

"Limiting Negro Education." *American Baptist Home Mission Monthly* 18 (Mar. 1896): 98–100, 205–9.

Little, Monroe H. "The Extra-Curricular Activities of Black College Students, 1868–1940." *Journal of Negro History* 65 (Spring 1980): 135–48.

Logan, Frenise A. "The Legal Status of Public School Education for Negroes in North Carolina, 1877–1894." *North Carolina Historical Review* 32 (July 1955): 346–57.

————. "The Movement in North Carolina to Establish a State Supported College for Negroes." *North Carolina Historical Review* 35 (Apr. 1958): 167–80.

Logan, Rayford W. "The Evolution of Private Colleges for Negroes." *Journal of Negro Education* 27 (Summer 1958): 213–20.

Logan, Thomas Muldrop. "The Opposition in the South to the Free-School System." *Journal of Social Science* 9 (Jan. 1878): 92–100.

Long, Herman H. "The Negro Public College in Tennessee." *Journal of Negro Education* 31 (Summer 1962): 341–48.

Lowe, W. A. "The Freedmen's Bureau and Education in Maryland." *Maryland Historical Magazine* 47 (1952): 29–39.

Ludlow, Helen W. "Hampton Normal and Agricultural Institute." *Harper's Magazine* 48 (Oct. 1873): 672–85.

Margo, Robert A. "Race Differences in Public School Expenditures: Disfranchisement and School Finance in Louisiana, 1890–1910." *Social Science History* 6 (Winter 1982): 9–33.

Martin, Sandy Dwayne. "The American Baptist Home Mission Society and Black Higher Education in the South, 1865–1920." *Foundations: A Baptist Journal of History, Theology and Ministry* 44 (Oct.–Dec. 1981): 310–27.

McCormick, J. Scott. "The Julius Rosenwald Fund." *Journal of Negro Education* 3 (Oct. 1934): 605–26.

McKinley, William. "Address at Tuskegee Institute, December 18, 1898." In John F. Slater Fund, *Proceedings, 1899,* pp. 41–44. New York: John F. Slater Fund, 1899.

McPherson, James M. "A Brief for Equality: The Abolitionist Reply to the Racist Myth, 1860–1865." In *The Antislavery Vanguard,* edited by Martin Duberman, pp. 156–77. Princeton: Princeton University Press, 1965.

————. "The New Puritanism: Values and Goals of Freedmen's Education in America." In *The University in Society,* edited by Lawrence Stone, 2:611–39. Princeton: Princeton University Press, 1974.

————. "White Liberals and Black Power in Negro Education, 1865–1915." *American Historical Review* 75 (June 1970): 1357–79.

Meier, August. "The Beginning of Industrial Education in Negro Schools." *Midwest Journal* 7 (Spring 1955): 23–44.

————. "Booker T. Washington and the Negro Press: With Special Reference to the Colored American Magazine." *Journal of Negro History* 37 (1958): 67–90.

———. "The Racial and Educational Thought of Kelly Miller, 1895–1915." *Journal of Negro Education* 29 (Spring 1960): 121–27.

Melish, J. Howard. "George Foster Peabody." *Religion in Life* 7 (Winter 1938): 85–96.

Meserve, Charles F. "Shaw University." *American Baptist Home Mission Monthly* 21 (Aug. 1889): 316.

Messner, William F. "Black Education in Louisiana, 1863–1865." *Civil War History* 22 (Mar. 1976): 41–59.

Miller, Kelly. "Negro Education and the Depression." *Journal of Negro Education* 2 (Jan. 1933): 1–4.

———. "The Past, Present and Future of the Negro College." *Journal of Negro Education* 2 (July 1933): 411–22.

Mitchell, E. C. "Higher Education and the Negro." *American Baptist Home Mission Monthly* 18 (Sept. 1896): 308.

Morgan, Thomas J. "Defects of Industrial Education." *American Baptist Home Mission Monthly* 22 (July 1900): 197–206.

———. "The Education of the Negroes." *American Baptist Home Mission Monthly* 17 (Oct. 1895): 368–73.

———. "The Higher Education of Colored Women." *American Baptist Home Mission Monthly* 18 (May 1896): 160.

———. "Negro Education." *American Baptist Home Mission Monthly* 22 (Jan. 1900): 3–4.

———. "Negro Preparation for Citizenship." *American Baptist Home Mission Monthly* 22 (Dec. 1900): 334–37.

Moton, Robert Russa. "Mr. R. C. Ogden's Interest in Negro Education." *Colored American Magazine* 11 (Nov. 1906): 293–94.

Myers, John B. "The Education of the Alabama Freedmen during Presidential Reconstruction, 1865–1867." *Journal of Negro Education* 40 (Spring 1971): 163–71.

"The Negro Common School in North Carolina." *Crisis* 34 (June 1927): 117–18.

"The Negro Common School, Mississippi." *Crisis* 33 (Dec. 1926): 96–97.

Newbold, N. C. "Common Schools for Negroes in the South." *Annals of the American Academy of Political and Social Science* 140 (1928): 209–23.

Newby, Robert G., and Tyack, David B. "Victims without Crimes: Some Historical Perspectives on Black Education." *Journal of Negro Education* 40 (Summer 1971): 192–206.

Nichols, Patricia C. "Black Women in the Rural South: Conservative and Innovative." *International Journal of the Sociology of Language* 17 (1978): 45–54.

Oak, Vishnu V. "Higher Education and the Negro." *Education* 53 (Nov. 1932): 176–81.

Ogden, Robert C. "Educational Conditions in the Southern States." *Educational Review* 23 (May 1902): 468–82.

Osborn, A. C. "Benedict College." *American Baptist Home Mission Monthly* 11 (Aug. 1889): 319.

Page, Walter Hines. "Booker T. Washington: The Characteristics of the Colored Leader Who Has Shown the Way to Solve the Hardest Problems of Our National Life." *Everybody's Magazine* 6 (Apr. 1902): 393–98.

————. "The Only Way to Allay Race Friction." *World's Work* 6 (Aug. 1903): 320–21.

Parker, Marjorie H. "Some Educational Activities of the Freedmen's Bureau." *Journal of Negro Education* 23 (Winter 1954): 9–21.

Patton, June O. "The Black Community of Augusta and the Struggle for Ware High School, 1880–1899." In *New Perspectives on Black Educational History*, edited by V. P. Franklin and James D. Anderson, pp. 45–59. Boston: G. K. Hall, 1978.

Pearce, Larry W. "The American Missionary Association and the Freedmen's Bureau in Arkansas, 1866–1868." *Arkansas Historical Quarterly* 30 (Autumn 1971): 241–59.

————. "The American Missionary Association and the Freedmen's Bureau in Arkansas, 1868–1878." *Arkansas Historical Quarterly* 31 (Autumn 1972): 246–61.

Peeps, J. M. Stephen. "Northern Philanthropy and the Emergence of Black Higher Education—Do-Gooders, Compromisers, or Co-Conspirators." *Journal of Negro Education*, 50 (Summer 1981): 251–69.

Perry, B. L., Jr. "Black Colleges and Universities in Florida: Past, Present, and Future." *Journal of Black Studies* 6 (Sept. 1975): 69–78.

Pierce, Edward L. "The Contrabands at Fortress Monroe." *Atlantic Monthly* 8 (Nov. 1861): 626–40.

Porter, Betty. "The History of Negro Education in Louisiana." *Louisiana Historical Quarterly* 25 (July 1942): 728–821.

Putney, Martha S. "The Baltimore Normal School for the Education of Black Teachers: Its Founders and Its Founding." *Maryland Historical Magazine* 72 (Summer 1977): 238–52.

————. "The Black Colleges in the Maryland State College System: Quest for Equal Opportunity, 1908–1975." *Maryland Historical Magazine* 75 (Dec. 1980): 335–43.

————. "The Formative Years of Maryland's First Black Postsecondary School [Bowie Normal School]." *Maryland Historical Magazine* 73 (Summer 1978): 168–79.

Rabinowitz, Howard N. "Half a Loaf: The Shift from White to Black Teachers in the Negro Schools of the Urban South, 1865–1890." *Journal of Southern History* 40 (Nov. 1974): 565–94.

Rachal, John R. "Gideonites and Freedmen: Adult Literacy Education at Port Royal, 1862–1865." *Journal of Negro Education* 55 (Fall 1986): 453–69.

Reid, Ira De A. "Lily-White Labor." *Opportunity* 7 (June 1930): 170–73.

"The Representation of the Colored South." *Illustrated American*, Sept. 1896, p. 404.

"Review of Crummell's *Common Sense in Common Schooling*." *A.M.E. Church Review* 3 (Jan. 1887): 319–20.

Rice, Elizabeth G. "A Yankee Teacher in the South: An Experience in the Early Days of Reconstruction." *Century Magazine*, May 1901, pp. 151–52.

Richardson, Joe M. "The American Missionary Association and Black Education in Civil War Missouri." *Missouri Historical Review* 69 (July 1975): 433–48.

———. "Fisk University, the First Critical Years." *Tennessee Historical Quarterly* 29 (Spring 1970): 24–41.

———. "Francis L. Cardoza: Black Educator during Reconstruction." *Journal of Negro Education* 48 (Winter 1979): 73–83.

———. "The Freedmen's Bureau and Negro Education in Florida." *Journal of Negro Education* 31 (Fall 1962): 460–67.

Roberts, S. O. "Negro Higher and Professional Education in Tennessee." *Journal of Negro Education* 17 (Summer 1948): 361–72.

Roy, Joseph E. "The Higher Education of the Negroes, No Mistake." In *First and Second Mohonk Conferences on the Negro Question, 1890–1891*, edited by Isabel C. Barrows, pp. 86–93. Reprint. New York: Negro Universities Press, 1969.

Sale, George E. "Education in Our Home Mission Schools." *American Baptist Home Mission Monthly* 18 (June 1896): 222–23.

———. "The Education of the Negro." *American Baptist Home Mission Monthly* 20 (Oct. 1898): 346–49.

Sawyer, R. McLaran. "The National Education Association and Negro Education, 1865–1884." *Journal of Negro Education* 39 (Fall 1970): 341–45.

Schweninger, Loren. "The American Missionary Association and Northern Philanthropy in Reconstruction Alabama." *Alabama Historical Quarterly* 32 (Fall–Winter 1970): 129–56.

Scott, Emmett J. "Twenty Years After: An Appraisal of Booker T. Washington." *Journal of Negro Education* 5 (Oct. 1936): 543–54.

Shannon, Samuel H. "Land-Grant College Legislation and Black Tennesseeans: A Case Study in the Politics of Education." *History of Education Quarterly* 22 (Summer 1982): 139–57.

Small, Sandra E. "The Yankee Schoolmarm in Freedmen's Schools: An Analysis of Attitudes." *Journal of Southern History* 45 (Aug. 1979): 381–402.

Smallwood, James. "Black Education in Reconstruction Texas: The Contributions of the Freedmen's Bureau and Benevolent Societies." *East Texas Histori-*

cal Journal 19 (Spring 1981): 17–40.

———. "Black Texans during Reconstruction: First Freedom." *East Texas Historical Journal* 14 (Spring 1976): 9–19.

Smith, T. Lynn. "The Redistribution of the Negro Population of the United States, 1910–1960." *Journal of Negro History* 51 (July 1966): 155–73.

Smith, Timothy L. "Native Blacks and Foreign Whites: Varying Responses to Educational Opportunity in America, 1880–1950." *Perspectives in American History* 6 (1972): 309–35.

Stowe, Harriet Beecher. "The Education of the Freedmen." *North American Review* 128 (June 1879): 605–15.

Streator, George. "Negro College Radicals." *Crisis* 41 (Jan. 1934): 47.

Sweat, Edward F. "Francis L. Cardoza—Profile of Integrity in Reconstruction Politics." *Journal of Negro History* 46 (Oct. 1961): 217–32.

———. "Some Notes on the Role of Negroes in the Establishment of Public Schools in South Carolina." *Phylon* 22 (1961): 160–66.

Taggart, Robert J. "Philanthropy and Black Public Education in Delaware, 1918–1930." *Pennsylvania Magazine of History and Biography* 103 (Oct. 1979): 467–83.

TeSelle, Eugene. "The Nashville Institute and Roger Williams University: Benevolence, Paternalism, and Black Consciousness, 1867–1910." *Tennessee Historical Quarterly* 41 (Winter 1982): 360–79.

Thomas, Jesse O. "Forces in Race Conflict." *Opportunity* 7 (Oct. 1929): 314–15.

Thompson, Charles H. "The Education of the Negro in the United States." *School and Society* 42 (9 Nov. 1935): 625–33.

———. "The Negro College: In Retrospect and in Prospect." *Journal of Negro Education* 27 (Spring 1958): 127–31.

———. "The Socio-Economic Status of Negro College Students." *Journal of Negro Education* 2 (Jan. 1933): 26–37.

Thompson, Ernest Trice. "Black Presbyterians, Education and Evangelism after the Civil War." *Journal of Presbyterian History* 51 (Summer 1973: 174–98.

Thornbrough, Emma L. "American Negro Newspapers, 1880–1914." *Business History Review* 40 (Winter 1966): 467–90.

———. "Booker T. Washington as Seen by His White Contemporaries." *Journal of Negro History* 53 (Jan. 1968): 161–82.

———. "More Light on Booker T. Washington and the New York Age." *Journal of Negro History* 43 (Jan. 1958): 34–50.

———. "The National Afro-American League, 1887–1908." *Journal of Southern History* 27 (Nov. 1961): 494–512.

Timberlake, C. L. "The Early Struggle for Education of the Blacks in the Commonwealth of Kentucky." *Register* 71 (July 1973): 225–52.

Turnbull, L. Minerva. "The Southern Educational Revolt." *William and Mary Quarterly Series*, 2d ser., 14 (Jan. 1934): 60–75.

"Tuskegee Normal School." *Christian Register*, July 1889, p. 430.

Tyack, David, and Lowe, Robert. "The Constitutional Moment: Reconstruction and Black Education in the South." *American Journal of Education* 94 (Feb. 1986): 236–56.

Vance, Joseph C. "Freedmen's Schools in Albemarle County during Reconstruction." *Virginia Magazine of History and Biography* 61 (Oct. 1953): 430–38.

Vaughn, William P. "Partners in Segregation: Barnas Sears and the Peabody Fund." *Civil War History* 10 (1964): 260–74.

Villard, Oswald G. "An Alabama Negro School." *American Monthly Review of Reviews* 26 (Dec. 1902): 711–14.

———. "William H. Baldwin, Jr." *South Atlantic Quarterly* 5 (Jan. 1906): 30–34.

Vincent, Charles. "Booker T. Washington's Tour of Louisiana, April, 1915." *Louisiana History* 22 (Spring 1981): 189–98.

Walker, Francis A. "Industrial Education." *Journal of Social Science* 19 (Dec. 1884): 117–31.

Ward, William Hayes. "Higher Education." *American Baptist Home Mission Monthly* 22 (Nov. 1900): 322.

Ware, Edward T. "Higher Education of Negroes in the United States." *Annals of the American Academy of Political and Social Science* 49 (Sept. 1913): 209–18.

"A Washington of To-Day." *Christian Endeavor World*, Apr. 1899, p. 589.

"Washington: The Moses of His Race." *Volunteers Gazette*, Oct. 1897, p. 6.

✓Washington, Booker T. "Education and Suffrage of Negroes." *Education* 19 (Sept. 1898): 49–50.

———. "Education Will Solve the Race Problem: A Reply." *North American Review* 171 (Aug. 1900): 221–32.

———. "The Educational Outlook in the South." *Journal of Proceedings and Addresses of the National Education Association* 23 (1885): 127.

———. "The Fruits of Industrial Training." *Atlantic Monthly* 92 (Oct. 1903): 453–62.

———. "Industrial Education and the Public Schools." *Annals of the American Academy of Political and Social Science* 49 (Sept. 1913): 219–32.

———. "National Negro Business League." *World's Work* 4 (Oct. 1902): 2671–75.

———. "The Relation of Industrial Education to National Progress." *Annals of the American Academy of Political and Social Science* 33 (Jan. 1909): 1–12.

———. "A University Education for Negroes." *Independent* 68 (24 Mar. 1910): 613–18.

Washington, Delo E. "Education of Freedmen and the Role of Self-Help in a Sea Island Setting, 1862–1982." *Agricultural History* 58 (July 1984): 442–55.

Wayland, H. L. "Instruction of the Colored Citizens." *Journal of Social Science* 34 (Nov. 1896): 78–83.

Wells, Guy F. "First School Survey." *Educational Review* 50 (Sept. 1915): 166.

Wennersten, John R., and Wennersten, Ruth Ellen. "Separate and Unequal: The Evolution of a Black Land Grant College in Maryland, 1890–1930." *Maryland Historical Magazine* 72 (Spring 1977): 110–17.

West, Earle H. "The Harris Brothers: Black Northern Teachers in the Reconstruction South." *Journal of Negro Education* 48 (Spring 1979): 126–38.

———. "The Peabody Fund and Negro Education, 1867–1880." *History of Education Quarterly* 6 (Summer 1966): 3–21.

Wheeler, Elizabeth L. "Isaac Fisher: The Frustrations of a Negro Educator at Branch Normal College, 1902–1911." *Arkansas Historical Quarterly* 41 (Spring 1982): 3–50.

White, Arthur O. "Booker T. Washington's Florida Incident, 1903–1904." *Florida Historical Quarterly* 51 (Jan. 1973): 227–49.

White, Kenneth B. "The Alabama Freedmen's Bureau and Black Education: The Myth of Opportunity." *Alabama Review* 33 (Apr. 1981): 107–24.

Wiener, Jonathan M. "Planter-Merchant Conflict in Reconstruction Alabama." *Past and Present* 68 (Aug. 1975): 73–94.

———. "Planter Persistence and Social Change: Alabama, 1850–1870." *Journal of Interdisciplinary History* 7 (Autumn 1976): 257.

Williams, Henry Sullivan. "The Development of the Negro Public School System in Missouri." *Journal of Negro Education* 5 (Apr. 1920): 137–65.

Winston, George T. "Industrial Training in Relation to the Negro Problem." *Proceedings of the Fourth Conference for Education in the South*, pp. 103–7. New York: Committee on Publication, 1901.

Woodman, Harold D. "Sequel to Slavery: The New History Views the Postbellum South." *Journal of Southern History* 43 (Nov. 1977): 523–54.

Woodward, Calvin M. "The Results of the St. Louis Manual Training School." *Journal of Proceedings and Addresses of the National Education Association* 28 (1889): 73–91.

Work, Monroe N. "Self-Help among Negroes." *Survey* 22 (7 Aug. 1909): 616–18.

Wright, Richard R., Jr. "The Negro in Unskilled Labor." *Annals of the American Academy of Political and Social Science* 49 (Sept. 1913): 19–25.

Wright, Stephen J. "The Development of the Hampton-Tuskegee Pattern of Higher Education." *Phylon* 10 (Dec. 1949): 334–42.

Wyatt-Brown, Bertram. "Black Schooling during Reconstruction." In *The Web of Southern Social Relations: Women, Family, and Education*, edited by Walter J. Fraser, Jr., R. Frank Saunders, Jr., and Jon L. Wakelyn, pp. 146–65. Athens: University of Georgia Press, 1985.

Dissertations and Theses

Alexander, Ann Field. "Black Protest in the New South: John Mitchell, Jr. (1863–1929) and the Richmond *Planet*." Ph.D. dissertation, Duke University, 1973.

Alexander, Philip Wade. "John Eaton, Jr., Preacher, Soldier, and Educator." Ph.D. dissertation, George Peabody College for Teachers, 1940.

Anderson, James Douglas. "Education for Servitude: The Social Purposes of Schooling in the Black South, 1870–1930." Ph.D. dissertation, University of Illinois at Urbana-Champaign, 1973.

Bahney, Robert Stanley. "Generals and Negroes: Education of Negroes by the Union Army, 1861–1865." Ph.D. dissertation, University of Michigan, 1965.

Beasley, Leon O. "A History of Education in Louisiana during the Reconstruction Period, 1862–1877." Ph.D. dissertation, Louisiana State University, 1957.

Berman, Edward Henry. "Education in Africa and America: A History of the Phelps-Stokes Fund, 1911–1945." Ed.D. dissertation, Columbia University, 1970.

Brownell, B. M. "The Urban Mind in the South: The Growth of Urban Consciousness." Ph.D. dissertation, University of North Carolina, 1969.

Butchart, Ronald Eugene. "Educating for Freedom: Northern Whites and the Origins of Black Education in the South, 1862–1875." Ph.D. dissertation, State University of New York at Binghamton, 1976.

Campbell, Clarice T. "History of Tougaloo College." Ph.D. dissertation, University of Michigan, 1970.

Chapman, Oscar James. "A Historical Study of Negro Land-Grant Colleges in Relationship with Their Social, Economic, Political, and Educational Backgrounds and a Program for Their Improvement." Ph.D. dissertation, Ohio State University, 1940.

Chase, Hal G. " 'Honey for Friends, Stings for Enemies': William Calvin Chase and the Washington *Bee*, 1882–1921." Ph.D. dissertation, University of Pennsylvania, 1973.

Clarke, Charles Morgan. "Philanthropic Foundations and Teacher Education in the South, 1867–1948." Ph.D. dissertation, University of North Carolina, 1948.

Crofts, Daniel Wallace. "The Blair Bill and the Elections Bill: The Congressional Aftermath to Reconstruction." Ph.D. dissertation, Yale University, 1968.

Danbom, David Byers. "The Industrialization of Agriculture, 1900–1930." Ph.D. dissertation, Stanford University, 1974.

DeBoer, Clara Merritt. "The Role of Afro-Americans in the Origin and Work of the American Missionary Association, 1839–1877." Ph.D. dissertation, Rutgers University, 1973.

Drake, Richard B. "The American Missionary Association and the Southern Negro, 1861–1888." Ph.D. dissertation, Emory University, 1957.

Enck, Henry Snyder. "The Burden Borne: Northern White Philanthropy and Southern Black Industrial Education, 1900–1915." Ph.D. dissertation, University of Cincinnati, 1970.

Hall, Clyde W. "A Survey of Industrial Education in the United States up to 1917." Ed.D. dissertation, Bradley University, 1953.

Horst, Samuel L. "Education for Manhood: The Education of Blacks in Virginia during the Civil War." Ph.D. dissertation, University of Virginia, 1977.

Johnson, Clifton H. "The American Missionary Association, 1846–1861: A Study of Christian Abolitionism." Ph.D. dissertation, University of North Carolina, 1959.

Johnson, Josie R. "An Historical Review of the Role Black Parents and the Black Community Played in Providing Schooling for Black Children in the South, 1865–1954." Ed.D. dissertation, University of Massachusetts, 1986.

Jones, Jacqueline. "The 'Great Opportunity': Northern Teachers and the Georgia Freedmen, 1865–73." Ph.D. dissertation, University of Wisconsin, 1976.

Lamon, Lester Crawford. "Negroes in Tennessee, 1900–1930." Ph.D. dissertation, University of North Carolina, 1971.

Lewis, William J. "The Educational Speaking of Jabez L. M. Curry." Ph.D. dissertation, University of Florida, 1955.

McMillian, Joseph Turner. "The Development of Higher Education for Blacks during the Late Nineteenth Century: A Study of the African Methodist Episcopal Church; Wilberforce University; American Missionary Association; Hampton Institute; and Fisk University." Ed.D. dissertation, Columbia University Teachers College, 1986.

Messner, William F. "The Federal Army and Blacks in the Gulf Department, 1862–1865." Ph.D. dissertation, University of Wisconsin, 1972.

Montgomery, William Edward. "Negro Churches in the South, 1865–1915." Ph.D. dissertation, University of Texas at Austin, 1975.

Morris, Robert C. "Reading, 'Riting and Reconstruction: Freedmen's Education in the South, 1865–1870." Ph.D. dissertation, University of Chicago, 1976.

Patton, June O. "Major Richard Robert Wright, Sr., and Black Higher Education in Georgia, 1880–1920." Ph.D. dissertation, University of Chicago, 1980.

Peck, Richard Connelley. "Jabez Lamar Monroe Curry: Educational Crusader." Ph.D. dissertation, George Peabody College for Teachers, 1942.

Rosen, Frederick B. "The Development of Negro Education in Florida during Reconstruction, 1865–1877." Ph.D. dissertation, University of Florida, 1974.

Rusnak, Robert Jay. "Walter Hines Page and *The World's Work*: 1900–1913." Ph.D. dissertation, University of California, Santa Barbara, 1973.

Sherer, Robert G., Jr. "Let Us Make Man: Negro Education in Nineteenth Century Alabama." Ph.D. dissertation, University of North Carolina, 1970.

Small, Sandra Eileen. "The Yankee Schoolmarm in Southern Freedmen's Schools, 1861–1871: The Career of a Stereotype." Ph.D. dissertation, Washington State University, 1976.

Smith, S. L. "The Relation of Farm Labor to School Term and Attendance." Master's thesis, George Peabody College for Teachers, 1918.

Stillman, Rachel Bryan. "Education in the Confederate States of America, 1861–1865." Ph.D. dissertation, University of Illinois at Urbana-Champaign, 1972.

Stokes, Allen Heath, Jr. "Black and White Labor and the Development of the Southern Textile Industry, 1800–1920." Ph.D. dissertation, University of South Carolina, 1977.

Thomas, Leland Clovis. "Some Aspects of Biracial Public Education in Georgia, 1900–1954." Ed.D. dissertation, George Peabody College for Teachers, 1960.

Westin, Richard B. "The State and Segregated Schools: Negro Public Education in North Carolina, 1863–1923." Ph.D. dissertation, Duke University, 1966.

White, Howard Ashley. "The Freedmen's Bureau in Louisiana." Ph.D. dissertation, Tulane University, 1955.

Williams, Gilbert Anthony. "The A.M.E. Christian Recorder: A Forum for the Social Ideas of Black Americans, 1854–1902." Ph.D. dissertation, University of Illinois at Urbana-Champaign, 1979.

Wright, C. T. "The Development of Education for Blacks in Georgia, 1865–1900." Ph.D. dissertation, Boston University, 1977.

INDEX

Abbott, Lyman, 71, 107
ABHMS. *See* American Baptist Home Mission Society
Accrediting agencies: and black colleges, 249–51
Adams, Charles Francis, 88
Adams, William W., 59
African Methodist Episcopal (AME) church, 13, 51; black colleges supported by, 67, 135, 240
African Methodist Episcopal Zion church, 67, 240
African Repository, 59
Afro-American Convention, 104
Agricultural labor: oppressive nature of in South, 20–25, 149–50, 152; numbers of blacks involved in in South, 44–45, 149–50; Hampton Idea for, 88–89. *See also* Child labor
Alabama: black education in, 23, 132, 135, 153, 161–63, 165, 172, 232
Alabama Baptist University, 132
Alabama Power Company, 232
Alabama State Normal School for Negroes, 232
Alderman, Edwin A., 83, 86, 99
Alexander's Magazine, 106
Alexandria, Va., 8
Allen University, 135, 240
Alvord, John W., 6–7, 9–10, 12–13, 15, 18–23, 26
AMA. *See* American Missionary Association
American Baptist Home Mission So-

ciety (ABHMS), 67–69, 132, 135, 240, 251–54
American Dilemma, An (Myrdal), 285
American Federation of Labor, 233
American Missionary Association (AMA), 5, 29, 30; and Hampton Institute, 36, 70; views of on black education, 67, 68, 241–43; colleges supported by, 134, 239–40
American Social Science Association, 68, 71
American Tract Society, 30
Antoine, C. C., 18
Arkansas: black education in, 106, 142, 206–11, 240; Rosenwald schools in, 168, 170
Arkansas Agricultural, Mechanical, and Normal College, 211
Arkansas Baptist College, 142, 211, 240
Armstrong, Richard, 38
Armstrong, Samuel Chapman, 70, 86, 87, 272; and origins of Hampton curriculum, 31, 33–40, 42–47, 49–55, 57, 72, 85, 273; black criticism of, 59–62, 64; and curricula other than Hampton's, 67; influence of on Washington, 73, 85, 102
Armstrong Association, 91
Arthur, George R., 207, 210, 229–30
Atlanta, Ga.: displacement of black workers in, 233–34
Atlanta Baptist College, 69
"Atlanta Compromise," 73, 103, 104
Atlanta Constitution, 100